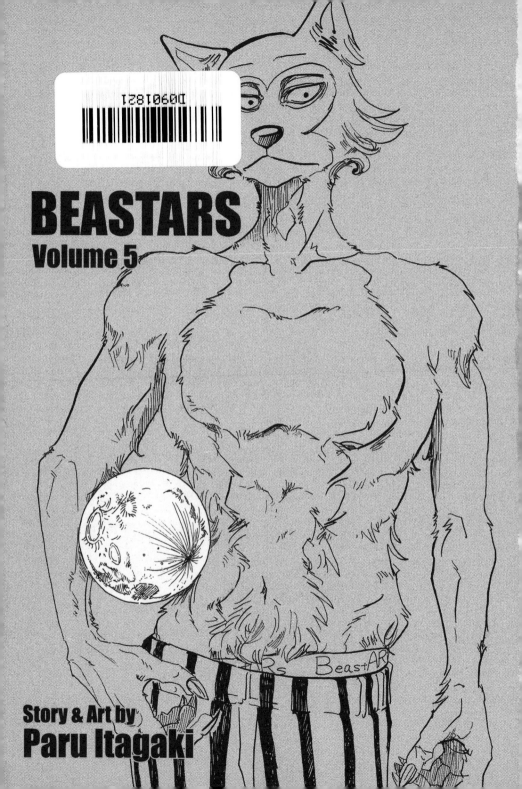

BEASTARS
Volume 5

Story & Art by
Paru Itagaki

STORY & CAST OF CHARACTERS

Cherryton Academy is an integrated boarding school for a diverse group of carnivores and herbivores. Recently, Tem, an alpaca member of the Drama Club, was slain and devoured on campus. The murderer has yet to be identified, and everyone's nerves are on edge.

The summer Meteor Festival is fast approaching, and gray wolf Legoshi is busy helping the Drama Club production crew prepare for the event. One day he sees red deer Louis and dwarf rabbit Haru together and realizes they have been intimate with each other. His jealousy makes him realize he is in love with Haru, but Haru is an herbivore—and Legoshi almost devoured her when they first met—so he tries to convince himself that the differences between them are insurmountable.

Meanwhile, gray wolf Juno has fallen in love with Legoshi. She tells Louis that she will become the next Beastar and make Legoshi hers. Louis loathes carnivores, but he still aspires to change the world for the better. Thus begins a slow battle for supremacy between a carnivore female and an herbivore male...

Legoshi finally vows to confess his love to Haru at the Meteor Festival...but on the eve of the event, Haru is kidnapped!

Legoshi

★ Gray wolf ♂
★ High school second-year
★ Member of the Drama Club production crew
★ Physically powerful yet emotionally sensitive
★ Struggles with his identity as a carnivore

B
E
A
S
T
A
R
S

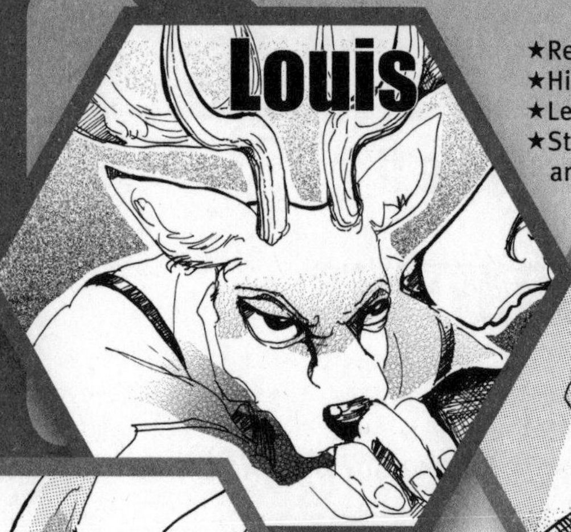

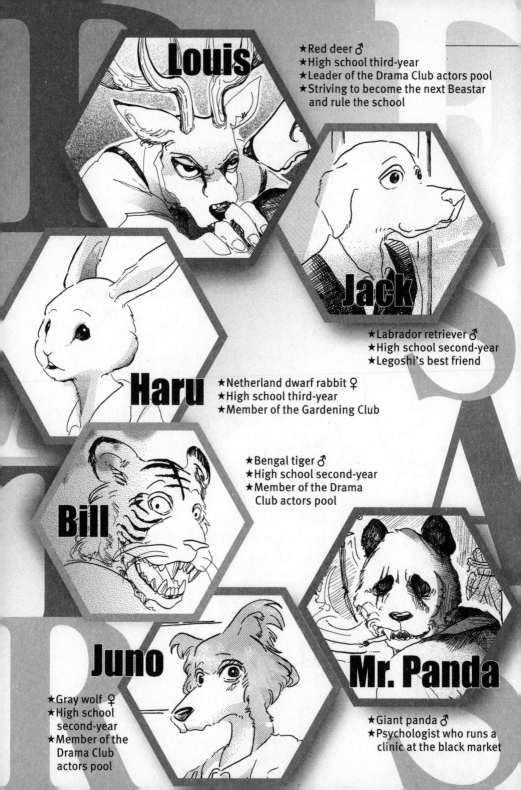

Louis

★Red deer ♂
★High school third-year
★Leader of the Drama Club actors pool
★Striving to become the next Beastar and rule the school

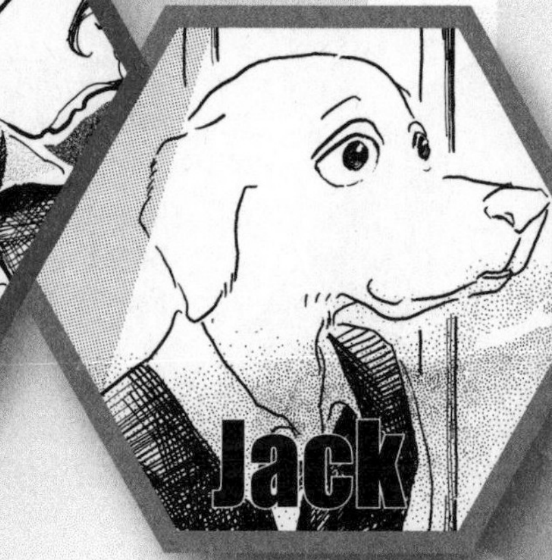

Jack

★Labrador retriever ♂
★High school second-year
★Legoshi's best friend

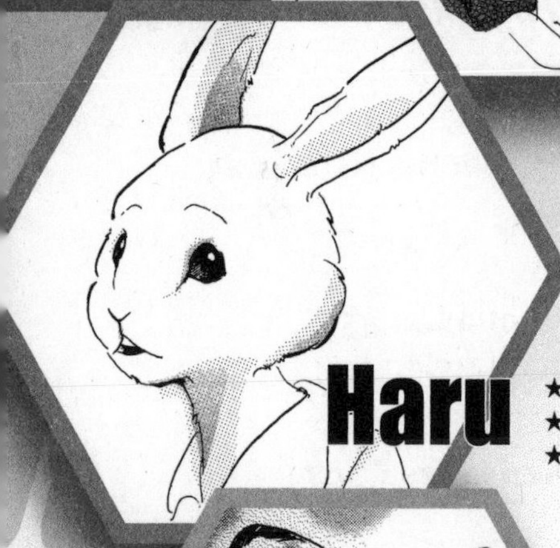

Haru

★Netherland dwarf rabbit ♀
★High school third-year
★Member of the Gardening Club

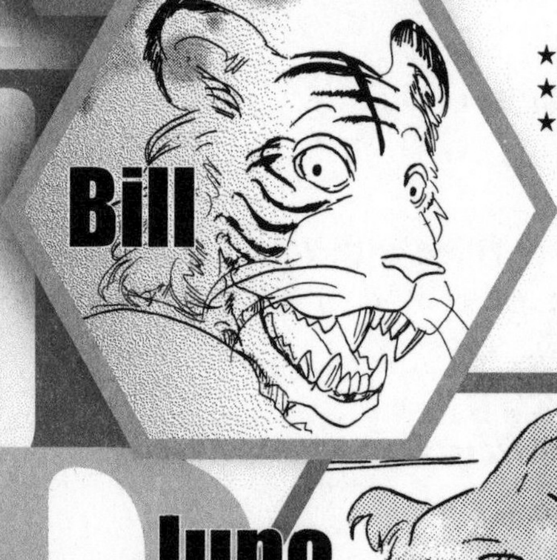

Bill

★Bengal tiger ♂
★High school second-year
★Member of the Drama Club actors pool

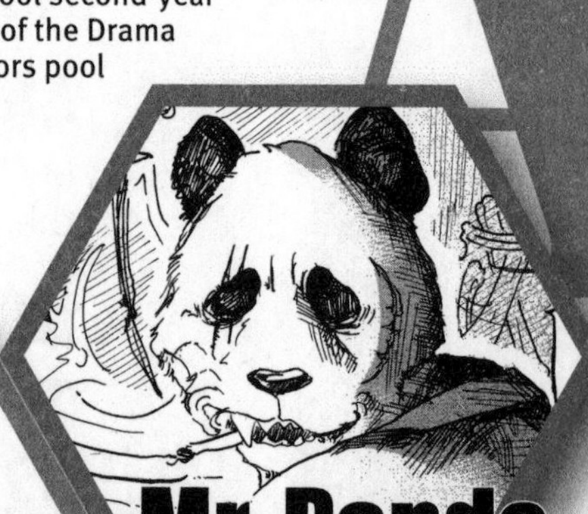

Mr. Panda

★Giant panda ♂
★Psychologist who runs a clinic at the black market

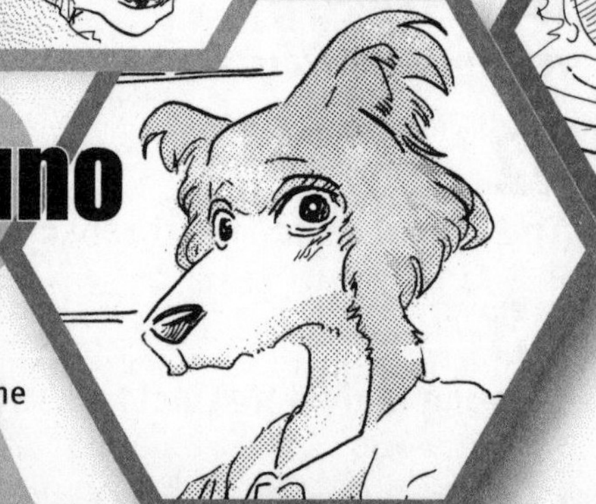

Juno

★Gray wolf ♀
★High school second-year
★Member of the Drama Club actors pool

BEASTARS
Volume 5

CONTENTS

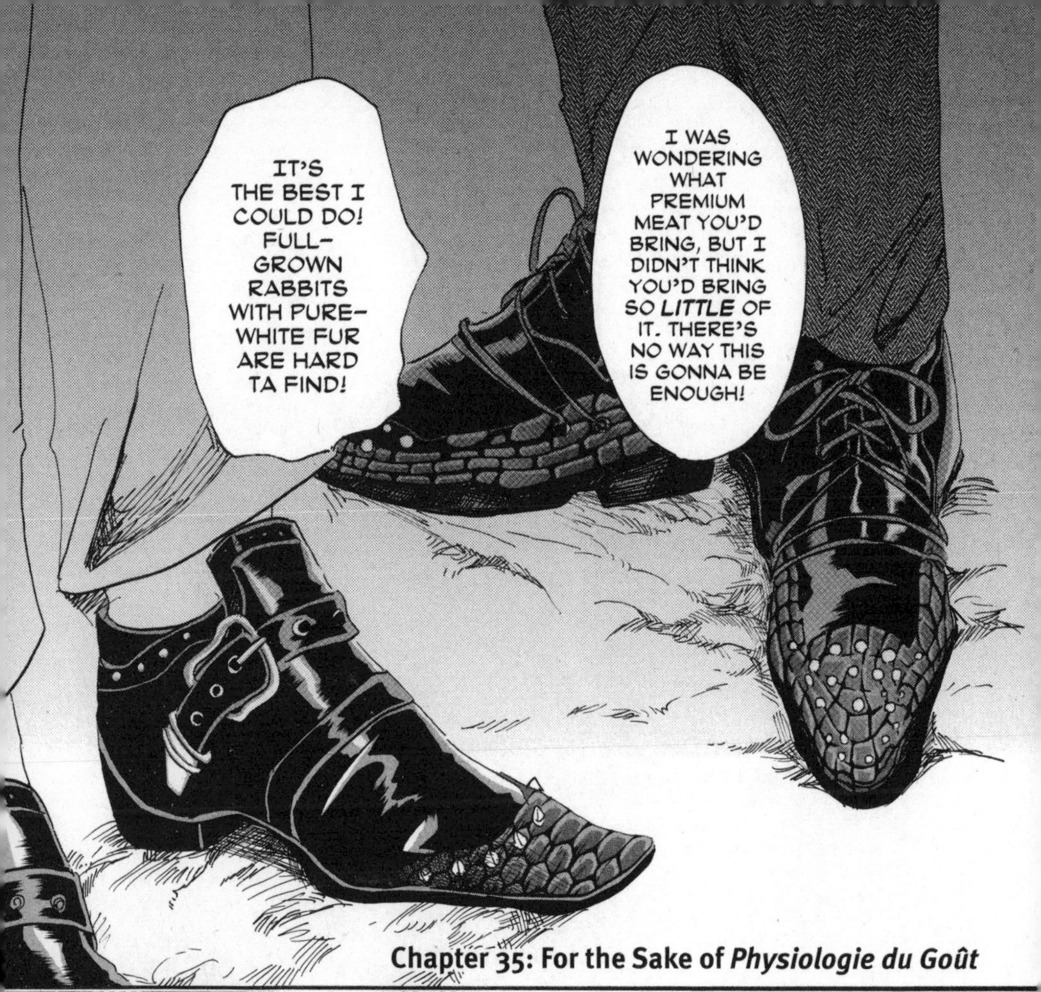
I WAS WONDERING WHAT PREMIUM MEAT YOU'D BRING, BUT I DIDN'T THINK YOU'D BRING SO *LITTLE* OF IT. THERE'S NO WAY THIS IS GONNA BE ENOUGH!
IT'S THE BEST I COULD DO! FULL-GROWN RABBITS WITH PURE-WHITE FUR ARE HARD TA FIND!

Chapter 35: For the Sake of *Physiologie du Goût*

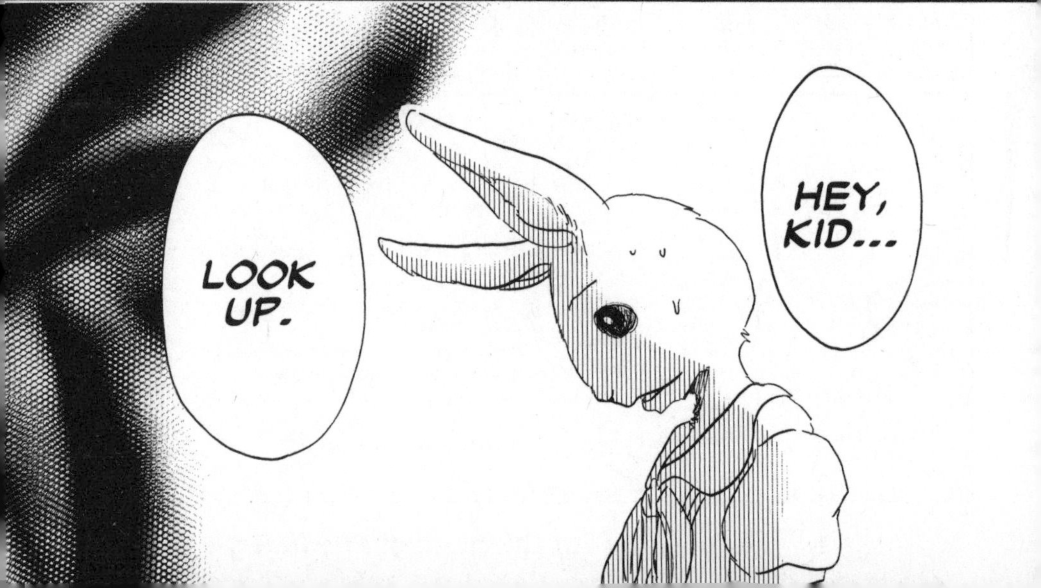
HEY, KID...
LOOK UP.

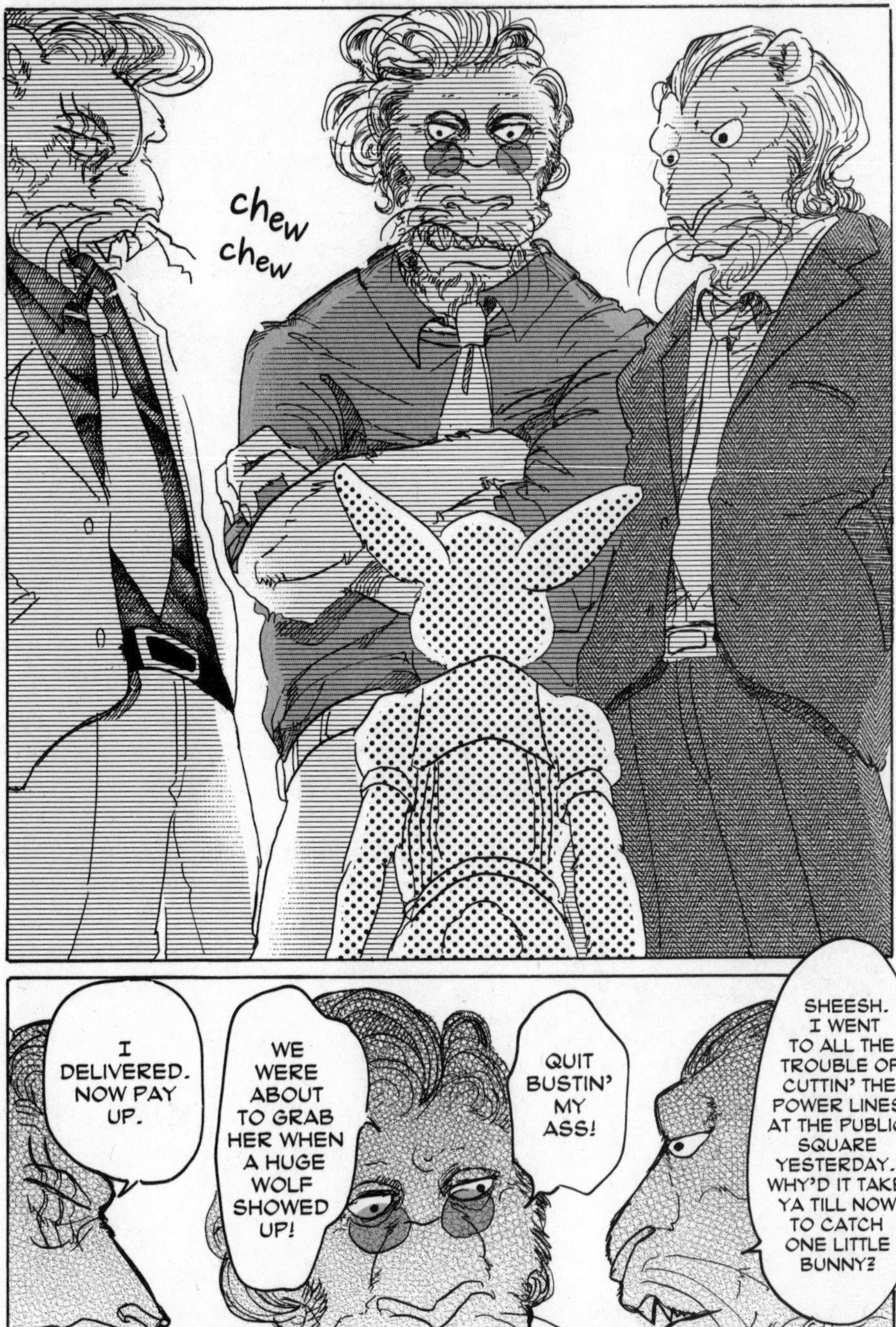
chew chew
SHEESH. I WENT TO ALL THE TROUBLE OF CUTTIN' THE POWER LINES AT THE PUBLIC SQUARE YESTERDAY. WHY'D IT TAKE YA TILL NOW TO CATCH ONE LITTLE BUNNY?
QUIT BUSTIN' MY ASS!
WE WERE ABOUT TO GRAB HER WHEN A HUGE WOLF SHOWED UP!
I DELIVERED. NOW PAY UP.

Chapter 35: For the Sake of *Physiologie du Goût*

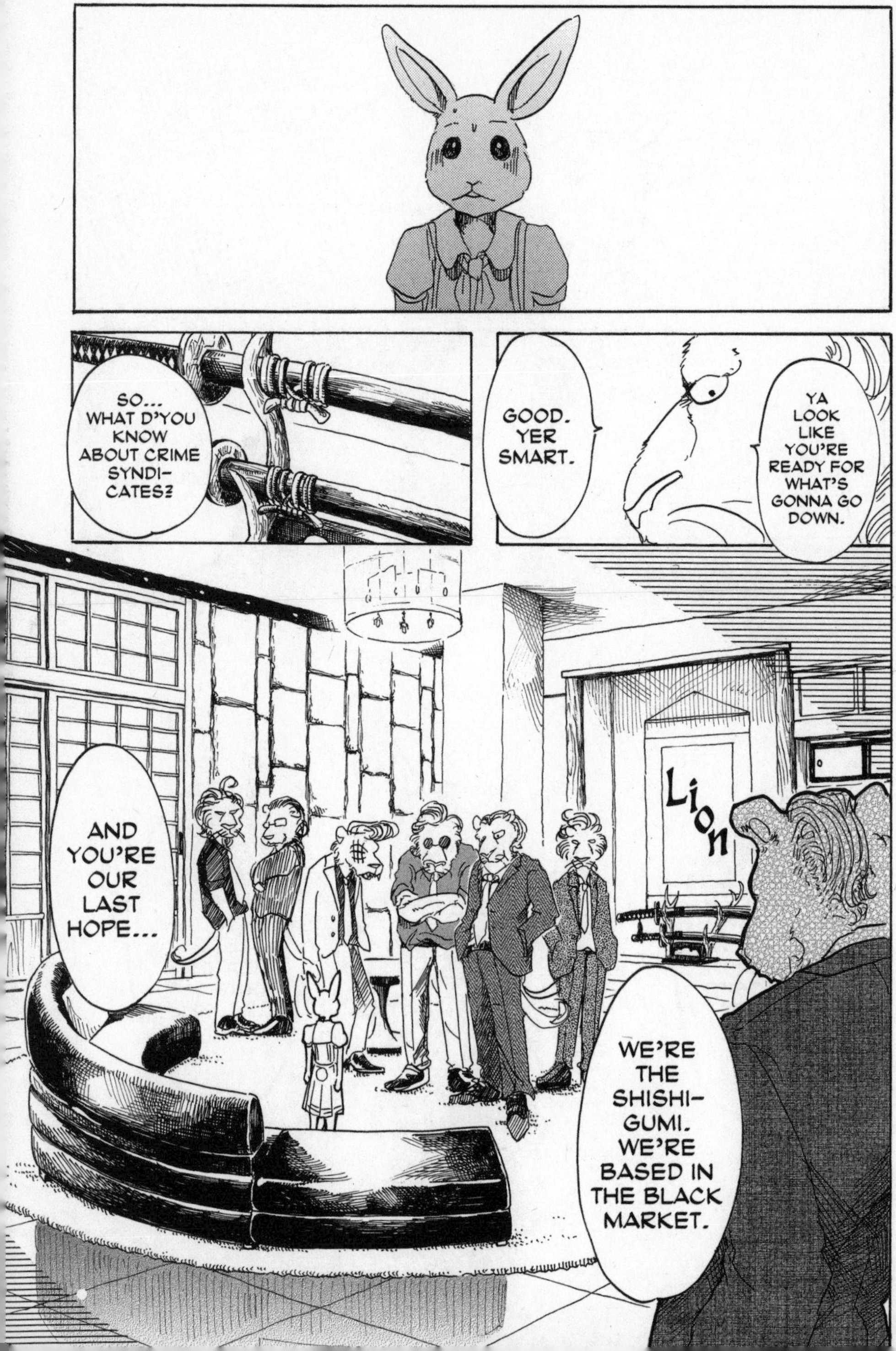
YA LOOK LIKE YOU'RE READY FOR WHAT'S GONNA GO DOWN.
GOOD. YER SMART.
SO... WHAT D'YOU KNOW ABOUT CRIME SYNDICATES?
Lion
WE'RE THE SHISHI-GUMI. WE'RE BASED IN THE BLACK MARKET.
AND YOU'RE OUR LAST HOPE...

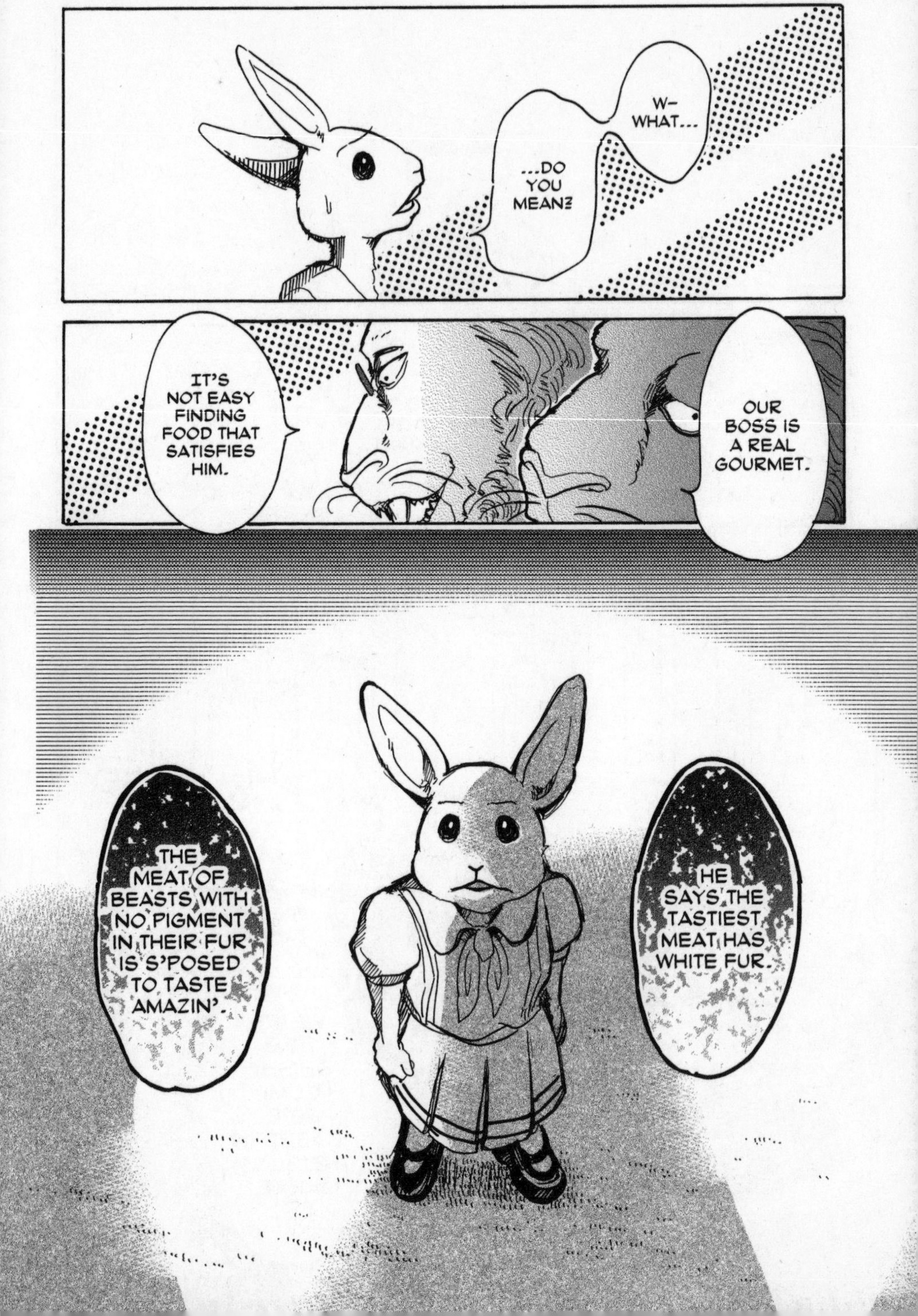
W- WHAT...
...DO YOU MEAN?
OUR BOSS IS A REAL GOURMET.
IT'S NOT EASY FINDING FOOD THAT SATISFIES HIM.
HE SAYS THE TASTIEST MEAT HAS WHITE FUR.
THE MEAT OF BEASTS WITH NO PIGMENT IN THEIR FUR IS S'POSED TO TASTE AMAZIN'.

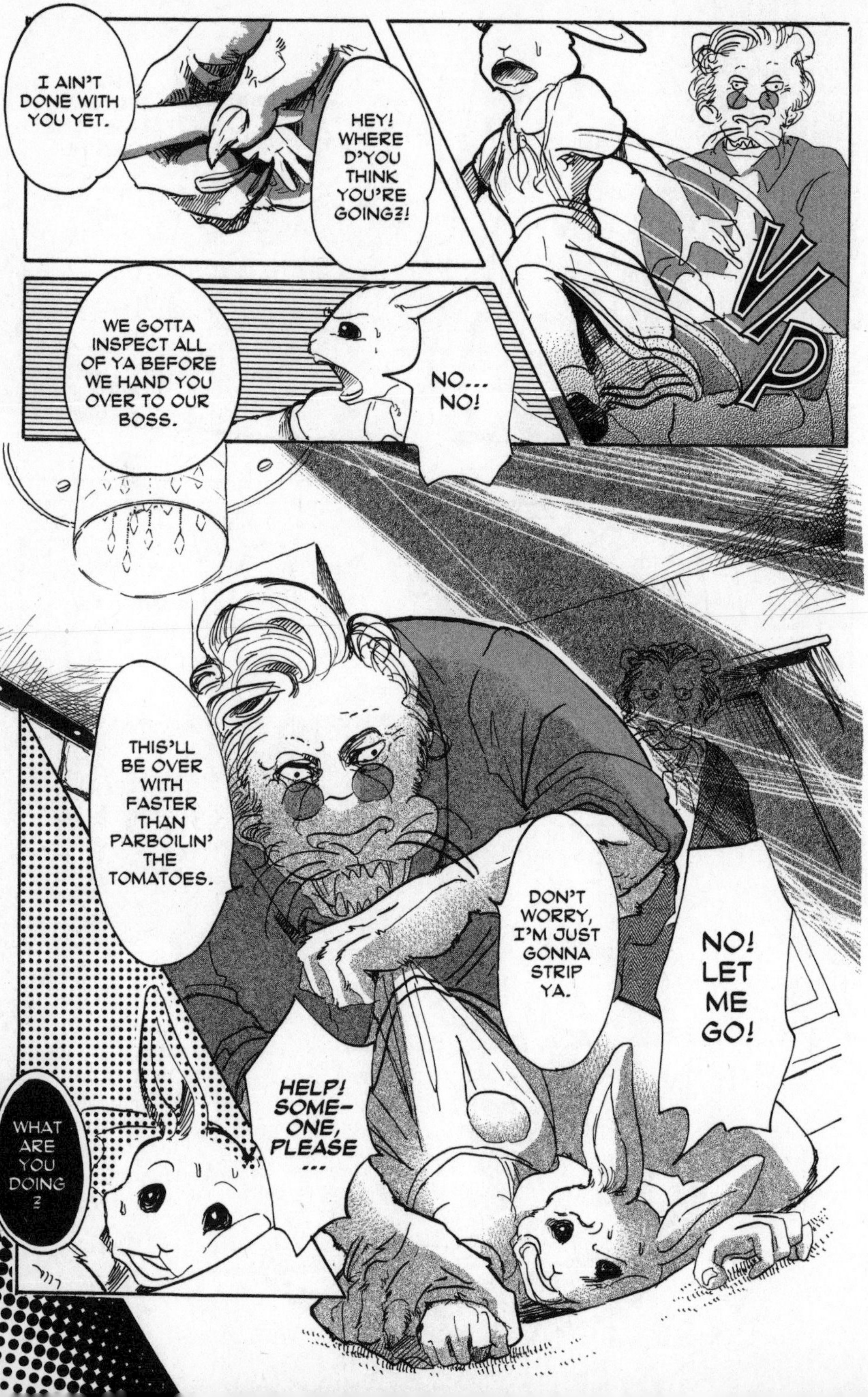
VIP
HEY! WHERE D'YOU THINK YOU'RE GOING?!
I AIN'T DONE WITH YOU YET.
NO... NO!
WE GOTTA INSPECT ALL OF YA BEFORE WE HAND YOU OVER TO OUR BOSS.
NO! LET ME GO!
DON'T WORRY, I'M JUST GONNA STRIP YA.
THIS'LL BE OVER WITH FASTER THAN PARBOILIN' THE TOMATOES.
HELP! SOME-ONE, PLEASE...
WHAT ARE YOU DOING?

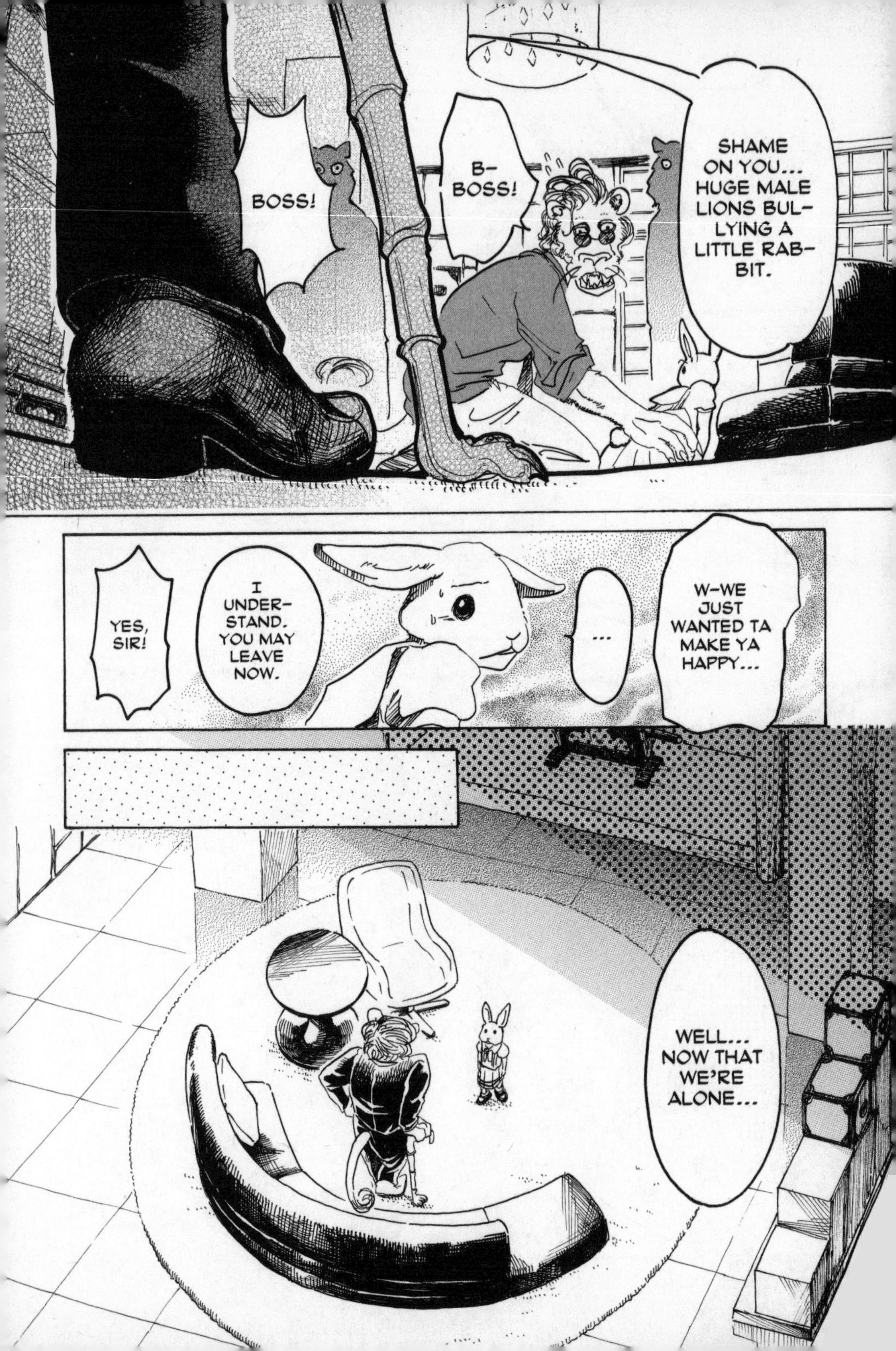
SHAME ON YOU... HUGE MALE LIONS BULLYING A LITTLE RABBIT.
B-BOSS!
BOSS!
W-WE JUST WANTED TA MAKE YA HAPPY...
...
I UNDERSTAND. YOU MAY LEAVE NOW.
YES, SIR!
WELL... NOW THAT WE'RE ALONE...

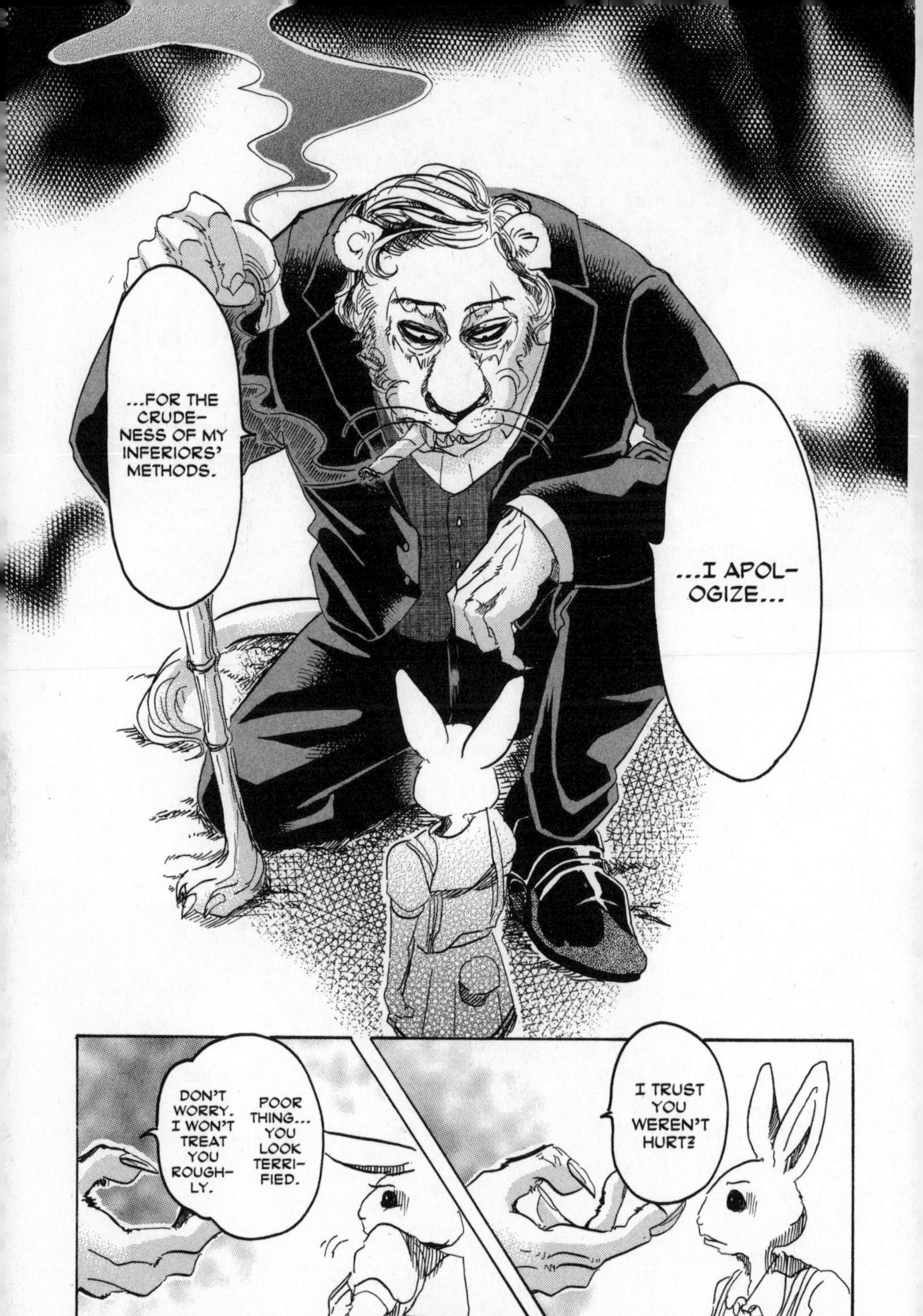
...I APOLOGIZE...
...FOR THE CRUDENESS OF MY INFERIORS' METHODS.
I TRUST YOU WEREN'T HURT?
POOR THING... YOU LOOK TERRIFIED.
DON'T WORRY. I WON'T TREAT YOU ROUGHLY.

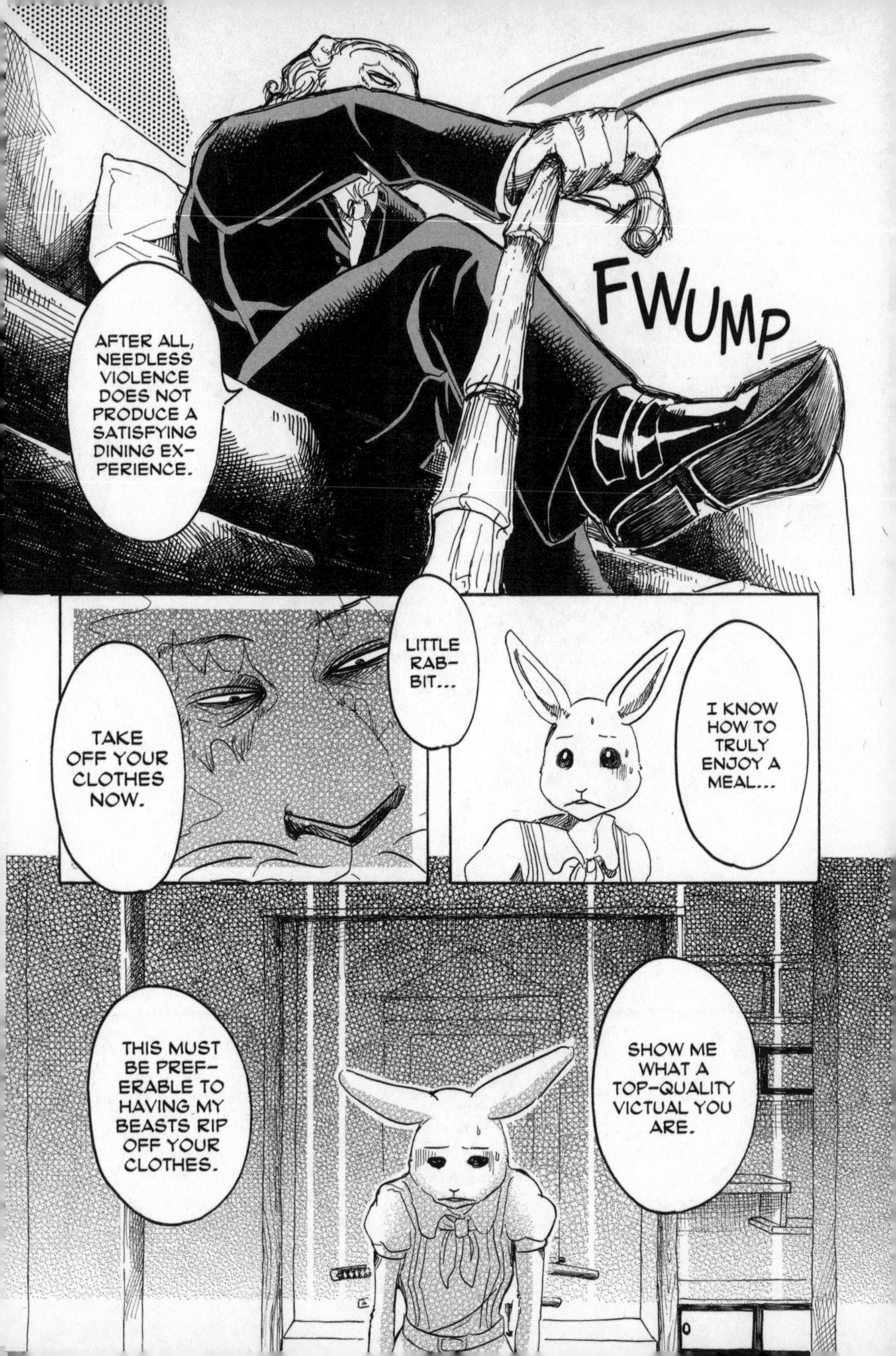
FWUMP
AFTER ALL, NEEDLESS VIOLENCE DOES NOT PRODUCE A SATISFYING DINING EXPERIENCE.
I KNOW HOW TO TRULY ENJOY A MEAL...
LITTLE RABBIT...
TAKE OFF YOUR CLOTHES NOW.
SHOW ME WHAT A TOP-QUALITY VICTUAL YOU ARE.
THIS MUST BE PREFERABLE TO HAVING MY BEASTS RIP OFF YOUR CLOTHES.

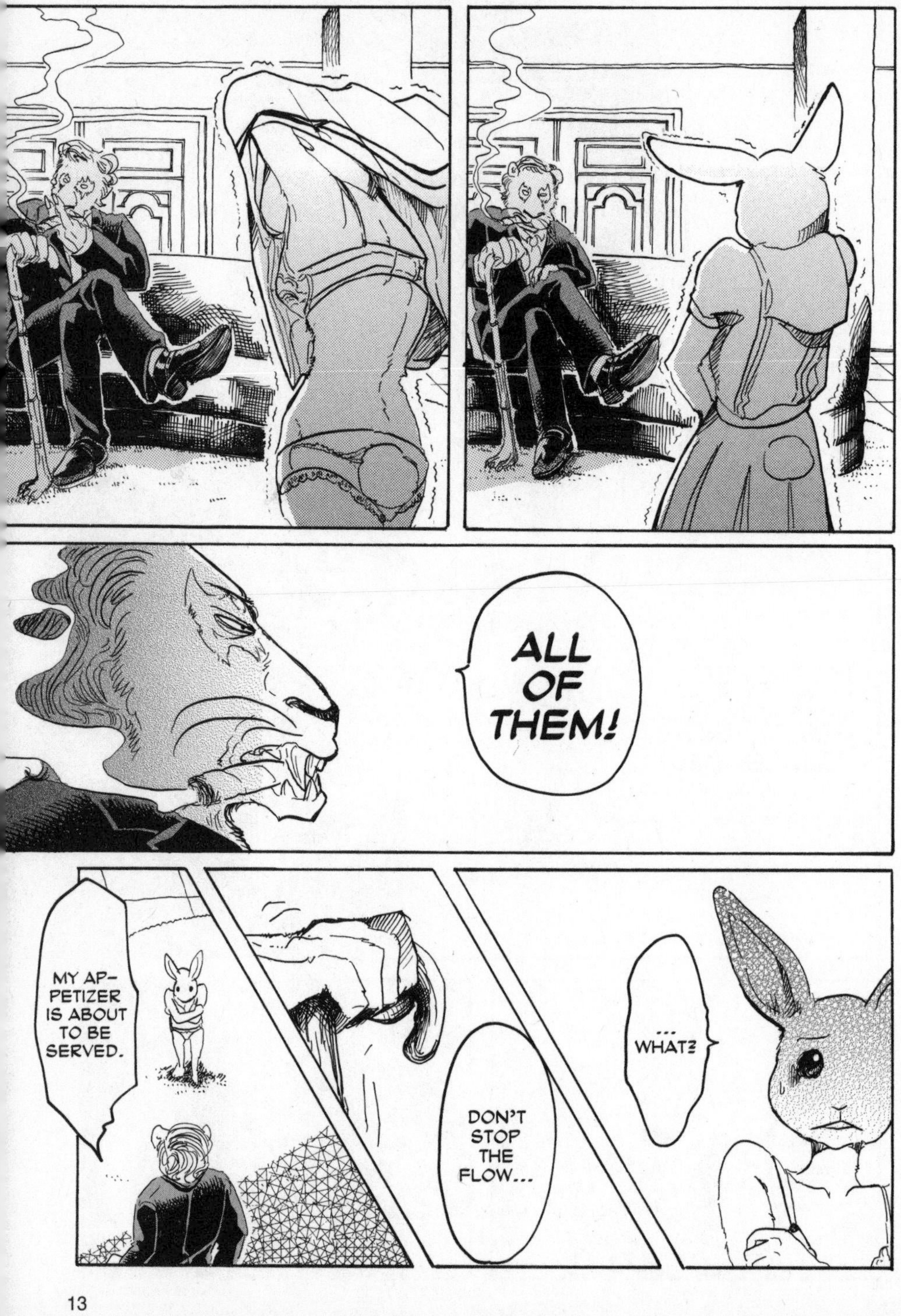
ALL OF THEM!
...WHAT?
DON'T STOP THE FLOW...
MY AP-PETIZER IS ABOUT TO BE SERVED.
...

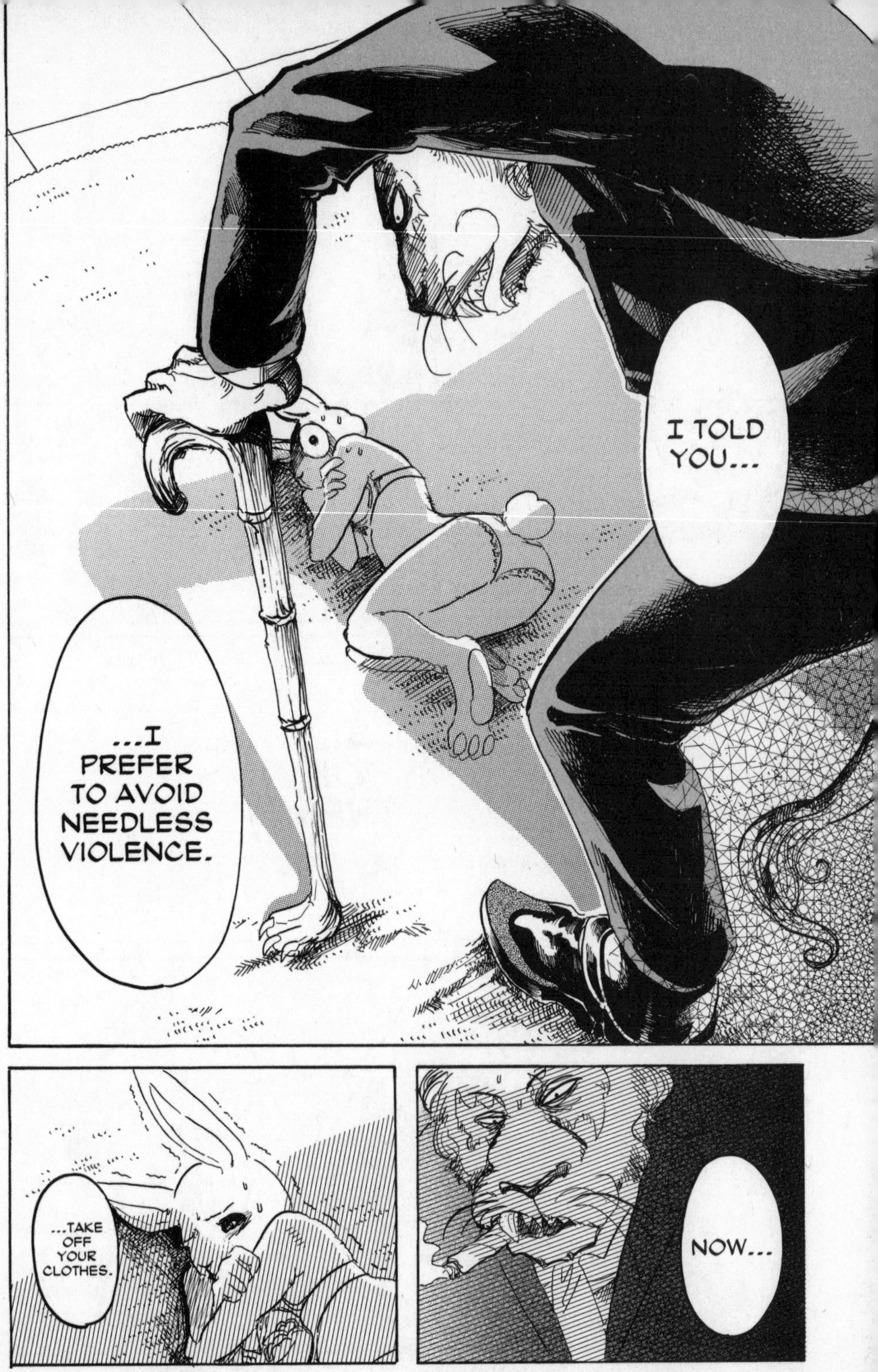
I TOLD YOU...
...I PREFER TO AVOID NEEDLESS VIOLENCE.
NOW...
...TAKE OFF YOUR CLOTHES.

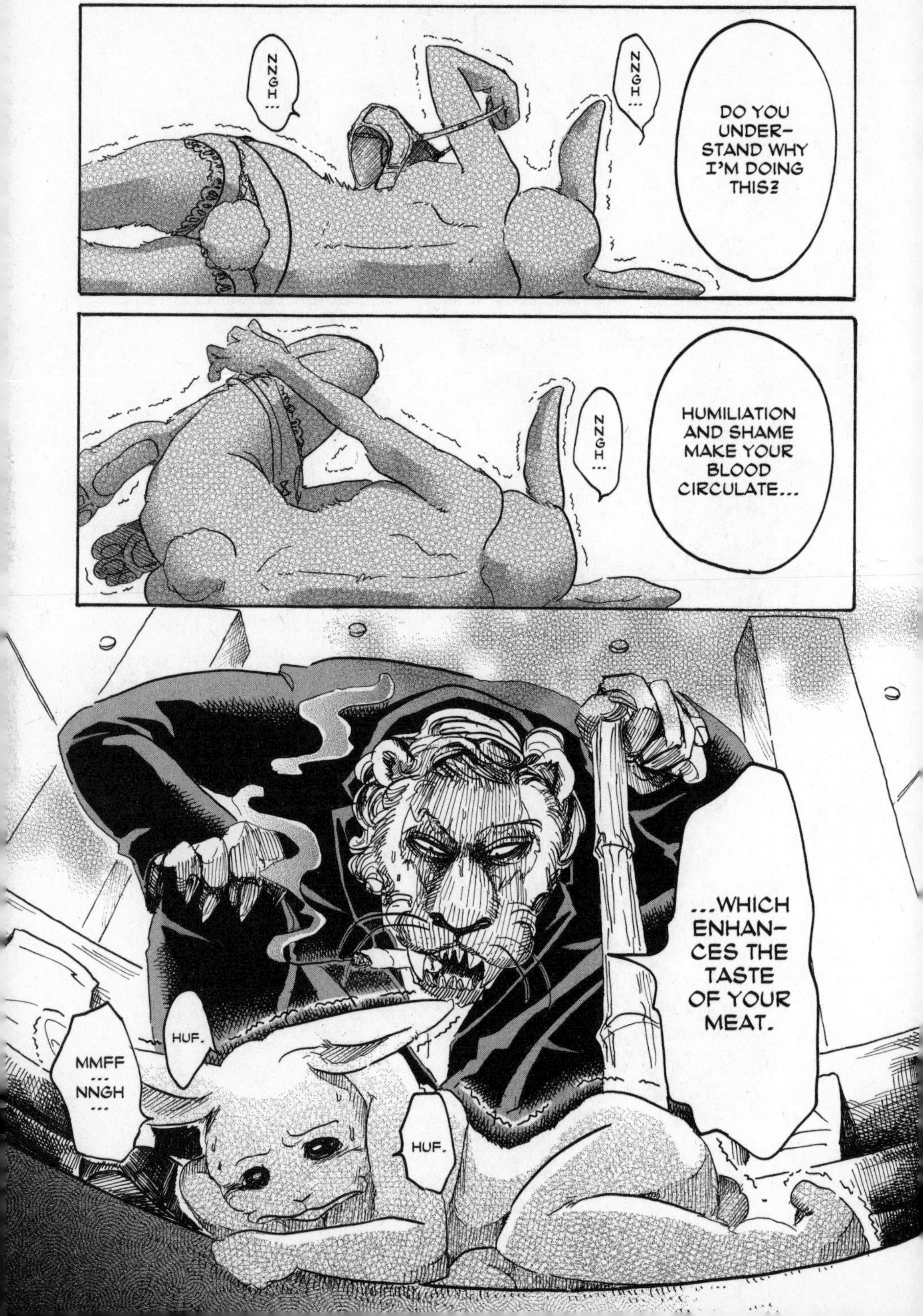
DO YOU UNDER-STAND WHY I'M DOING THIS?
NNGH...
NNGH...
HUMILIATION AND SHAME MAKE YOUR BLOOD CIRCULATE...
NNGH...
...WHICH ENHAN-CES THE TASTE OF YOUR MEAT.
HUF.
HUF.
MMFF... NNGH...

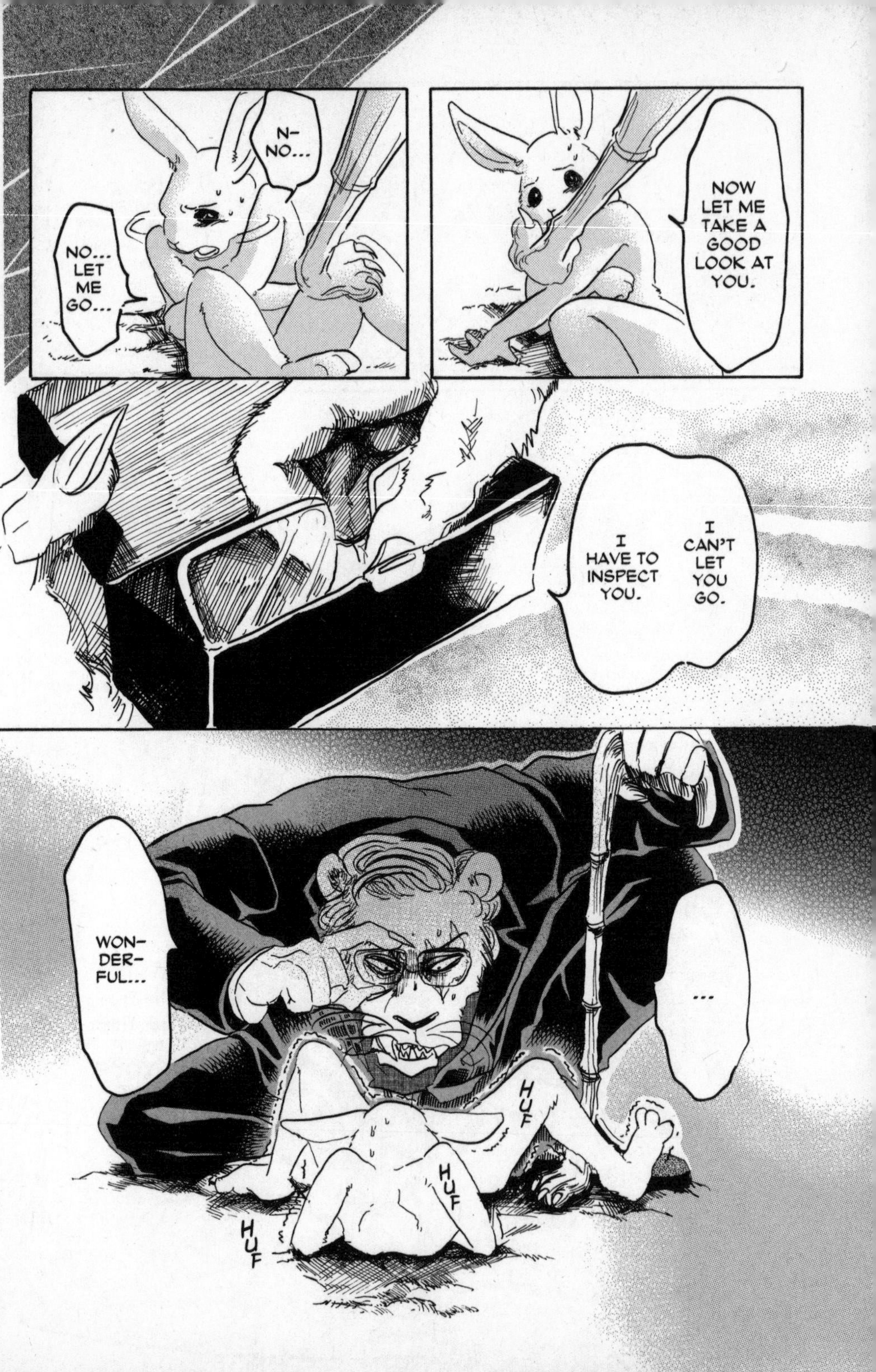
NOW LET ME TAKE A GOOD LOOK AT YOU.
N- NO...
NO... LET ME GO...
I CAN'T LET YOU GO.
I HAVE TO INSPECT YOU.
...
WON-DER-FUL...
HUF
HUF
HUF

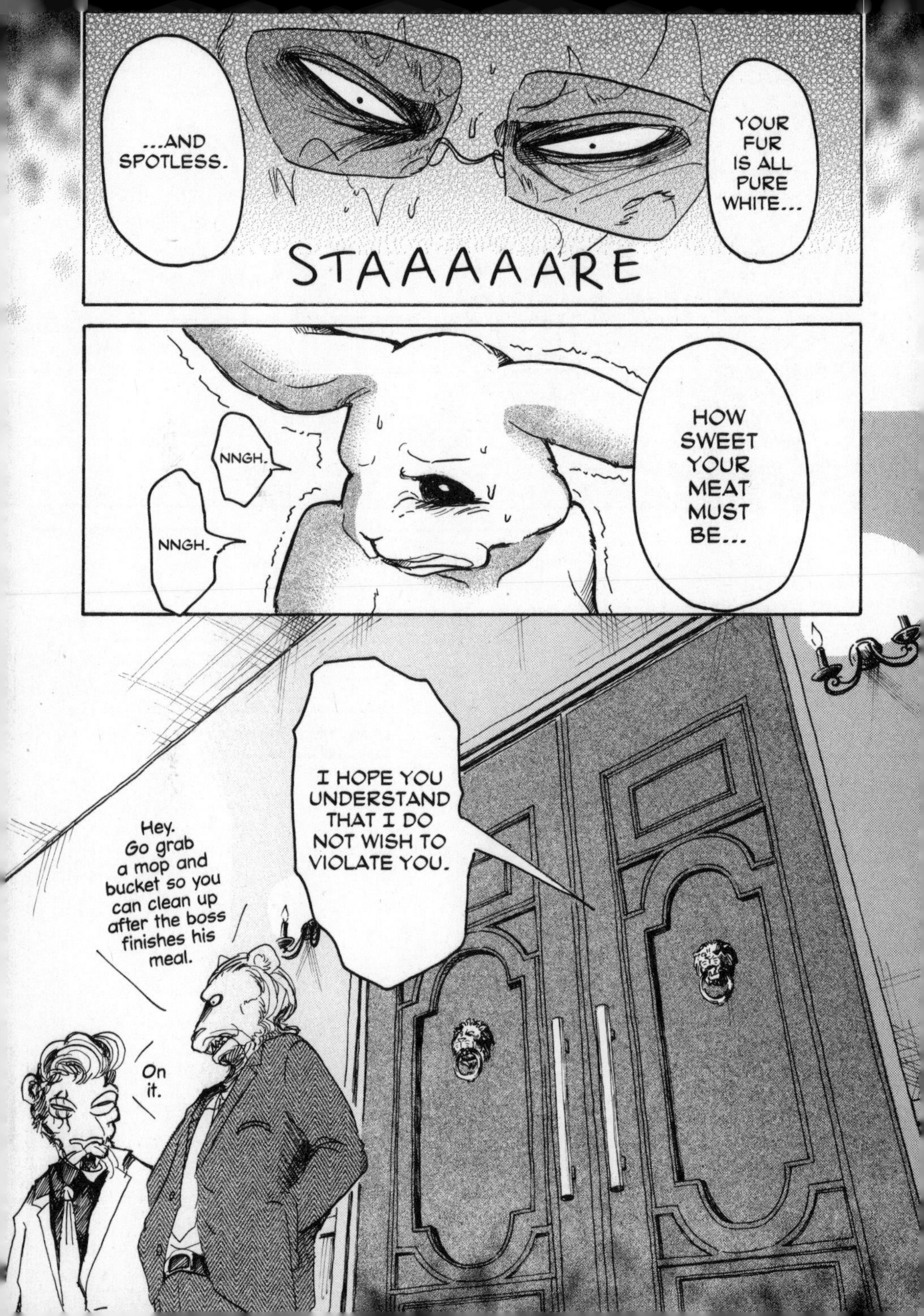
YOUR FUR IS ALL PURE WHITE...
...AND SPOTLESS.
STAAAAARE
HOW SWEET YOUR MEAT MUST BE...
NNGH.
NNGH.
I HOPE YOU UNDERSTAND THAT I DO NOT WISH TO VIOLATE YOU.
Hey. Go grab a mop and bucket so you can clean up after the boss finishes his meal.
On it.

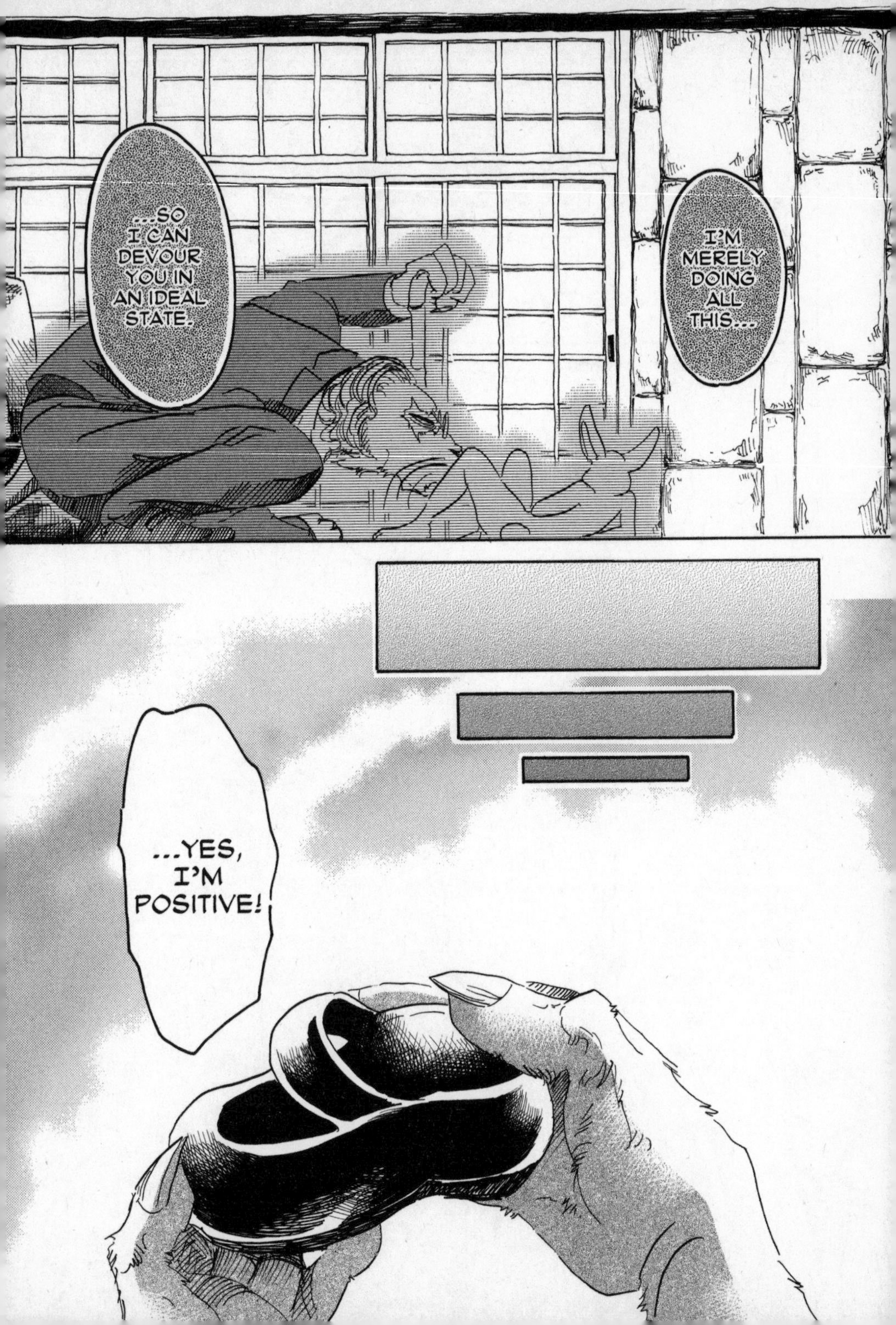
I'M MERELY DOING ALL THIS...
...SO I CAN DEVOUR YOU IN AN IDEAL STATE.
...YES, I'M POSITIVE!

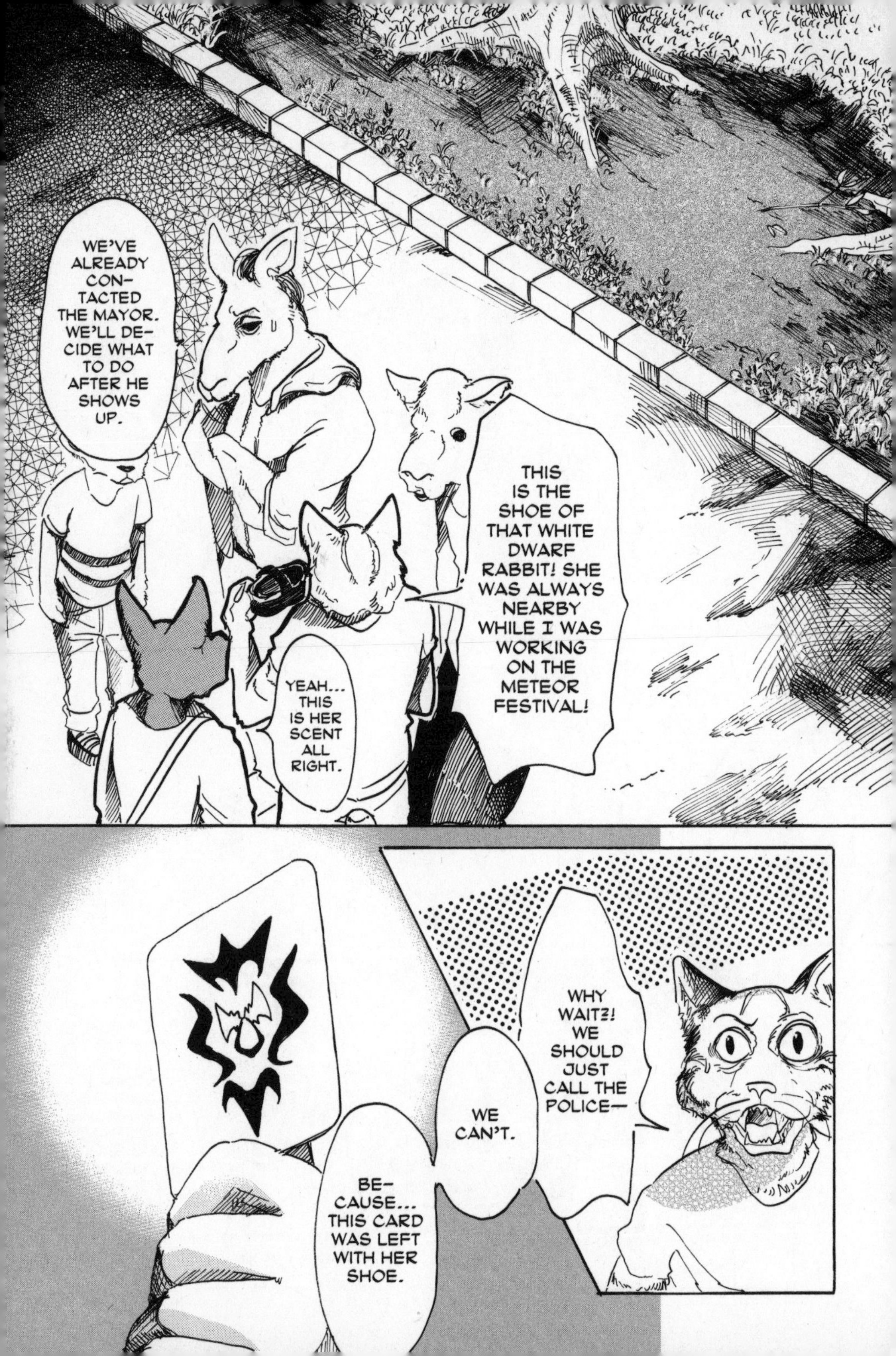
THIS IS THE SHOE OF THAT WHITE DWARF RABBIT! SHE WAS ALWAYS NEARBY WHILE I WAS WORKING ON THE METEOR FESTIVAL!
YEAH... THIS IS HER SCENT ALL RIGHT.
WE'VE ALREADY CON-TACTED THE MAYOR. WE'LL DE-CIDE WHAT TO DO AFTER HE SHOWS UP.
WHY WAIT?! WE SHOULD JUST CALL THE POLICE—
WE CAN'T.
BE-CAUSE... THIS CARD WAS LEFT WITH HER SHOE.

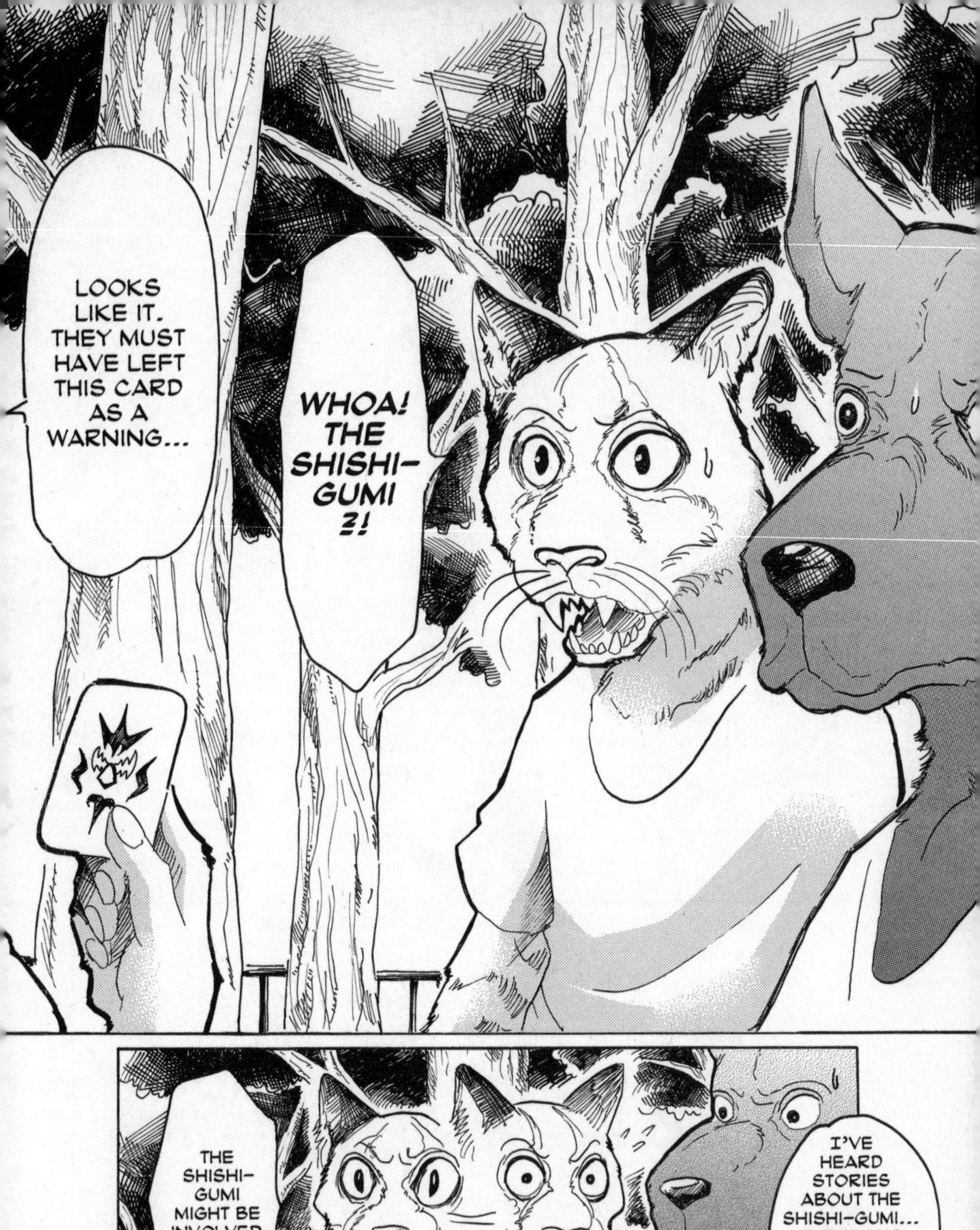
WHOA! THE SHISHI-GUMI ?!
LOOKS LIKE IT. THEY MUST HAVE LEFT THIS CARD AS A WARNING...
I'VE HEARD STORIES ABOUT THE SHISHI-GUMI... THEY HANG FRESHLY SEVERED HEADS OF HERBIVORES IN FRONT OF THEIR HEAD-QUARTERS TO KEEP BEASTS AWAY.
JERK! HOW COULD YOU SAY THAT IN FRONT OF A HORSE ?!
THE SHISHI-GUMI MIGHT BE INVOLVED, BUT A GIRL HAS BEEN KID-NAPPED!

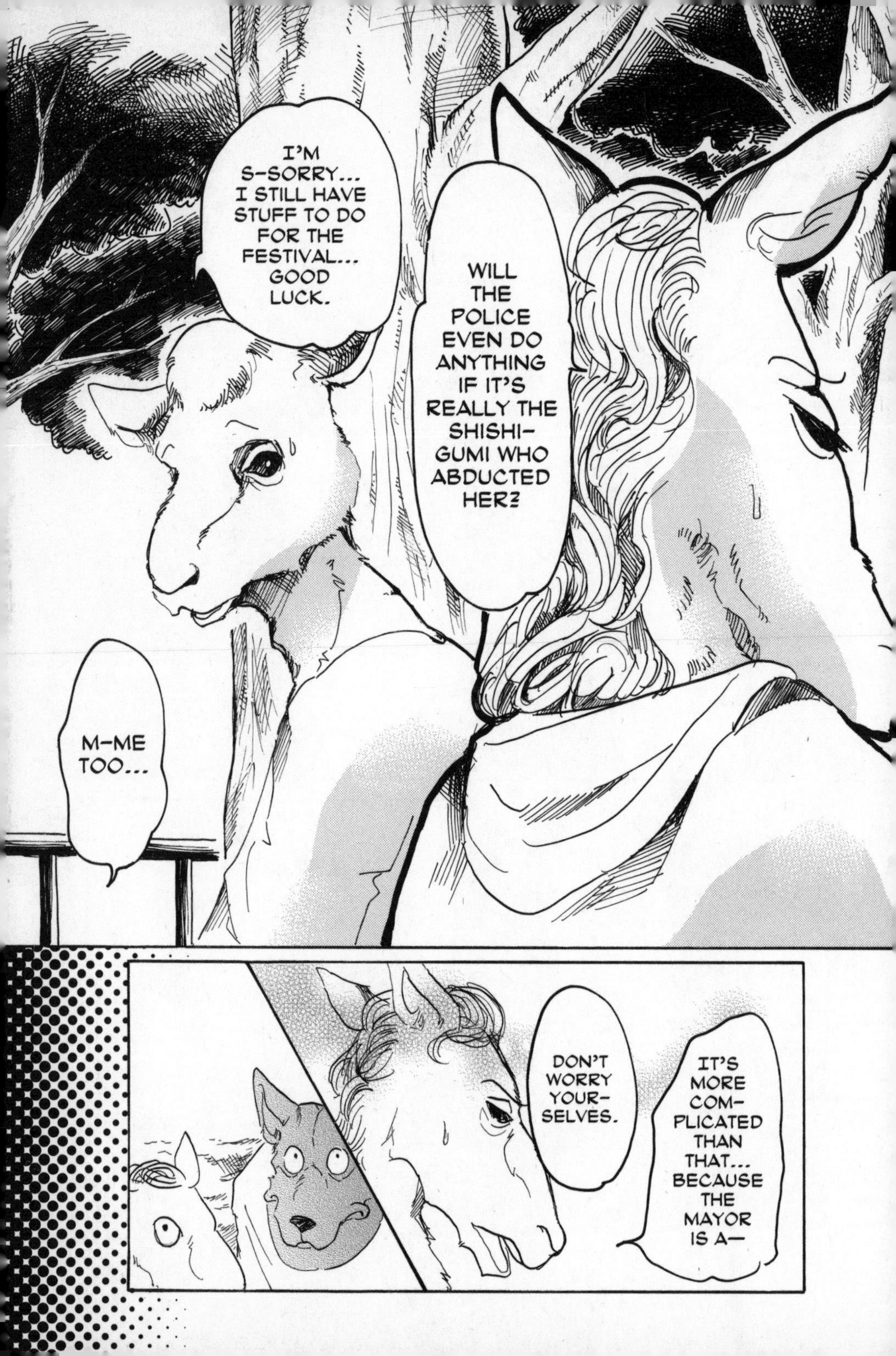
WILL THE POLICE EVEN DO ANYTHING IF IT'S REALLY THE SHISHI-GUMI WHO ABDUCTED HER?
I'M S-SORRY... I STILL HAVE STUFF TO DO FOR THE FESTIVAL... GOOD LUCK.
M-ME TOO...
IT'S MORE COM-PLICATED THAN THAT... BECAUSE THE MAYOR IS A—
DON'T WORRY YOUR-SELVES.

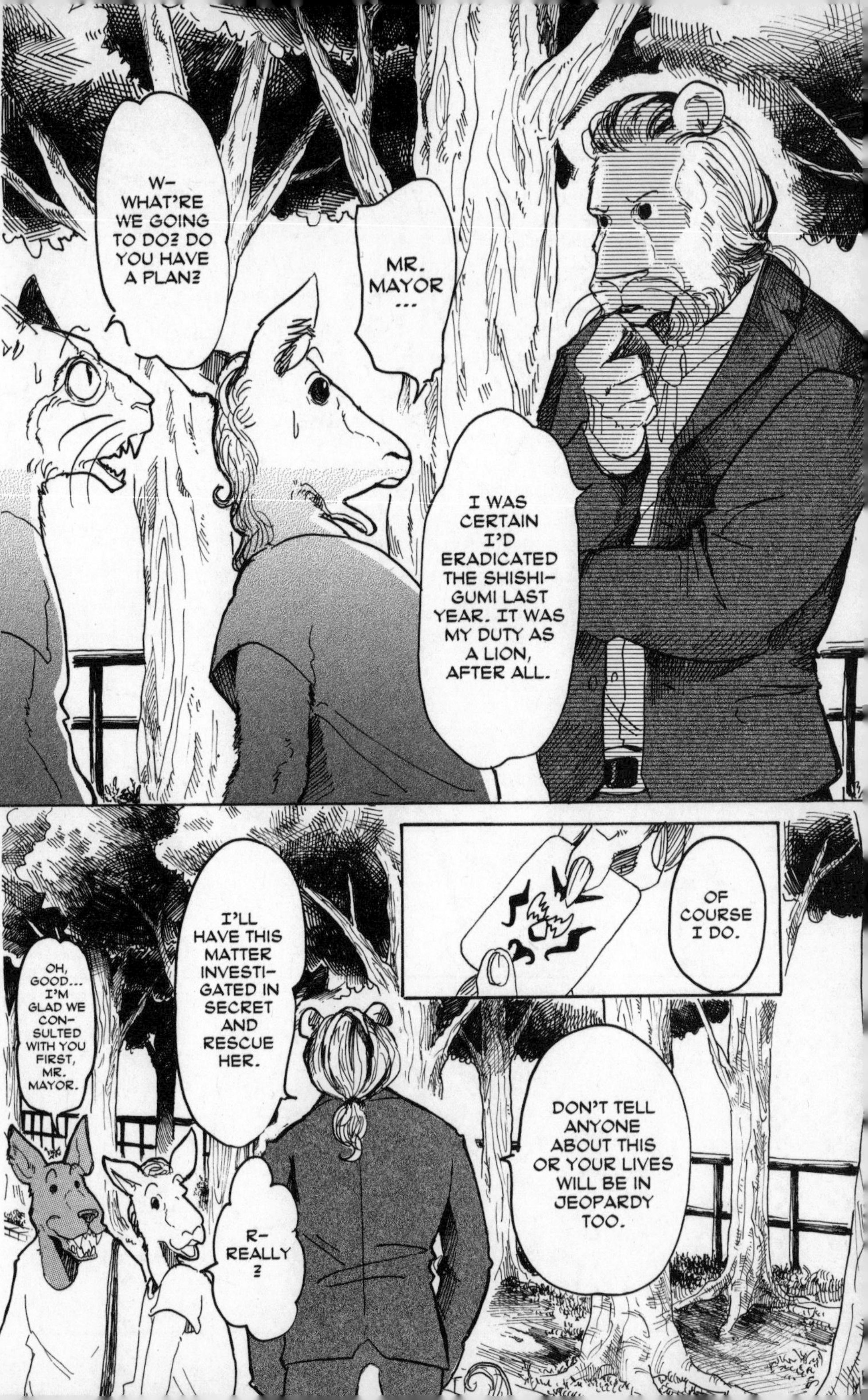
MR. MAYOR...
W-WHAT'RE WE GOING TO DO? DO YOU HAVE A PLAN?
I WAS CERTAIN I'D ERADICATED THE SHISHI-GUMI LAST YEAR. IT WAS MY DUTY AS A LION, AFTER ALL.
OF COURSE I DO.
I'LL HAVE THIS MATTER INVESTI-GATED IN SECRET AND RESCUE HER.
OH, GOOD... I'M GLAD WE CON-SULTED WITH YOU FIRST, MR. MAYOR.
R-REALLY?
DON'T TELL ANYONE ABOUT THIS OR YOUR LIVES WILL BE IN JEOPARDY TOO.

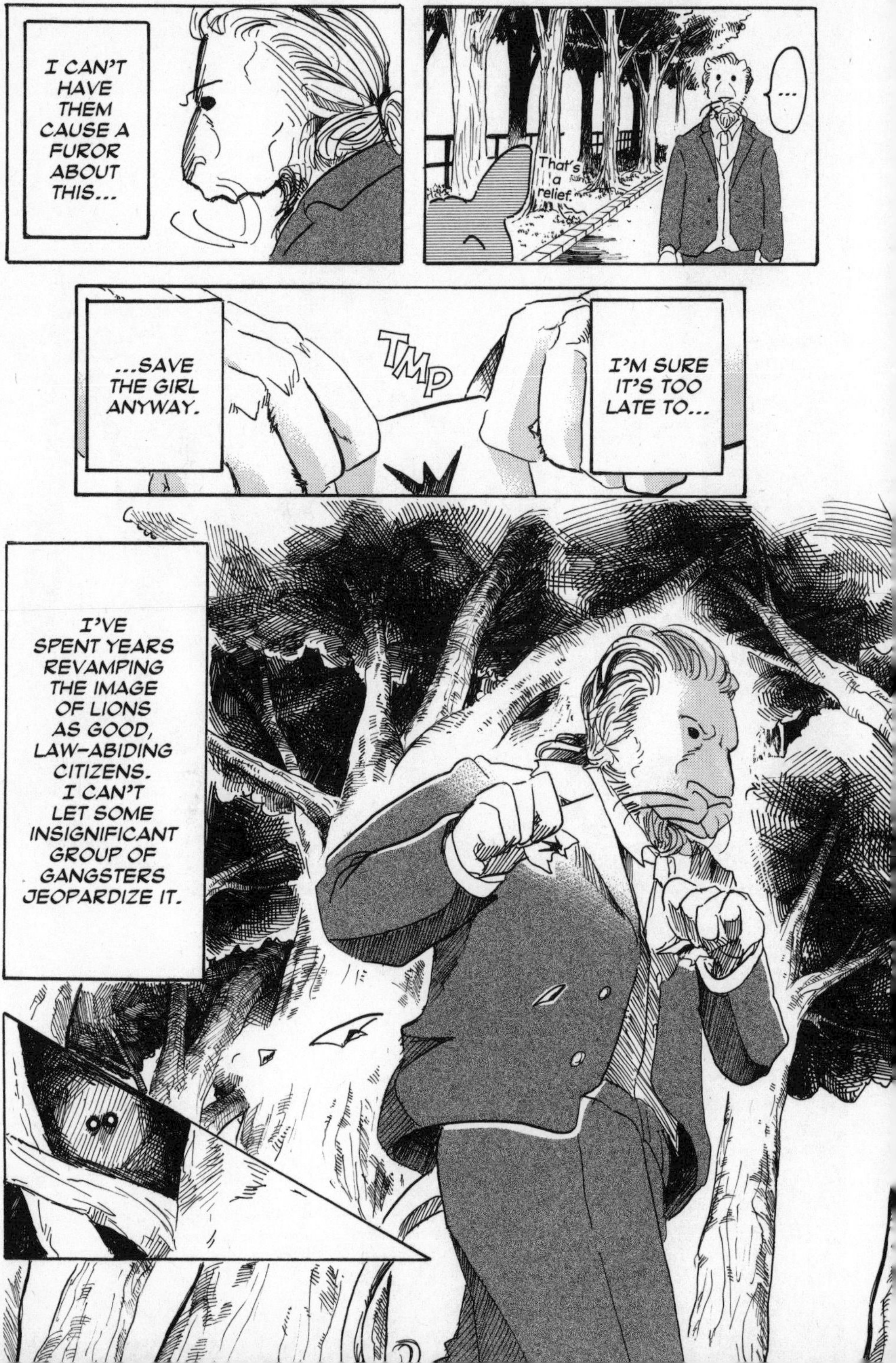
...
That's a relief.
I CAN'T HAVE THEM CAUSE A FUROR ABOUT THIS...
I'M SURE IT'S TOO LATE TO...
TMP
...SAVE THE GIRL ANYWAY.
I'VE SPENT YEARS REVAMPING THE IMAGE OF LIONS AS GOOD, LAW-ABIDING CITIZENS. I CAN'T LET SOME INSIGNIFICANT GROUP OF GANGSTERS JEOPARDIZE IT.

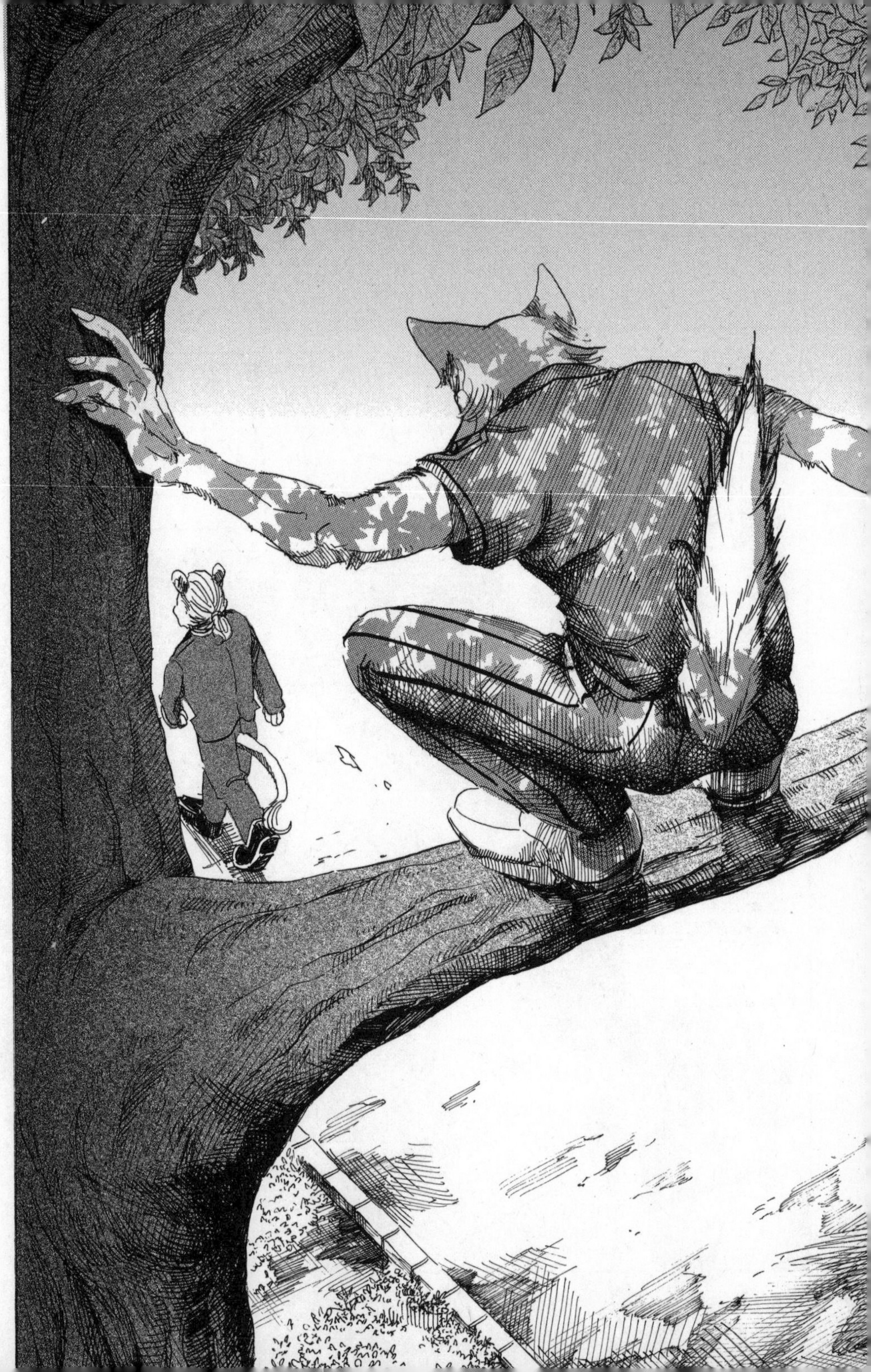

Chapter 36: What Spills Over from His Fists

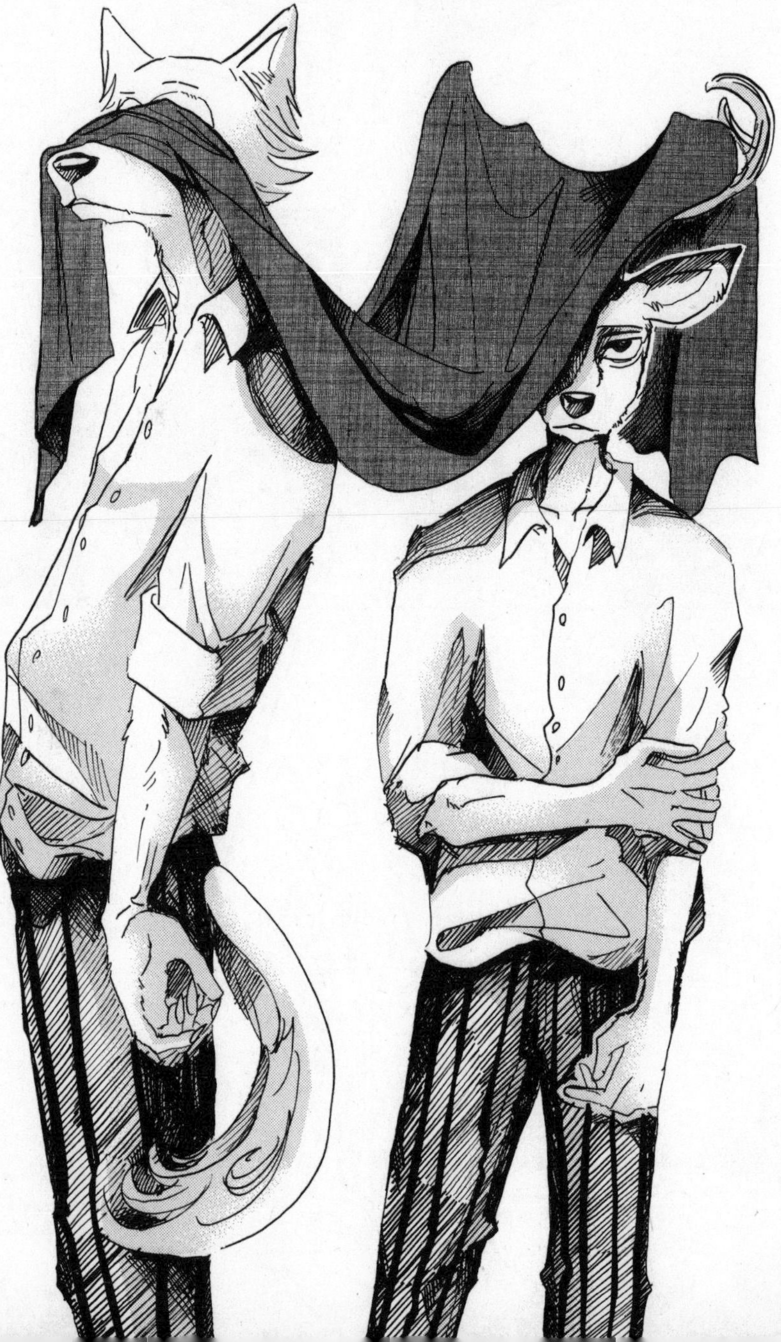

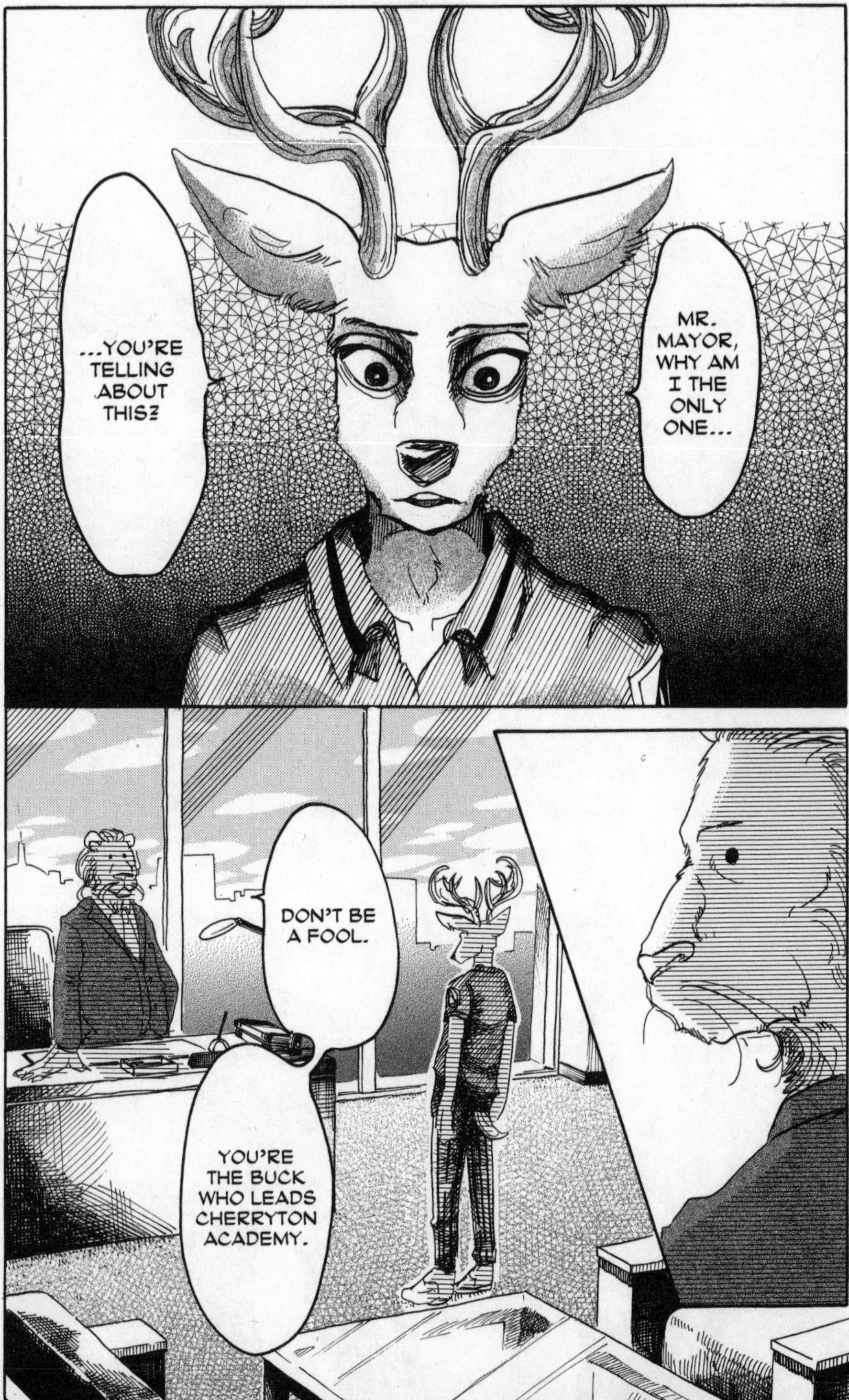
MR. MAYOR, WHY AM I THE ONLY ONE...
...YOU'RE TELLING ABOUT THIS?
DON'T BE A FOOL.
YOU'RE THE BUCK WHO LEADS CHERRYTON ACADEMY.

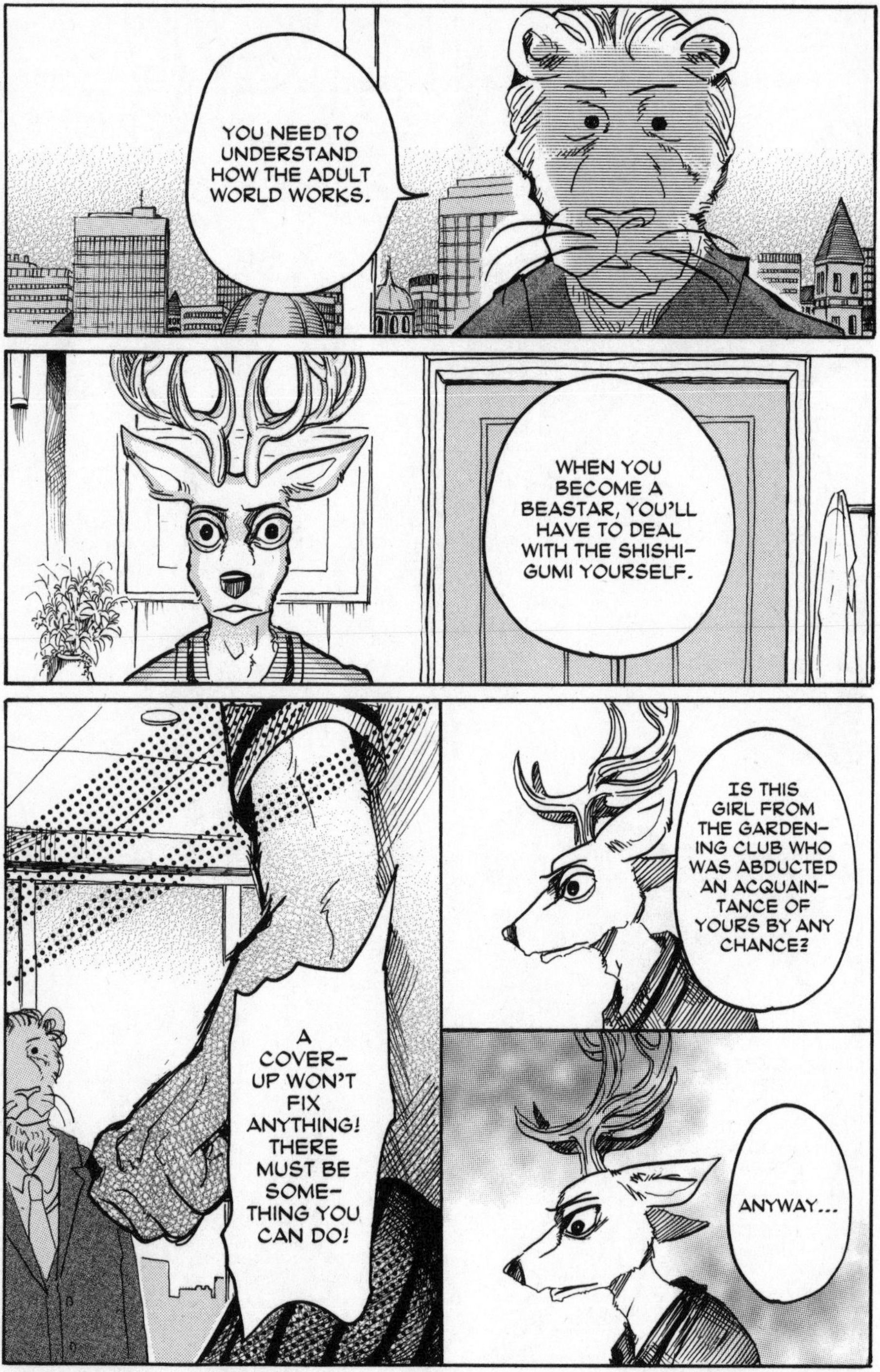
YOU NEED TO UNDERSTAND HOW THE ADULT WORLD WORKS.
WHEN YOU BECOME A BEASTAR, YOU'LL HAVE TO DEAL WITH THE SHISHI-GUMI YOURSELF.
IS THIS GIRL FROM THE GARDEN-ING CLUB WHO WAS ABDUCTED AN ACQUAIN-TANCE OF YOURS BY ANY CHANCE?
ANYWAY...
A COVER-UP WON'T FIX ANYTHING! THERE MUST BE SOME-THING YOU CAN DO!

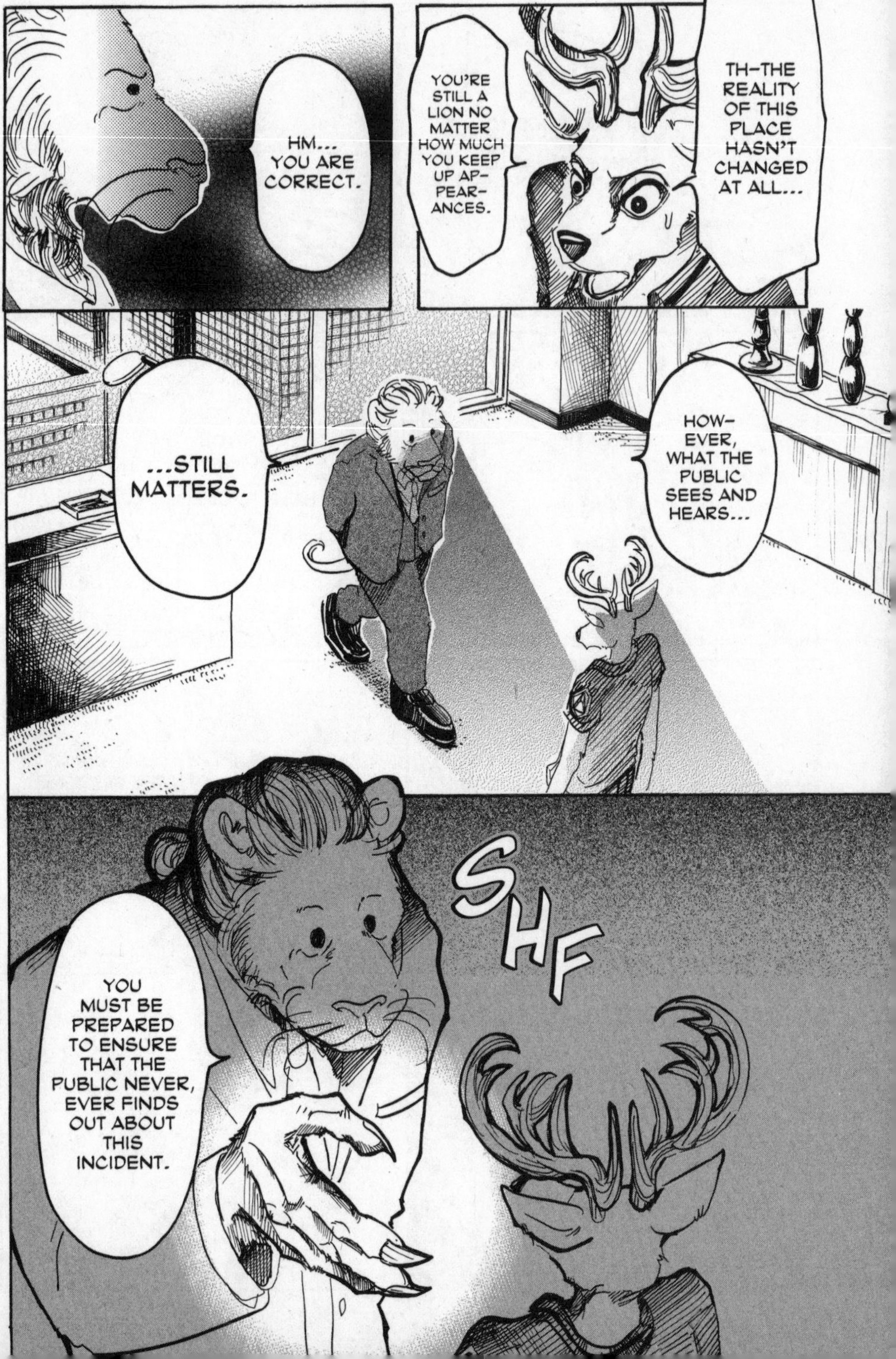
TH-THE REALITY OF THIS PLACE HASN'T CHANGED AT ALL...
YOU'RE STILL A LION NO MATTER HOW MUCH YOU KEEP UP AP-PEAR-ANCES.
HM... YOU ARE CORRECT.
HOW-EVER, WHAT THE PUBLIC SEES AND HEARS...
...STILL MATTERS.
SHF
YOU MUST BE PREPARED TO ENSURE THAT THE PUBLIC NEVER, EVER FINDS OUT ABOUT THIS INCIDENT.

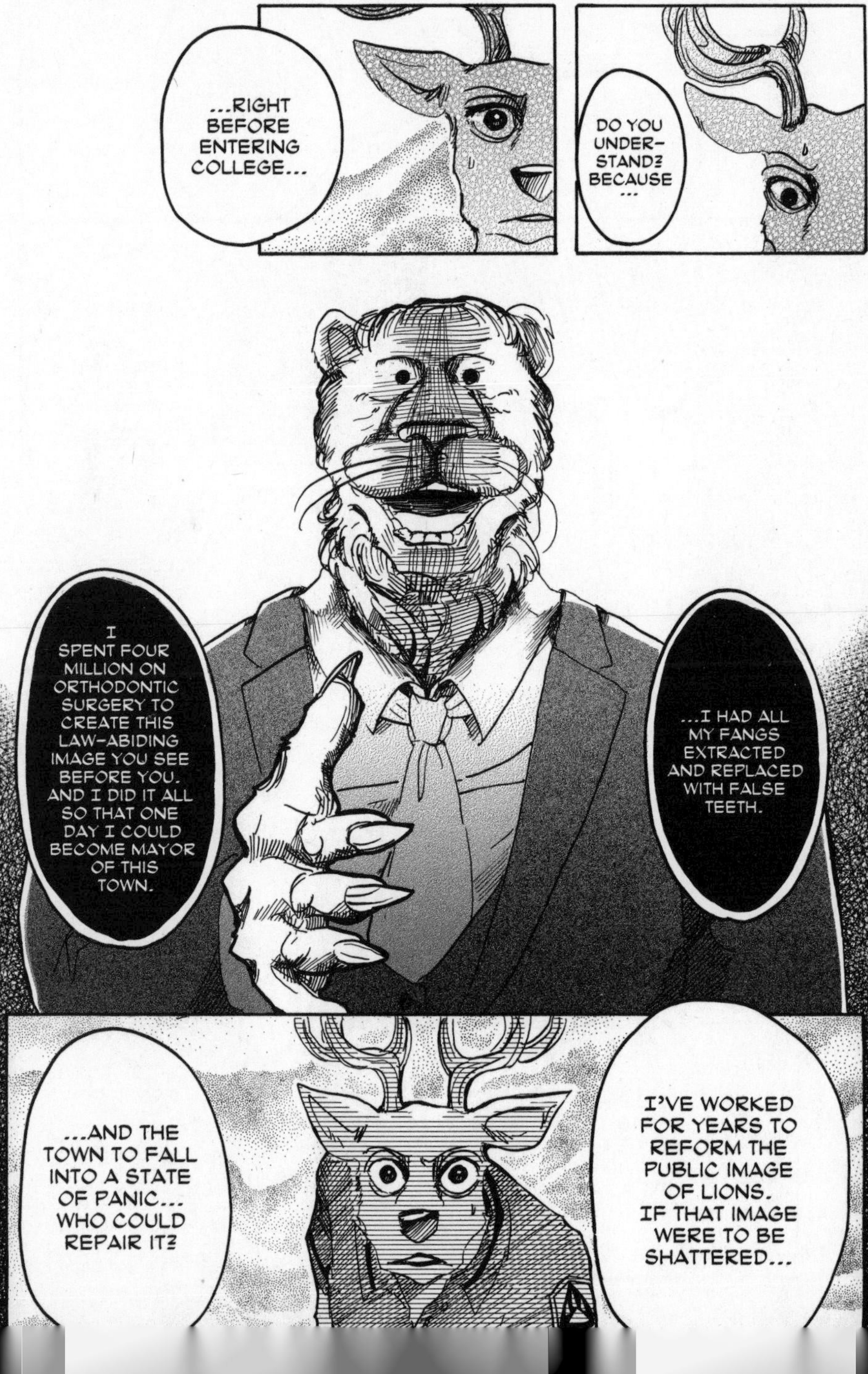
DO YOU UNDERSTAND? BECAUSE...
...RIGHT BEFORE ENTERING COLLEGE...
...I HAD ALL MY FANGS EXTRACTED AND REPLACED WITH FALSE TEETH.
I SPENT FOUR MILLION ON ORTHODONTIC SURGERY TO CREATE THIS LAW-ABIDING IMAGE YOU SEE BEFORE YOU. AND I DID IT ALL SO THAT ONE DAY I COULD BECOME MAYOR OF THIS TOWN.
I'VE WORKED FOR YEARS TO REFORM THE PUBLIC IMAGE OF LIONS. IF THAT IMAGE WERE TO BE SHATTERED...
...AND THE TOWN TO FALL INTO A STATE OF PANIC... WHO COULD REPAIR IT?

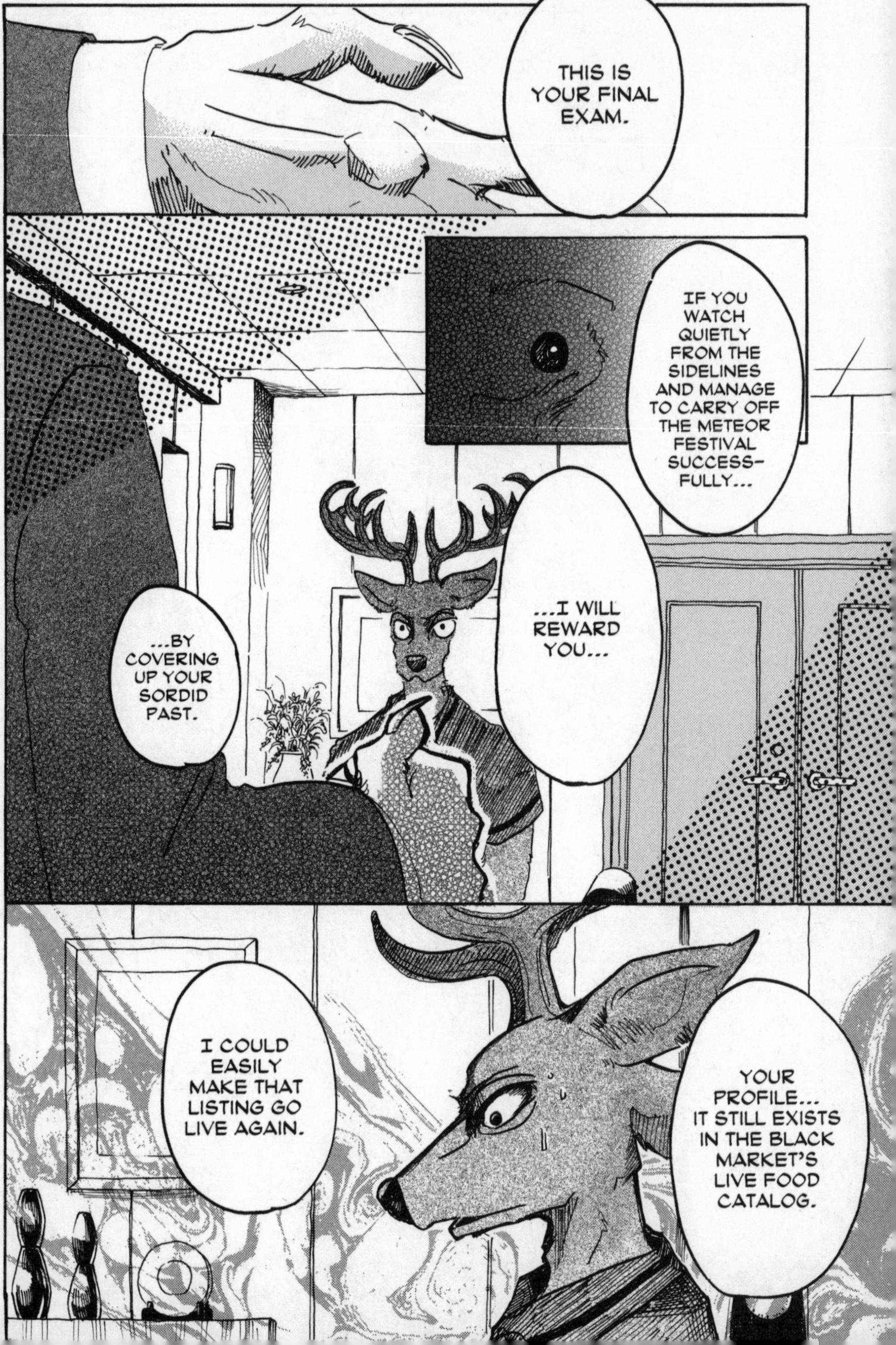
THIS IS YOUR FINAL EXAM.
IF YOU WATCH QUIETLY FROM THE SIDELINES AND MANAGE TO CARRY OFF THE METEOR FESTIVAL SUCCESS-FULLY...
...I WILL REWARD YOU...
...BY COVERING UP YOUR SORDID PAST.
YOUR PROFILE... IT STILL EXISTS IN THE BLACK MARKET'S LIVE FOOD CATALOG.
I COULD EASILY MAKE THAT LISTING GO LIVE AGAIN.

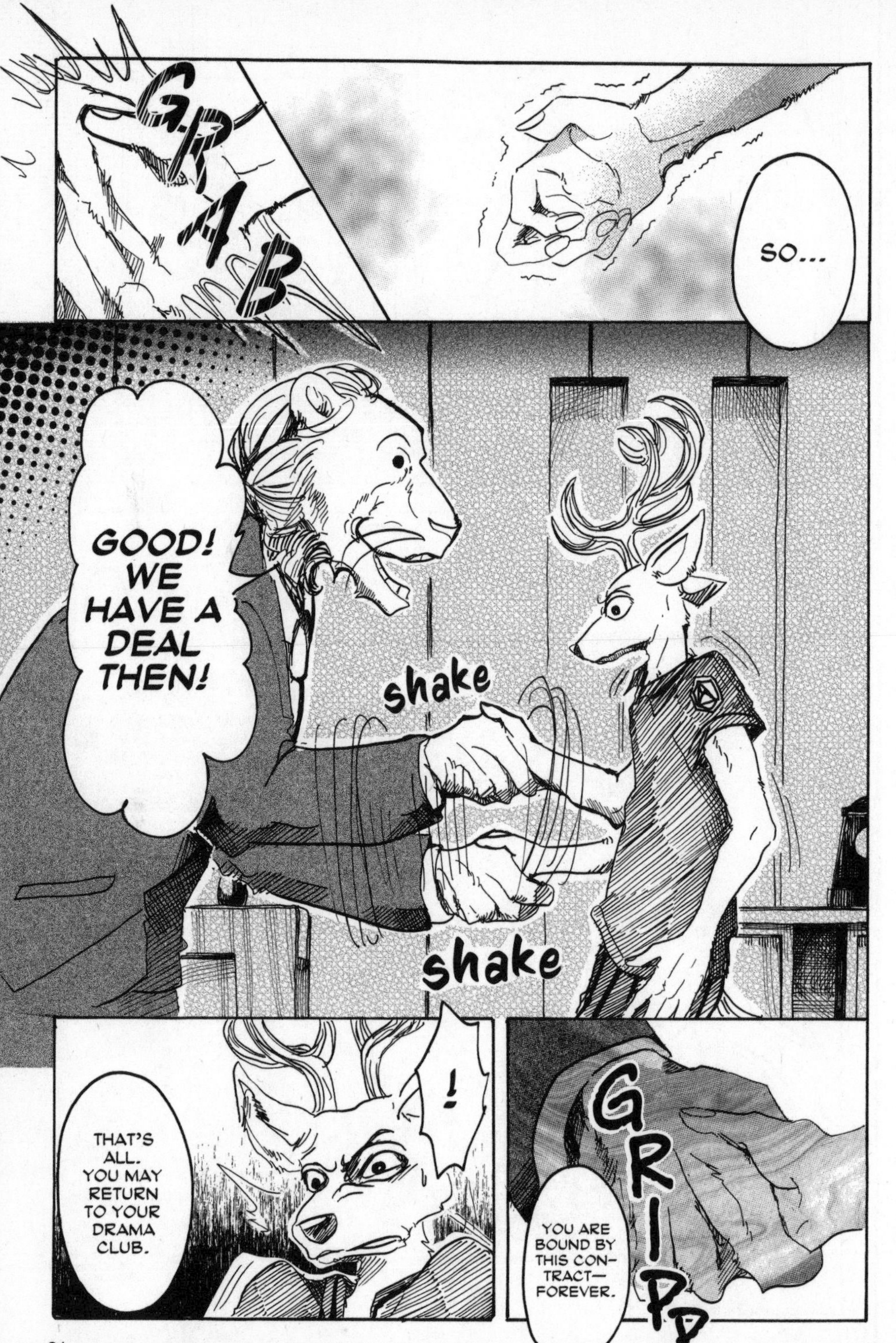
SO...
GRAB
GOOD! WE HAVE A DEAL THEN!
shake
shake
GRIPP
YOU ARE BOUND BY THIS CON-TRACT—FOREVER.
!
THAT'S ALL. YOU MAY RETURN TO YOUR DRAMA CLUB.

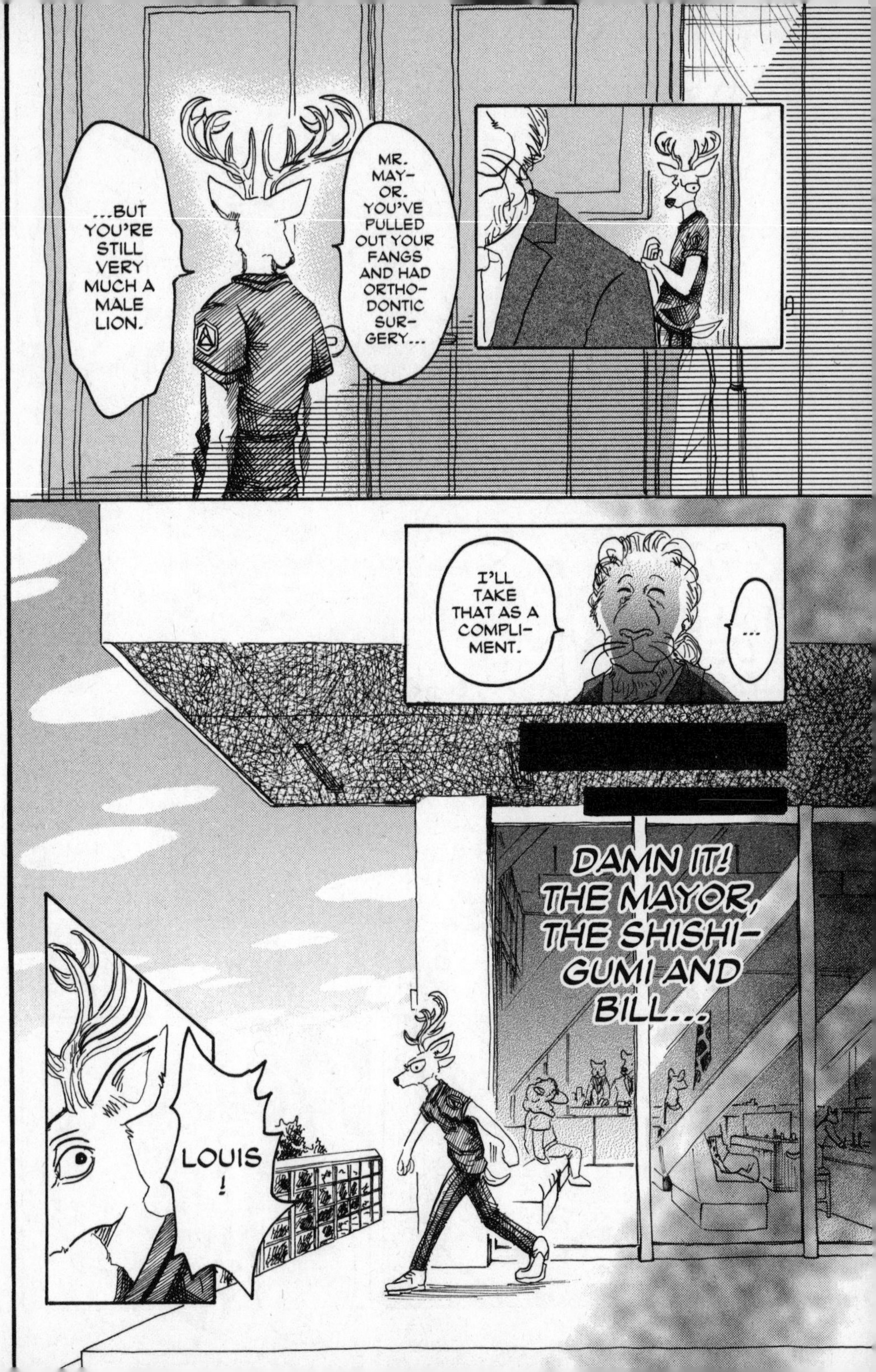
MR. MAYOR. YOU'VE PULLED OUT YOUR FANGS AND HAD ORTHODONTIC SURGERY...
...BUT YOU'RE STILL VERY MUCH A MALE LION.
...
I'LL TAKE THAT AS A COMPLIMENT.
[redacted]
DAMN IT! THE MAYOR, THE SHISHI-GUMI AND BILL...
LOUIS!

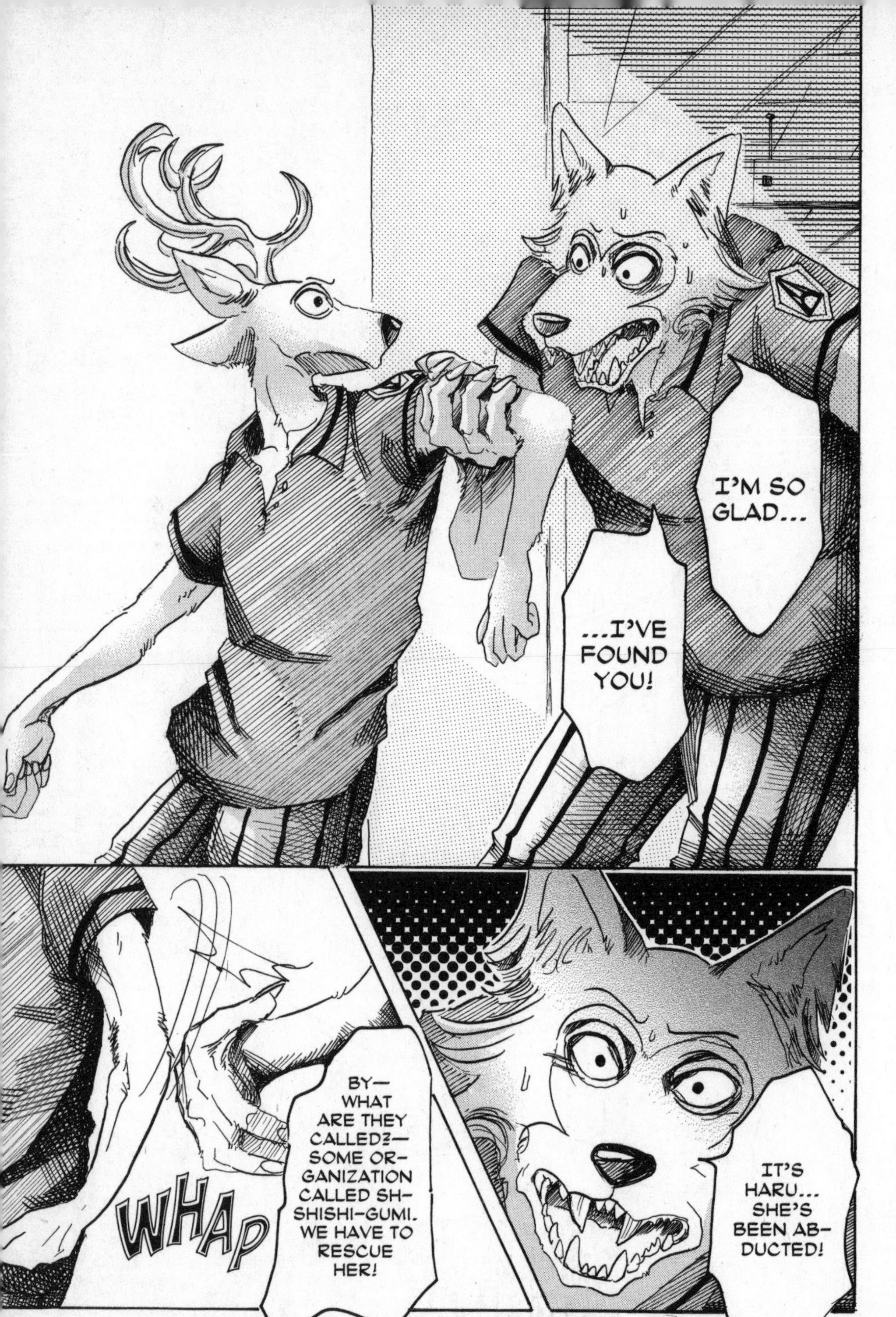
I'M SO GLAD...
...I'VE FOUND YOU!
IT'S HARU... SHE'S BEEN ABDUCTED!
BY— WHAT ARE THEY CALLED?— SOME OR-GANIZATION CALLED SH-SHISHI-GUMI. WE HAVE TO RESCUE HER!
WHAP

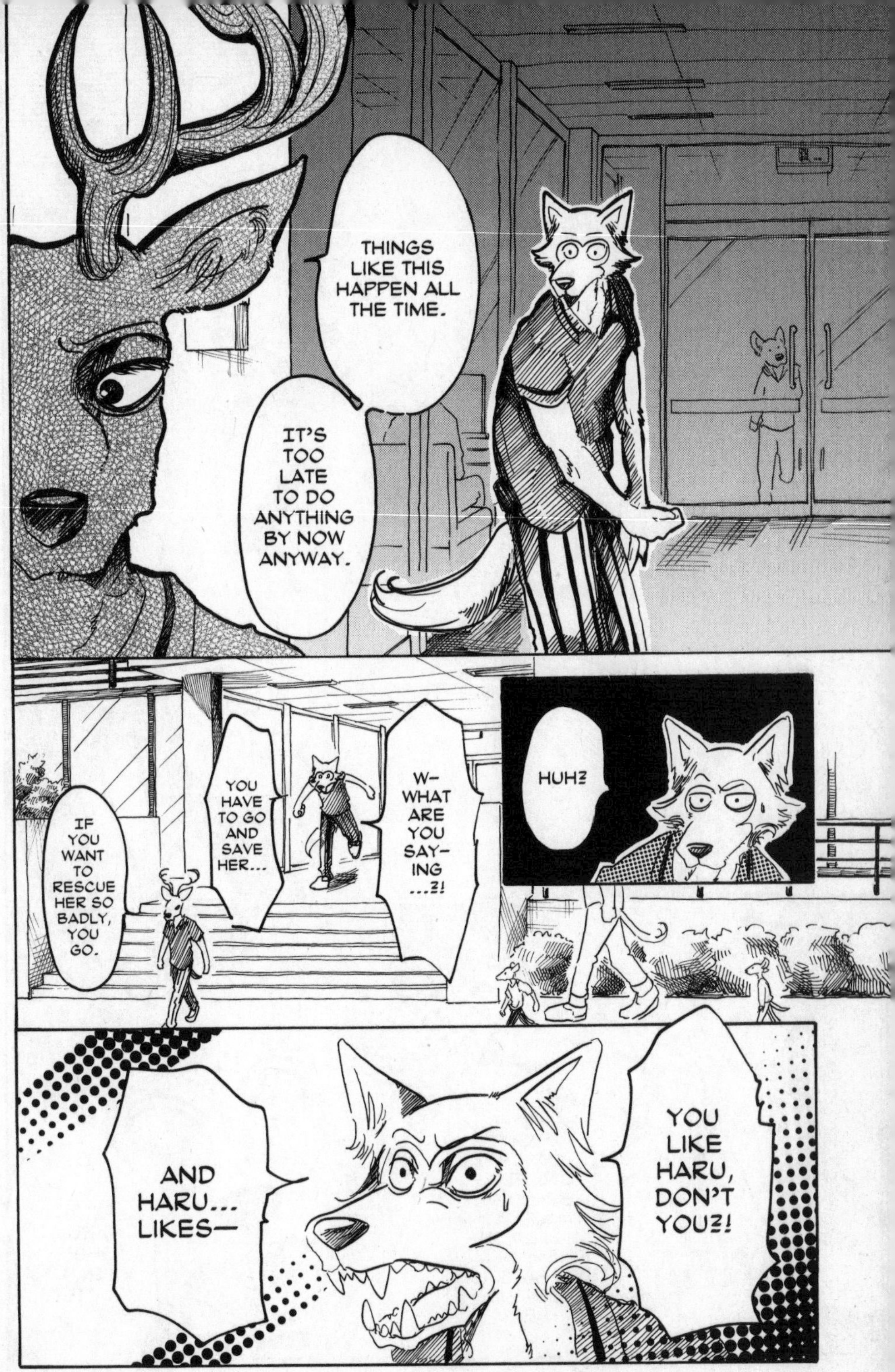
THINGS LIKE THIS HAPPEN ALL THE TIME.
IT'S TOO LATE TO DO ANYTHING BY NOW ANYWAY.
HUH?
W-WHAT ARE YOU SAYING...?!
YOU HAVE TO GO AND SAVE HER...
IF YOU WANT TO RESCUE HER SO BADLY, YOU GO.
YOU LIKE HARU, DON'T YOU?!
AND HARU... LIKES—

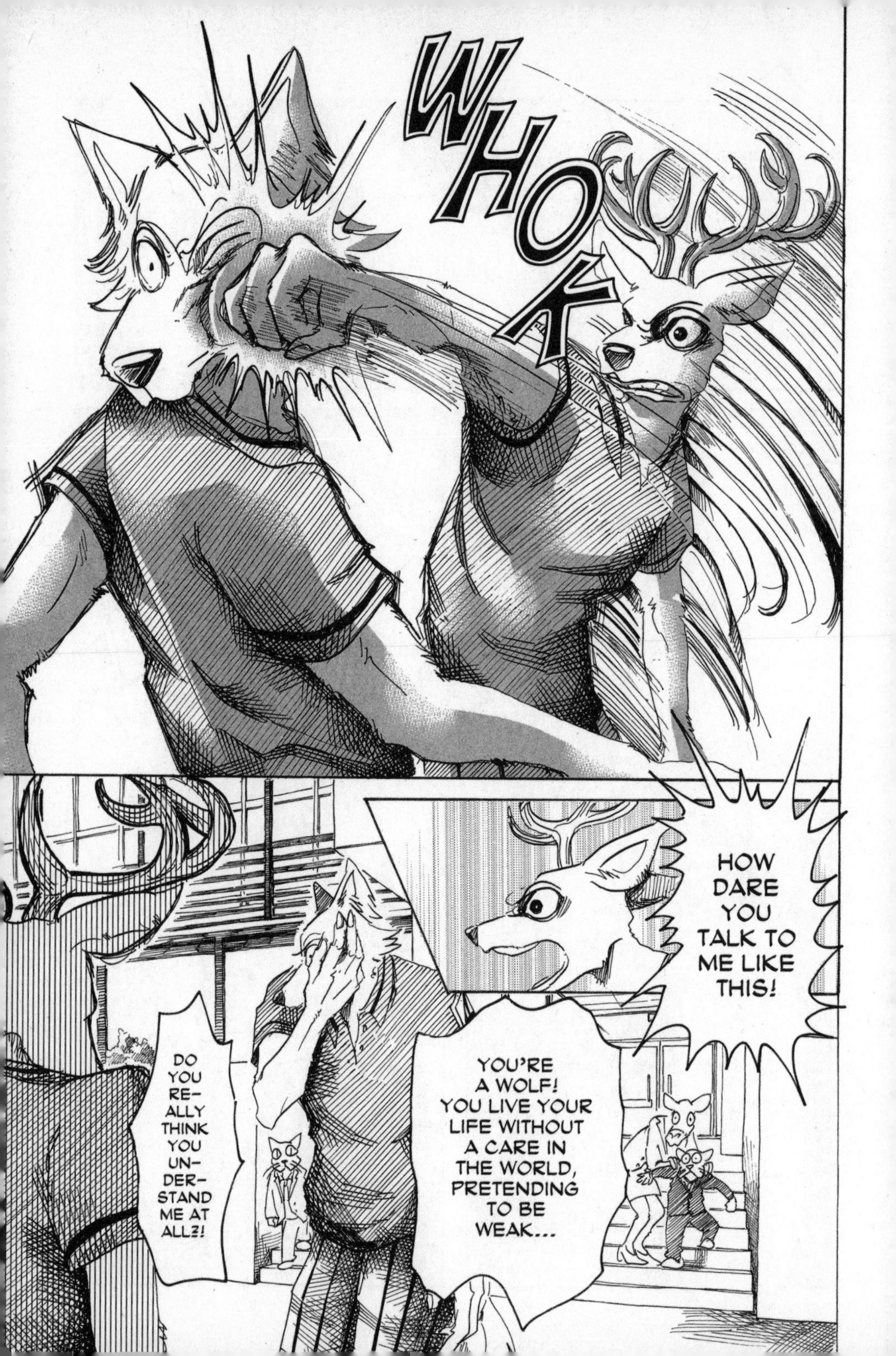
WHOK
HOW DARE YOU TALK TO ME LIKE THIS!
YOU'RE A WOLF! YOU LIVE YOUR LIFE WITHOUT A CARE IN THE WORLD, PRETENDING TO BE WEAK...
DO YOU RE-ALLY THINK YOU UN-DER-STAND ME AT ALL?!

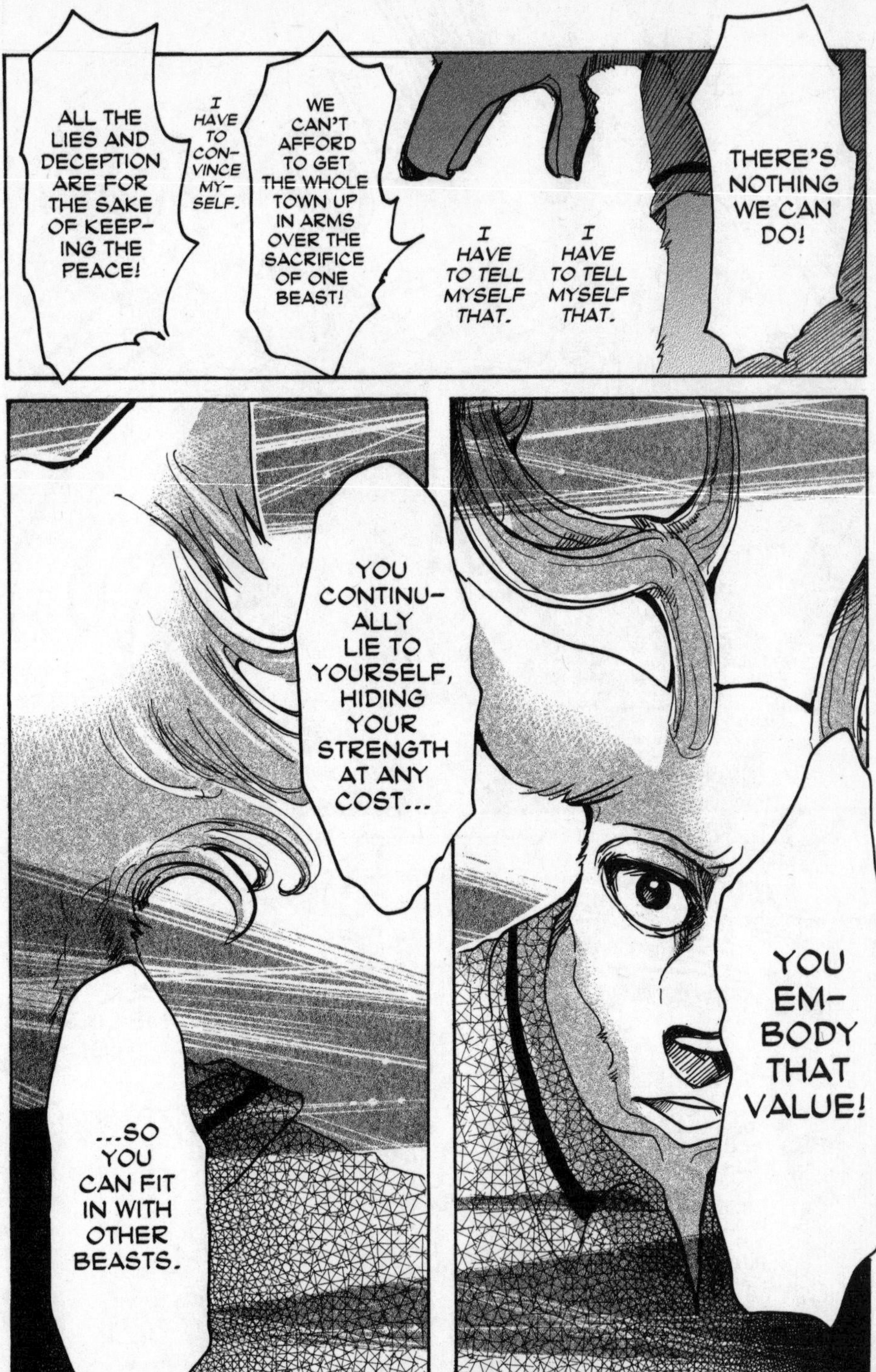
THERE'S NOTHING WE CAN DO!
I HAVE TO TELL MYSELF THAT.
I HAVE TO TELL MYSELF THAT.
WE CAN'T AFFORD TO GET THE WHOLE TOWN UP IN ARMS OVER THE SACRIFICE OF ONE BEAST!
I HAVE TO CONVINCE MYSELF.
ALL THE LIES AND DECEPTION ARE FOR THE SAKE OF KEEPING THE PEACE!
YOU EMBODY THAT VALUE!
YOU CONTINUALLY LIE TO YOURSELF, HIDING YOUR STRENGTH AT ANY COST...
...SO YOU CAN FIT IN WITH OTHER BEASTS.

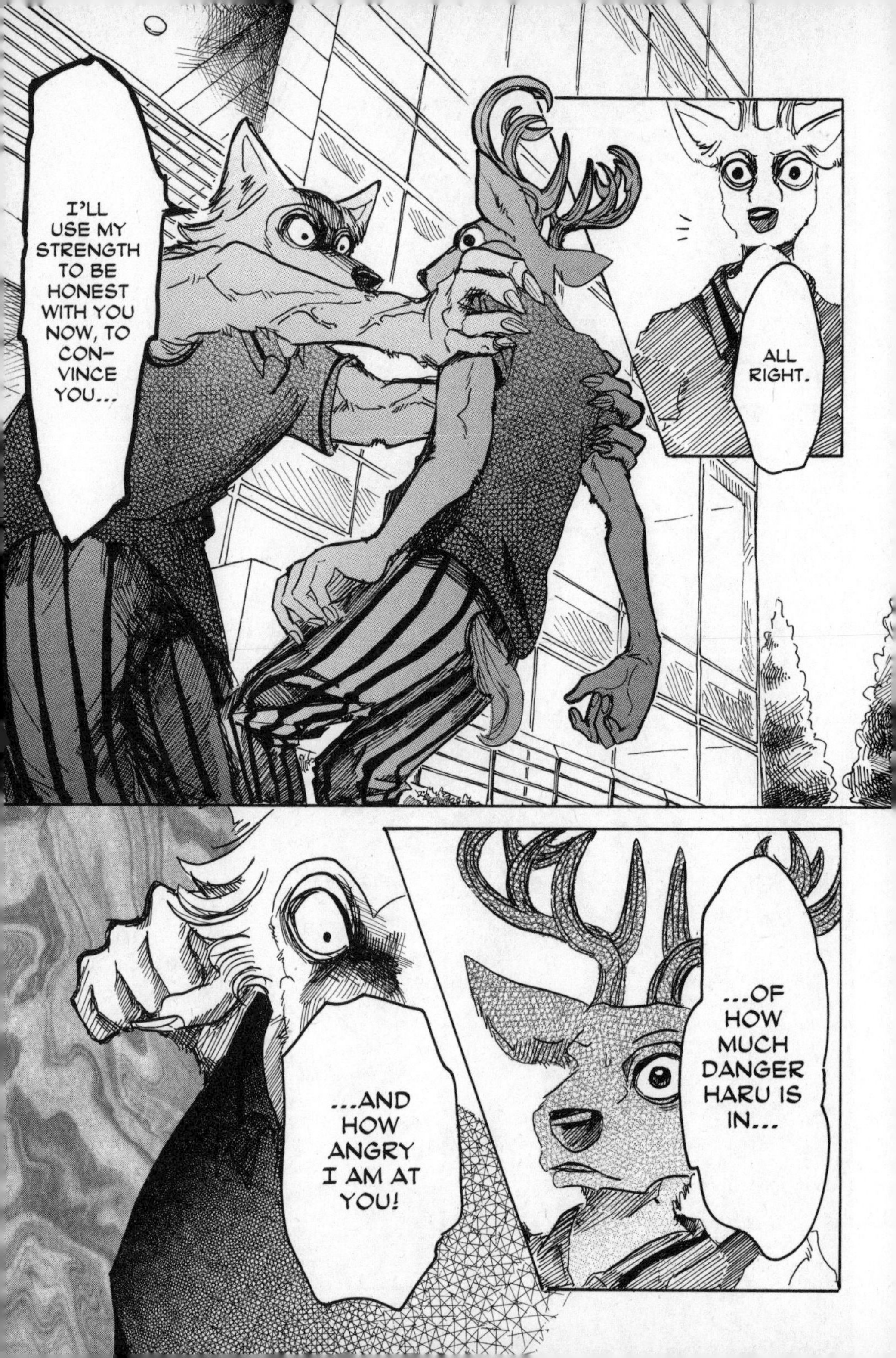
ALL RIGHT.
I'LL USE MY STRENGTH TO BE HONEST WITH YOU NOW, TO CON-VINCE YOU...
...OF HOW MUCH DANGER HARU IS IN...
...AND HOW ANGRY I AM AT YOU!

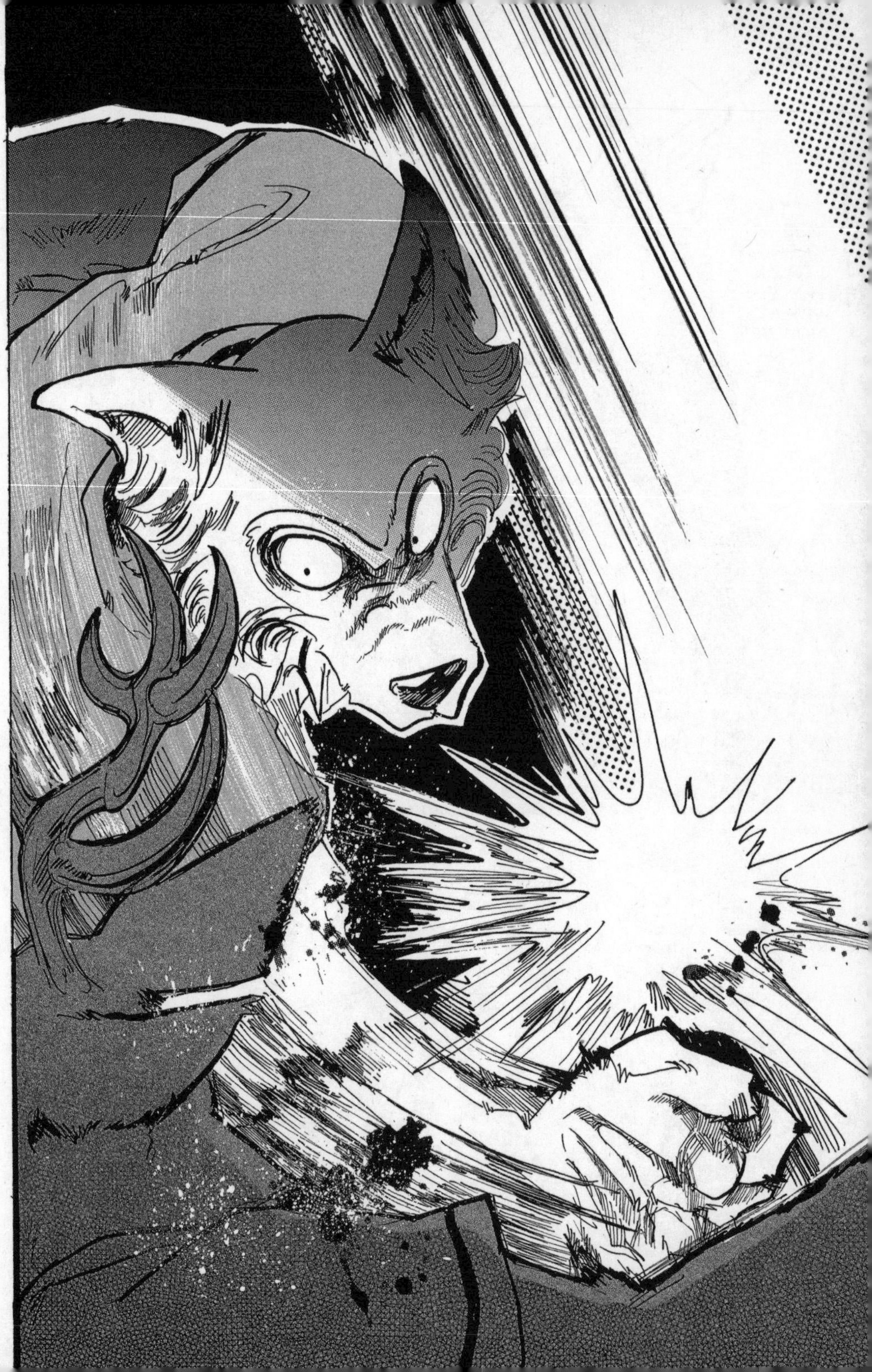

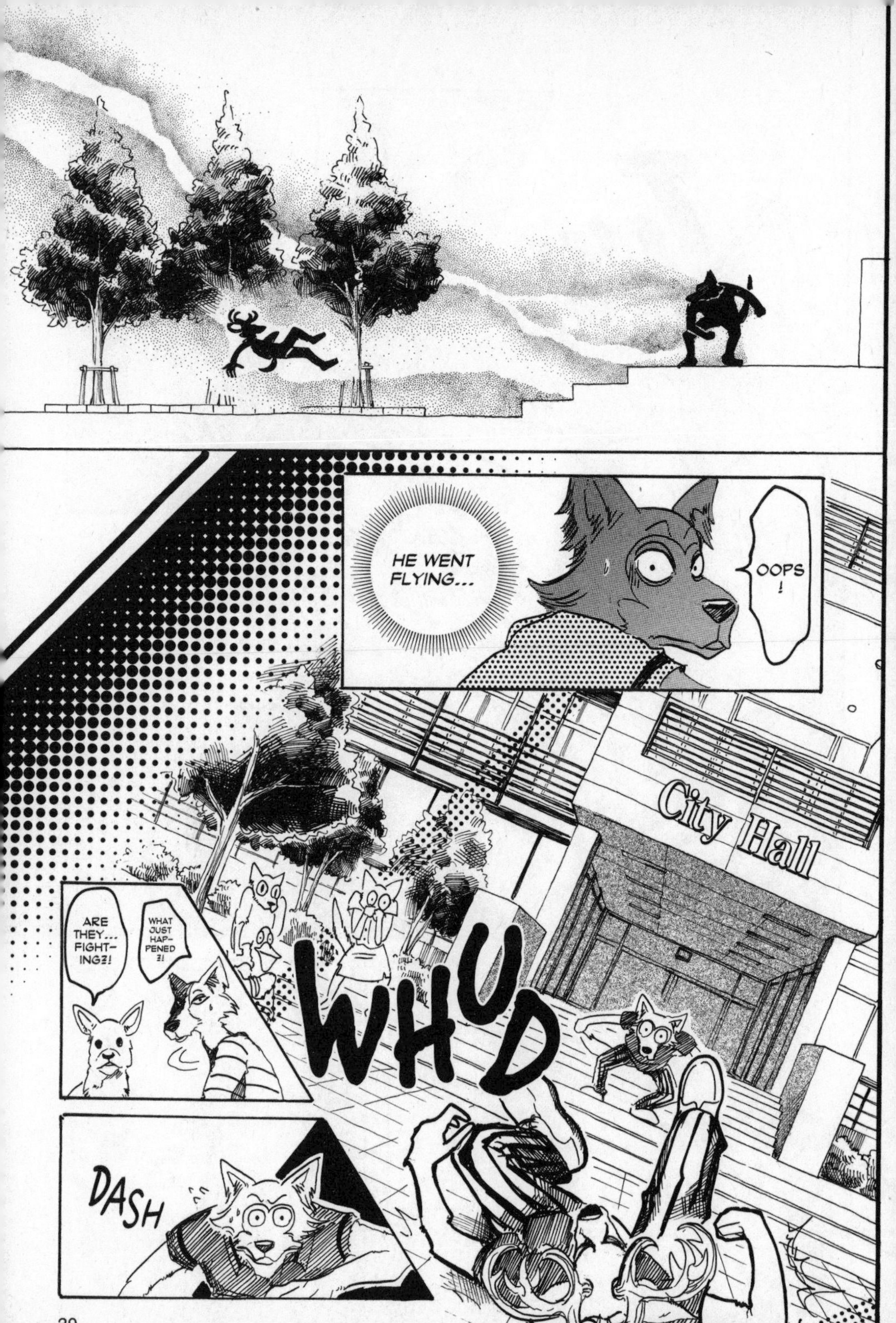
OOPS!
HE WENT FLYING...
City Hall
WHUD
WHAT JUST HAP-PENED?!
ARE THEY... FIGHT-ING?!
DASH

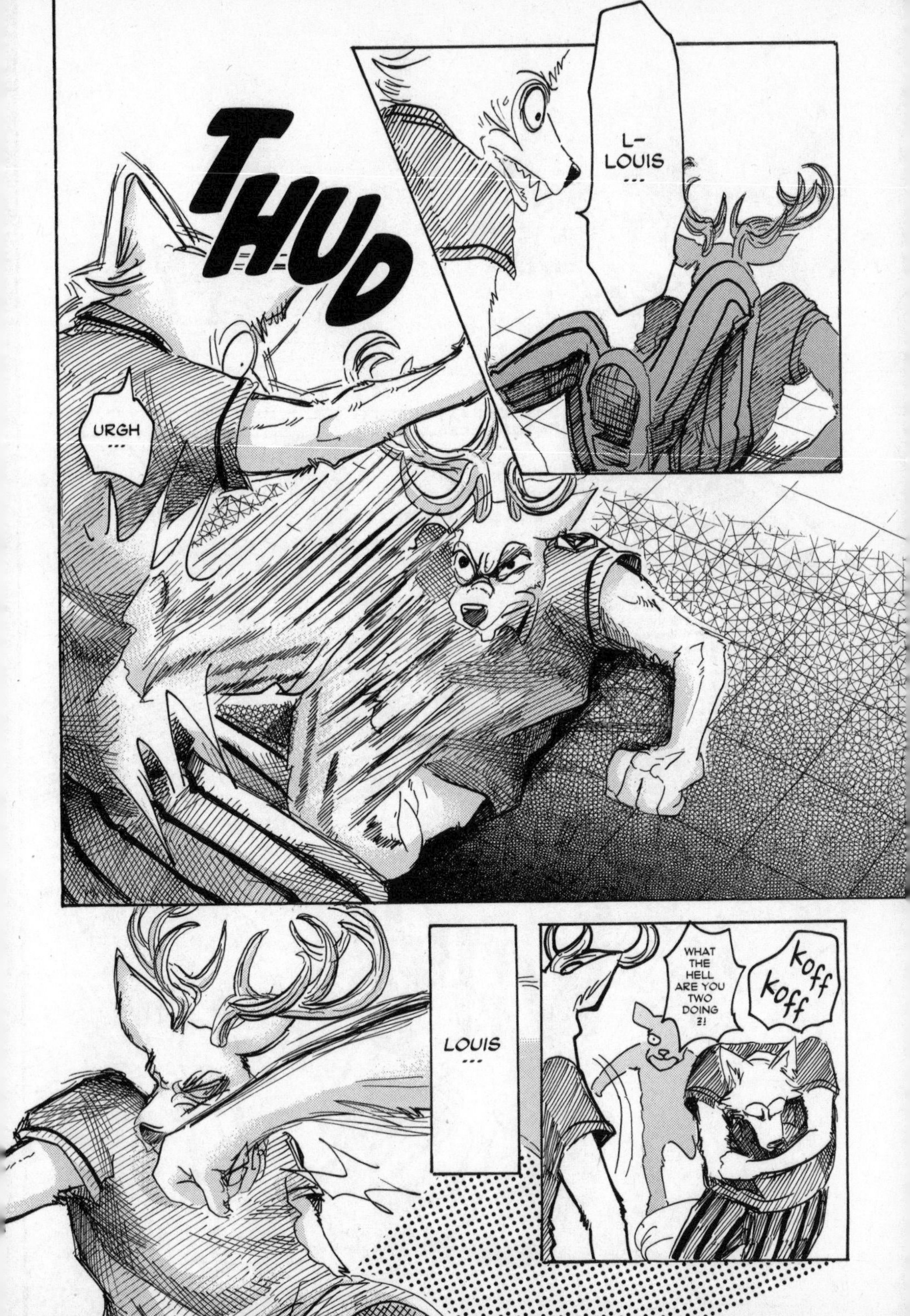
L–
LOUIS

THUD
URGH
---
koff koff
WHAT THE HELL ARE YOU TWO DOING ?!
LOUIS

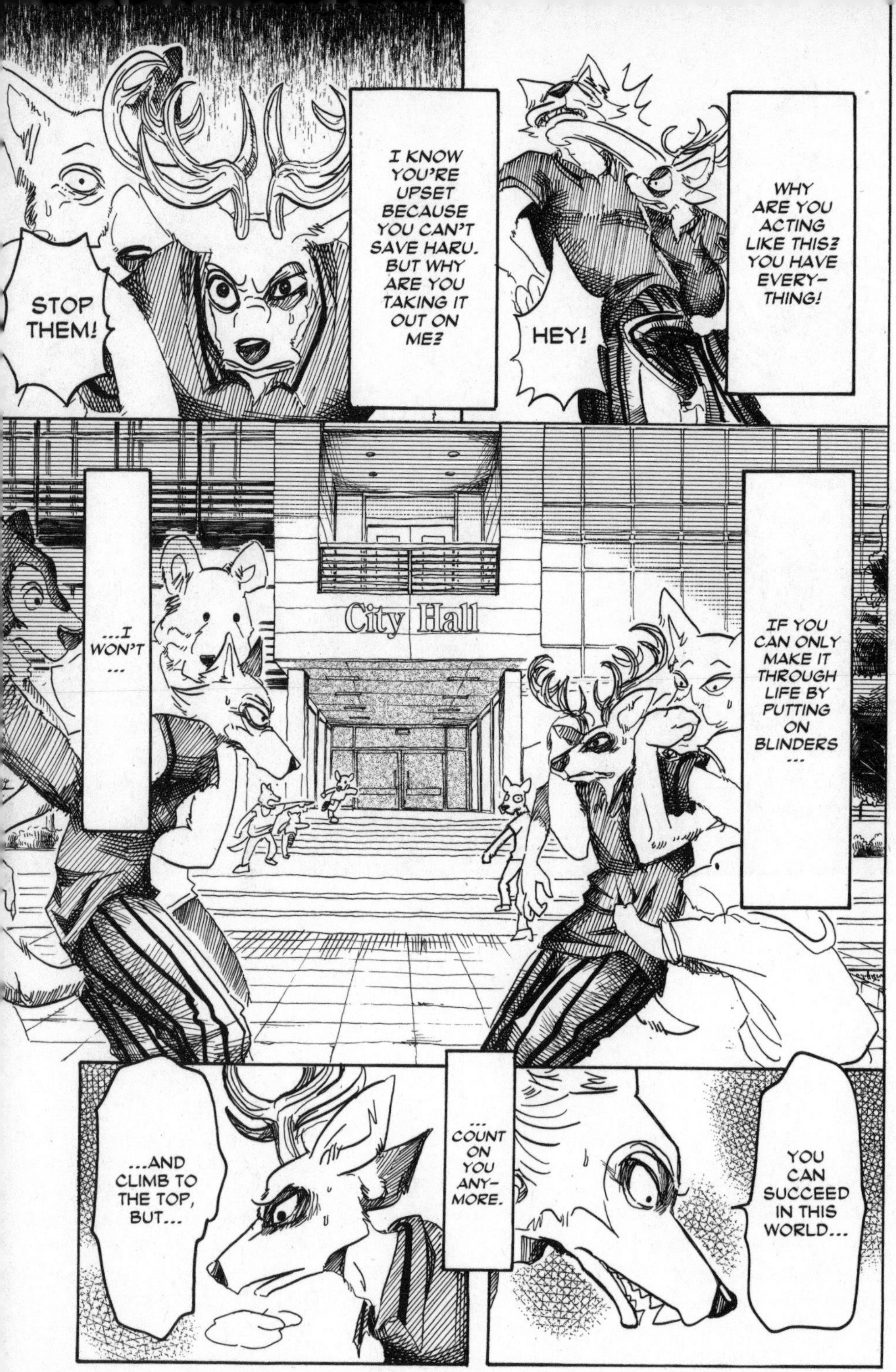
WHY ARE YOU ACTING LIKE THIS? YOU HAVE EVERY-THING!
HEY!
I KNOW YOU'RE UPSET BECAUSE YOU CAN'T SAVE HARU. BUT WHY ARE YOU TAKING IT OUT ON ME?
STOP THEM!
IF YOU CAN ONLY MAKE IT THROUGH LIFE BY PUTTING ON BLINDERS...
City Hall
...I WON'T...
YOU CAN SUCCEED IN THIS WORLD...
...COUNT ON YOU ANY-MORE.
...AND CLIMB TO THE TOP, BUT...

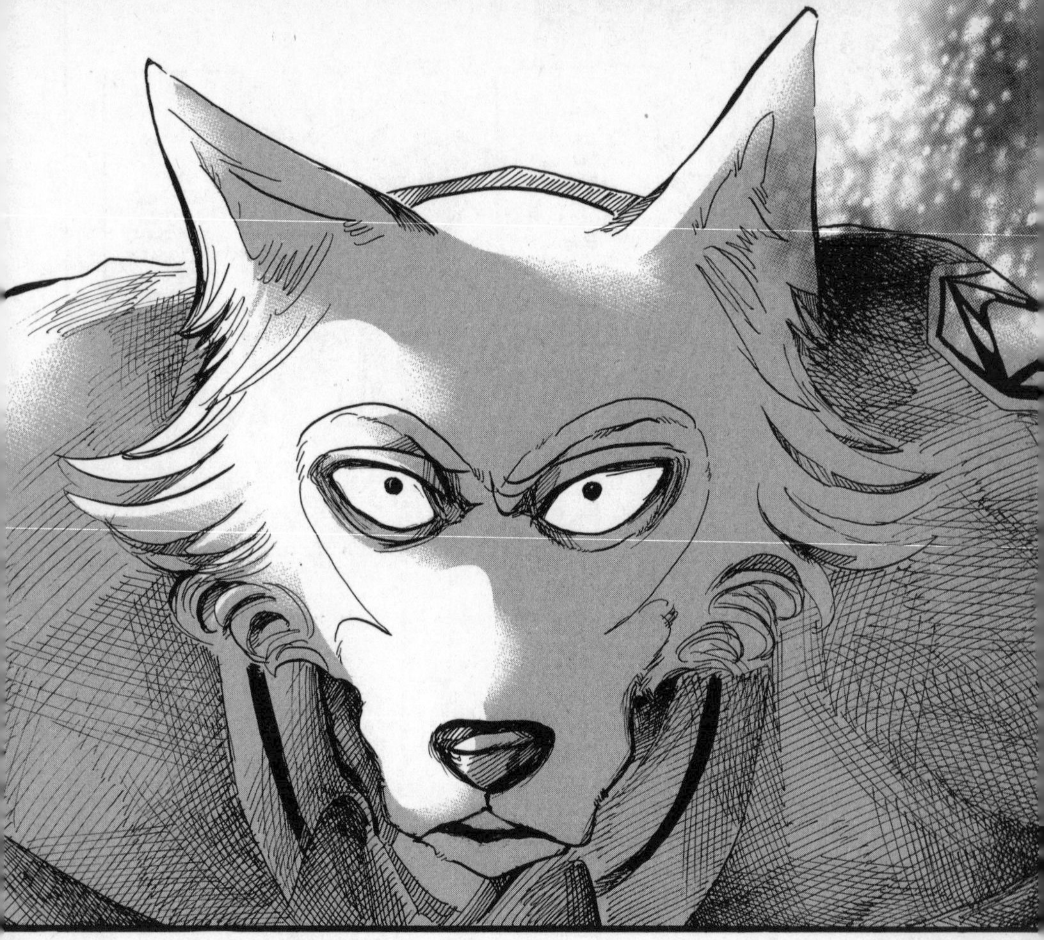
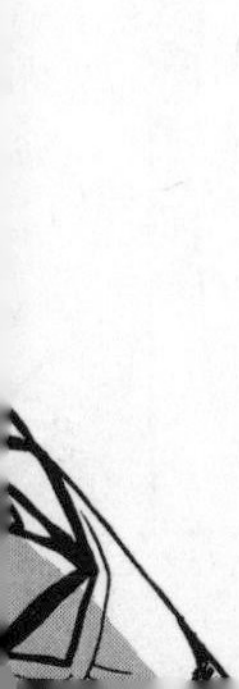

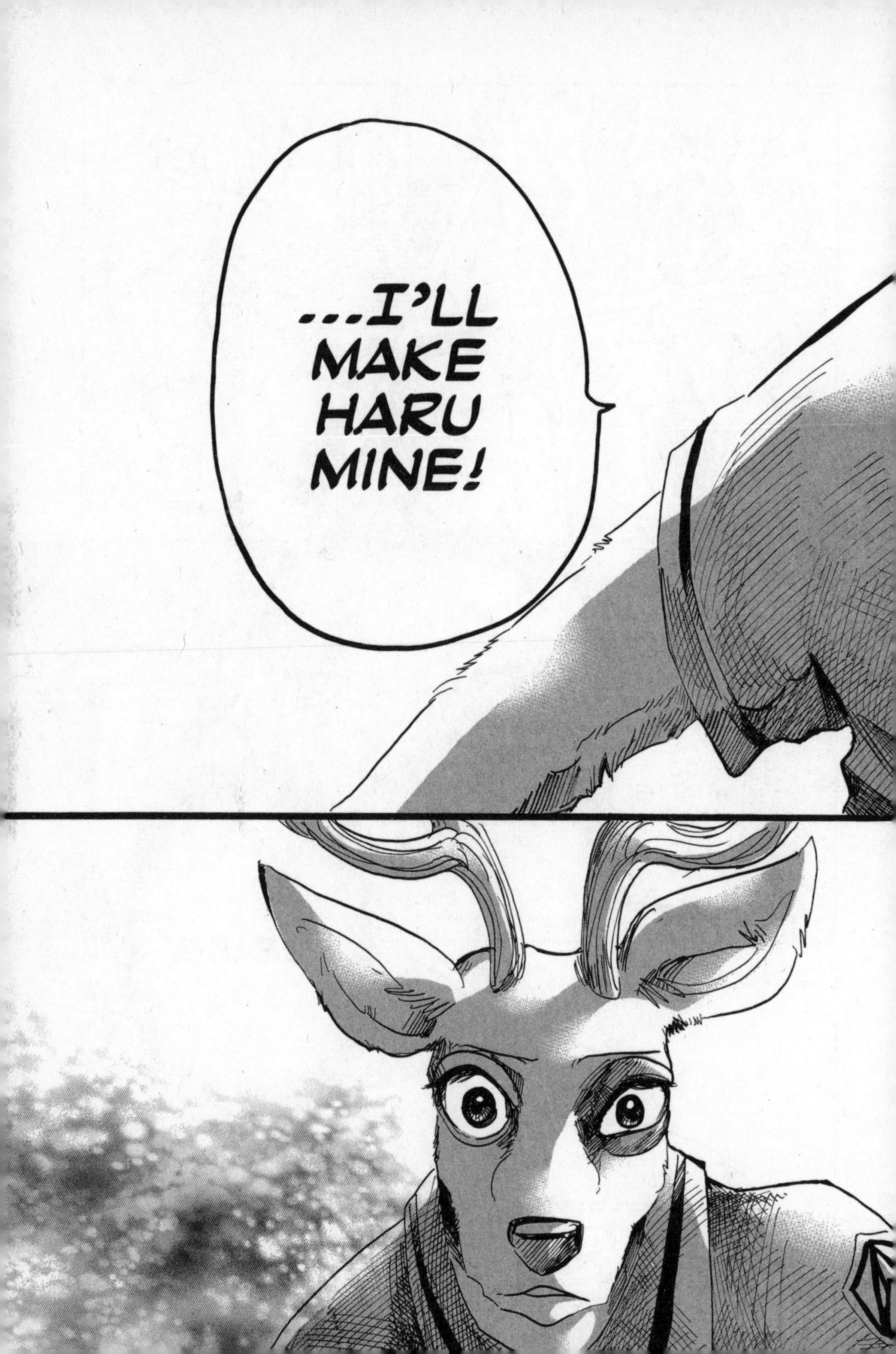
...I'LL MAKE HARU MINE!

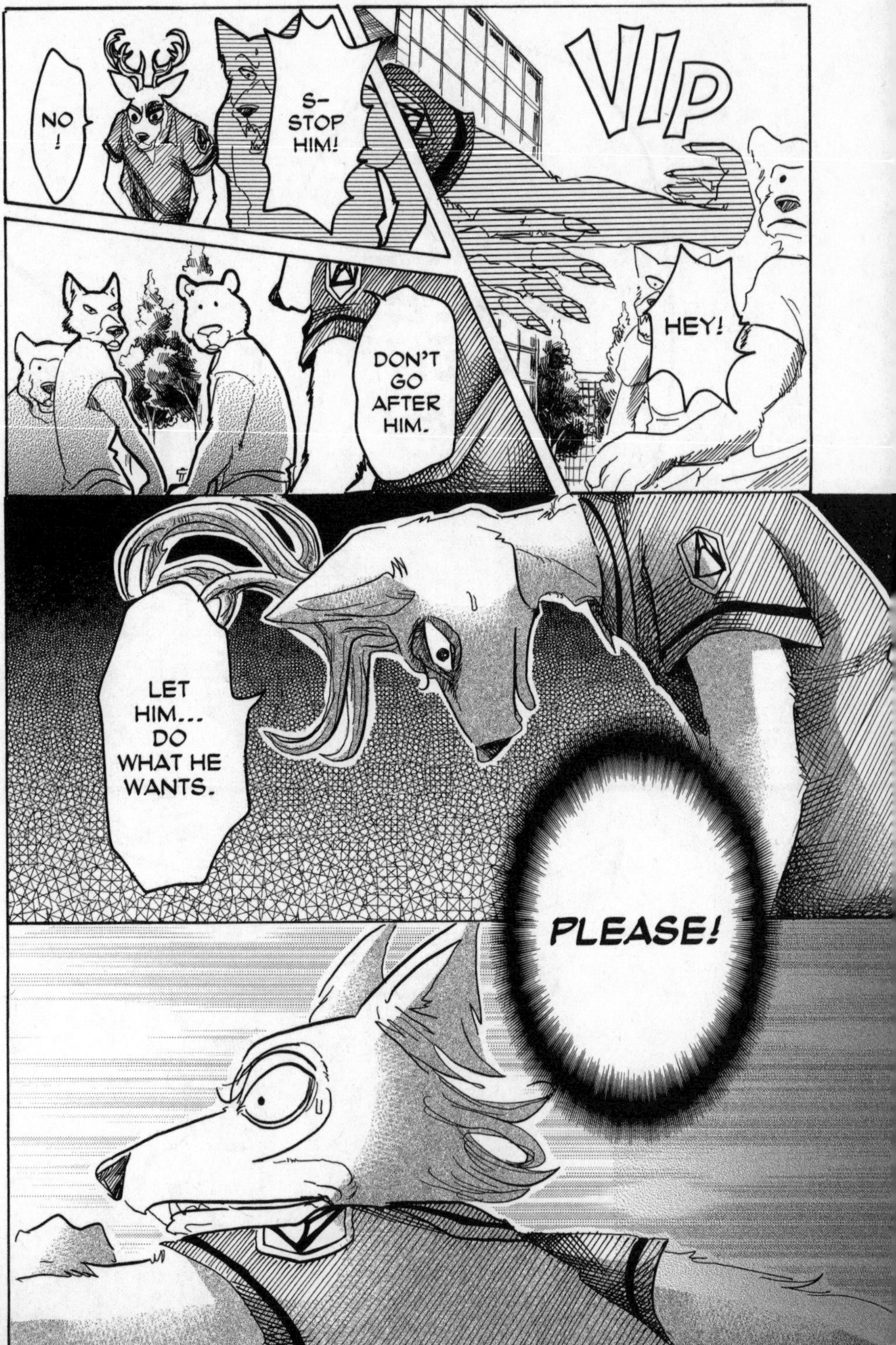
VIP
S-STOP HIM!
NO!
HEY!
DON'T GO AFTER HIM.
LET HIM... DO WHAT HE WANTS.
PLEASE!

Chapter 37: Guided by Rain Clouds

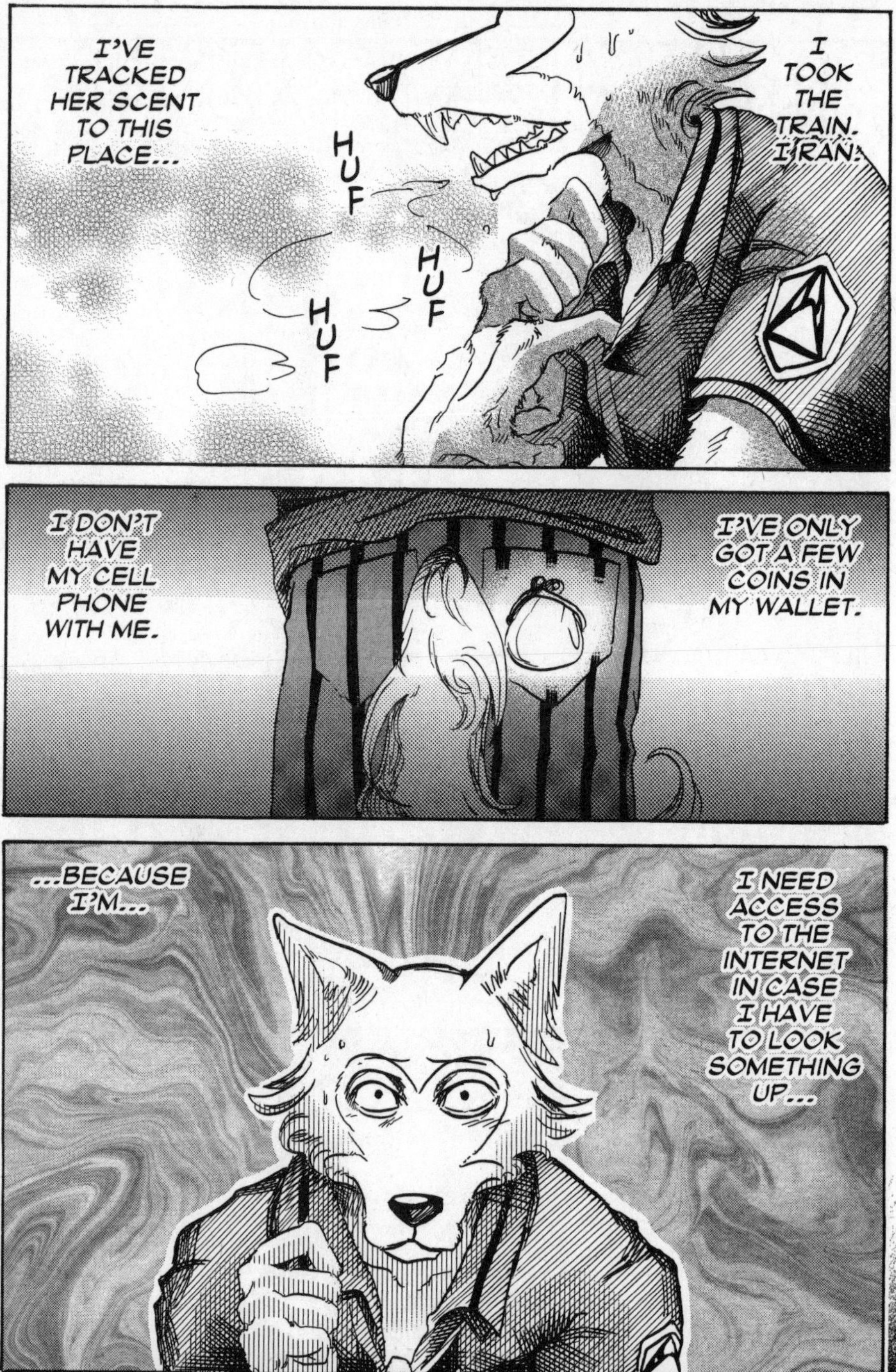
I TOOK THE TRAIN. I RAN.
I'VE TRACKED HER SCENT TO THIS PLACE...
HUF
HUF
HUF
I'VE ONLY GOT A FEW COINS IN MY WALLET.
I DON'T HAVE MY CELL PHONE WITH ME.
I NEED ACCESS TO THE INTERNET IN CASE I HAVE TO LOOK SOMETHING UP...
...BECAUSE I'M...

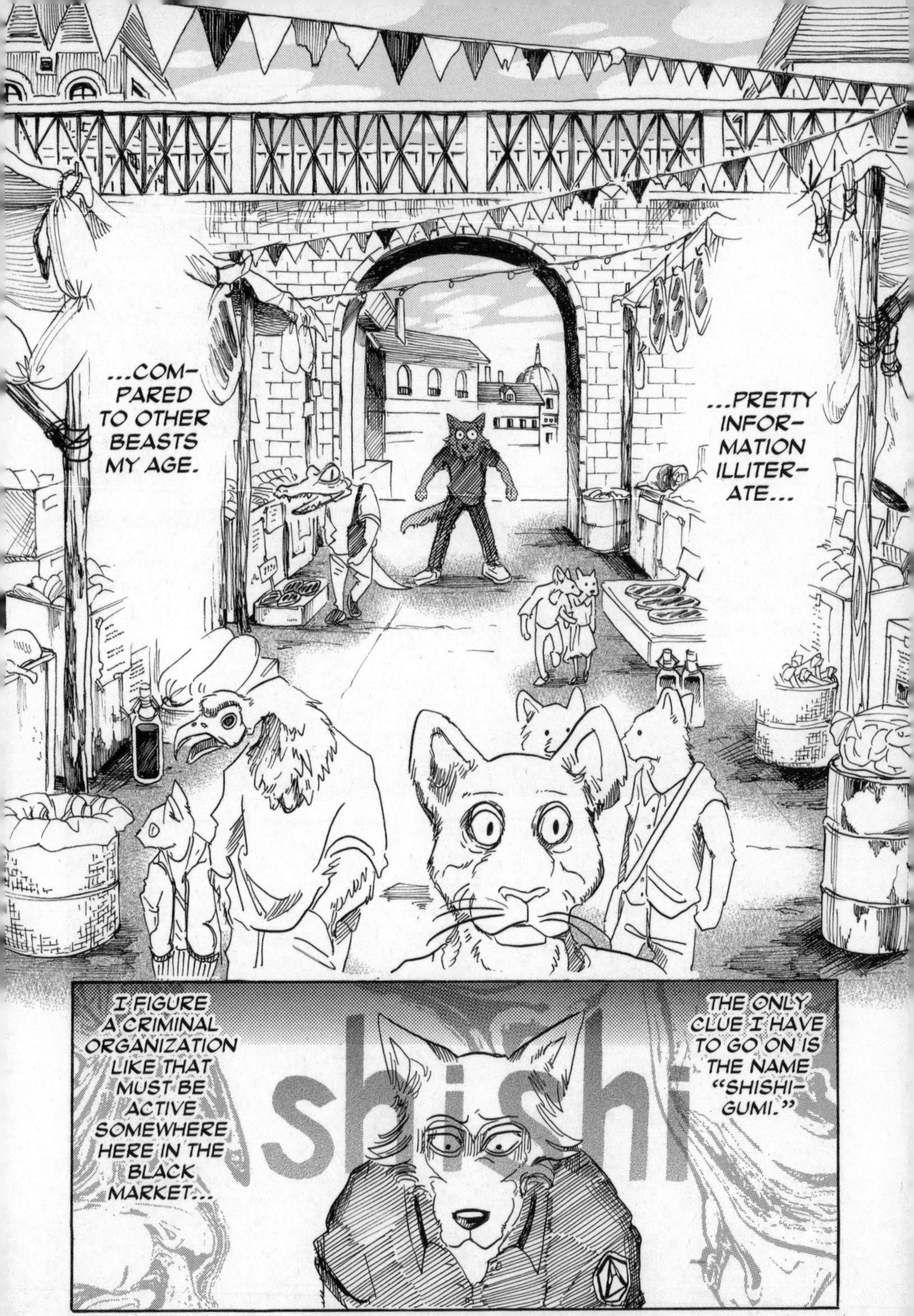
...PRETTY INFORMATION ILLITERATE...
...COMPARED TO OTHER BEASTS MY AGE.
THE ONLY CLUE I HAVE TO GO ON IS THE NAME "SHISHI-GUMI."
shishi
I FIGURE A CRIMINAL ORGANIZATION LIKE THAT MUST BE ACTIVE SOMEWHERE HERE IN THE BLACK MARKET...

Chapter 37: Guided by Rain Clouds

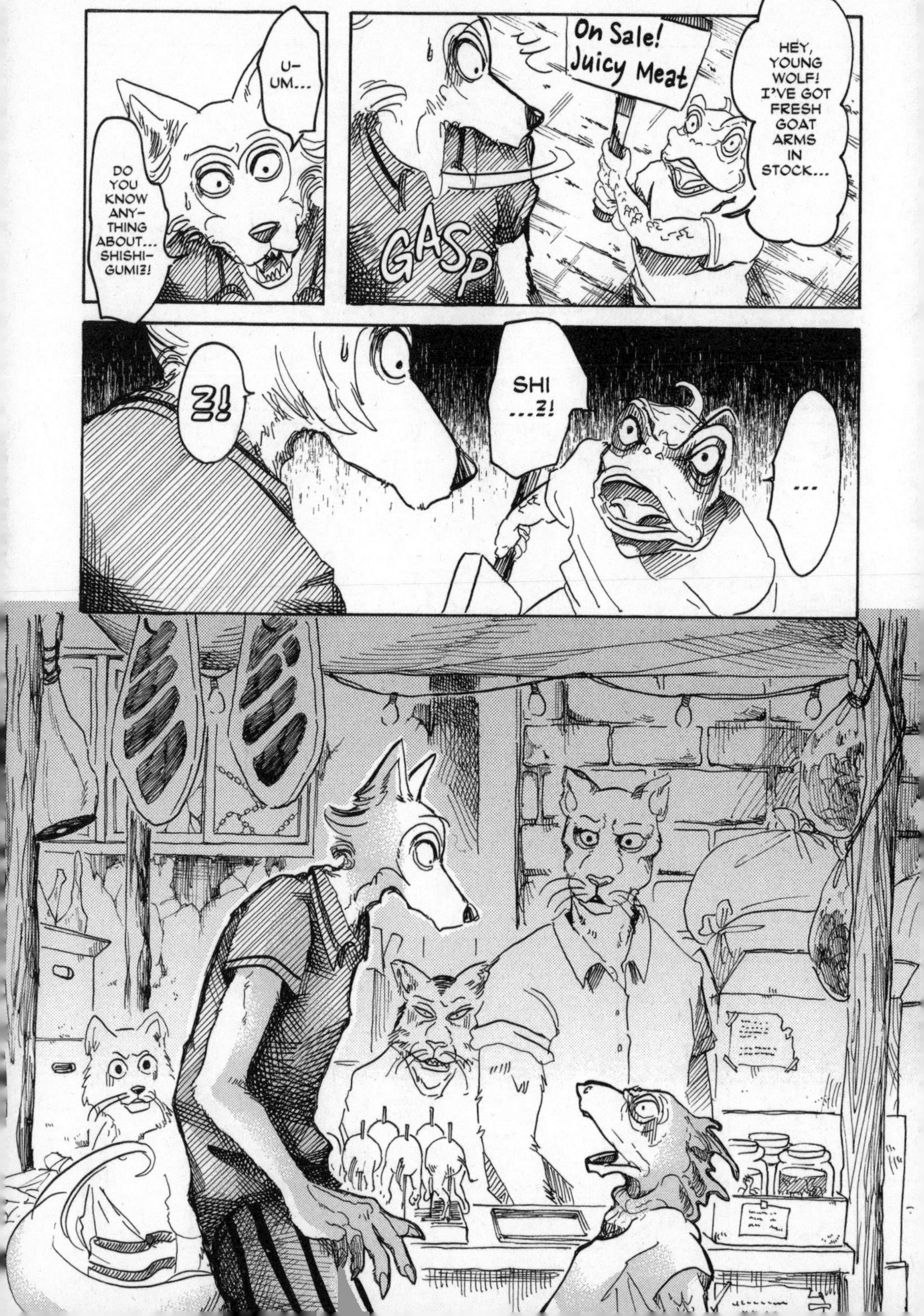
HEY, YOUNG WOLF! I'VE GOT FRESH GOAT ARMS IN STOCK...
On Sale! Juicy Meat
GASP
U-UM...
DO YOU KNOW ANYTHING ABOUT... SHISHI-GUMI?!
...
SHI ...?!
?!

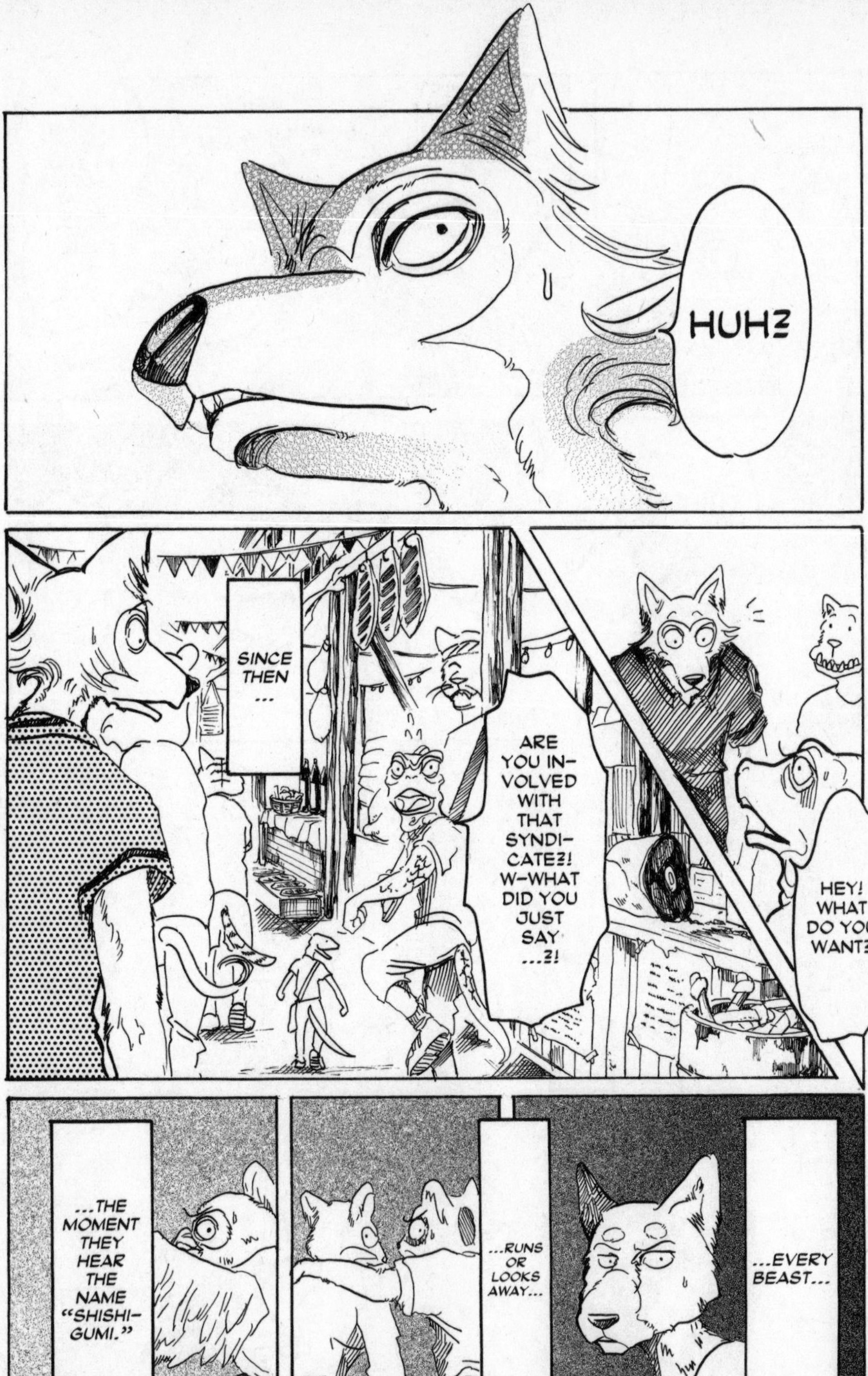
HUH?
HEY! WHAT DO YOU WANT?
SINCE THEN...
ARE YOU INVOLVED WITH THAT SYNDICATE?! W-WHAT DID YOU JUST SAY...?!
...EVERY BEAST...
...RUNS OR LOOKS AWAY...
...THE MOMENT THEY HEAR THE NAME "SHISHI-GUMI."

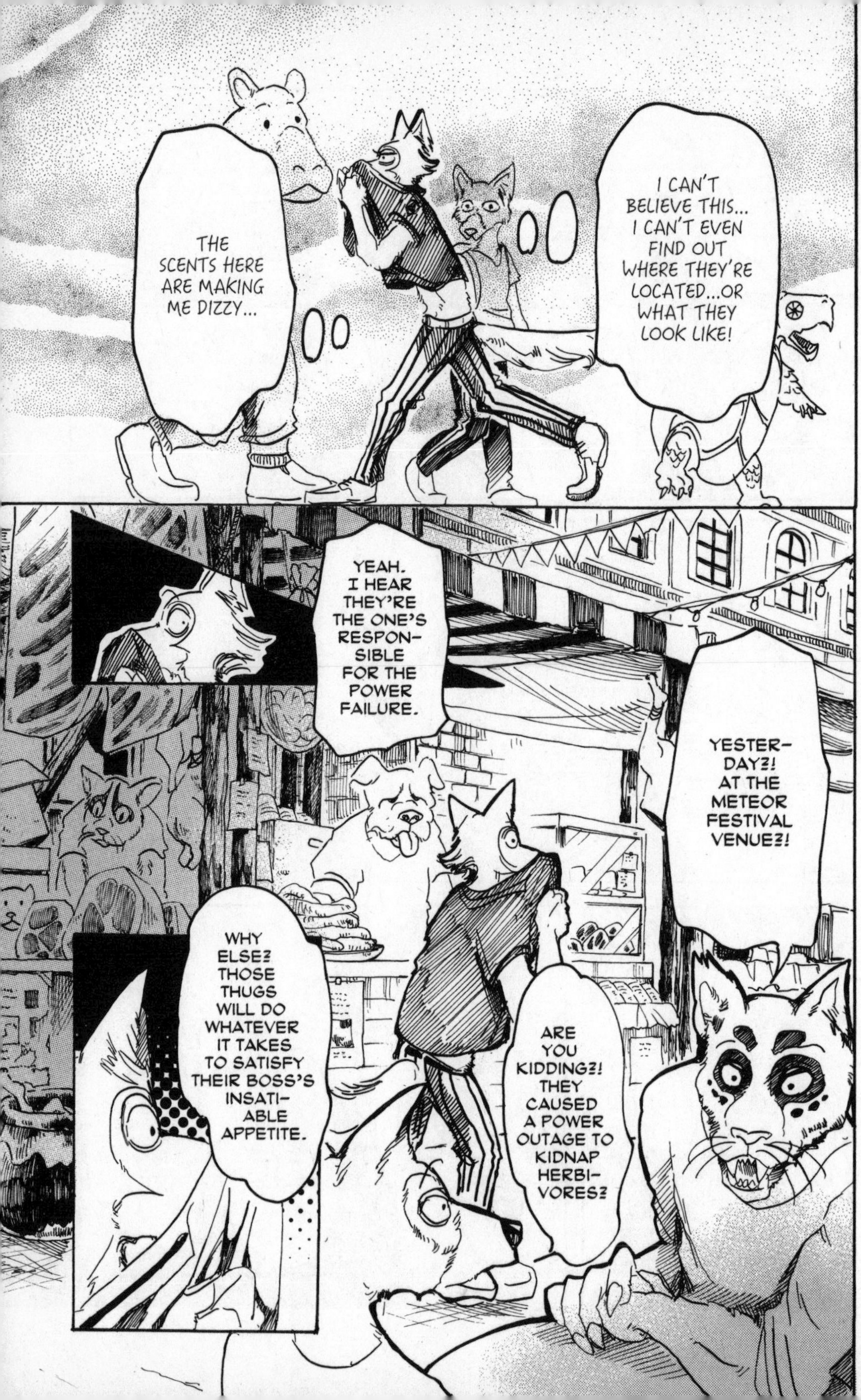
I CAN'T BELIEVE THIS... I CAN'T EVEN FIND OUT WHERE THEY'RE LOCATED...OR WHAT THEY LOOK LIKE!
THE SCENTS HERE ARE MAKING ME DIZZY...
YESTER-DAY?! AT THE METEOR FESTIVAL VENUE?!
YEAH. I HEAR THEY'RE THE ONE'S RESPON-SIBLE FOR THE POWER FAILURE.
ARE YOU KIDDING?! THEY CAUSED A POWER OUTAGE TO KIDNAP HERBI-VORES?
WHY ELSE? THOSE THUGS WILL DO WHATEVER IT TAKES TO SATISFY THEIR BOSS'S INSATI-ABLE APPETITE.

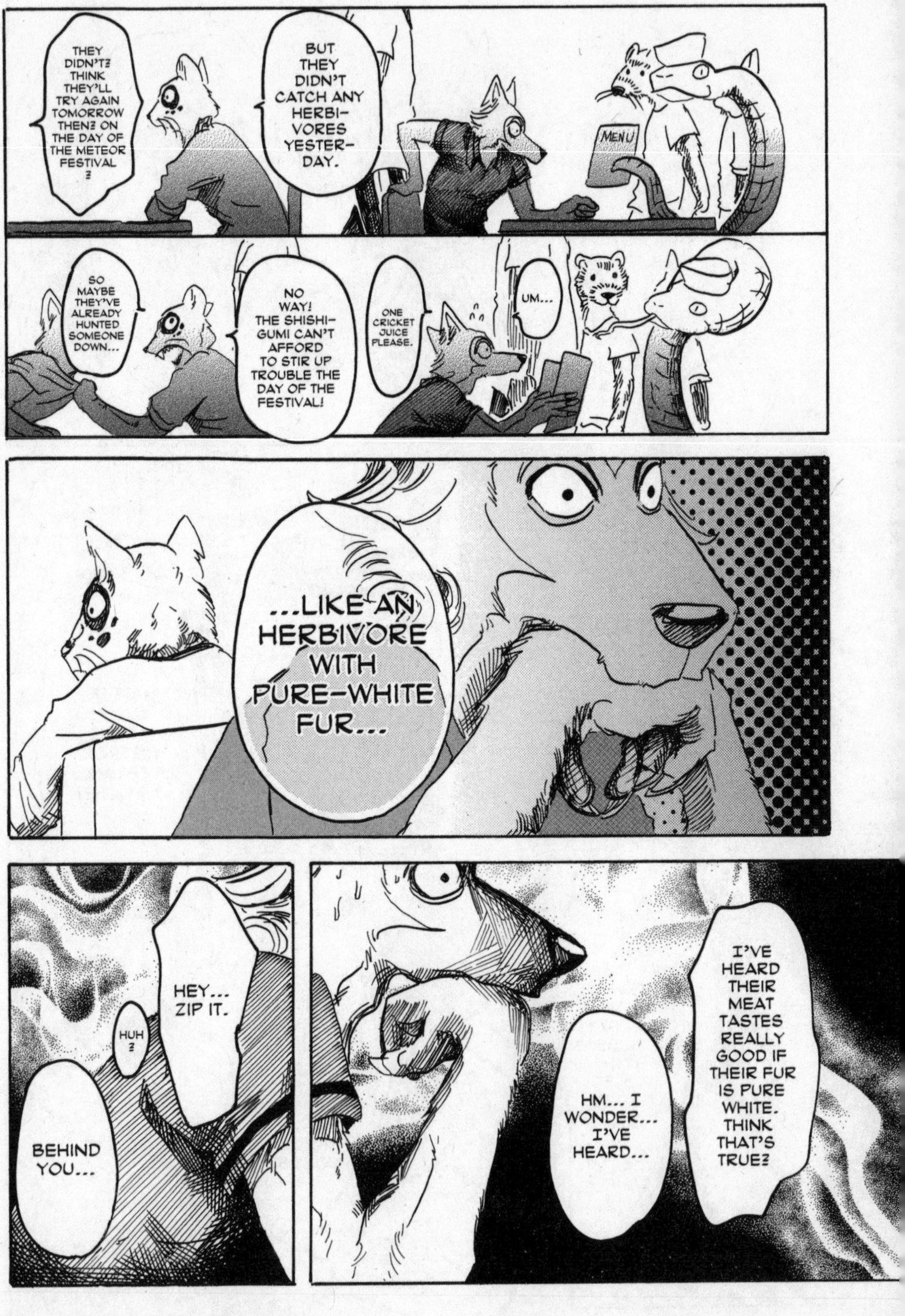
MENU
BUT THEY DIDN'T CATCH ANY HERBIVORES YESTERDAY.
THEY DIDN'T? THINK THEY'LL TRY AGAIN TOMORROW THEN? ON THE DAY OF THE METEOR FESTIVAL?
UM...
ONE CRICKET JUICE PLEASE.
NO WAY! THE SHISHIGUMI CAN'T AFFORD TO STIR UP TROUBLE THE DAY OF THE FESTIVAL!
SO MAYBE THEY'VE ALREADY HUNTED SOMEONE DOWN...
...LIKE AN HERBIVORE WITH PURE-WHITE FUR...
I'VE HEARD THEIR MEAT TASTES REALLY GOOD IF THEIR FUR IS PURE WHITE. THINK THAT'S TRUE?
HM... I WONDER... I'VE HEARD...
HEY... ZIP IT.
HUH?
BEHIND YOU...

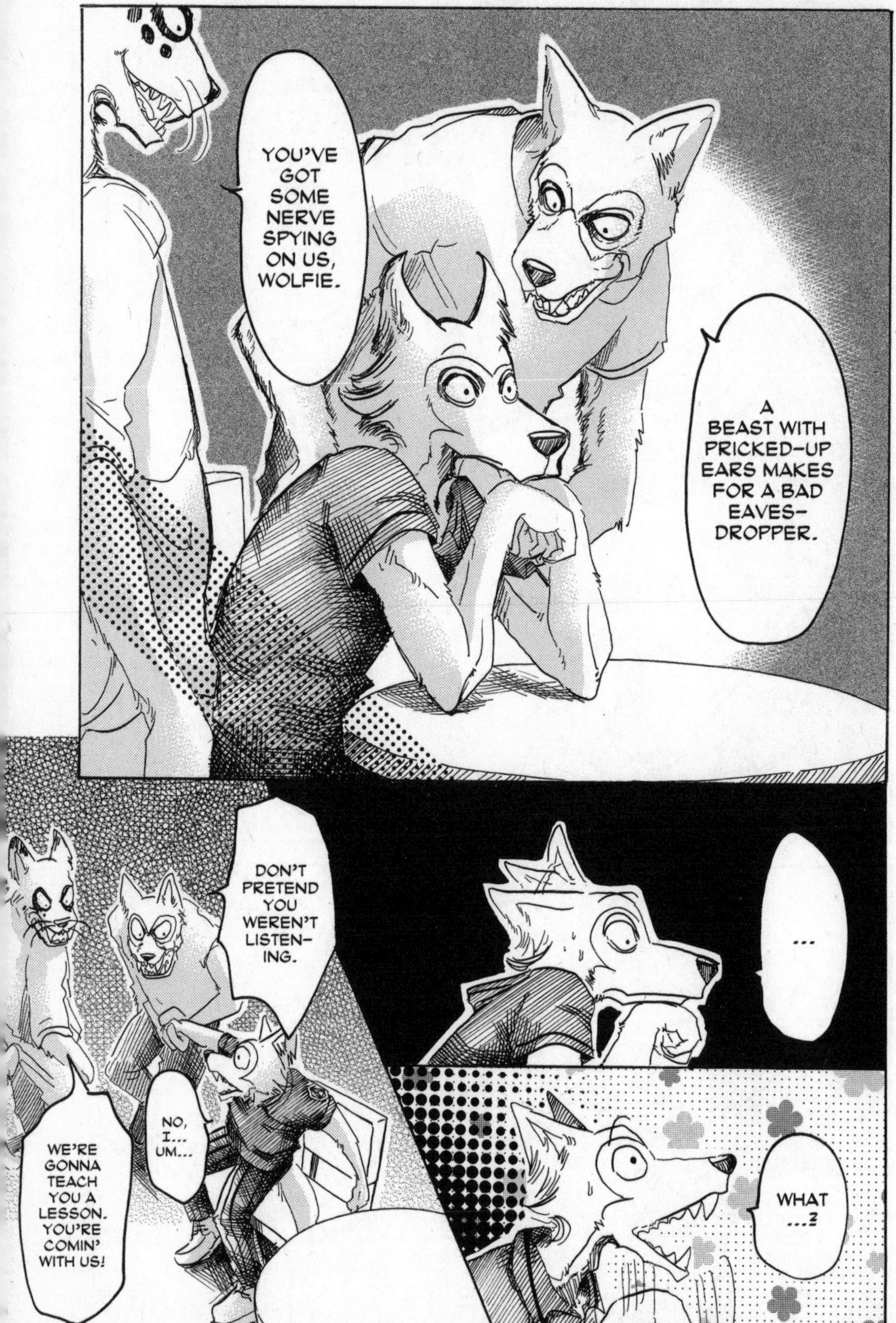
A BEAST WITH PRICKED-UP EARS MAKES FOR A BAD EAVES-DROPPER.
YOU'VE GOT SOME NERVE SPYING ON US, WOLFIE.
...
WHAT ...?
DON'T PRETEND YOU WEREN'T LISTEN-ING.
NO, I... UM...
WE'RE GONNA TEACH YOU A LESSON. YOU'RE COMIN' WITH US!

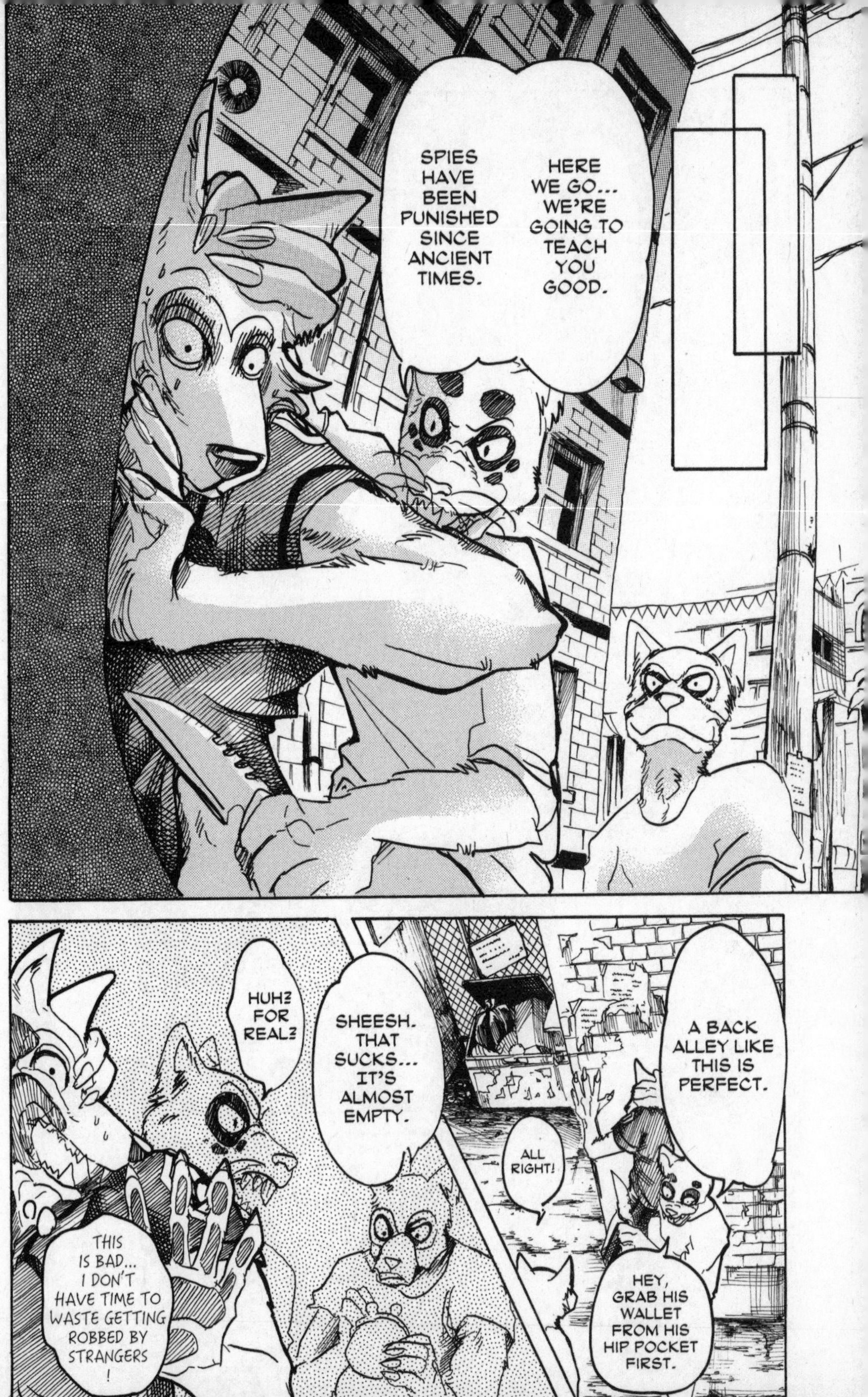
HERE WE GO... WE'RE GOING TO TEACH YOU GOOD.
SPIES HAVE BEEN PUNISHED SINCE ANCIENT TIMES.
A BACK ALLEY LIKE THIS IS PERFECT.
ALL RIGHT!
HEY, GRAB HIS WALLET FROM HIS HIP POCKET FIRST.
SHEESH. THAT SUCKS... IT'S ALMOST EMPTY.
HUH? FOR REAL?
THIS IS BAD... I DON'T HAVE TIME TO WASTE GETTING ROBBED BY STRANGERS!

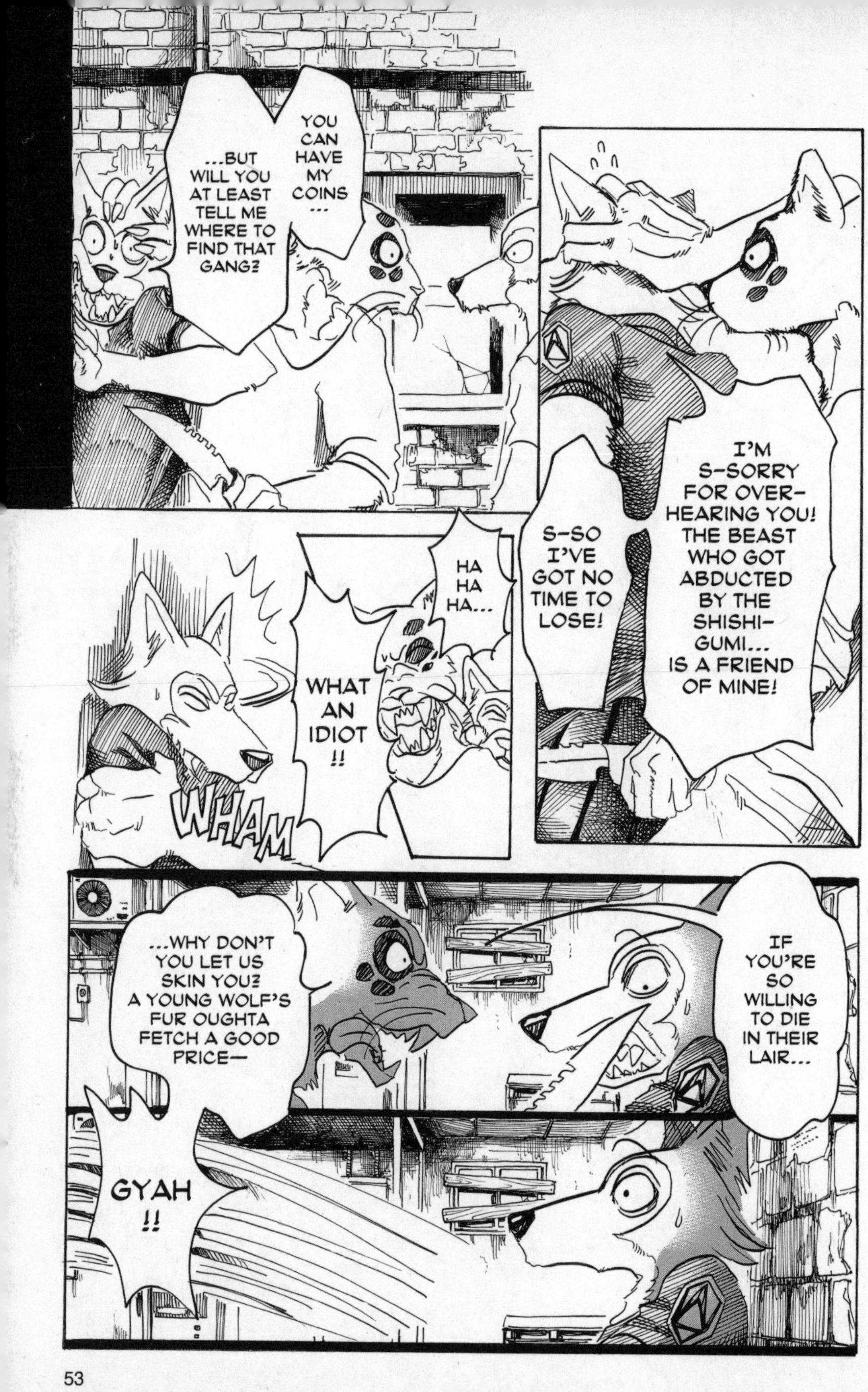
YOU CAN HAVE MY COINS...
...BUT WILL YOU AT LEAST TELL ME WHERE TO FIND THAT GANG?
I'M S-SORRY FOR OVER-HEARING YOU! THE BEAST WHO GOT ABDUCTED BY THE SHISHI-GUMI... IS A FRIEND OF MINE!
S-SO I'VE GOT NO TIME TO LOSE!
HA HA HA...
WHAT AN IDIOT!!
WHAM
IF YOU'RE SO WILLING TO DIE IN THEIR LAIR...
...WHY DON'T YOU LET US SKIN YOU? A YOUNG WOLF'S FUR OUGHTA FETCH A GOOD PRICE—
GYAH!!

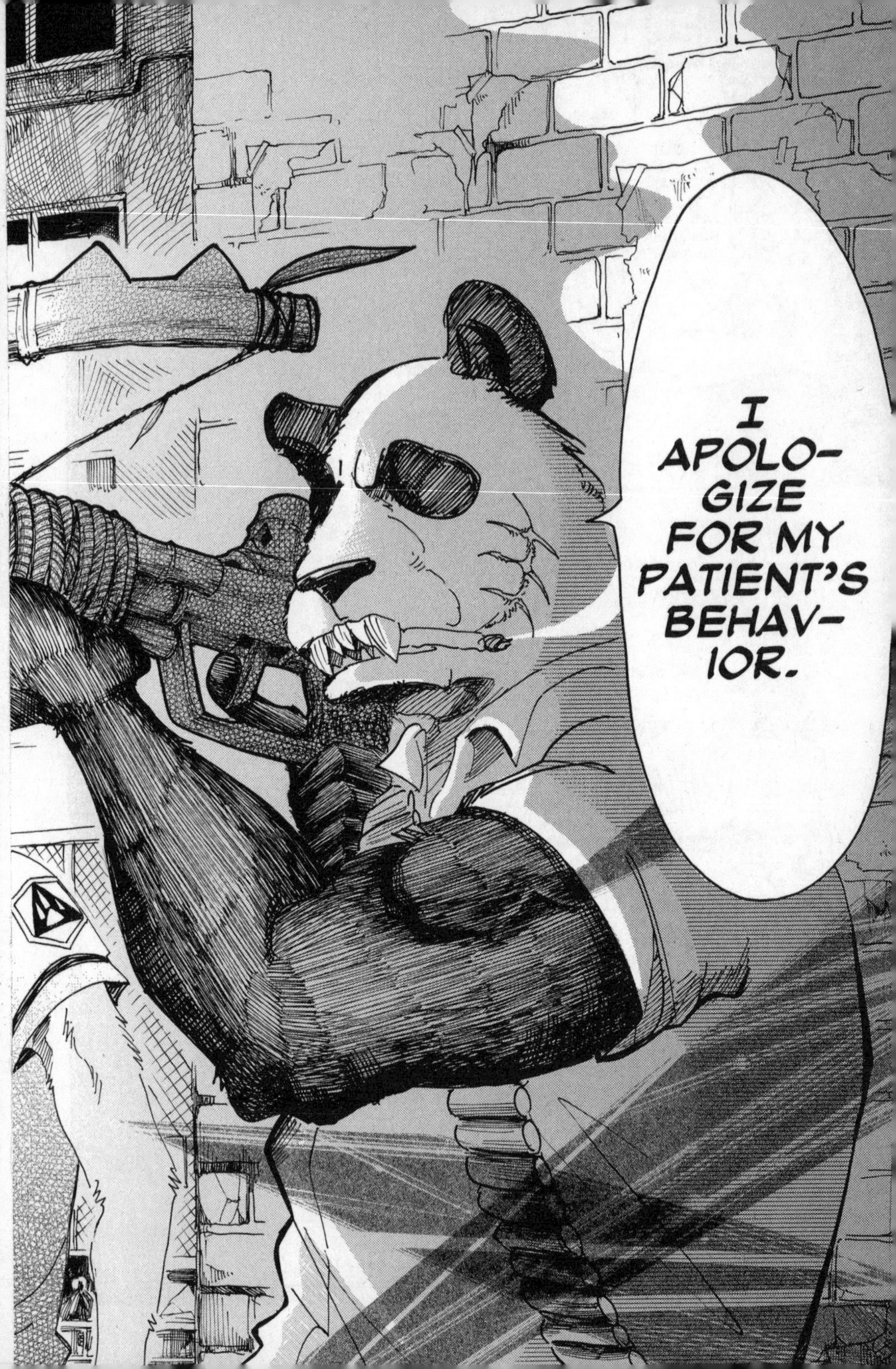
I APOLOGIZE FOR MY PATIENT'S BEHAVIOR.

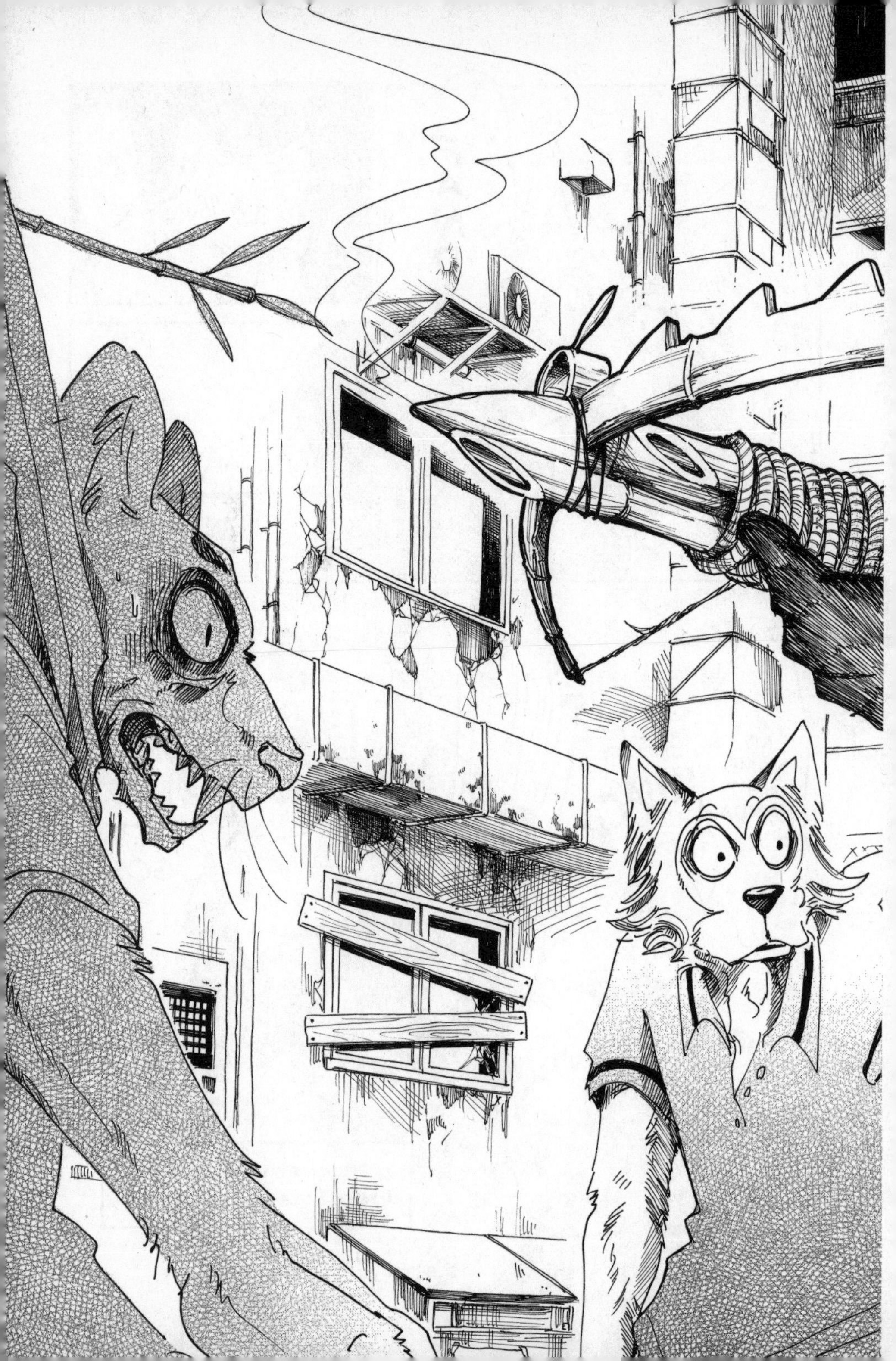

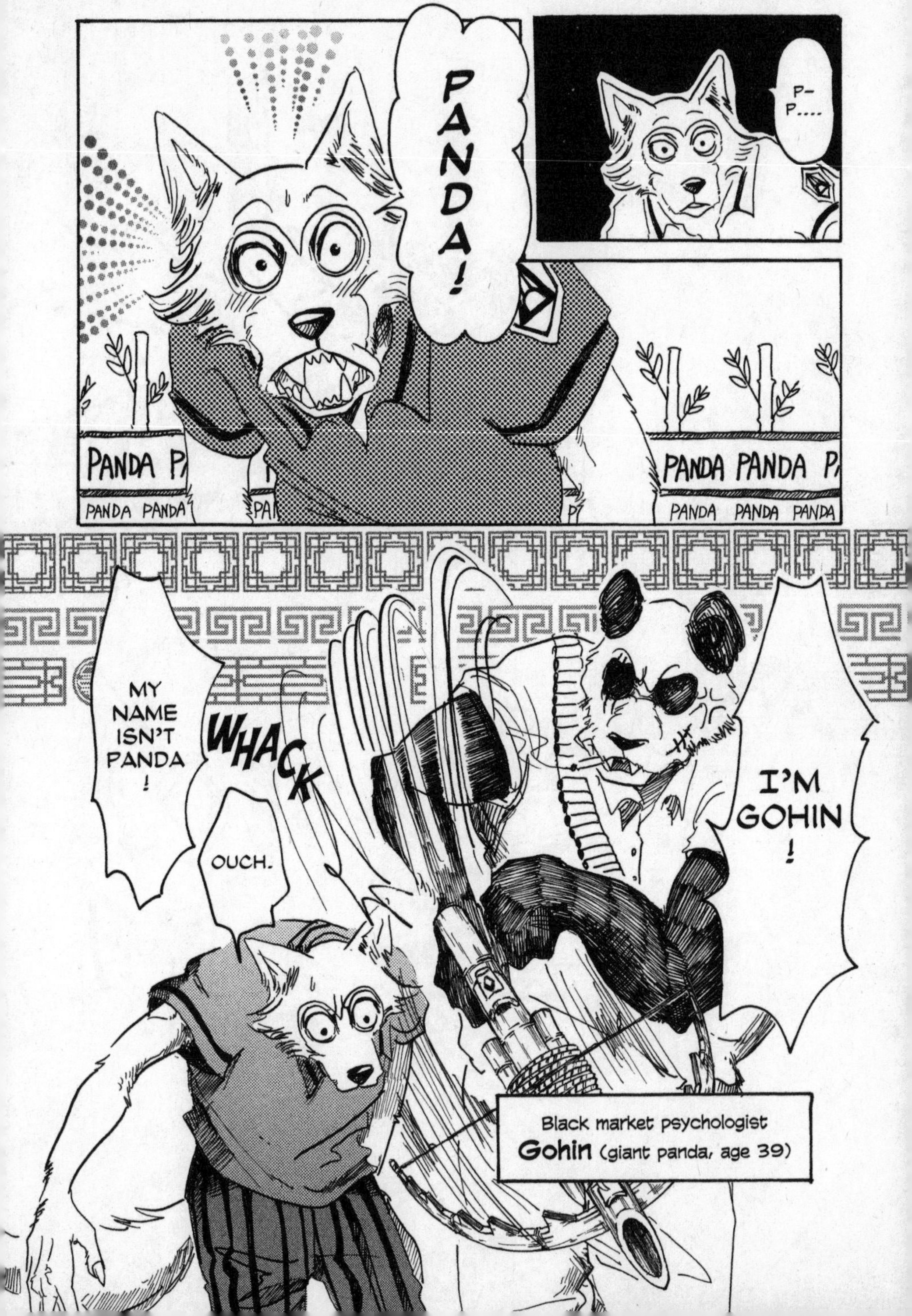
P– P....
PANDA!
PANDA PA
PANDA PANDA
PANDA PANDA PA
PANDA PANDA PANDA
I'M GOHIN!
MY NAME ISN'T PANDA!
WHACK
OUCH.
Black market psychologist
Gohin (giant panda, age 39)

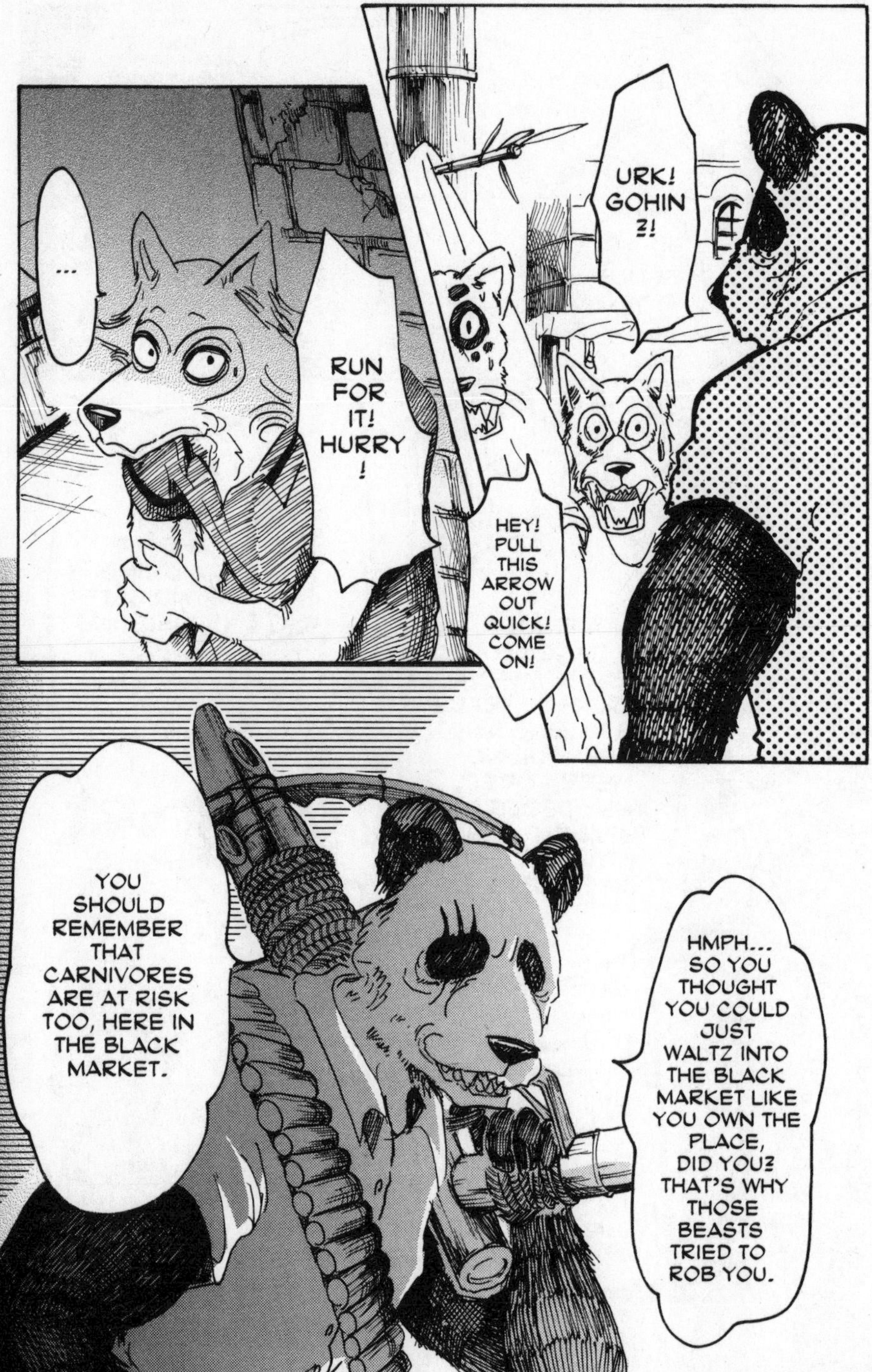
URK! GOHIN?!
HEY! PULL THIS ARROW OUT QUICK! COME ON!
RUN FOR IT! HURRY!
...
HMPH... SO YOU THOUGHT YOU COULD JUST WALTZ INTO THE BLACK MARKET LIKE YOU OWN THE PLACE, DID YOU? THAT'S WHY THOSE BEASTS TRIED TO ROB YOU.
YOU SHOULD REMEMBER THAT CARNIVORES ARE AT RISK TOO, HERE IN THE BLACK MARKET.

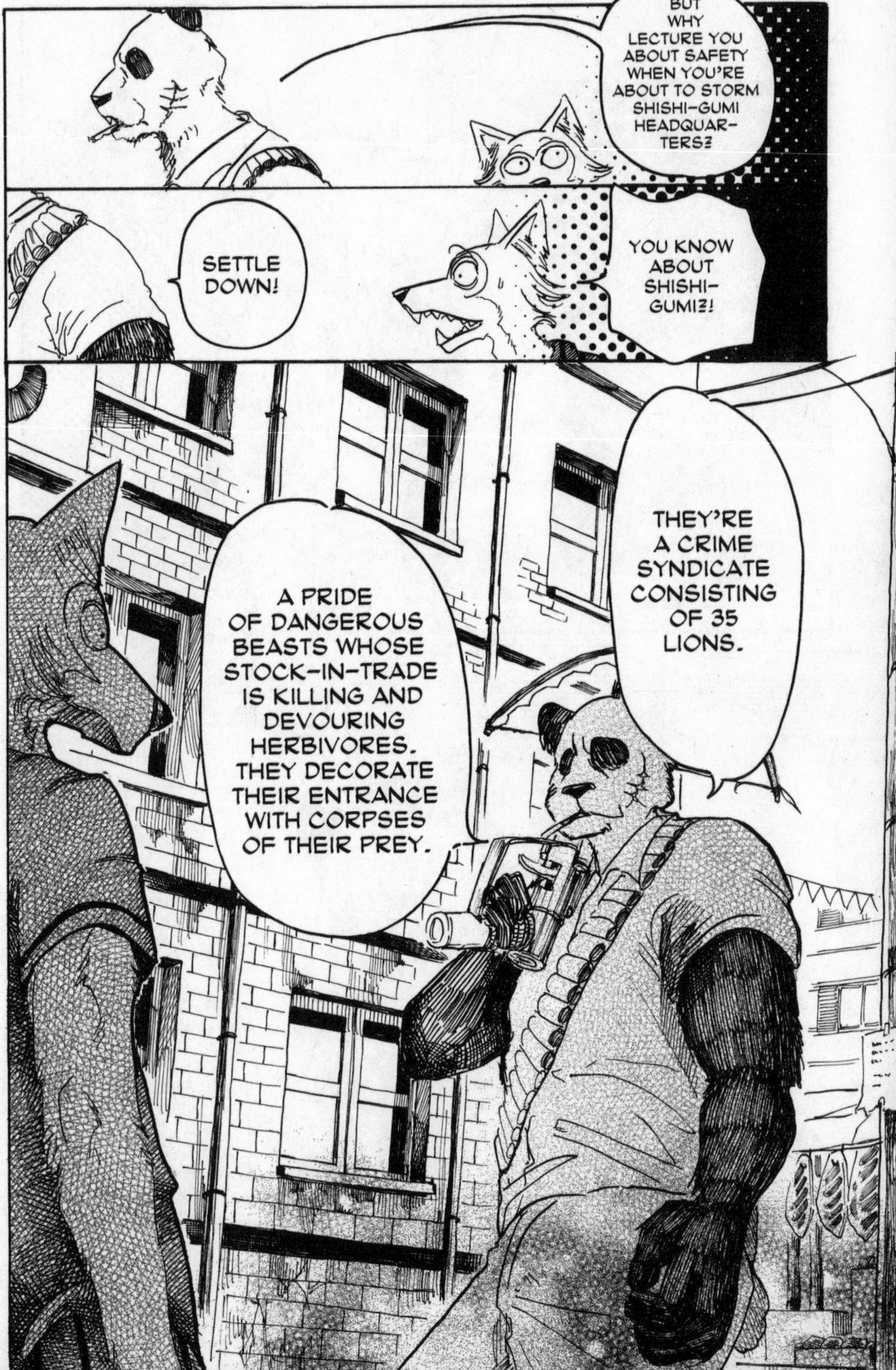
BUT WHY LECTURE YOU ABOUT SAFETY WHEN YOU'RE ABOUT TO STORM SHISHI-GUMI HEADQUARTERS?
YOU KNOW ABOUT SHISHI-GUMI?!
SETTLE DOWN!
THEY'RE A CRIME SYNDICATE CONSISTING OF 35 LIONS.
A PRIDE OF DANGEROUS BEASTS WHOSE STOCK-IN-TRADE IS KILLING AND DEVOURING HERBIVORES. THEY DECORATE THEIR ENTRANCE WITH CORPSES OF THEIR PREY.

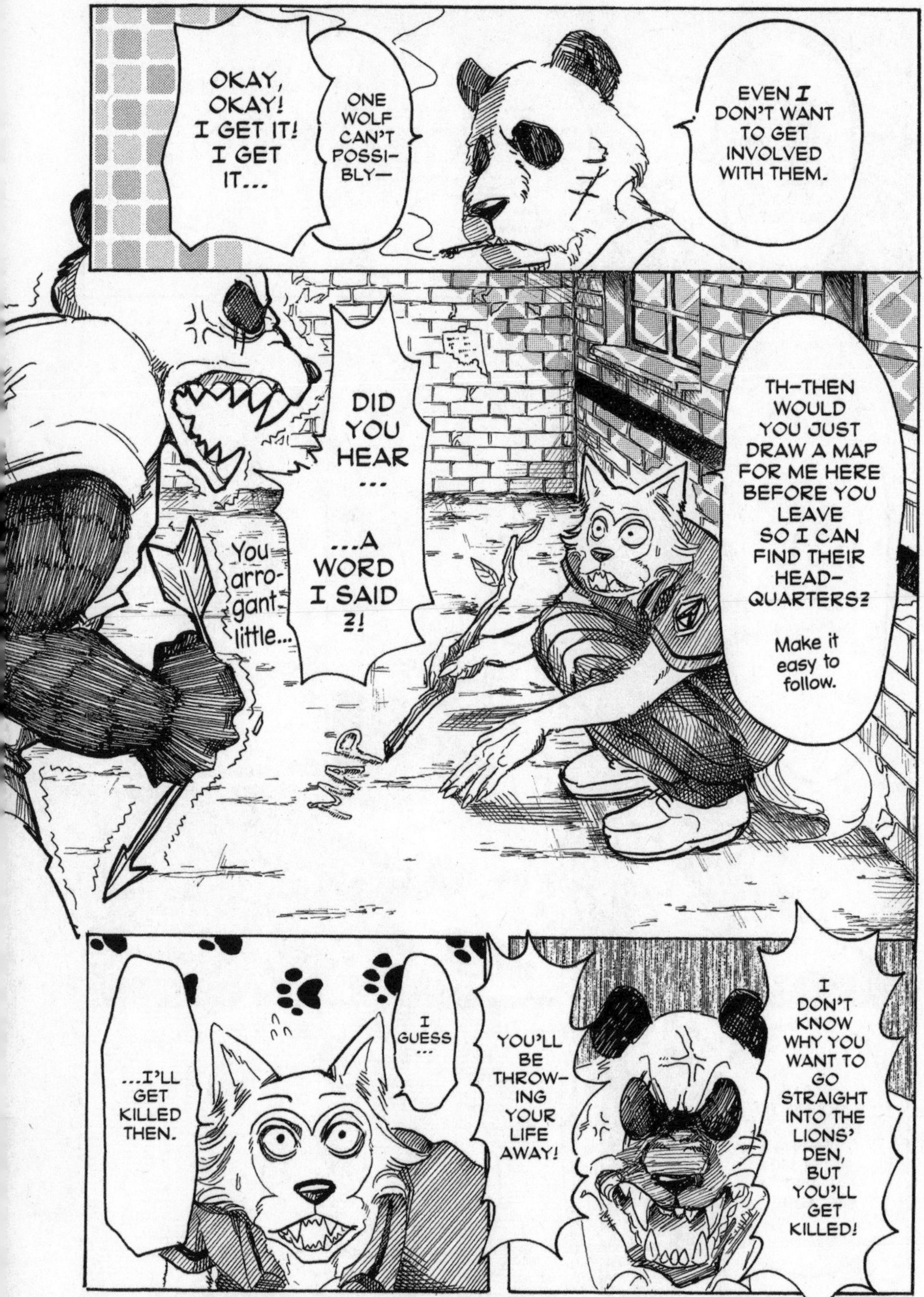
EVEN I DON'T WANT TO GET INVOLVED WITH THEM.
ONE WOLF CAN'T POSSIBLY—
OKAY, OKAY! I GET IT! I GET IT...
TH-THEN WOULD YOU JUST DRAW A MAP FOR ME HERE BEFORE YOU LEAVE SO I CAN FIND THEIR HEADQUARTERS?
Make it easy to follow.
DID YOU HEAR... ...A WORD I SAID?!
You arrogant little...
I DON'T KNOW WHY YOU WANT TO GO STRAIGHT INTO THE LIONS' DEN, BUT YOU'LL GET KILLED!
YOU'LL BE THROWING YOUR LIFE AWAY!
I GUESS...
...I'LL GET KILLED THEN.

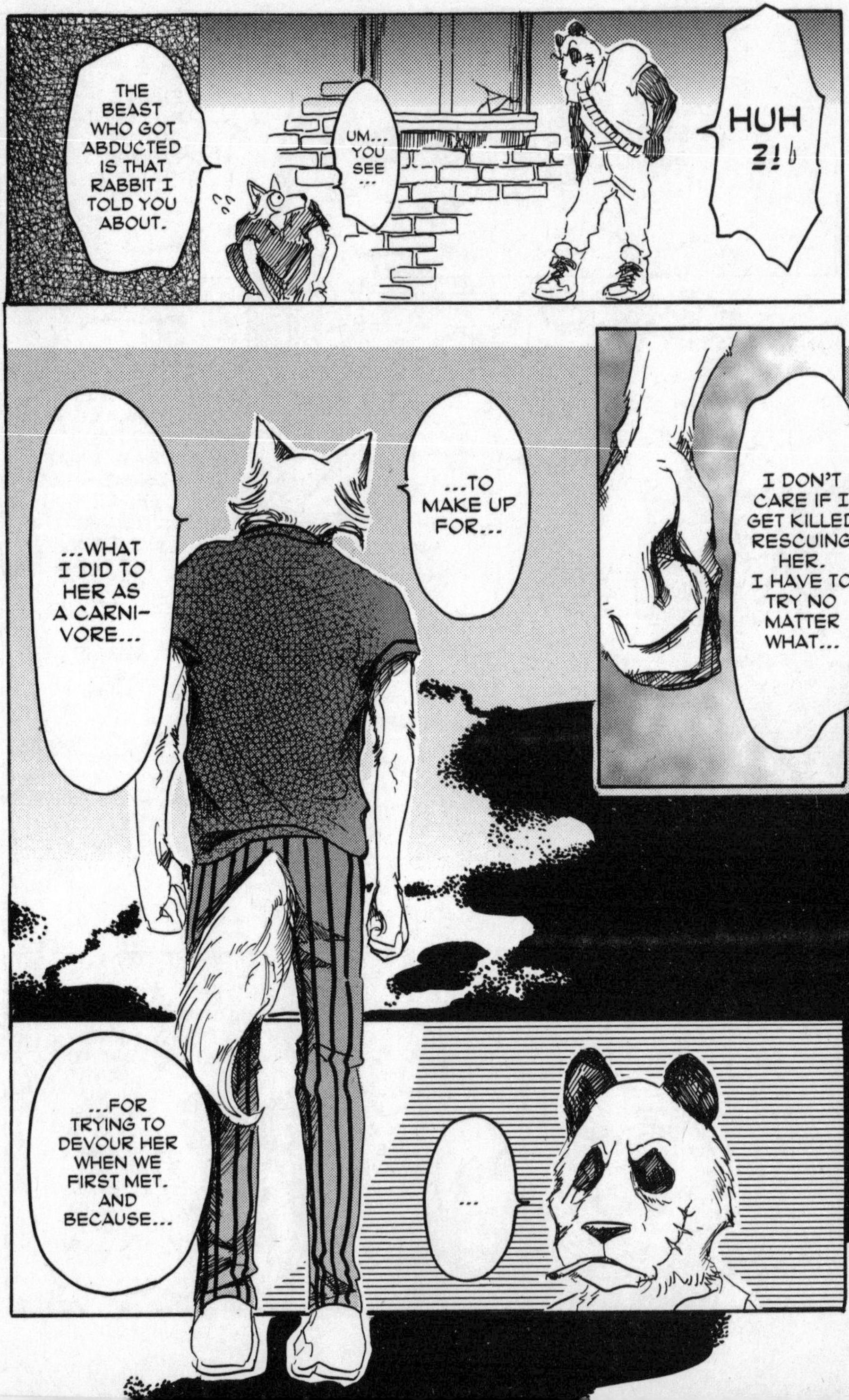
HUH ?!
UM... YOU SEE ...
THE BEAST WHO GOT ABDUCTED IS THAT RABBIT I TOLD YOU ABOUT.
I DON'T CARE IF I GET KILLED RESCUING HER. I HAVE TO TRY NO MATTER WHAT...
...TO MAKE UP FOR...
...WHAT I DID TO HER AS A CARNIVORE...
...
...FOR TRYING TO DEVOUR HER WHEN WE FIRST MET. AND BECAUSE...

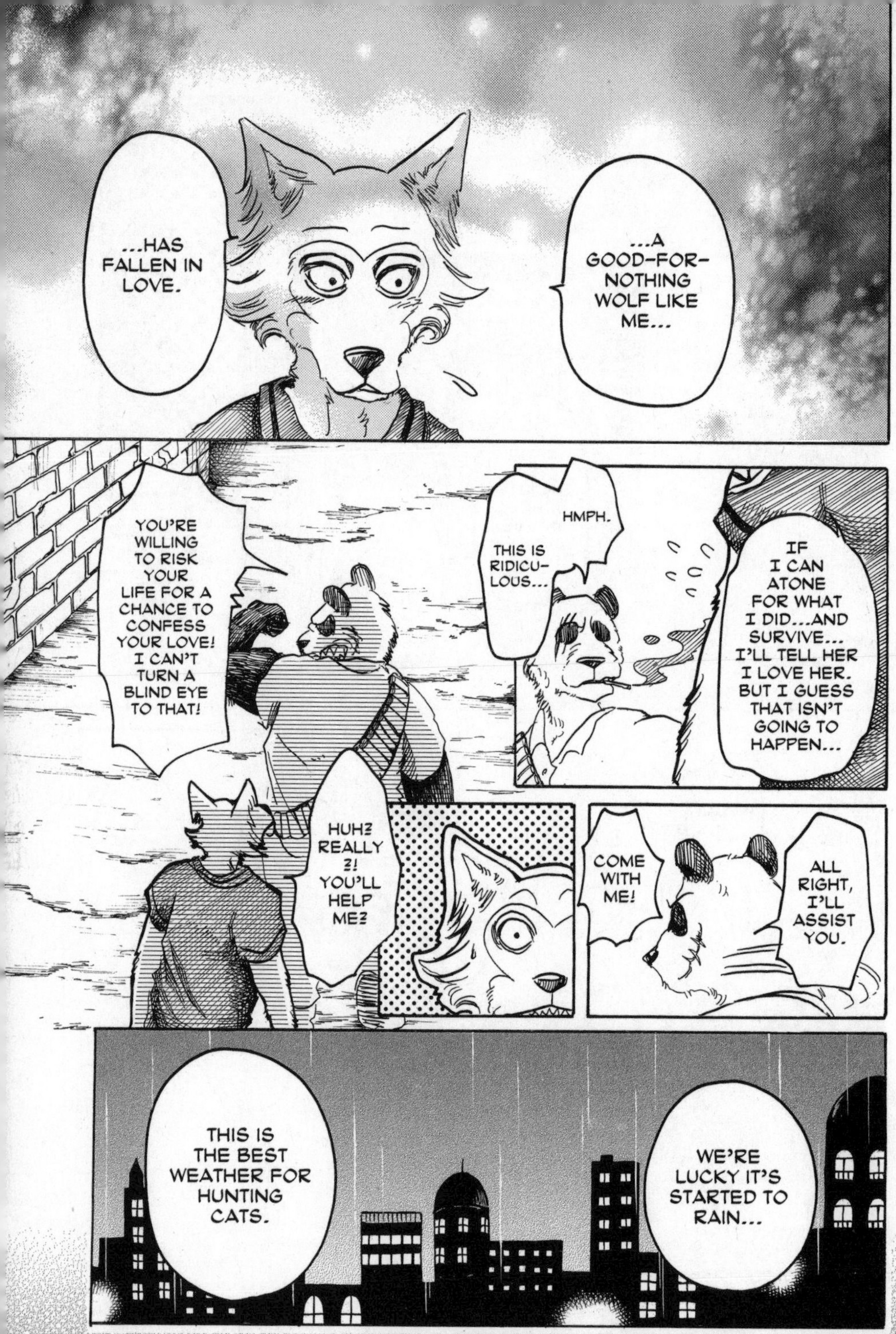
...A GOOD-FOR-NOTHING WOLF LIKE ME...
...HAS FALLEN IN LOVE.
IF I CAN ATONE FOR WHAT I DID...AND SURVIVE... I'LL TELL HER I LOVE HER. BUT I GUESS THAT ISN'T GOING TO HAPPEN...
HMPH.
THIS IS RIDICULOUS...
ALL RIGHT, I'LL ASSIST YOU.
COME WITH ME!
HUH? REALLY?! YOU'LL HELP ME?
YOU'RE WILLING TO RISK YOUR LIFE FOR A CHANCE TO CONFESS YOUR LOVE! I CAN'T TURN A BLIND EYE TO THAT!
WE'RE LUCKY IT'S STARTED TO RAIN...
THIS IS THE BEST WEATHER FOR HUNTING CATS.

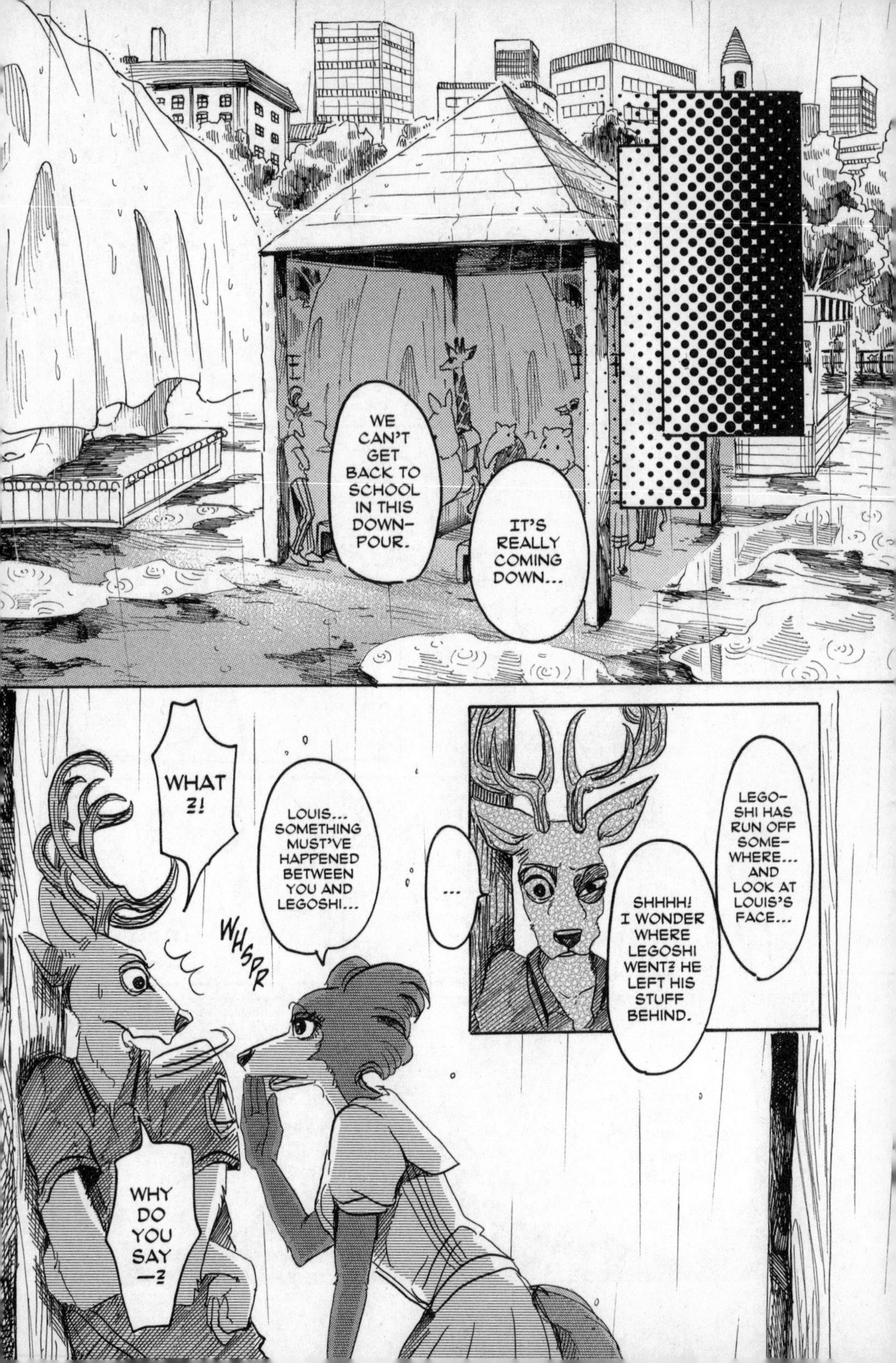
IT'S REALLY COMING DOWN...
WE CAN'T GET BACK TO SCHOOL IN THIS DOWN-POUR.
LEGO-SHI HAS RUN OFF SOME-WHERE... AND LOOK AT LOUIS'S FACE...
SHHHH! I WONDER WHERE LEGOSHI WENT? HE LEFT HIS STUFF BEHIND.
...
LOUIS... SOMETHING MUST'VE HAPPENED BETWEEN YOU AND LEGOSHI...
WHSPR
WHAT?!
WHY DO YOU SAY—?

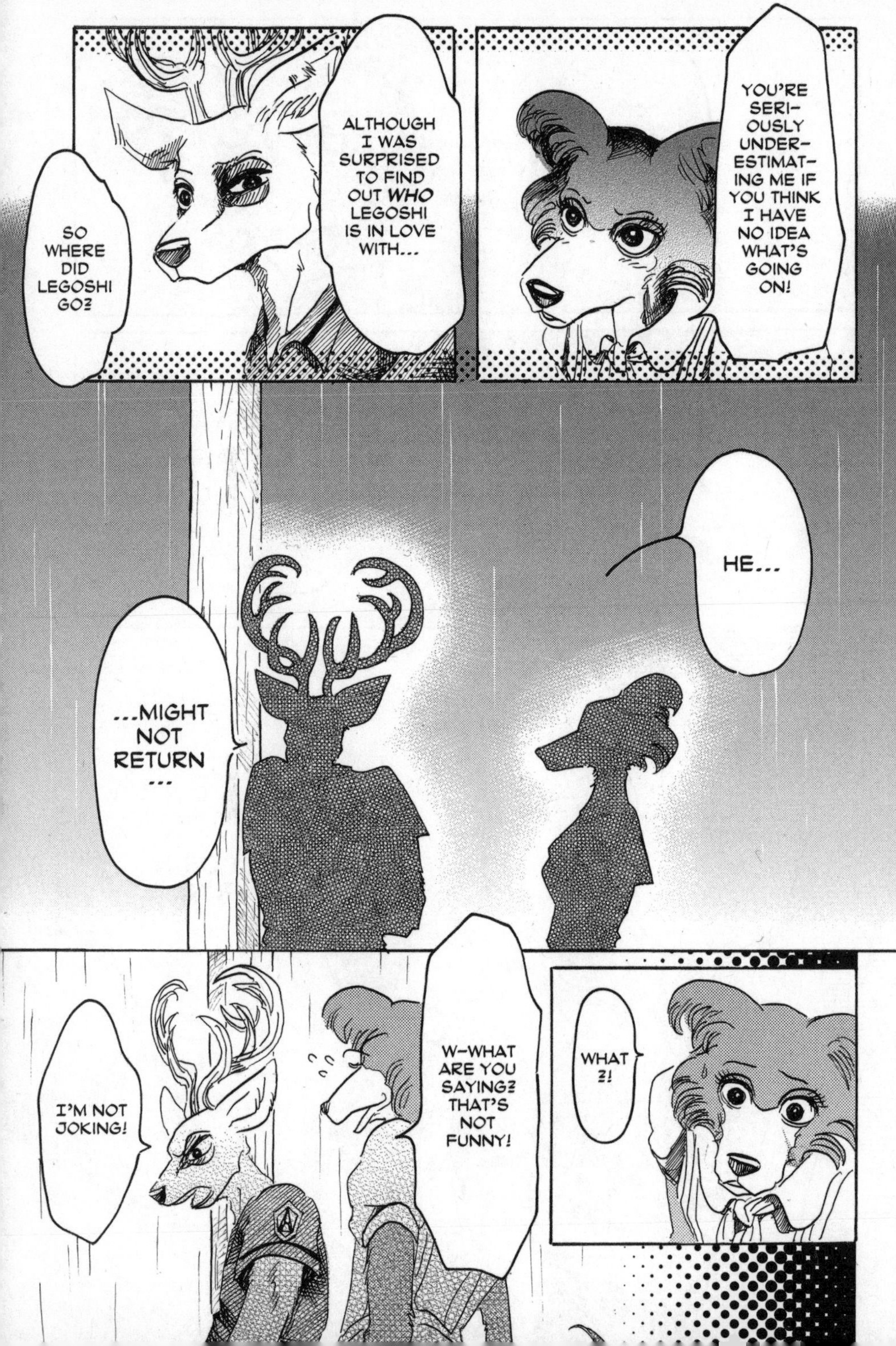
YOU'RE SERIOUSLY UNDERESTIMATING ME IF YOU THINK I HAVE NO IDEA WHAT'S GOING ON!
ALTHOUGH I WAS SURPRISED TO FIND OUT *WHO* LEGOSHI IS IN LOVE WITH...
SO WHERE DID LEGOSHI GO?
HE...
...MIGHT NOT RETURN...
WHAT?!
W-WHAT ARE YOU SAYING? THAT'S NOT FUNNY!
I'M NOT JOKING!

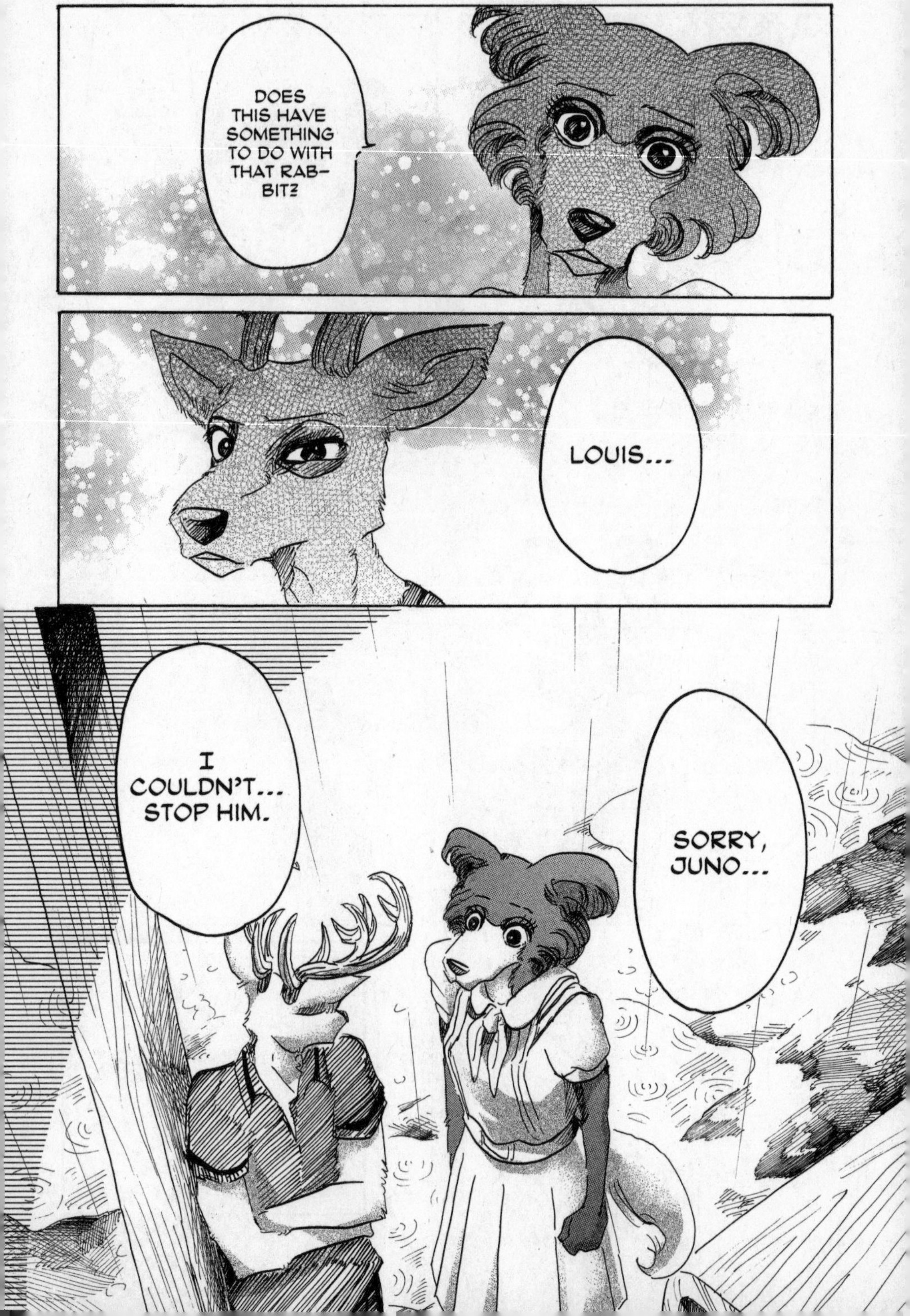
DOES THIS HAVE SOMETHING TO DO WITH THAT RAB-BIT?
LOUIS...
SORRY, JUNO...
I COULDN'T... STOP HIM.

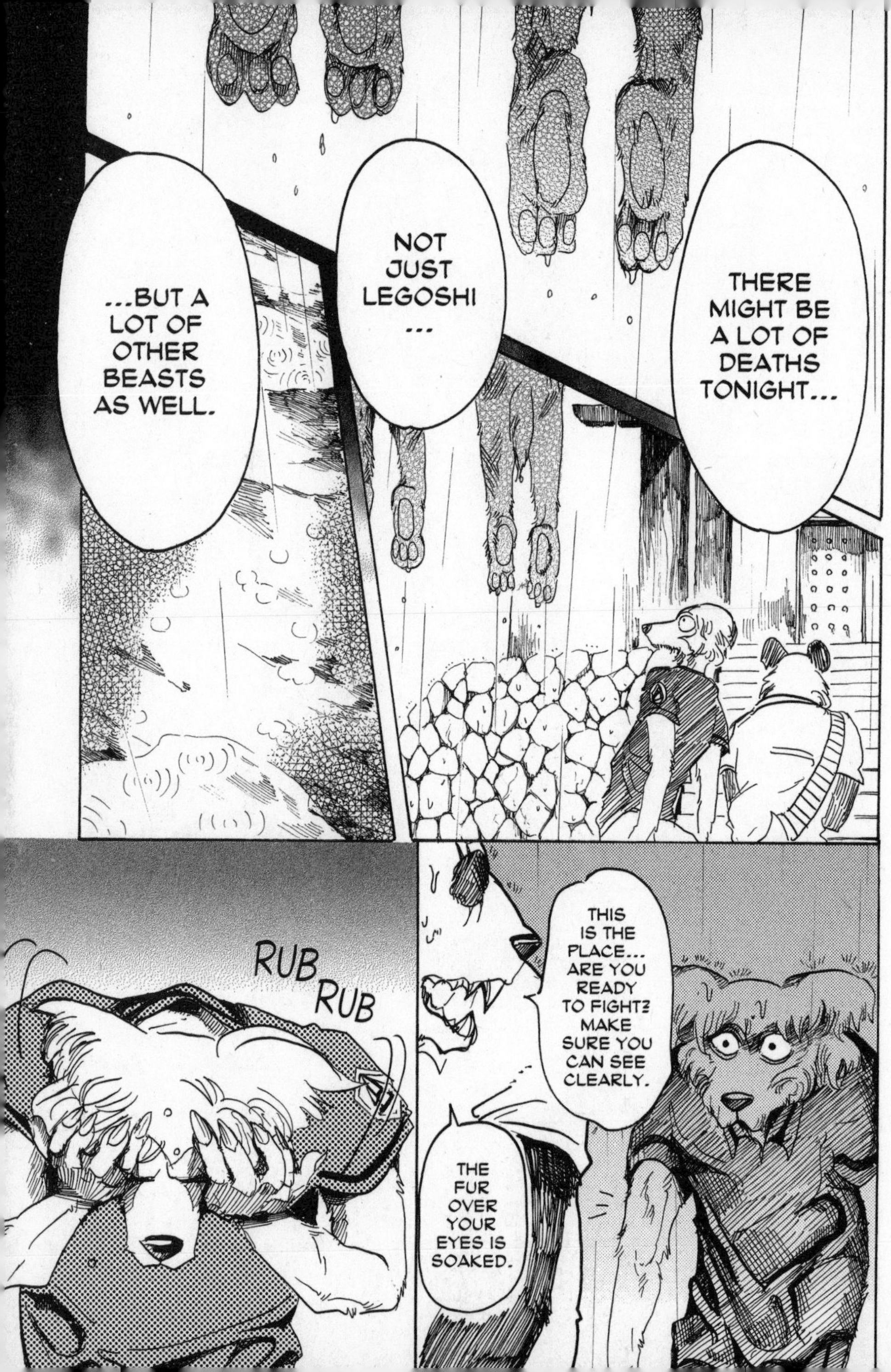
THERE MIGHT BE A LOT OF DEATHS TONIGHT...
NOT JUST LEGOSHI...
...BUT A LOT OF OTHER BEASTS AS WELL.
THIS IS THE PLACE... ARE YOU READY TO FIGHT? MAKE SURE YOU CAN SEE CLEARLY.
THE FUR OVER YOUR EYES IS SOAKED.
RUB RUB

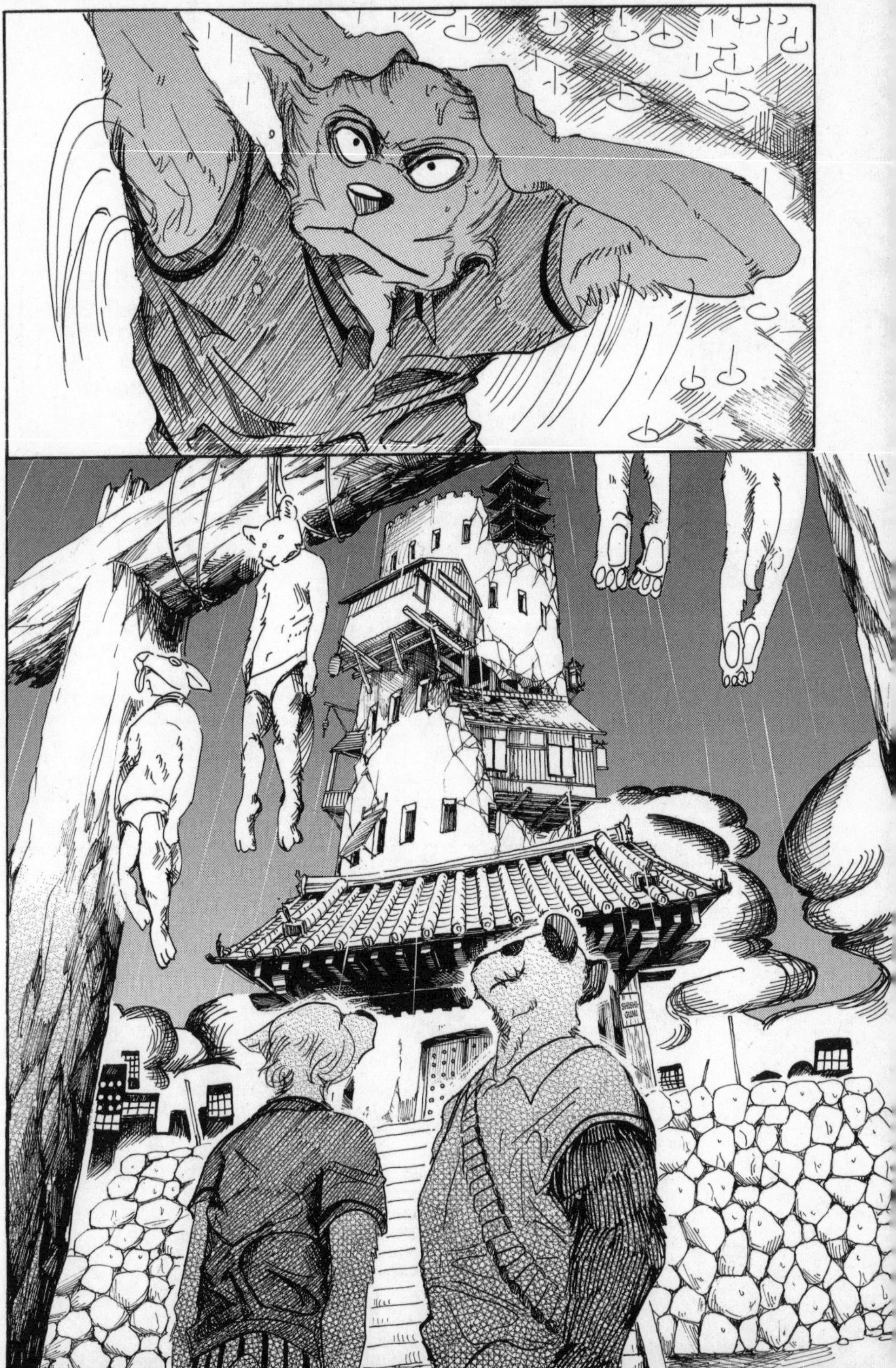
SHISHI-GUMI

Chapter 38: White Fur on Ruled Lines

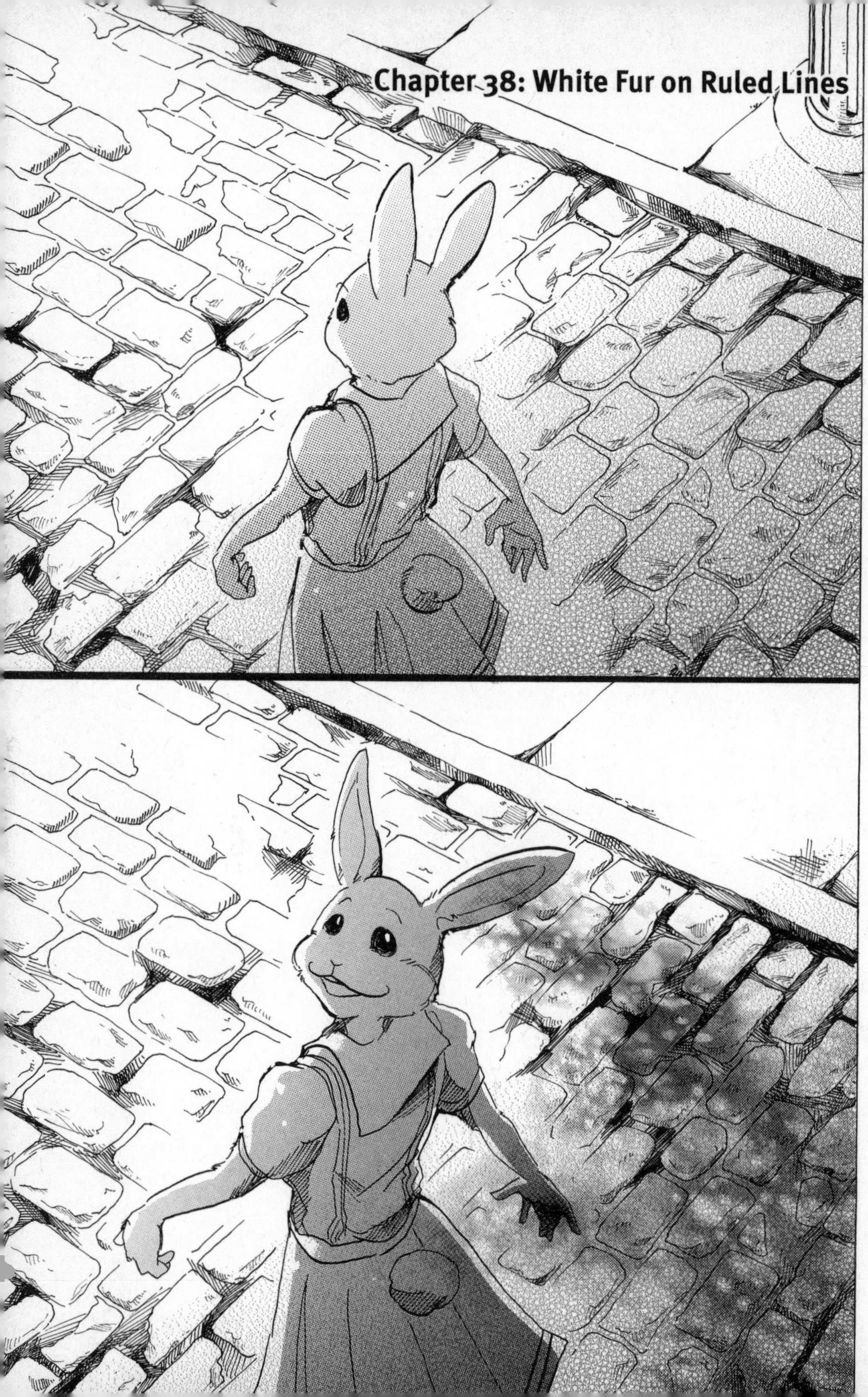

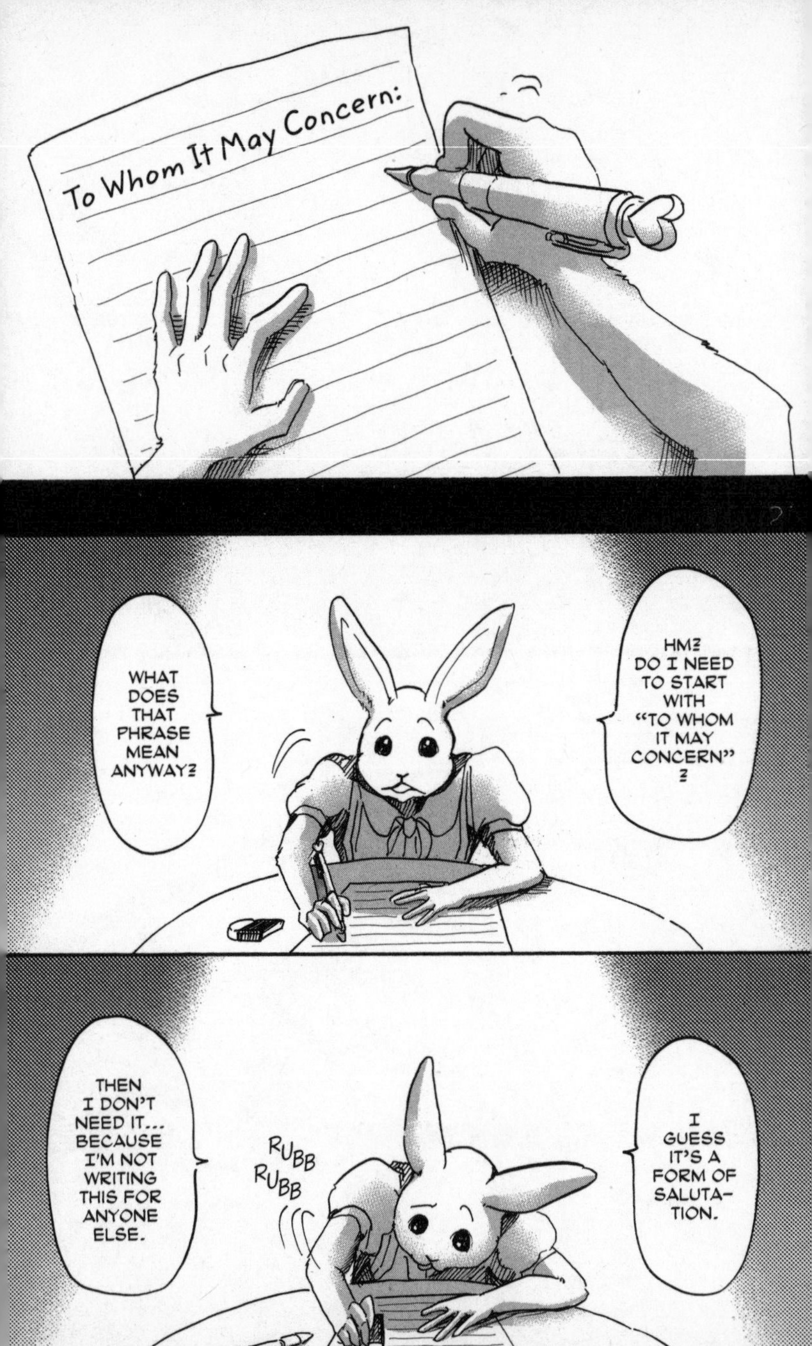
To Whom It May Concern:
HM? DO I NEED TO START WITH "TO WHOM IT MAY CONCERN" ?
WHAT DOES THAT PHRASE MEAN ANYWAY?
I GUESS IT'S A FORM OF SALUTATION.
RUBB RUBB
THEN I DON'T NEED IT... BECAUSE I'M NOT WRITING THIS FOR ANYONE ELSE.

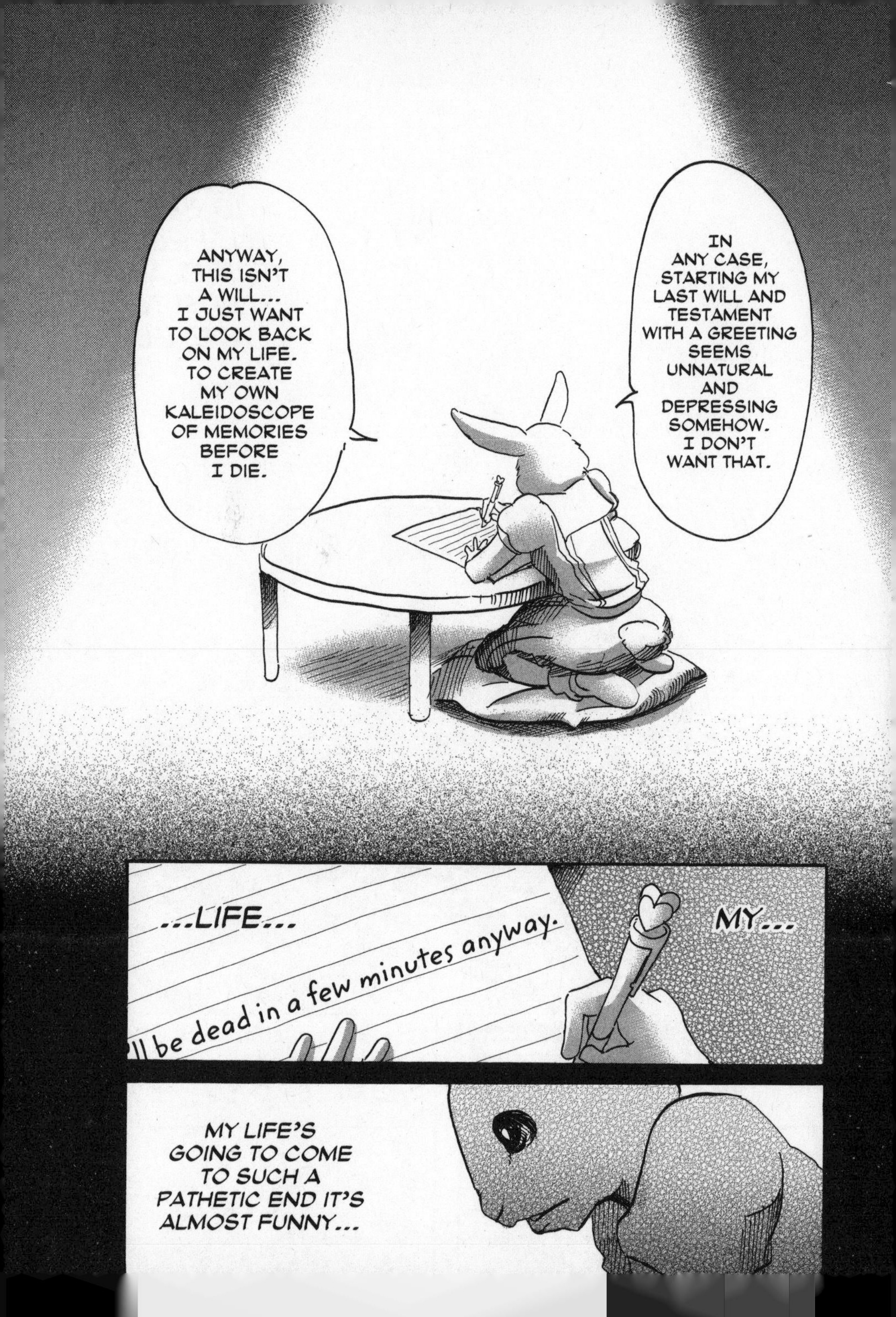
IN ANY CASE, STARTING MY LAST WILL AND TESTAMENT WITH A GREETING SEEMS UNNATURAL AND DEPRESSING SOMEHOW. I DON'T WANT THAT.
ANYWAY, THIS ISN'T A WILL... I JUST WANT TO LOOK BACK ON MY LIFE. TO CREATE MY OWN KALEIDOSCOPE OF MEMORIES BEFORE I DIE.
MY...
ll be dead in a few minutes anyway.
...LIFE...
MY LIFE'S GOING TO COME TO SUCH A PATHETIC END IT'S ALMOST FUNNY...

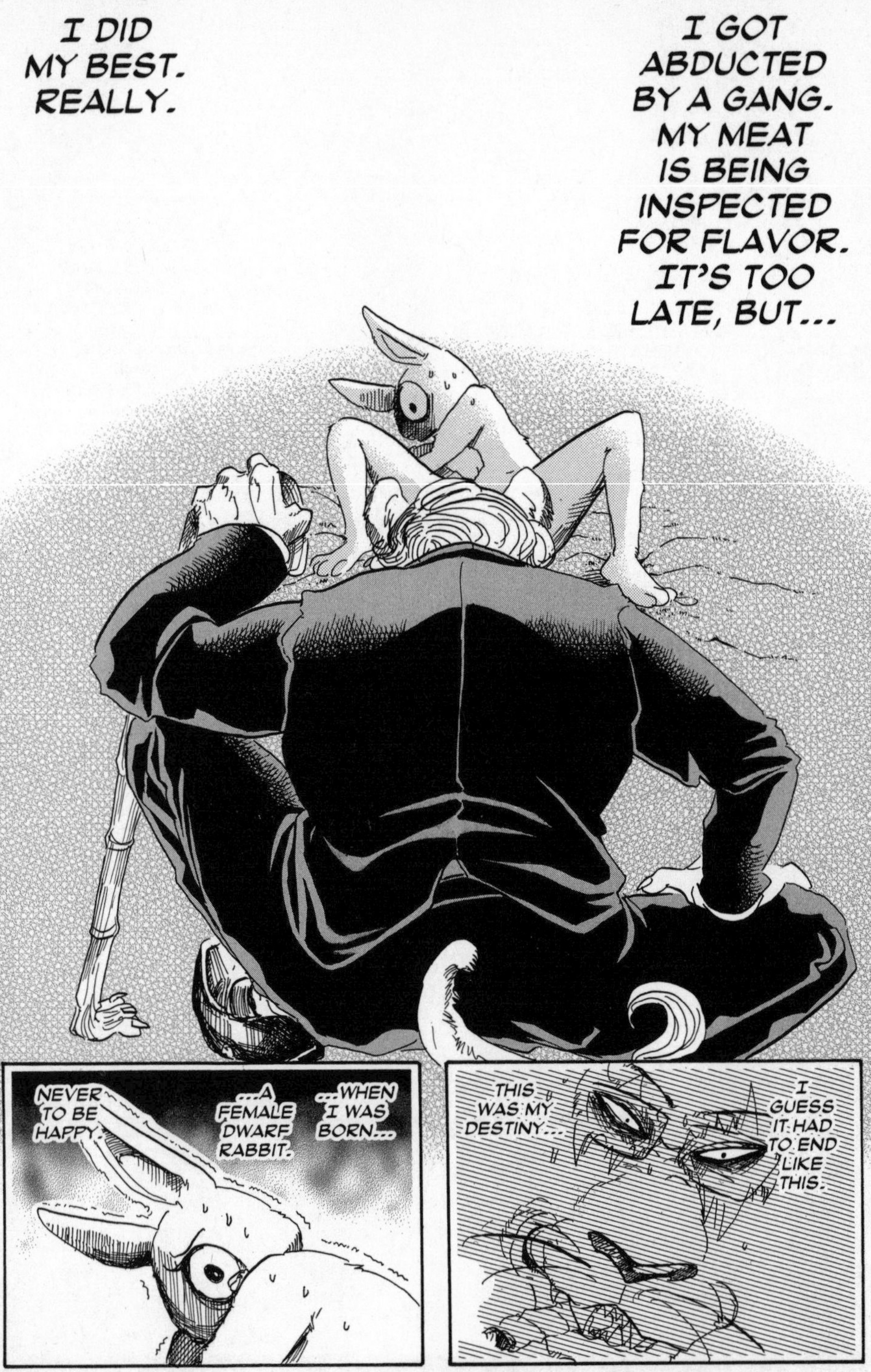
I GOT ABDUCTED BY A GANG. MY MEAT IS BEING INSPECTED FOR FLAVOR. IT'S TOO LATE, BUT...
I DID MY BEST. REALLY.
I GUESS IT HAD TO END LIKE THIS.
THIS WAS MY DESTINY...
...WHEN I WAS BORN...
...A FEMALE DWARF RABBIT.
NEVER TO BE HAPPY.

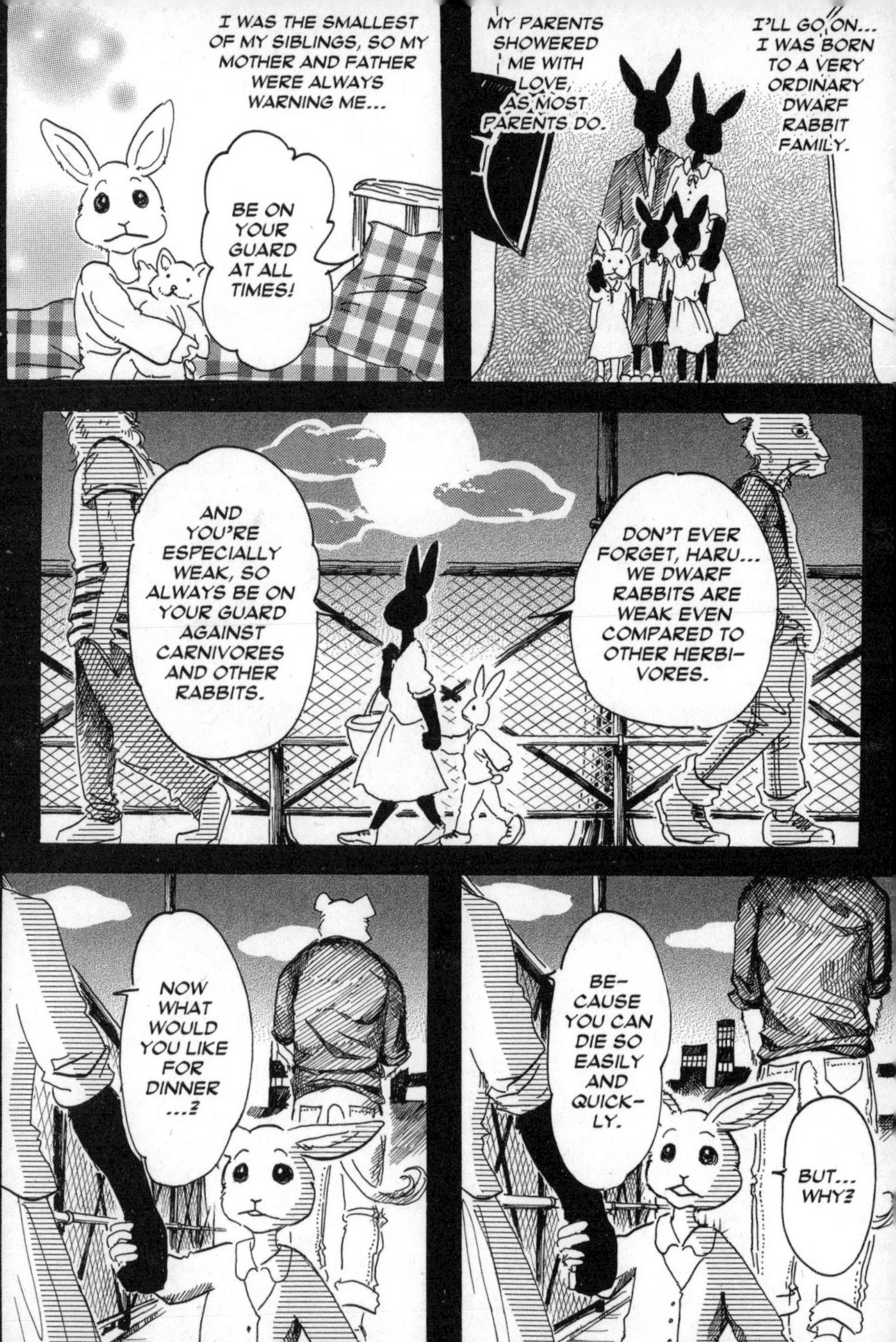
I'LL GO ON... I WAS BORN TO A VERY ORDINARY DWARF RABBIT FAMILY.
MY PARENTS SHOWERED ME WITH LOVE, AS MOST PARENTS DO.
I WAS THE SMALLEST OF MY SIBLINGS, SO MY MOTHER AND FATHER WERE ALWAYS WARNING ME...
BE ON YOUR GUARD AT ALL TIMES!
DON'T EVER FORGET, HARU... WE DWARF RABBITS ARE WEAK EVEN COMPARED TO OTHER HERBI-VORES.
AND YOU'RE ESPECIALLY WEAK, SO ALWAYS BE ON YOUR GUARD AGAINST CARNIVORES AND OTHER RABBITS.
BUT... WHY?
BE-CAUSE YOU CAN DIE SO EASILY AND QUICK-LY.
NOW WHAT WOULD YOU LIKE FOR DINNER ...?

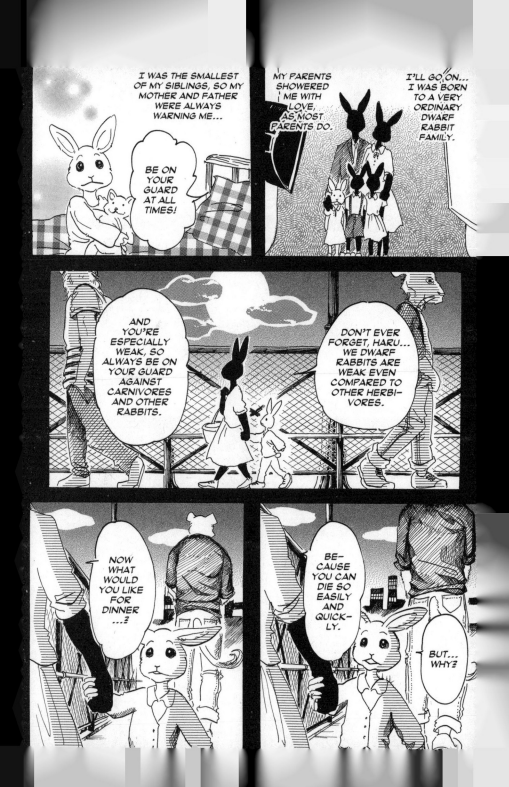

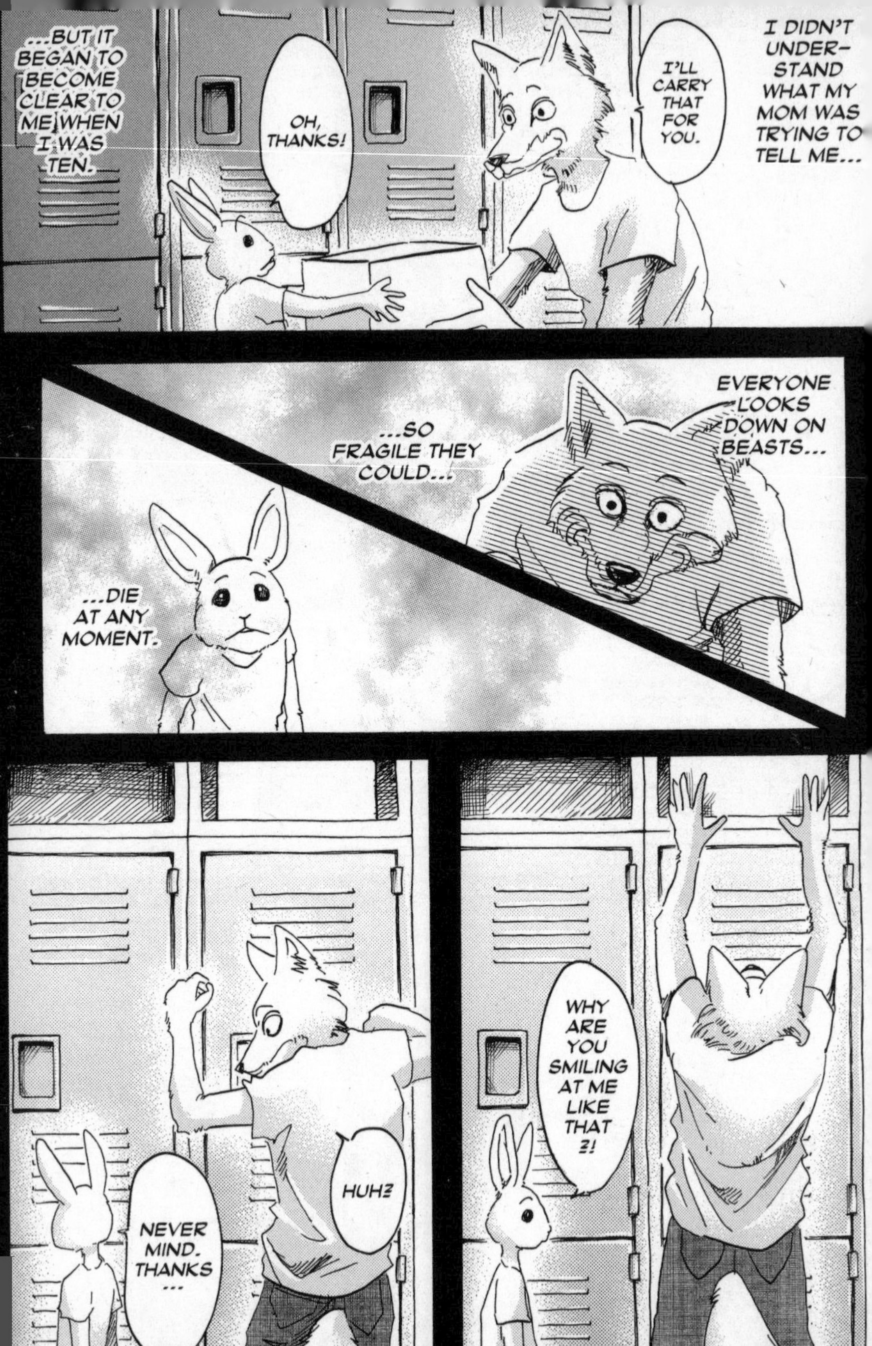
I DIDN'T UNDER-STAND WHAT MY MOM WAS TRYING TO TELL ME...
I'LL CARRY THAT FOR YOU.
OH, THANKS!
...BUT IT BEGAN TO BECOME CLEAR TO ME WHEN I WAS TEN.
EVERYONE LOOKS DOWN ON BEASTS...
...SO FRAGILE THEY COULD...
...DIE AT ANY MOMENT.
WHY ARE YOU SMILING AT ME LIKE THAT?!
HUH?
NEVER MIND. THANKS...

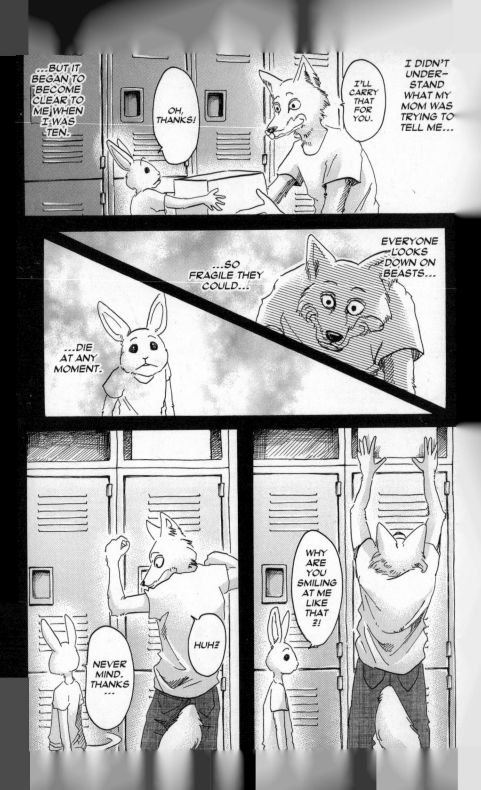

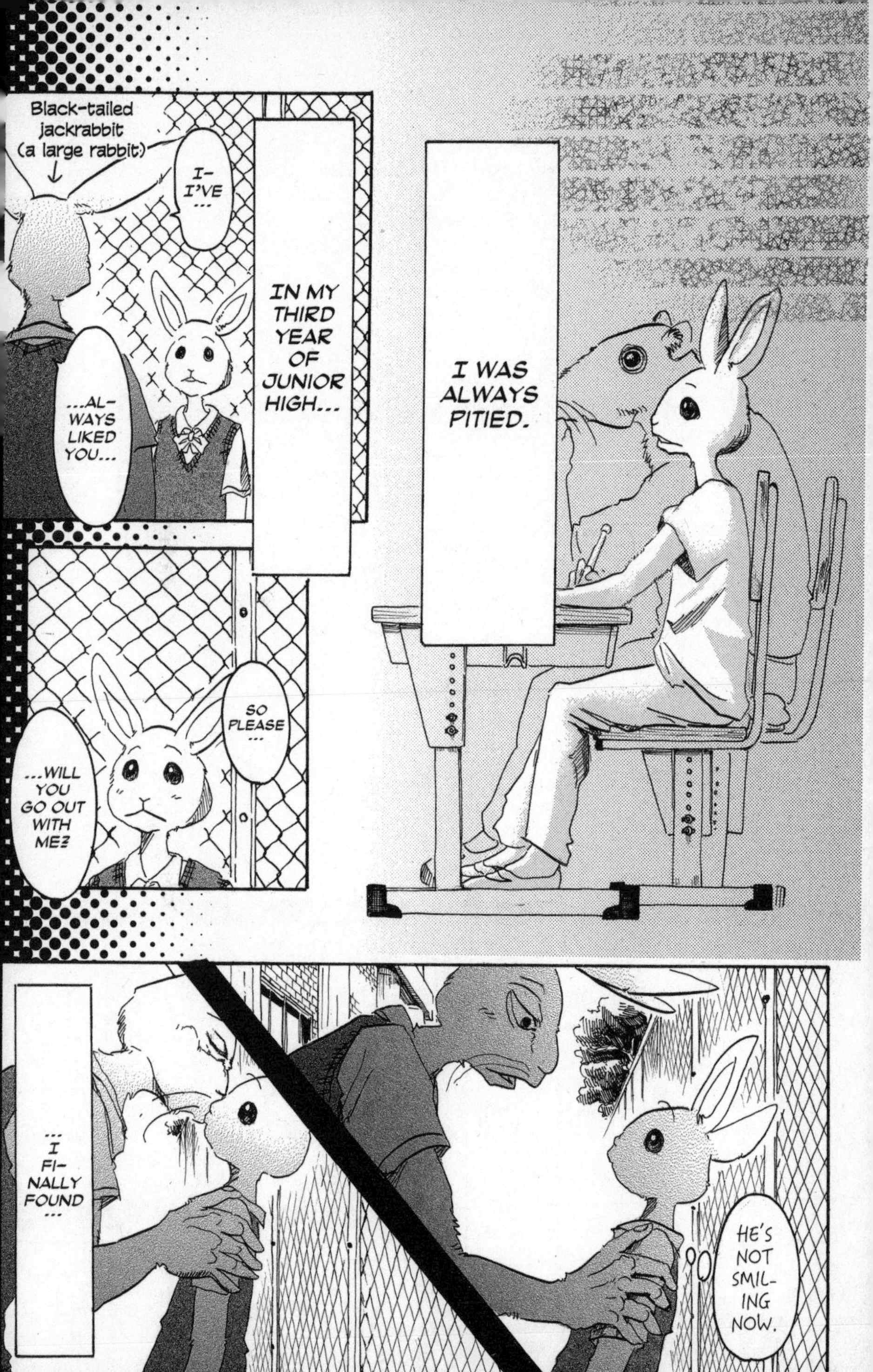
I WAS ALWAYS PITIED.
IN MY THIRD YEAR OF JUNIOR HIGH...
Black-tailed jackrabbit (a large rabbit)
I- I'VE...
...AL-WAYS LIKED YOU...
SO PLEASE...
...WILL YOU GO OUT WITH ME?
HE'S NOT SMIL-ING NOW.
...I FI-NALLY FOUND...

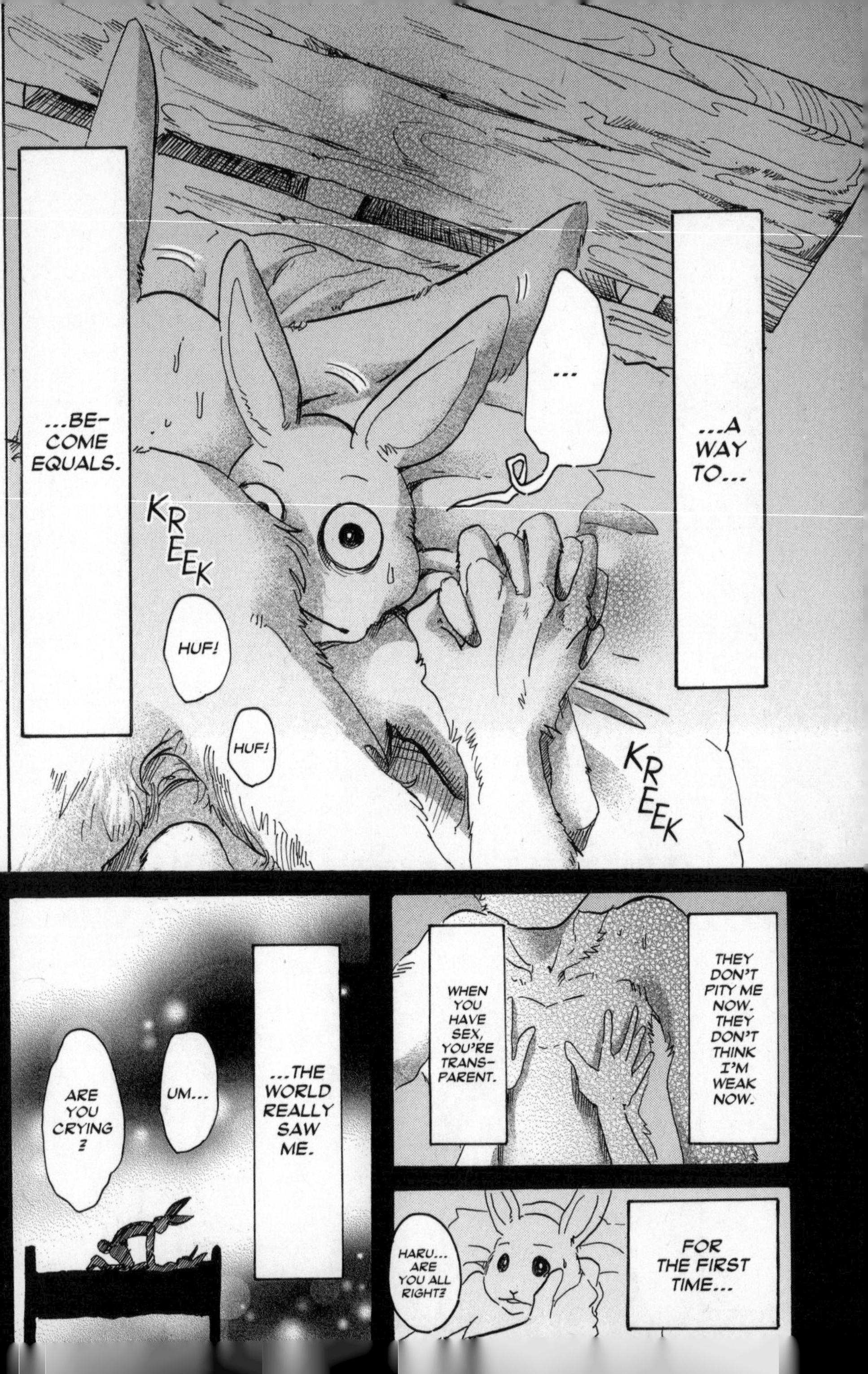
...A WAY TO...
...
...BE-COME EQUALS.
KREEK
HUF!
HUF!
KREEK
THEY DON'T PITY ME NOW. THEY DON'T THINK I'M WEAK NOW.
WHEN YOU HAVE SEX, YOU'RE TRANS-PARENT.
FOR THE FIRST TIME...
HARU... ARE YOU ALL RIGHT?
...THE WORLD REALLY SAW ME.
UM...
ARE YOU CRYING?

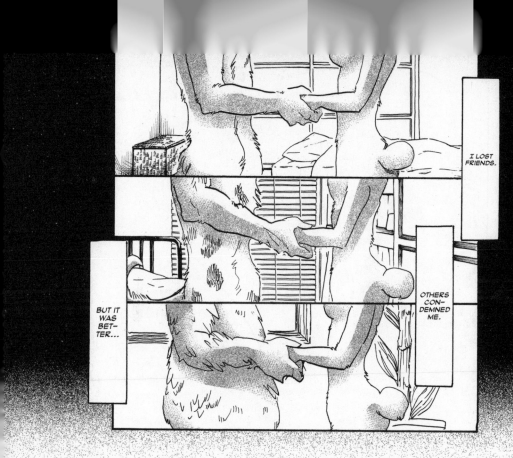

I LOST FRIENDS.

OTHERS CON-DEMNED ME.

BUT IT WAS BET-TER...

...PITIED.

...THAN BEING...

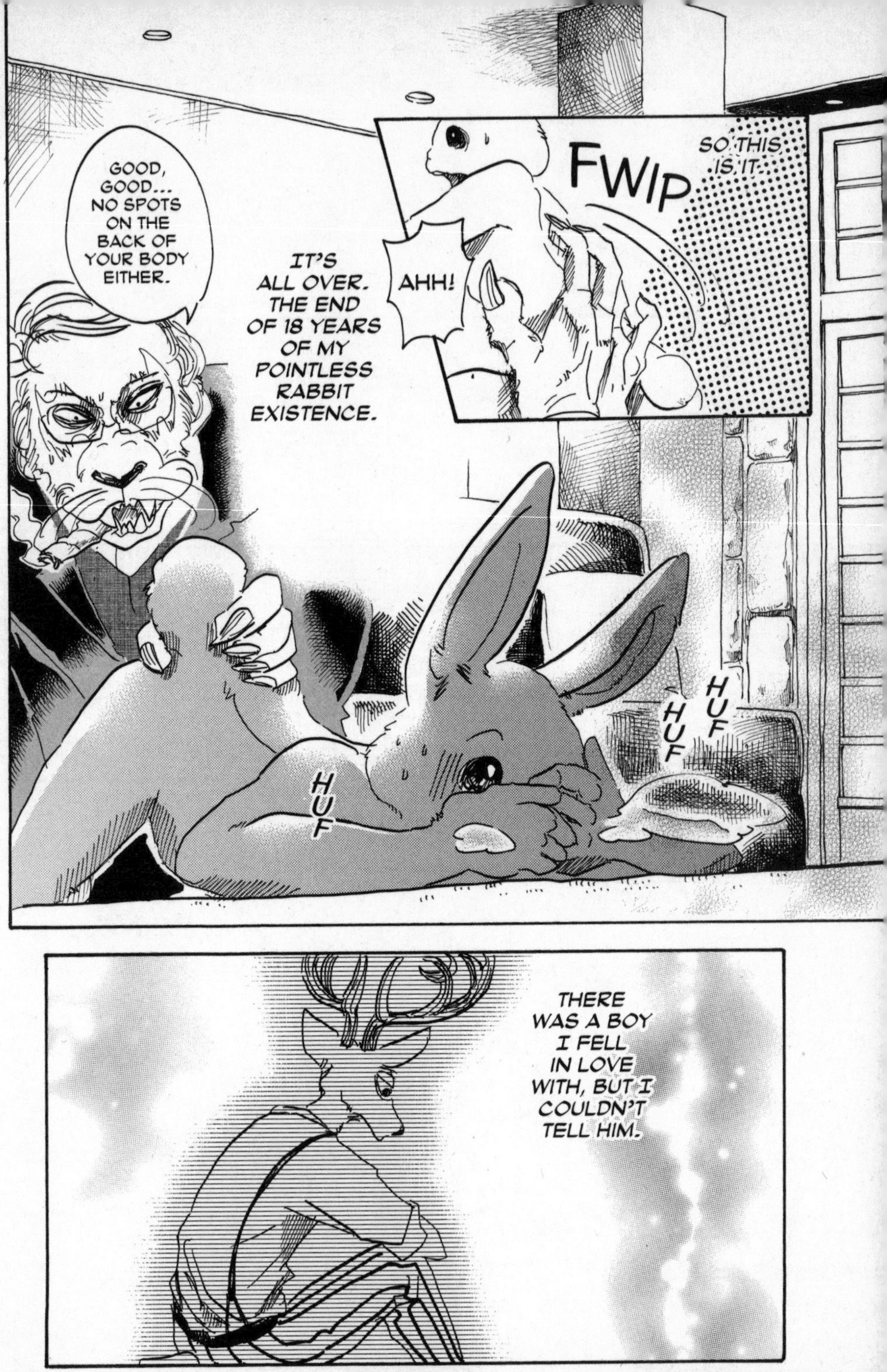
SO THIS IS IT...
FWIP
AHH!
IT'S ALL OVER. THE END OF 18 YEARS OF MY POINTLESS RABBIT EXISTENCE.
GOOD, GOOD... NO SPOTS ON THE BACK OF YOUR BODY EITHER.
HUF HUF
HUF
THERE WAS A BOY I FELL IN LOVE WITH, BUT I COULDN'T TELL HIM.

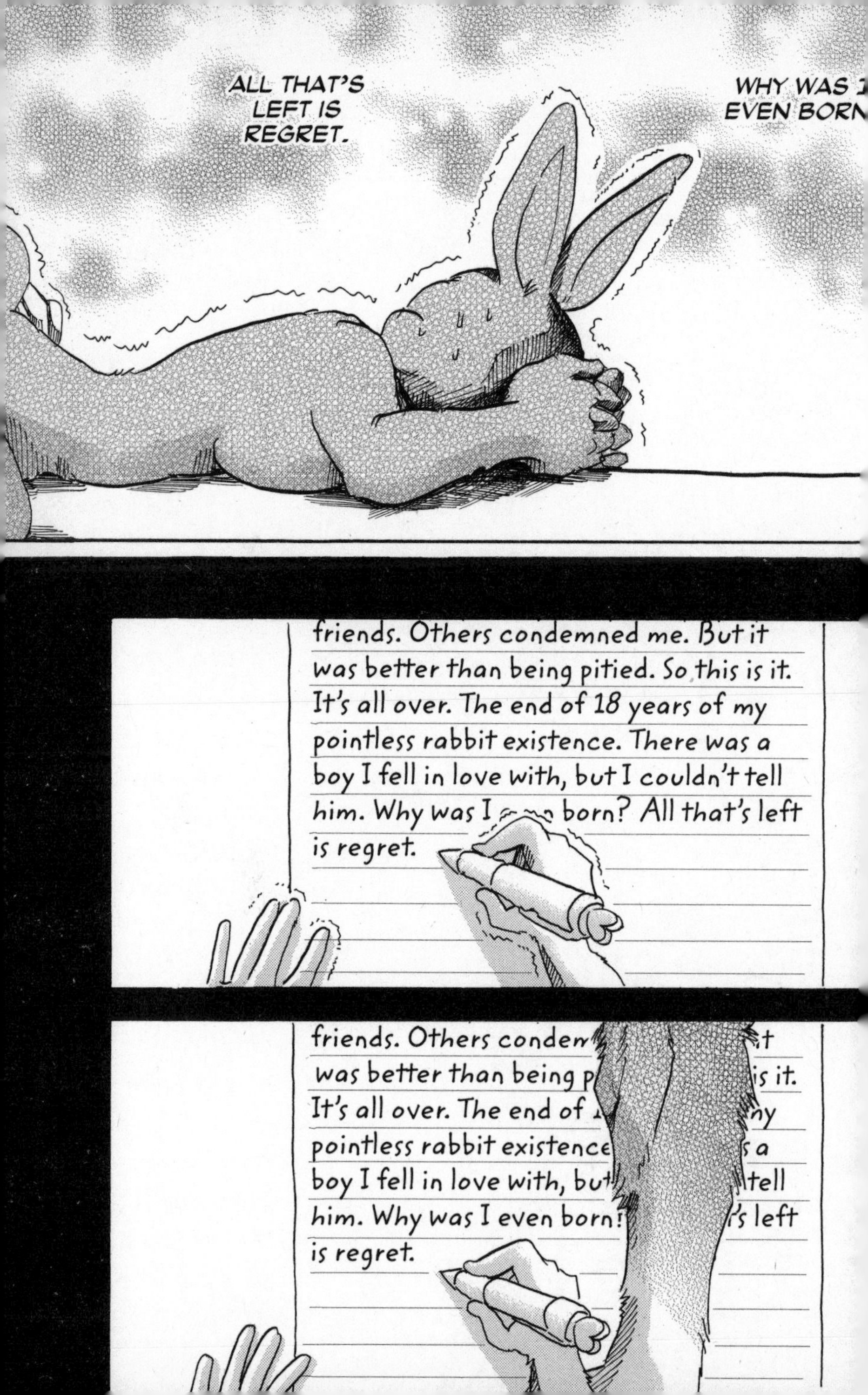
WHY WAS I EVEN BORN
ALL THAT'S LEFT IS REGRET.
friends. Others condemned me. But it was better than being pitied. So this is it. It's all over. The end of 18 years of my pointless rabbit existence. There was a boy I fell in love with, but I couldn't tell him. Why was I born? All that's left is regret.
friends. Others condem
was better than being p
is it.
It's all over. The end of
pointless rabbit existence
boy I fell in love with, but
tell
him. Why was I even born
's left
is regret.

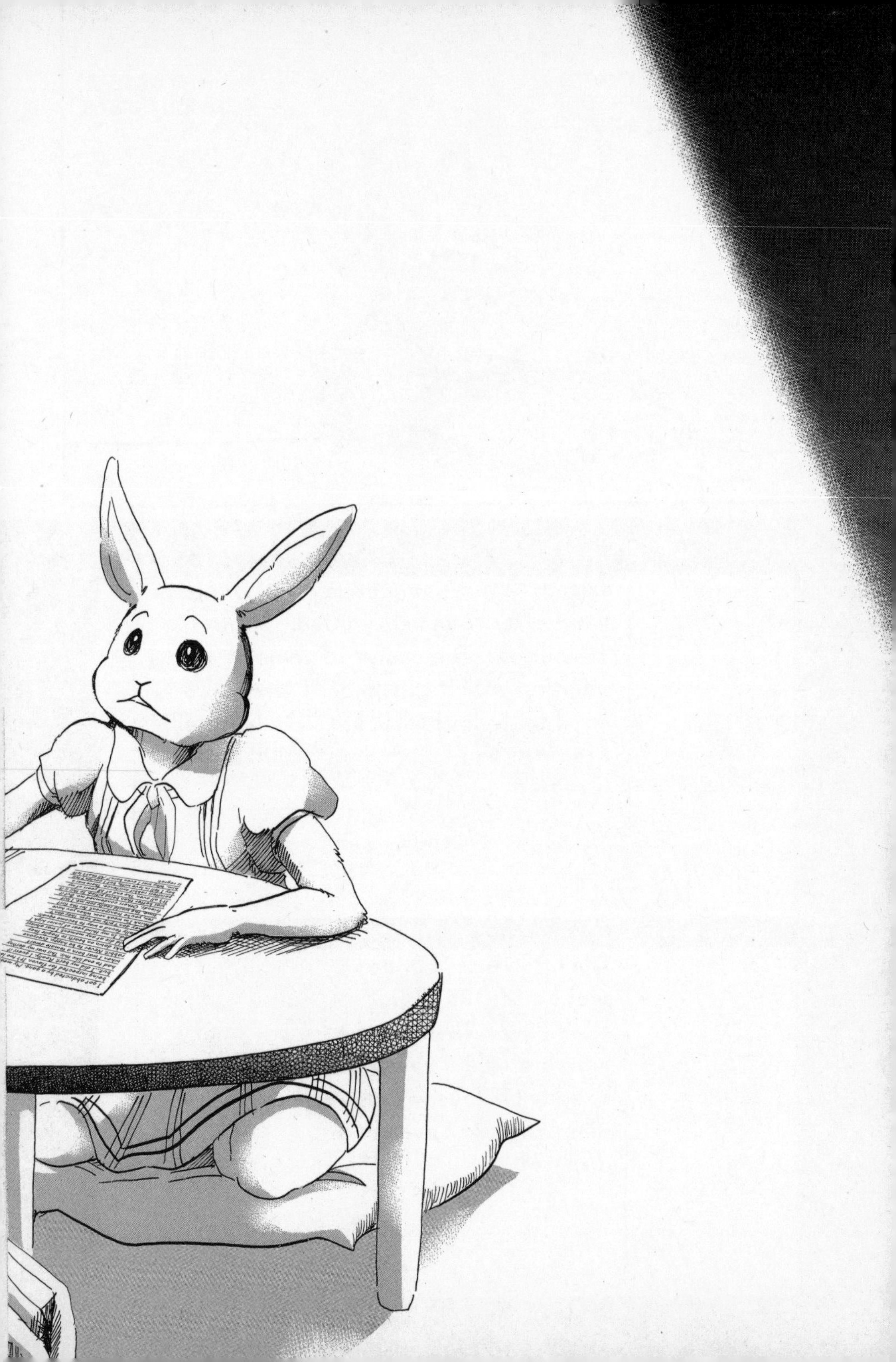

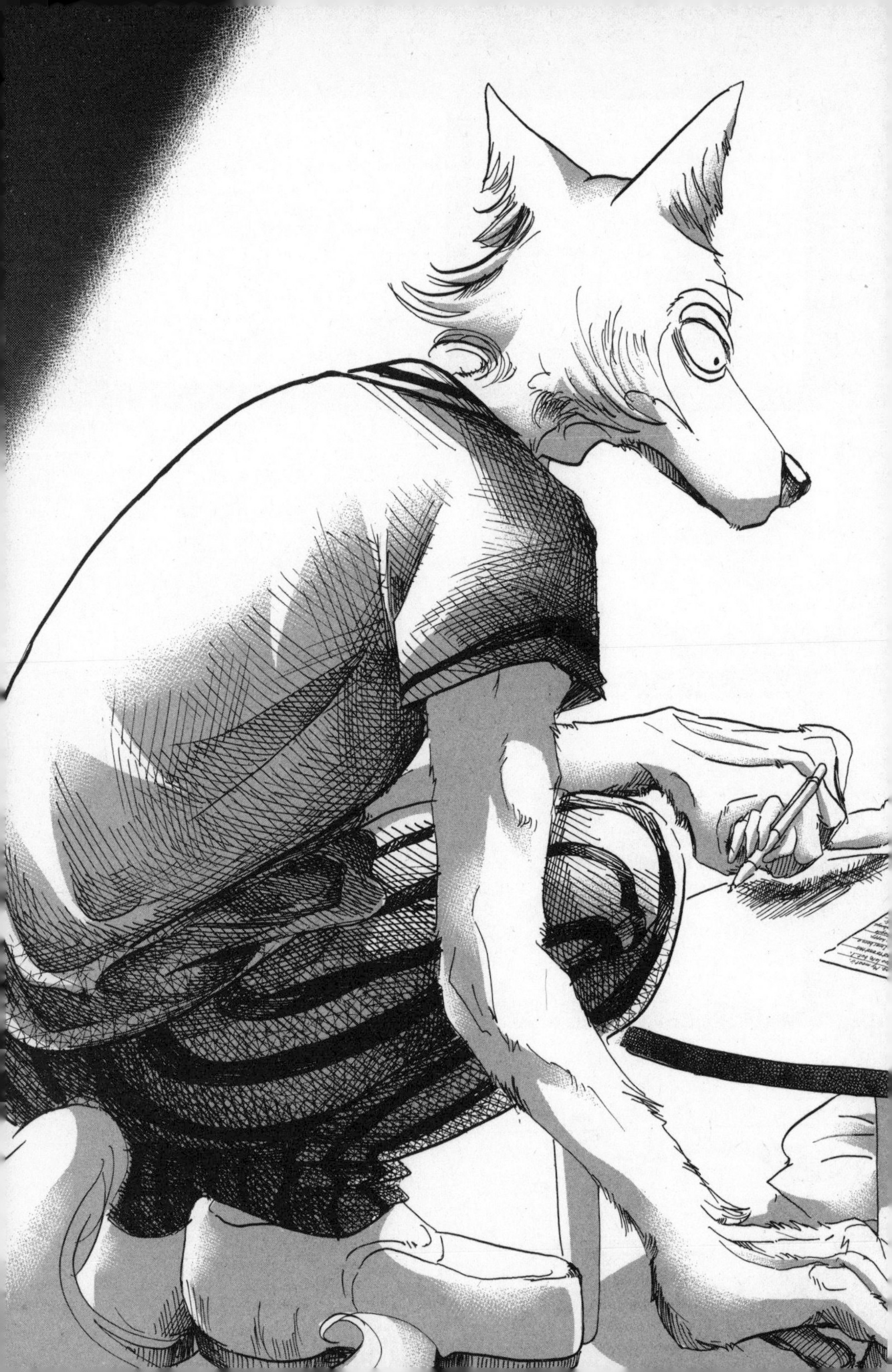

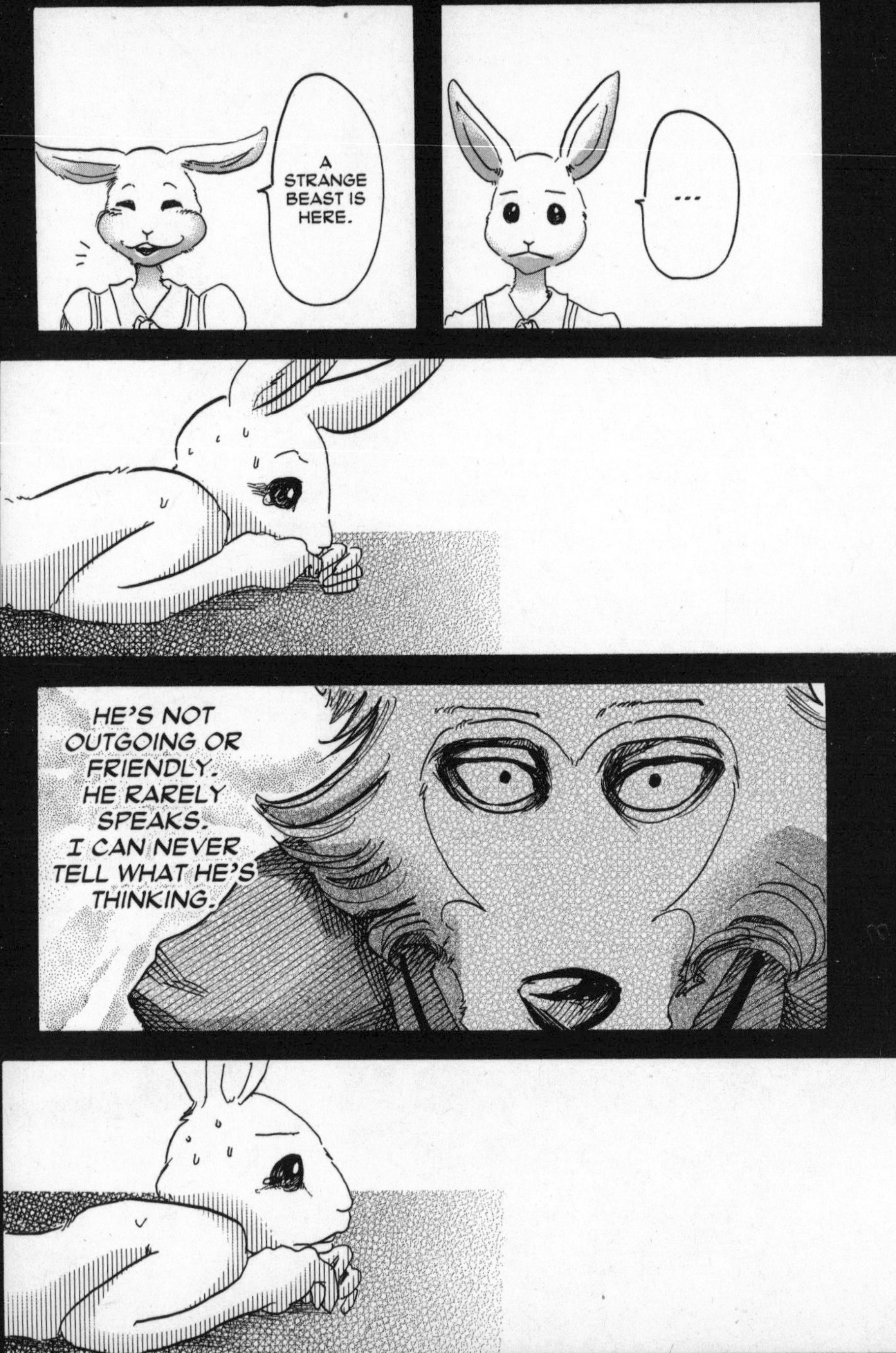
...
A STRANGE BEAST IS HERE.
HE'S NOT OUTGOING OR FRIENDLY. HE RARELY SPEAKS. I CAN NEVER TELL WHAT HE'S THINKING.

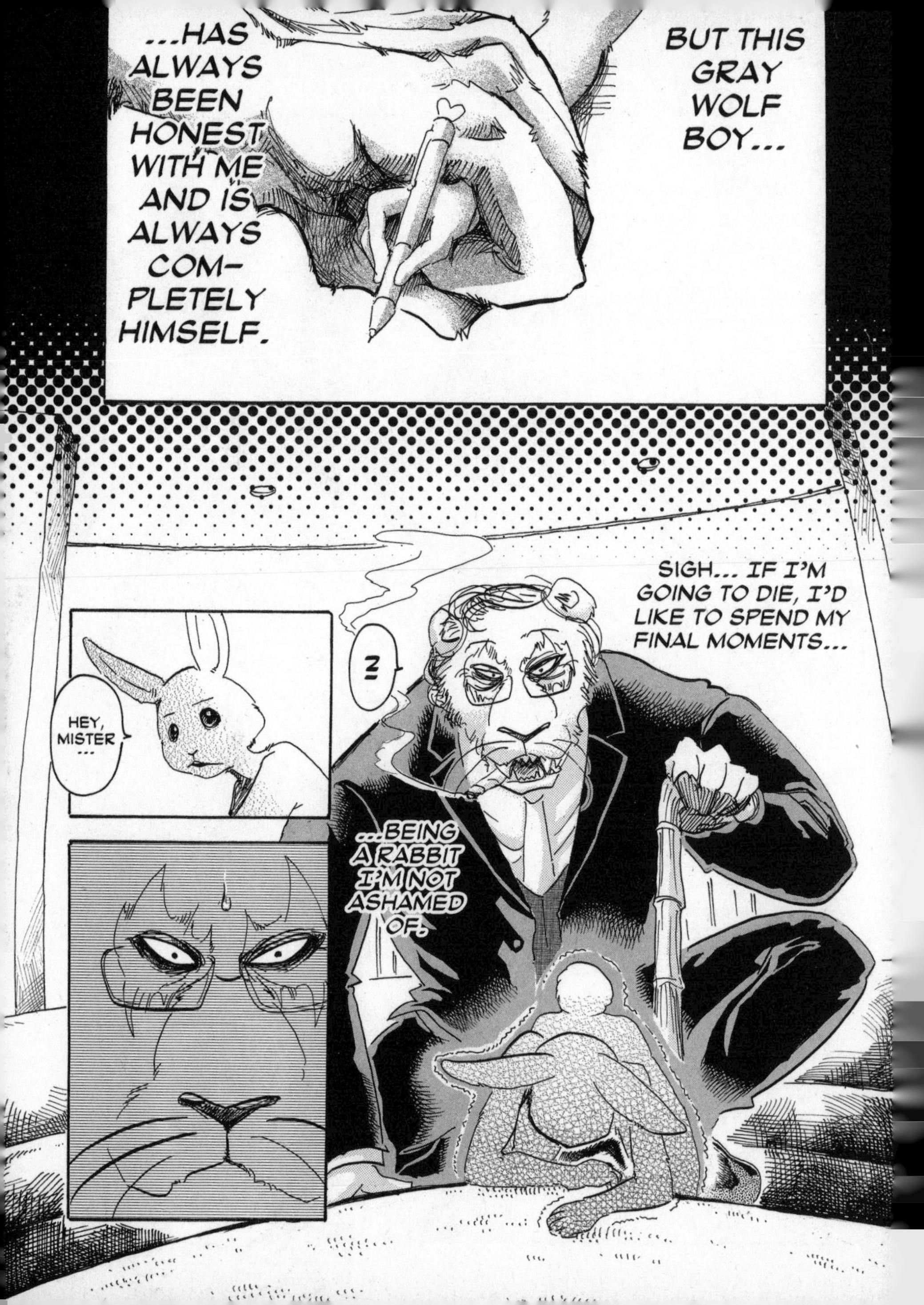
BUT THIS GRAY WOLF BOY...
...HAS ALWAYS BEEN HONEST WITH ME AND IS ALWAYS COM-PLETELY HIMSELF.
SIGH... IF I'M GOING TO DIE, I'D LIKE TO SPEND MY FINAL MOMENTS...
...BEING A RABBIT I'M NOT ASHAMED OF.
HEY, MISTER...
?

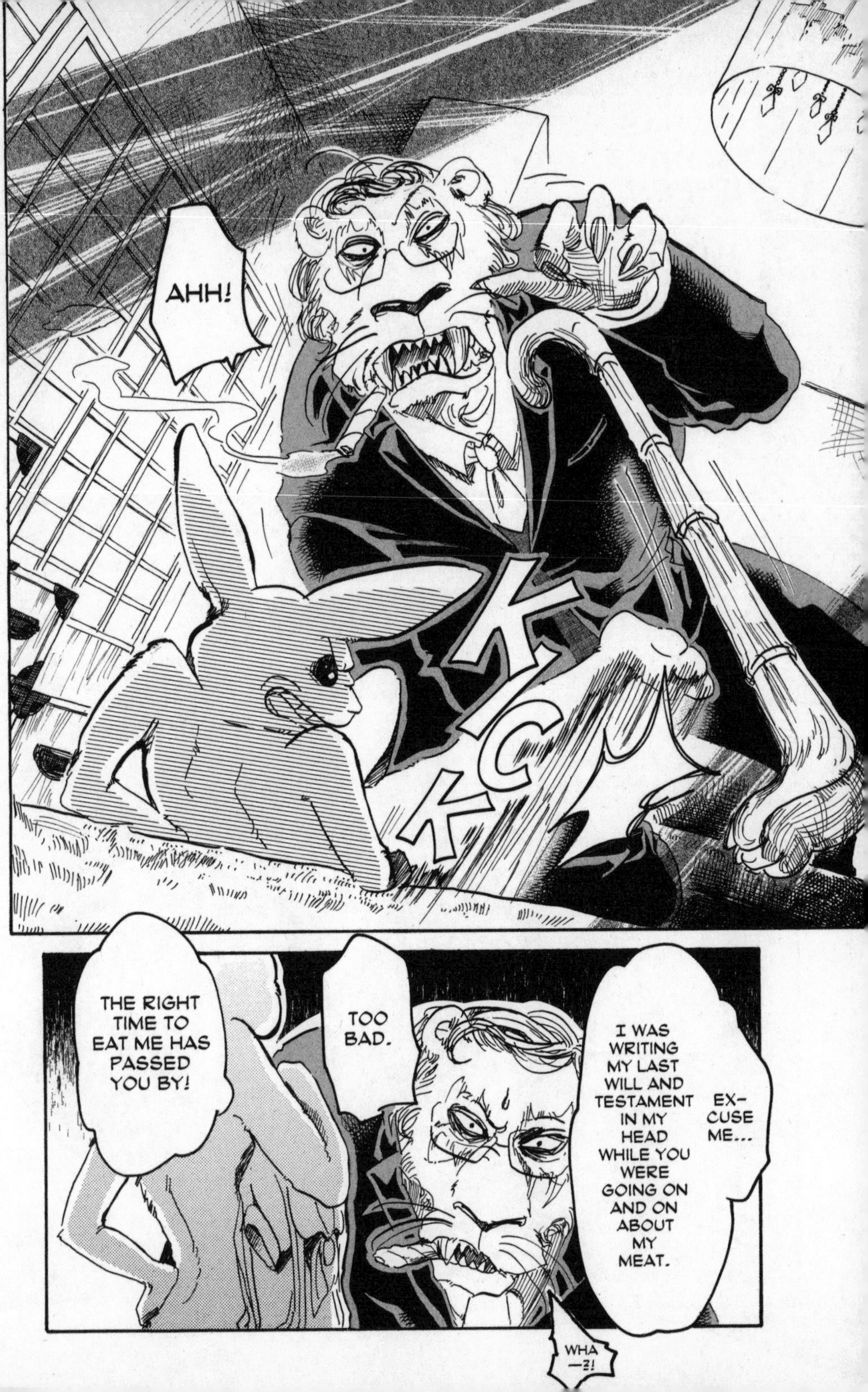
AHH!
KCK
EX-CUSE ME...
I WAS WRITING MY LAST WILL AND TESTAMENT IN MY HEAD WHILE YOU WERE GOING ON AND ON ABOUT MY MEAT.
TOO BAD.
THE RIGHT TIME TO EAT ME HAS PASSED YOU BY!
WHA—?!

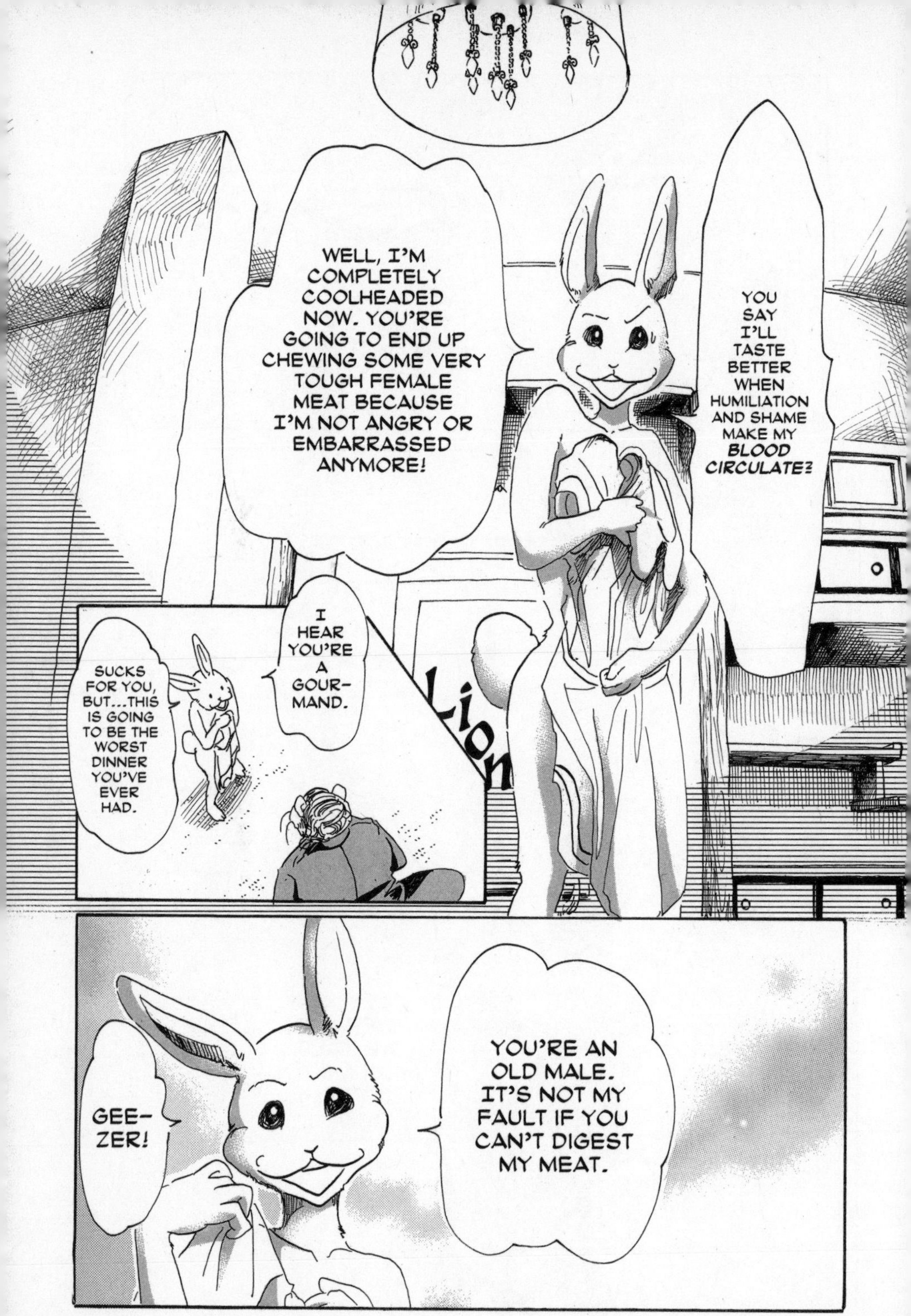
YOU SAY I'LL TASTE BETTER WHEN HUMILIATION AND SHAME MAKE MY *BLOOD CIRCULATE*?
WELL, I'M COMPLETELY COOLHEADED NOW. YOU'RE GOING TO END UP CHEWING SOME VERY TOUGH FEMALE MEAT BECAUSE I'M NOT ANGRY OR EMBARRASSED ANYMORE!
Lion
I HEAR YOU'RE A GOUR-MAND.
SUCKS FOR YOU, BUT...THIS IS GOING TO BE THE WORST DINNER YOU'VE EVER HAD.
YOU'RE AN OLD MALE. IT'S NOT MY FAULT IF YOU CAN'T DIGEST MY MEAT.
GEE-ZER!

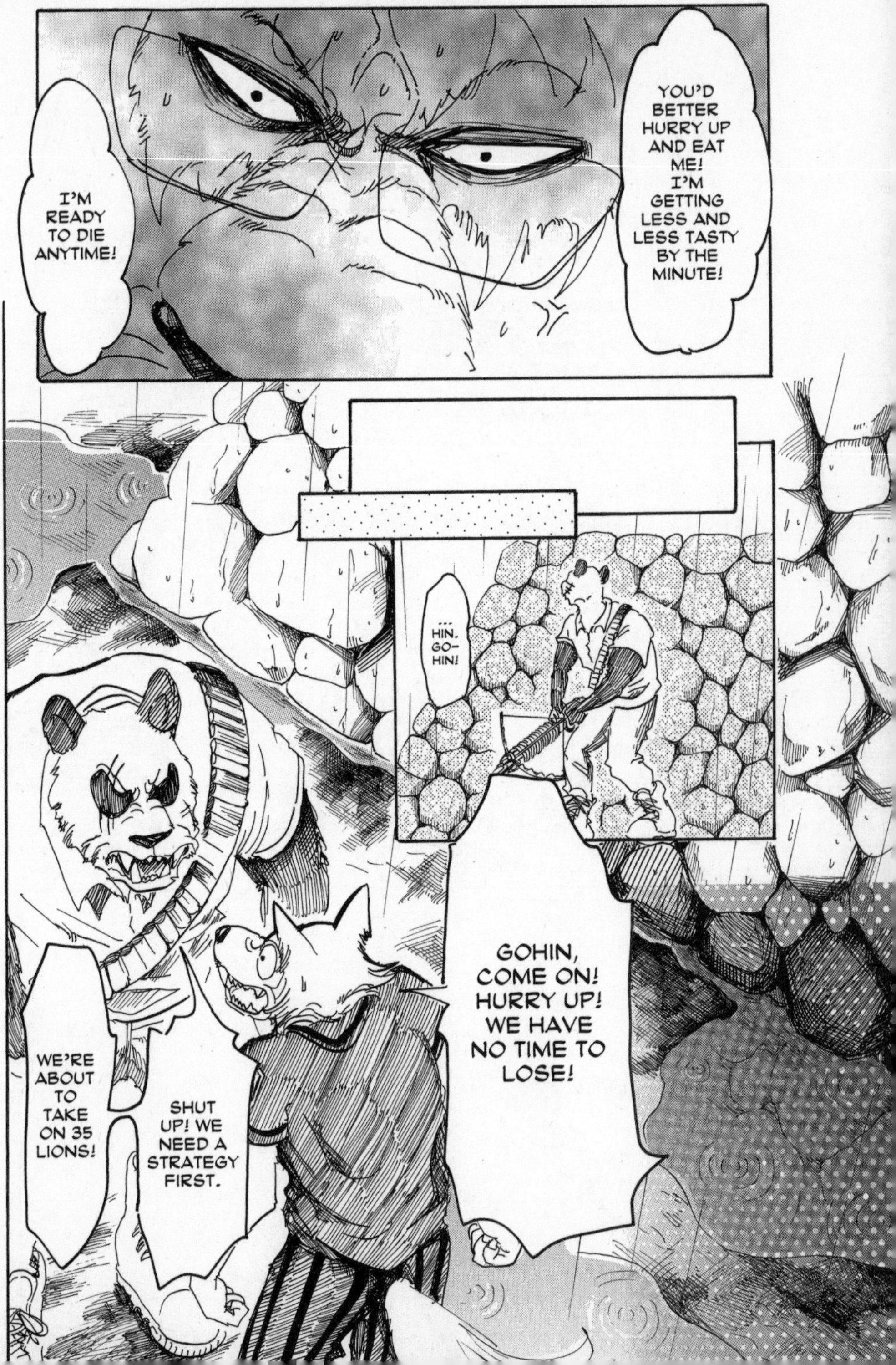
YOU'D BETTER HURRY UP AND EAT ME! I'M GETTING LESS AND LESS TASTY BY THE MINUTE!
I'M READY TO DIE ANYTIME!
...HIN. GOHIN!
GOHIN, COME ON! HURRY UP! WE HAVE NO TIME TO LOSE!
SHUT UP! WE NEED A STRATEGY FIRST.
WE'RE ABOUT TO TAKE ON 35 LIONS!

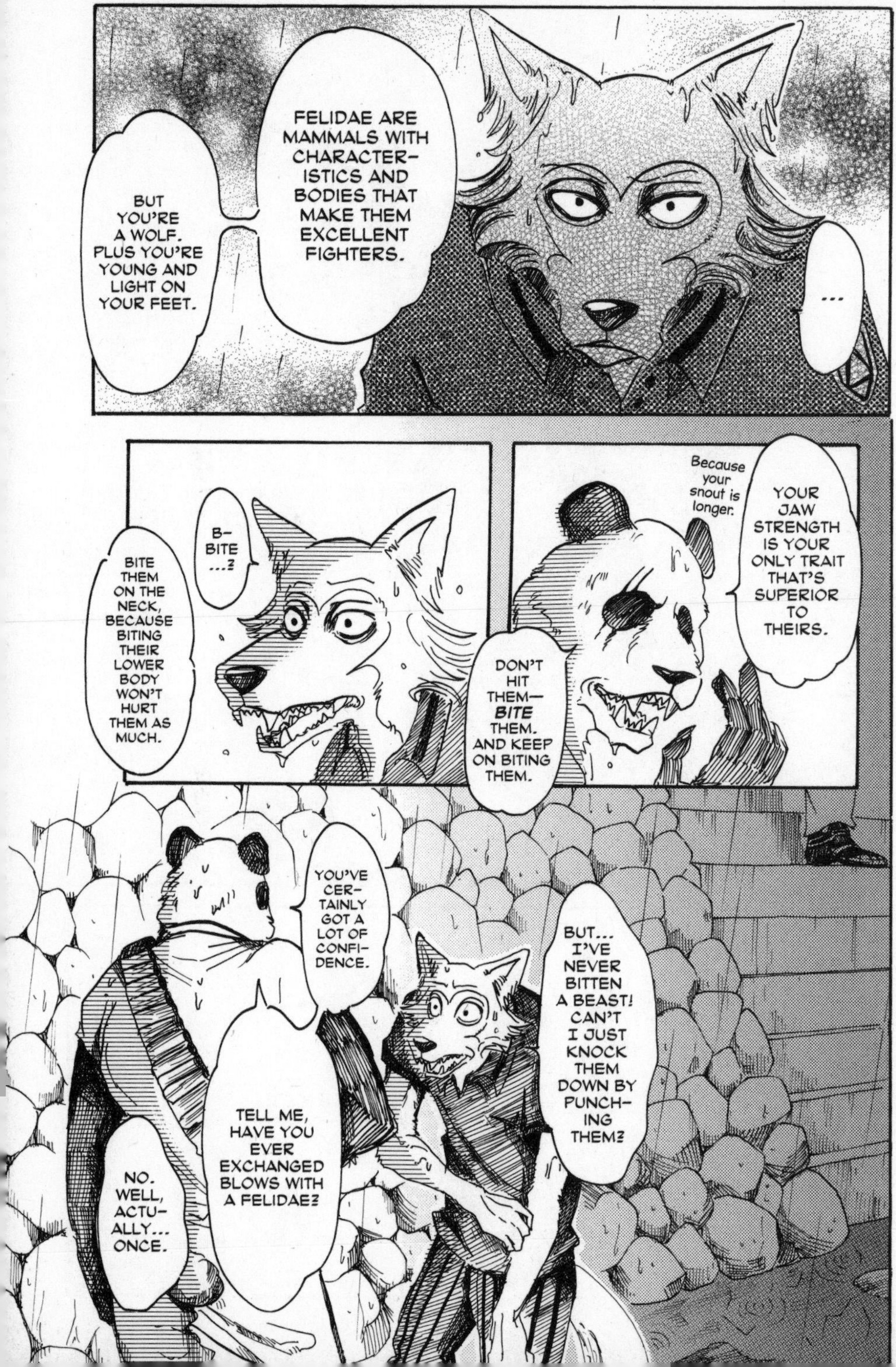
...
FELIDAE ARE MAMMALS WITH CHARACTERISTICS AND BODIES THAT MAKE THEM EXCELLENT FIGHTERS.
BUT YOU'RE A WOLF. PLUS YOU'RE YOUNG AND LIGHT ON YOUR FEET.
YOUR JAW STRENGTH IS YOUR ONLY TRAIT THAT'S SUPERIOR TO THEIRS.
Because your snout is longer.
DON'T HIT THEM— *BITE* THEM. AND KEEP ON BITING THEM.
B-BITE...?
BITE THEM ON THE NECK, BECAUSE BITING THEIR LOWER BODY WON'T HURT THEM AS MUCH.
BUT... I'VE NEVER BITTEN A BEAST! CAN'T I JUST KNOCK THEM DOWN BY PUNCHING THEM?
YOU'VE CERTAINLY GOT A LOT OF CONFIDENCE.
TELL ME, HAVE YOU EVER EXCHANGED BLOWS WITH A FELIDAE?
NO. WELL, ACTUALLY... ONCE.

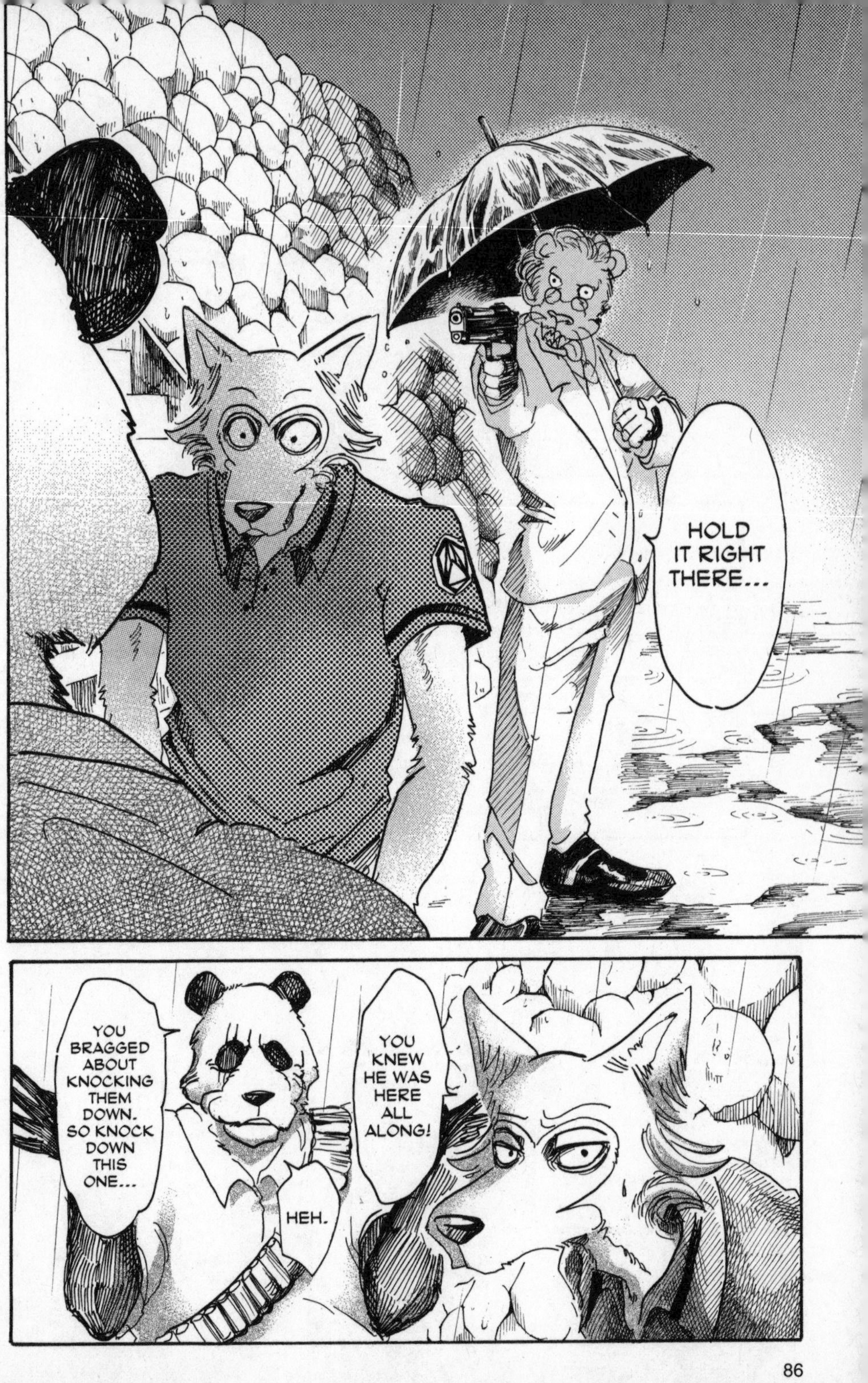
HOLD IT RIGHT THERE...
YOU KNEW HE WAS HERE ALL ALONG!
YOU BRAGGED ABOUT KNOCKING THEM DOWN. SO KNOCK DOWN THIS ONE...
HEH.

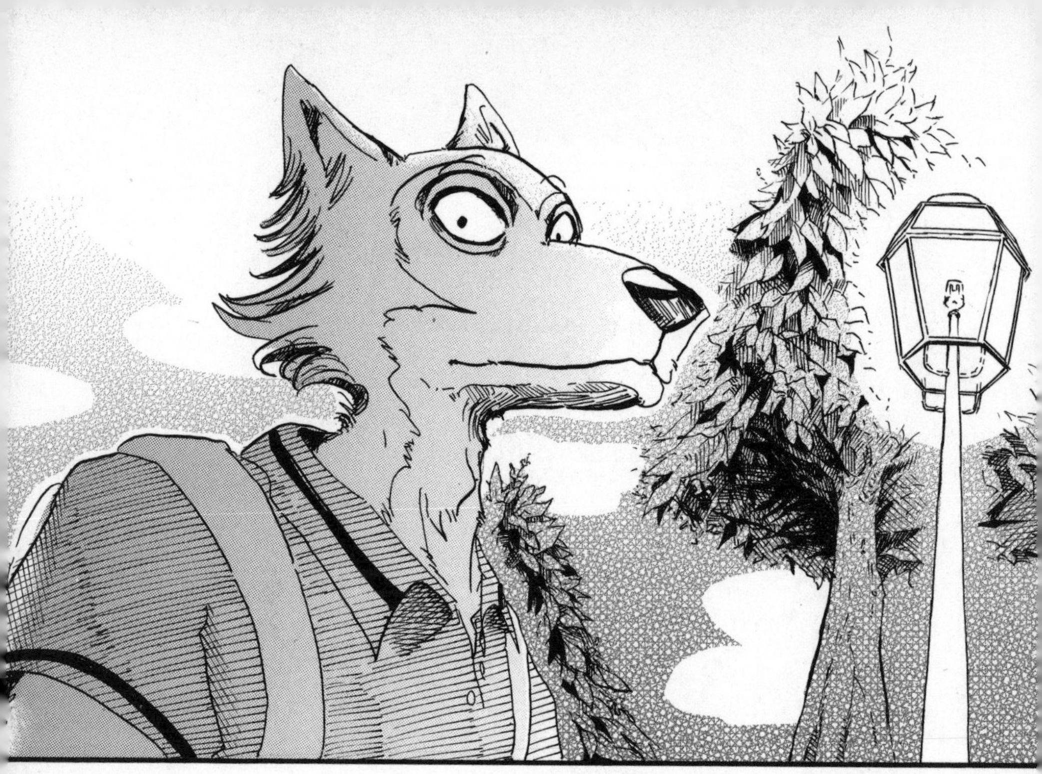

Chapter 39: I Want to Capture You

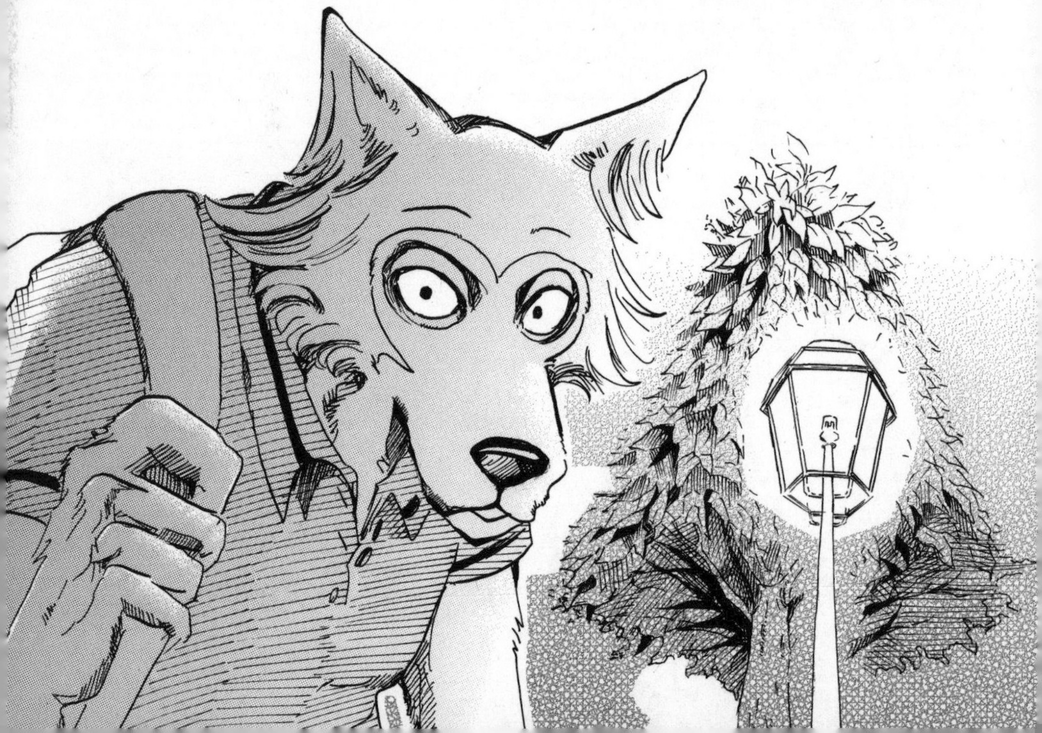

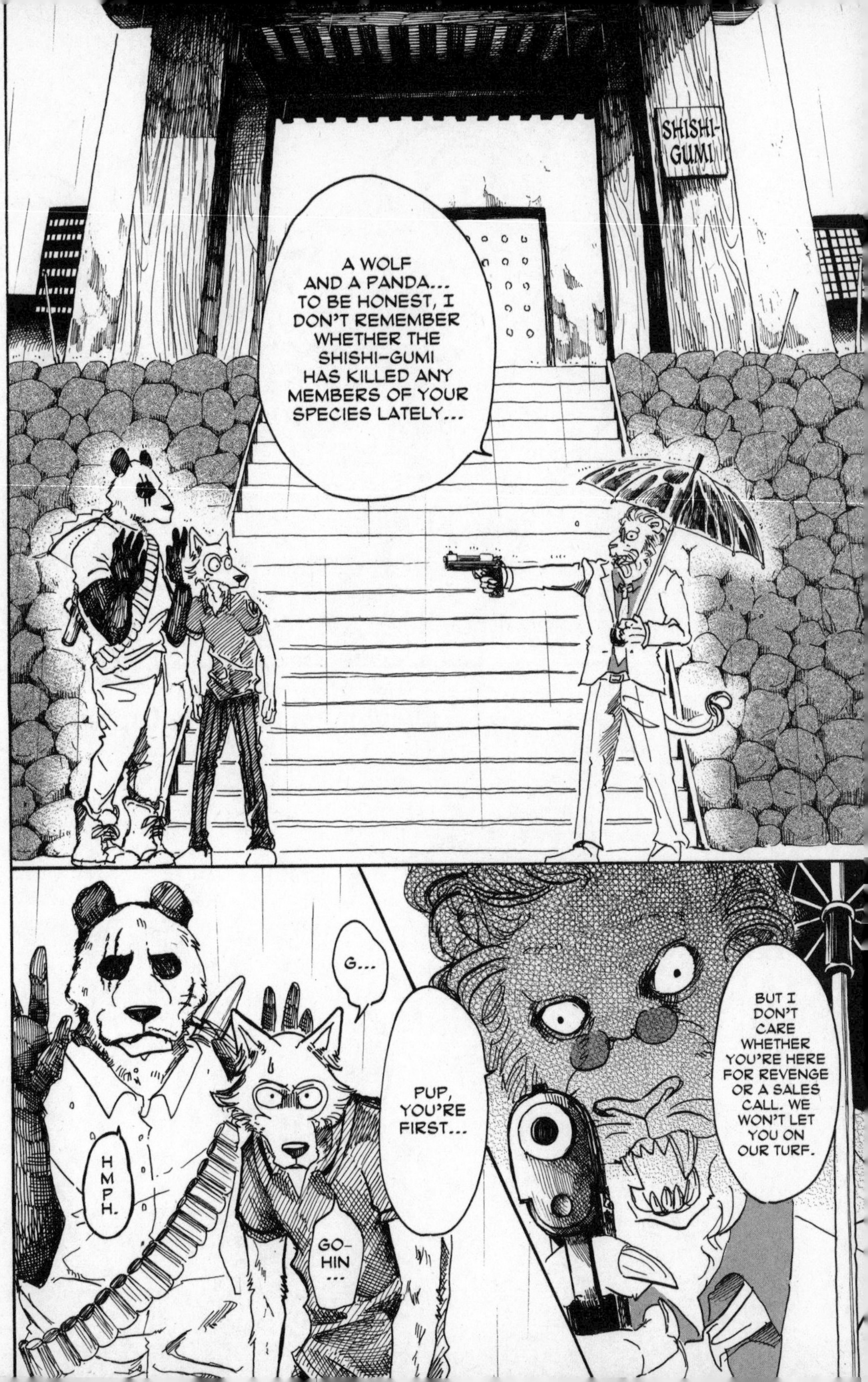
SHISHI-GUMI
A WOLF AND A PANDA... TO BE HONEST, I DON'T REMEMBER WHETHER THE SHISHI-GUMI HAS KILLED ANY MEMBERS OF YOUR SPECIES LATELY...
BUT I DON'T CARE WHETHER YOU'RE HERE FOR REVENGE OR A SALES CALL. WE WON'T LET YOU ON OUR TURF.
PUP, YOU'RE FIRST...
G...
GO-HIN...
HMPH.

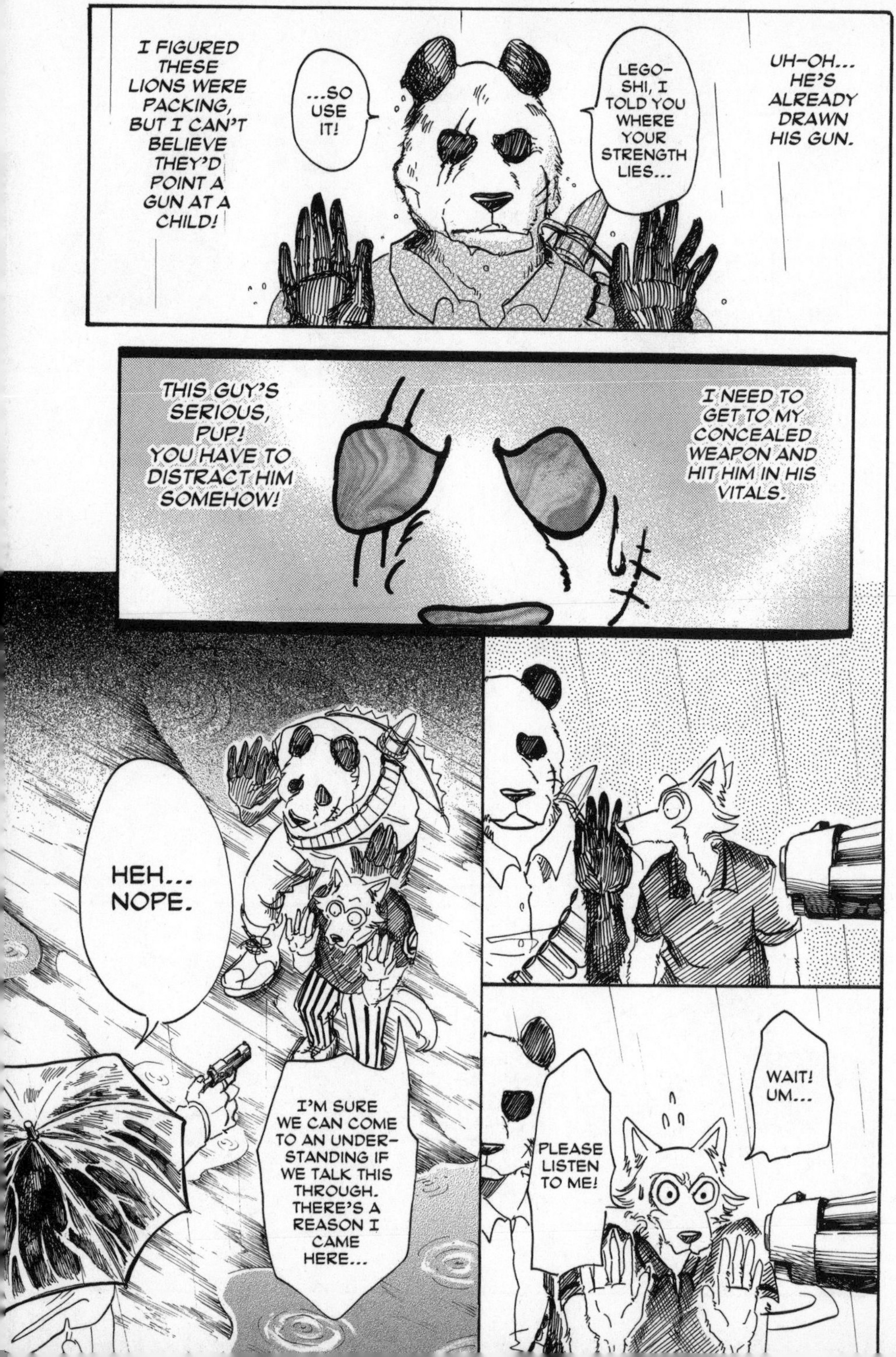
UH-OH... HE'S ALREADY DRAWN HIS GUN.
LEGO-SHI, I TOLD YOU WHERE YOUR STRENGTH LIES...
...SO USE IT!
I FIGURED THESE LIONS WERE PACKING, BUT I CAN'T BELIEVE THEY'D POINT A GUN AT A CHILD!
I NEED TO GET TO MY CONCEALED WEAPON AND HIT HIM IN HIS VITALS.
THIS GUY'S SERIOUS, PUP! YOU HAVE TO DISTRACT HIM SOMEHOW!
WAIT! UM...
PLEASE LISTEN TO ME!
I'M SURE WE CAN COME TO AN UNDER-STANDING IF WE TALK THIS THROUGH. THERE'S A REASON I CAME HERE...
HEH... NOPE.

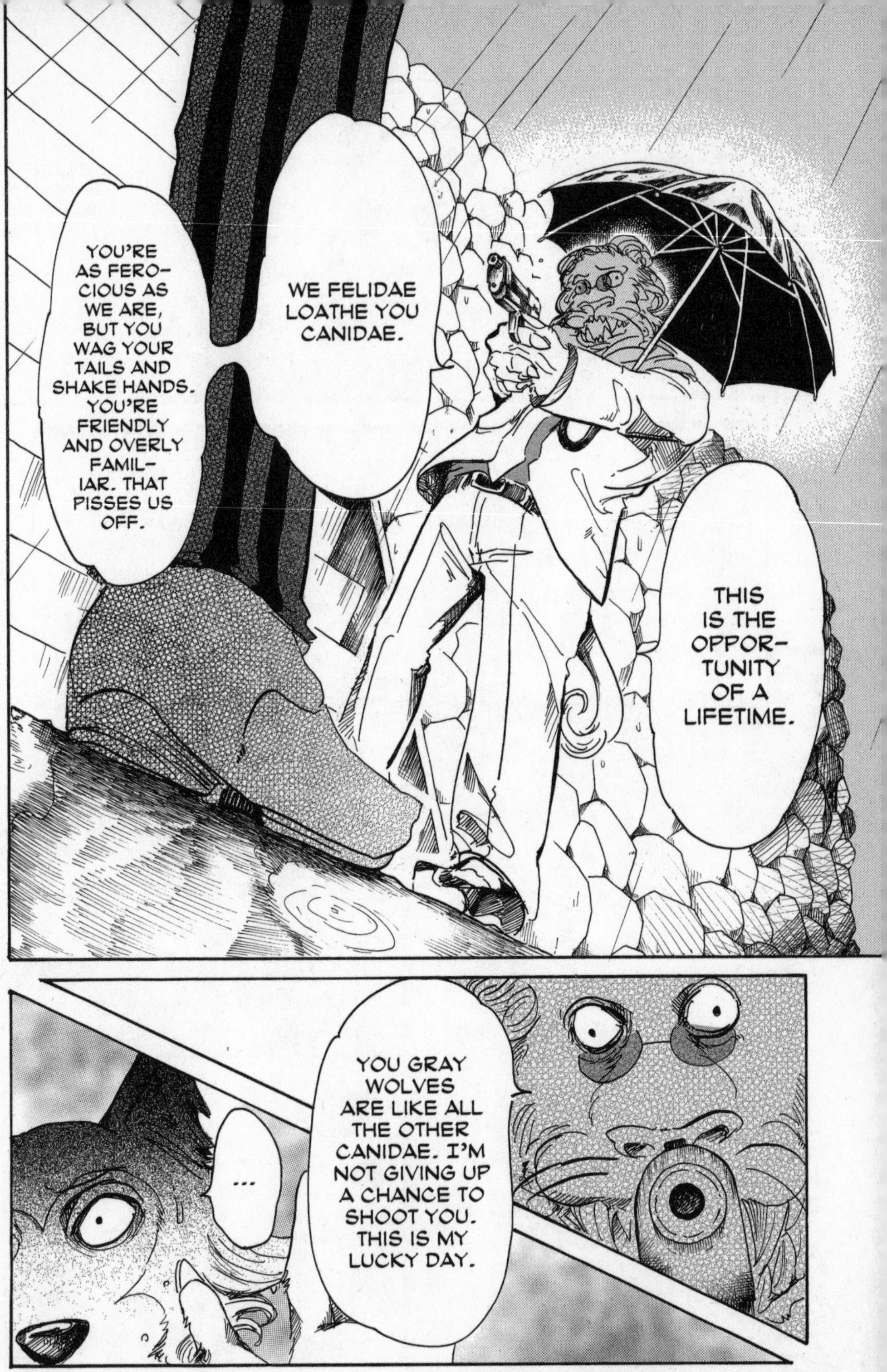
WE FELIDAE LOATHE YOU CANIDAE.
YOU'RE AS FEROCIOUS AS WE ARE, BUT YOU WAG YOUR TAILS AND SHAKE HANDS. YOU'RE FRIENDLY AND OVERLY FAMILIAR. THAT PISSES US OFF.
THIS IS THE OPPORTUNITY OF A LIFETIME.
YOU GRAY WOLVES ARE LIKE ALL THE OTHER CANIDAE. I'M NOT GIVING UP A CHANCE TO SHOOT YOU. THIS IS MY LUCKY DAY.
...

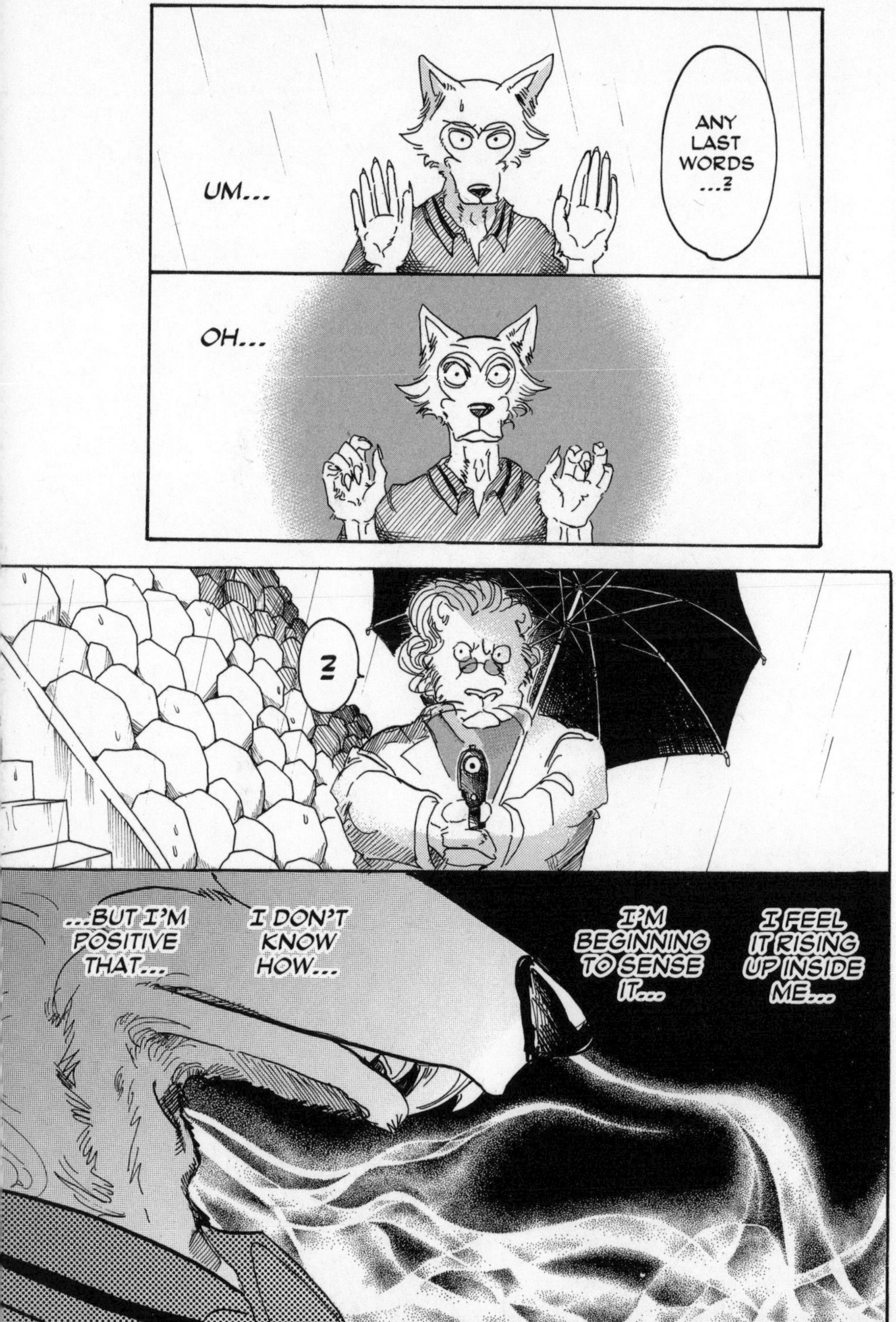
ANY LAST WORDS...?
UM...
OH...
?
I FEEL IT RISING UP INSIDE ME...
I'M BEGINNING TO SENSE IT...
I DON'T KNOW HOW...
...BUT I'M POSITIVE THAT...

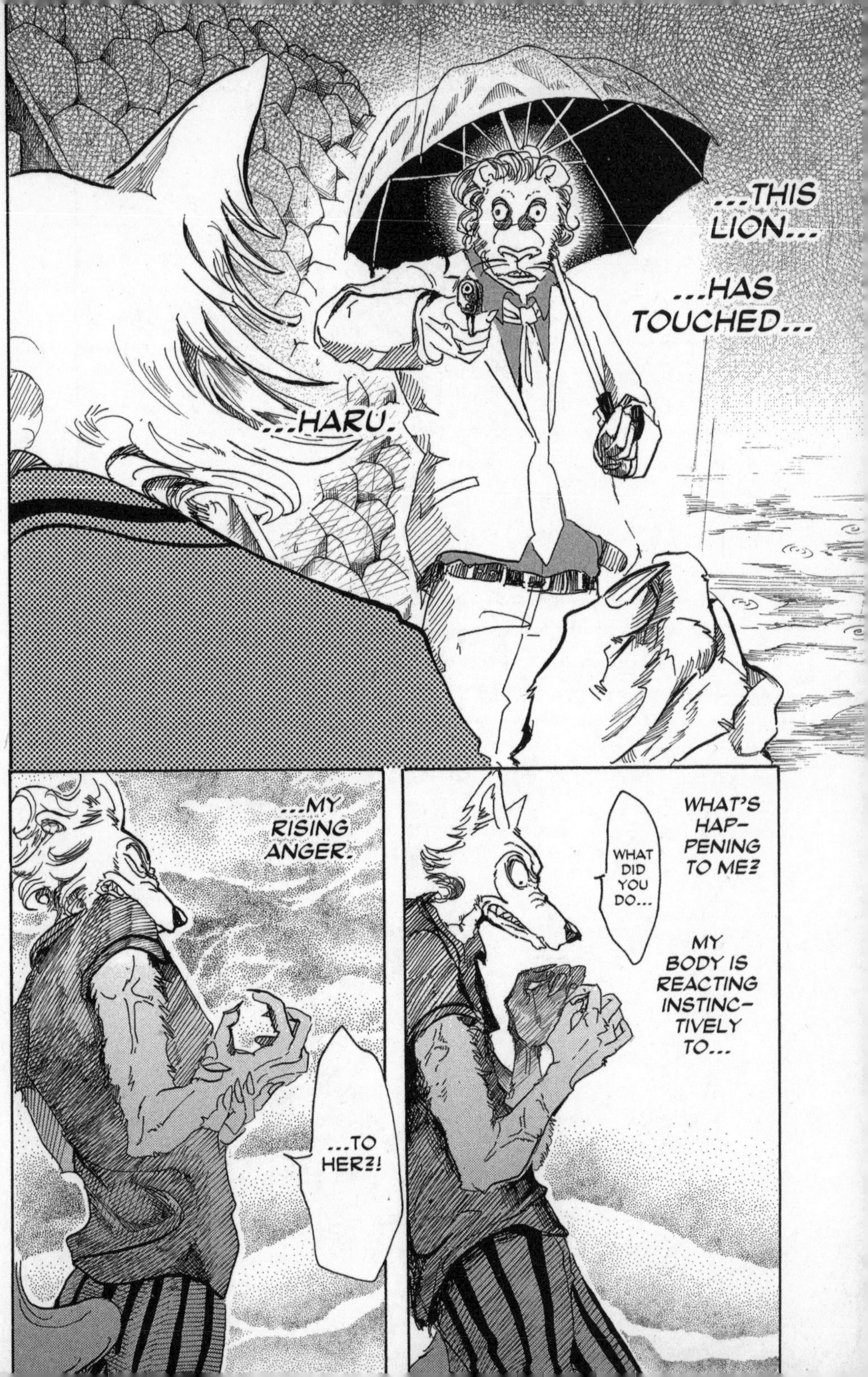
...THIS LION...
...HAS TOUCHED...
...HARU.
WHAT'S HAP-PENING TO ME?
WHAT DID YOU DO...
MY BODY IS REACTING INSTINC-TIVELY TO...
...MY RISING ANGER.
...TO HER?!

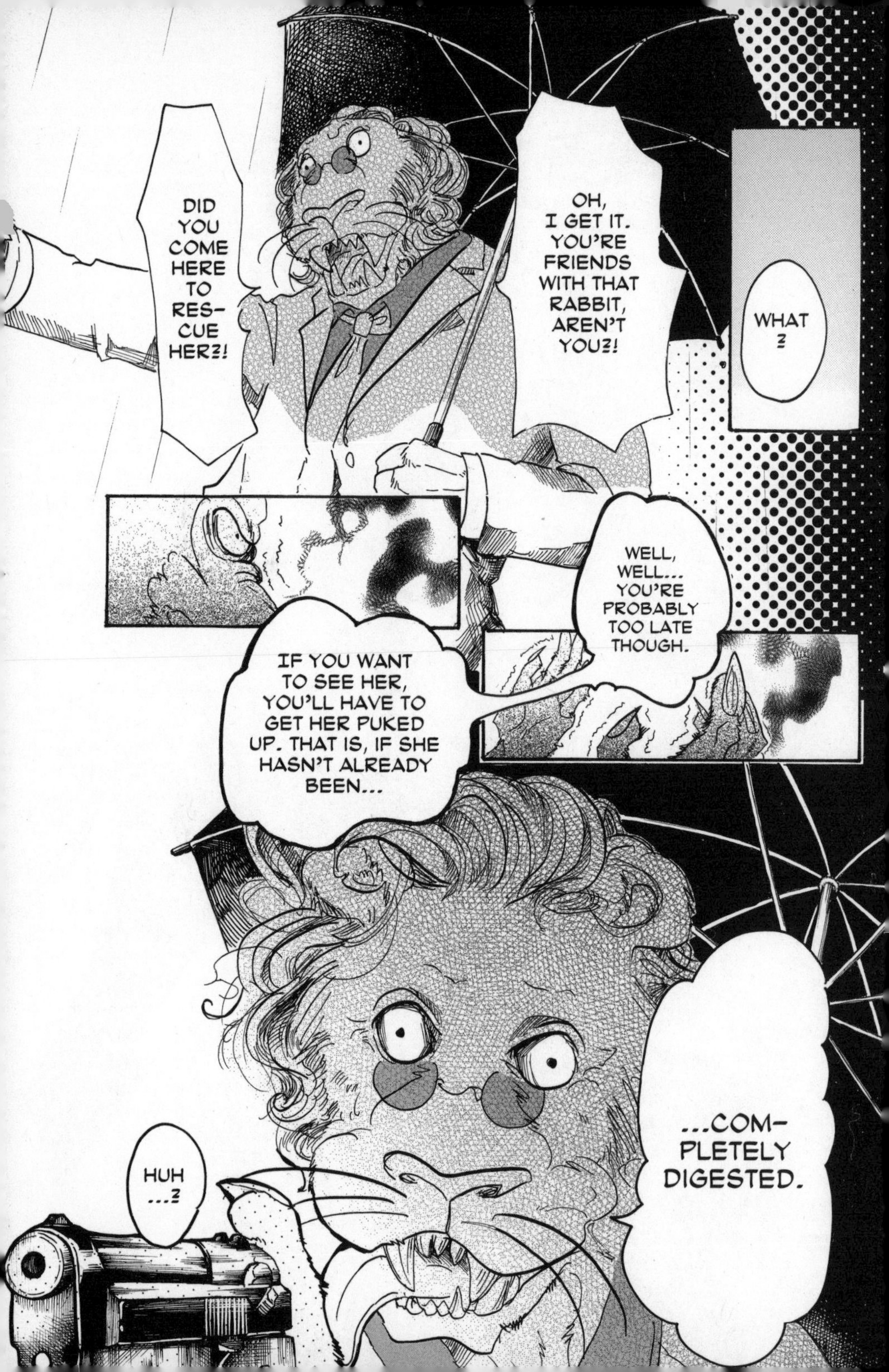
WHAT?
OH, I GET IT. YOU'RE FRIENDS WITH THAT RABBIT, AREN'T YOU?!
DID YOU COME HERE TO RES-CUE HER?!
WELL, WELL... YOU'RE PROBABLY TOO LATE THOUGH.
IF YOU WANT TO SEE HER, YOU'LL HAVE TO GET HER PUKED UP. THAT IS, IF SHE HASN'T ALREADY BEEN...
...COM-PLETELY DIGESTED.
HUH ...?

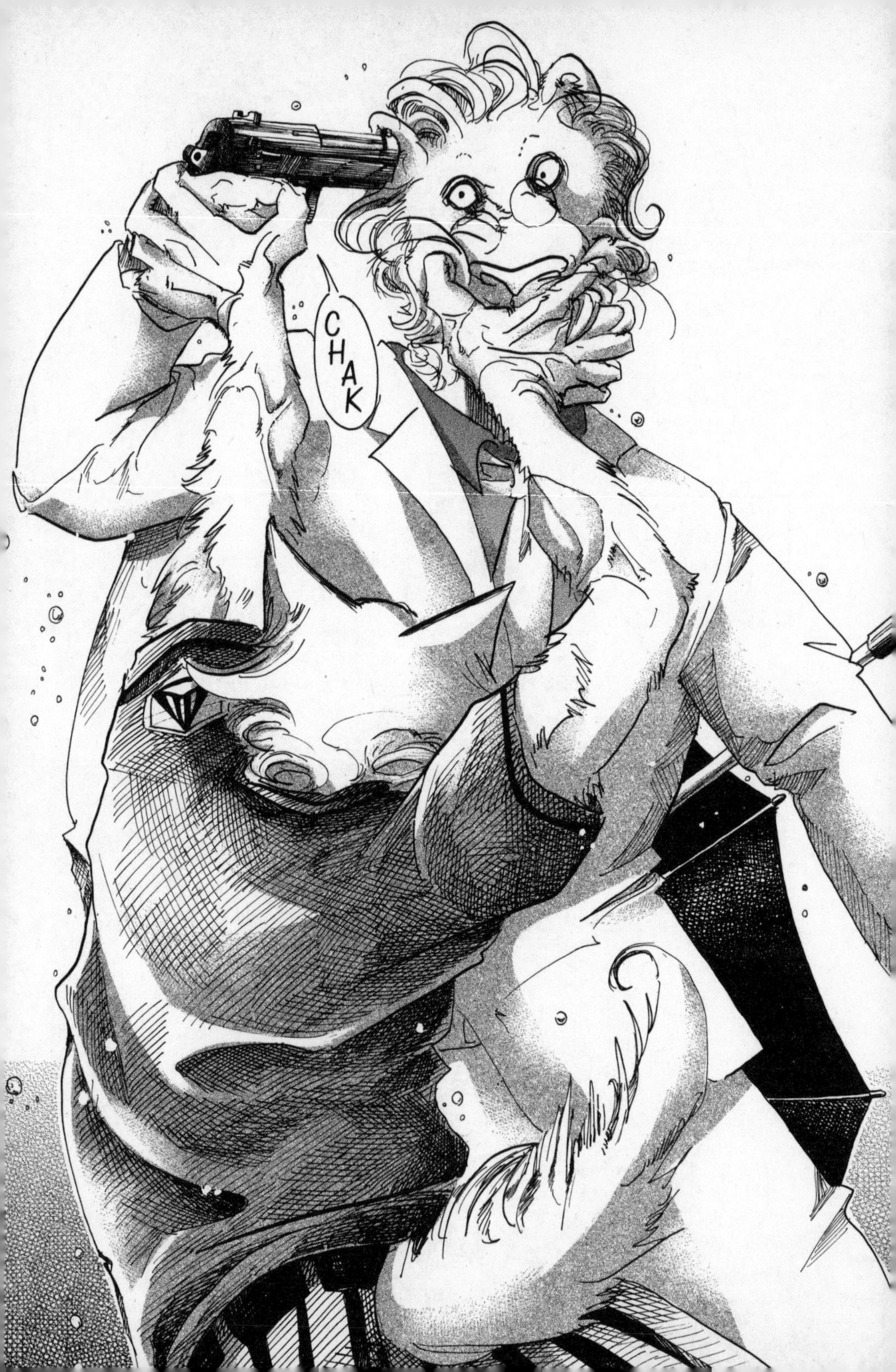
CHAK

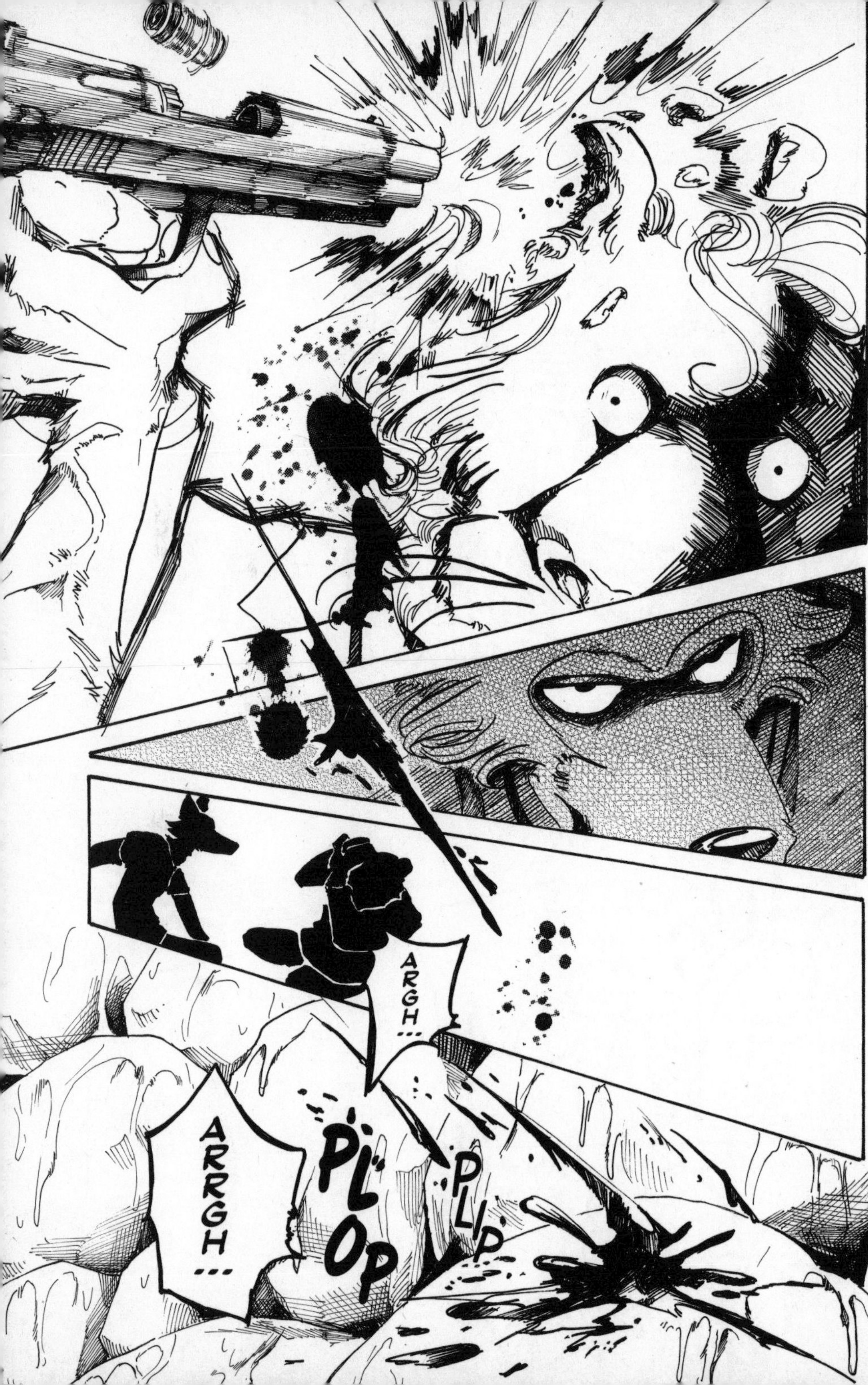
ARGH...
PLIP
PLOP
ARRGH...

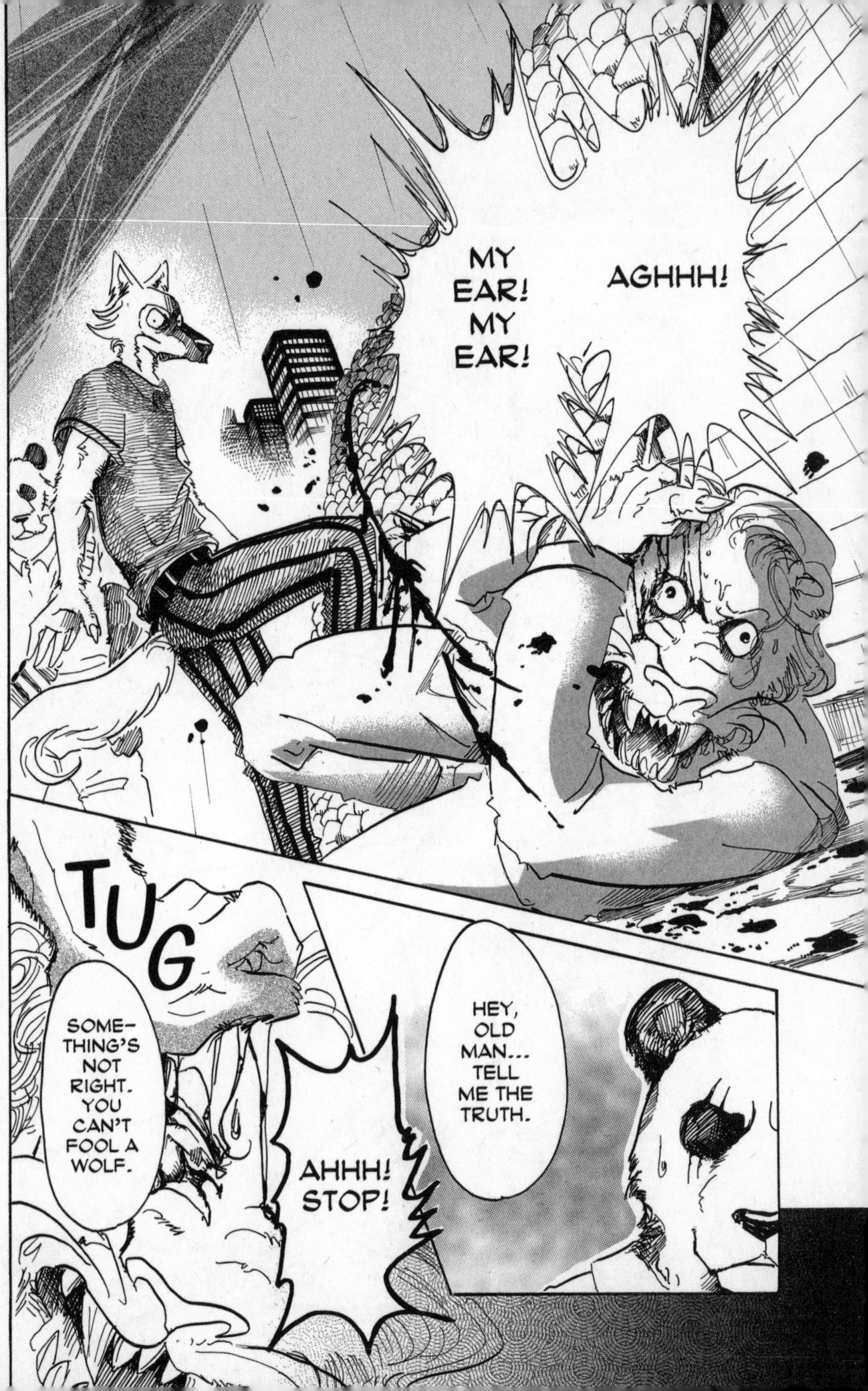
AGHHH!
MY EAR! MY EAR!
HEY, OLD MAN... TELL ME THE TRUTH.
TUG
AHHH! STOP!
SOME-THING'S NOT RIGHT. YOU CAN'T FOOL A WOLF.

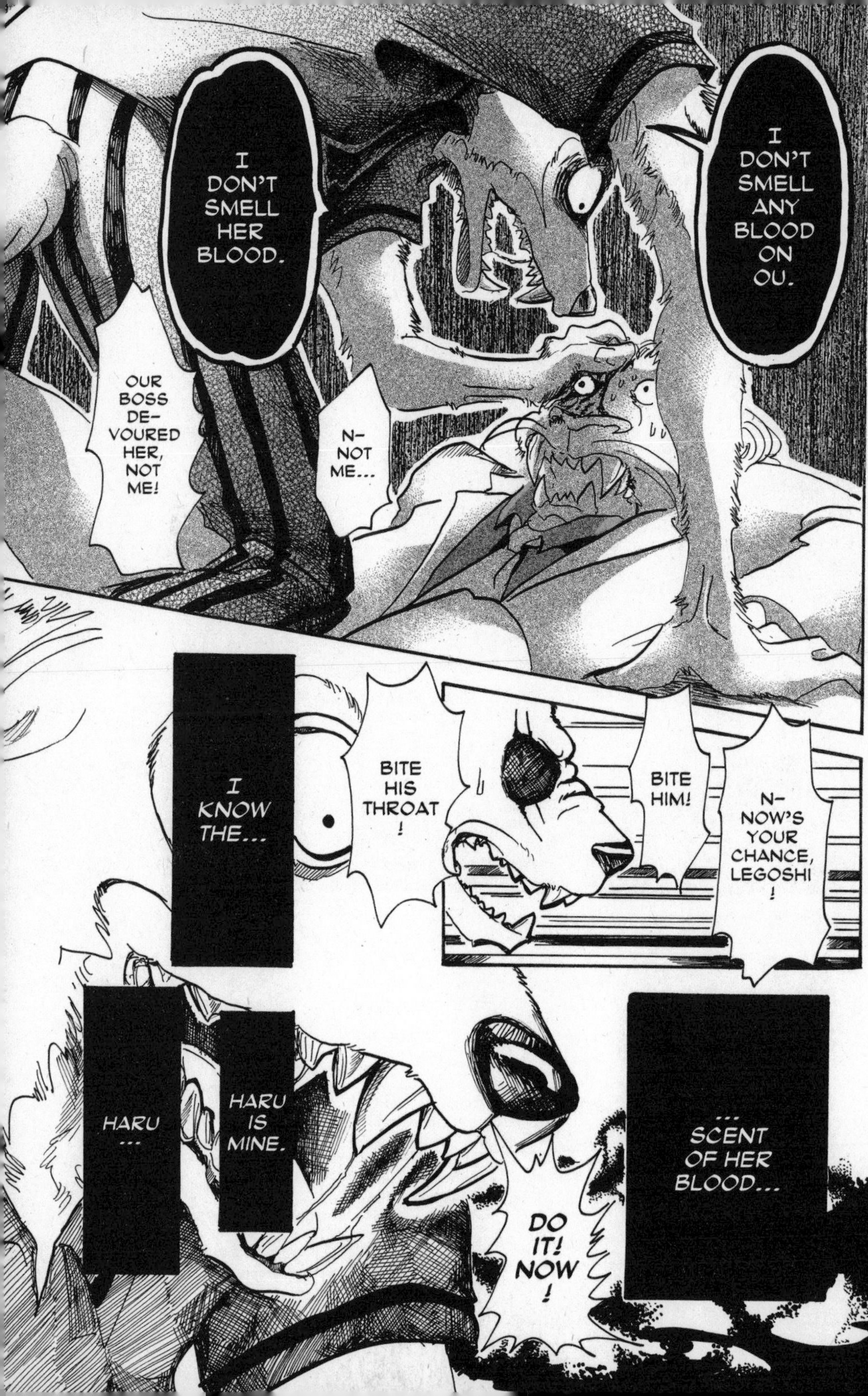
I DON'T SMELL ANY BLOOD ON OU.
I DON'T SMELL HER BLOOD.
N-NOT ME...
OUR BOSS DE-VOURED HER, NOT ME!
N-NOW'S YOUR CHANCE, LEGOSHI!
BITE HIM!
BITE HIS THROAT!
I KNOW THE...
...SCENT OF HER BLOOD...
DO IT! NOW!
HARU IS MINE.
HARU...

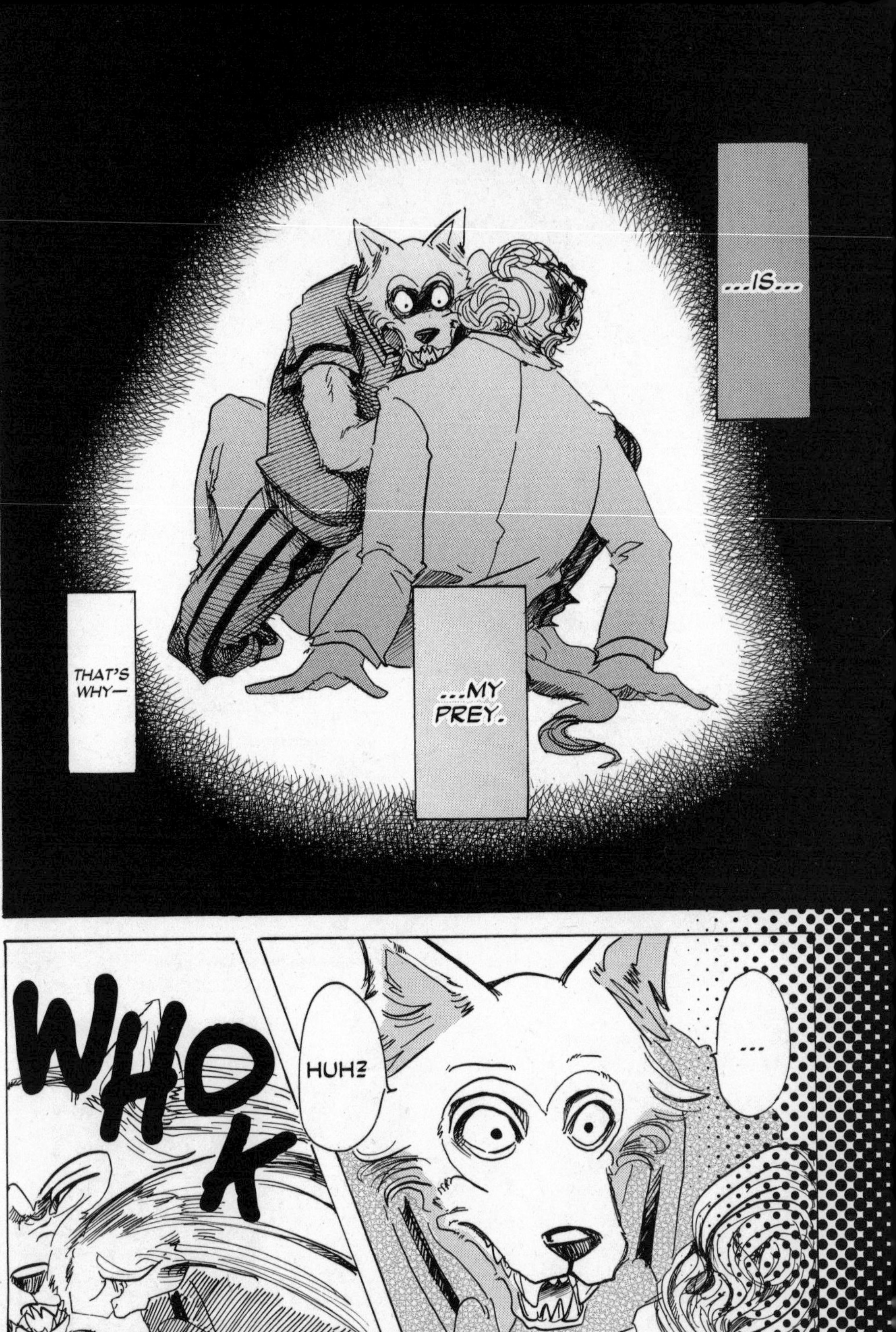
...IS...
...MY PREY.
THAT'S WHY—
...
HUH?
WHOK

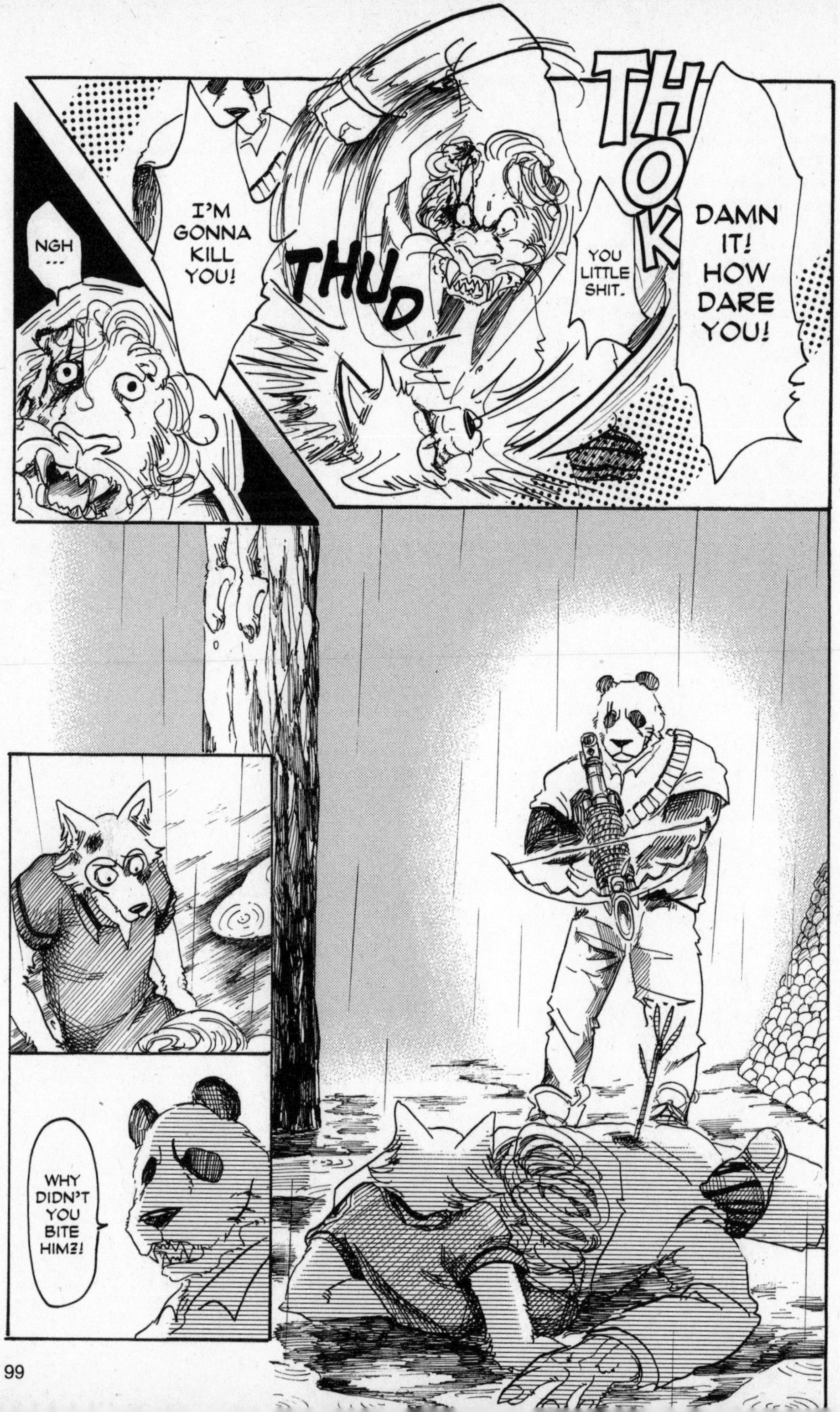
THOK
DAMN IT! HOW DARE YOU!
YOU LITTLE SHIT.
THUD
I'M GONNA KILL YOU!
NGH...
WHY DIDN'T YOU BITE HIM?!

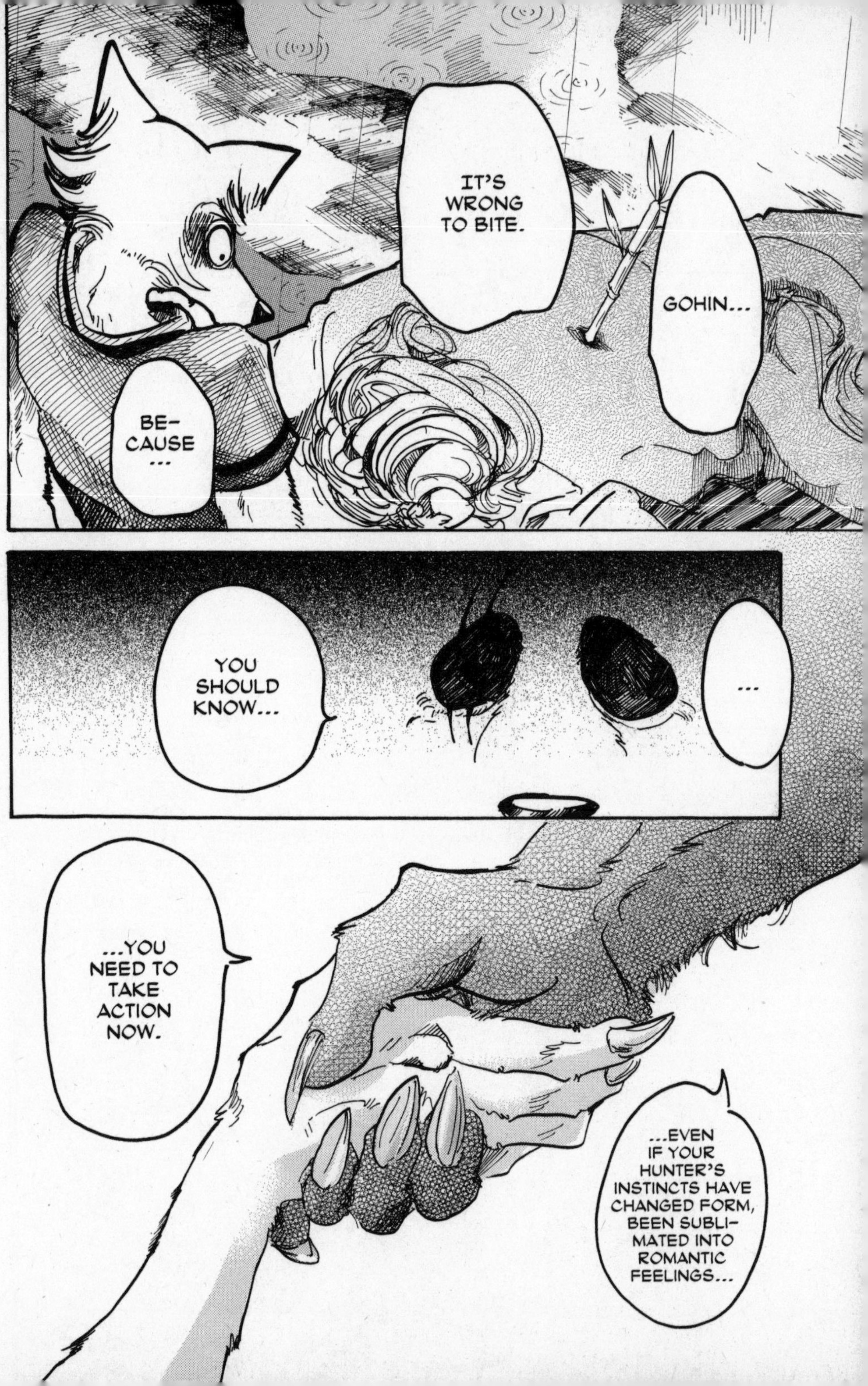
GOHIN...
IT'S WRONG TO BITE.
BE-CAUSE...
...
YOU SHOULD KNOW...
...EVEN IF YOUR HUNTER'S INSTINCTS HAVE CHANGED FORM, BEEN SUBLI-MATED INTO ROMANTIC FEELINGS...
...YOU NEED TO TAKE ACTION NOW.

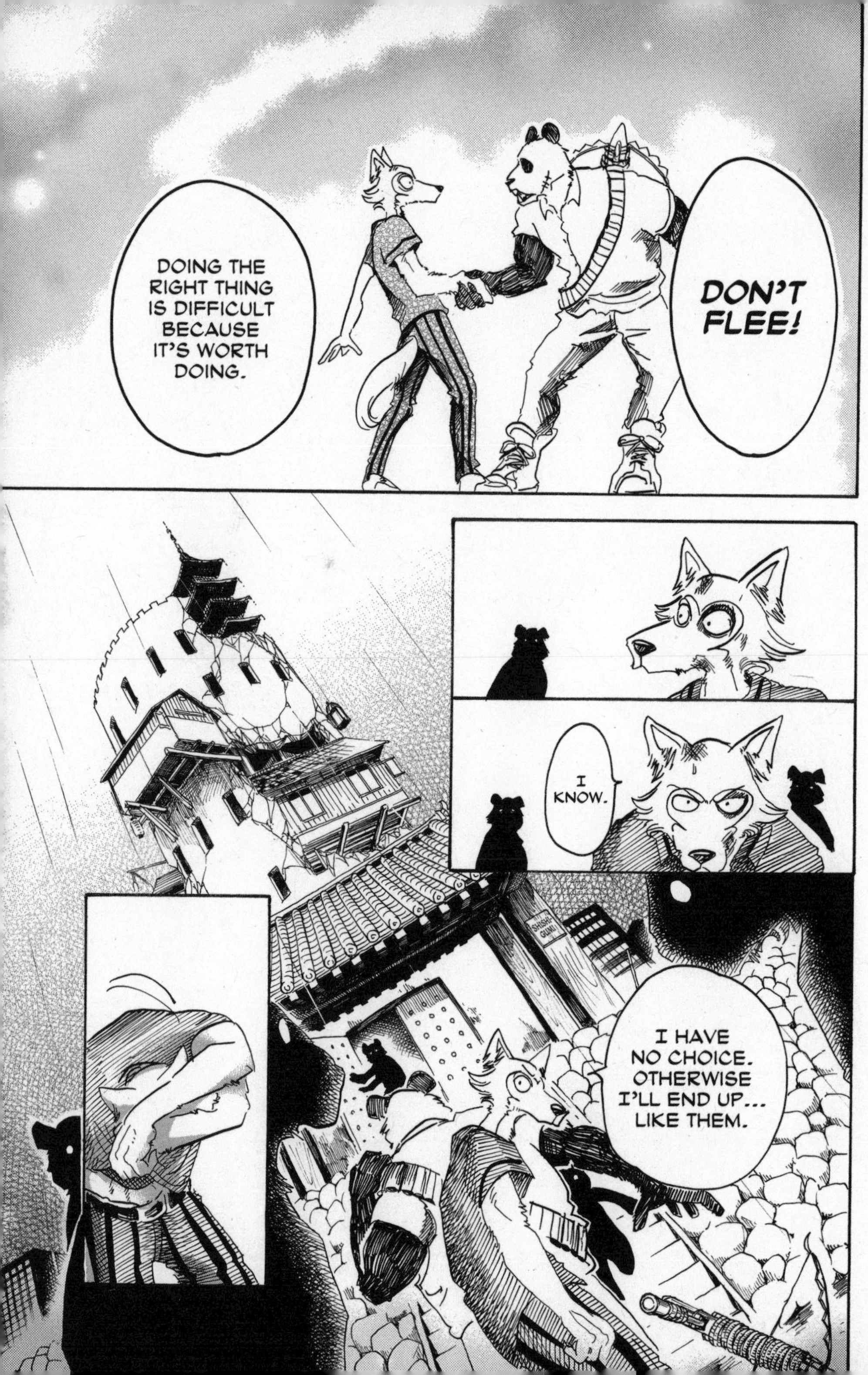
DON'T FLEE!
DOING THE RIGHT THING IS DIFFICULT BECAUSE IT'S WORTH DOING.
I KNOW.
I HAVE NO CHOICE. OTHERWISE I'LL END UP... LIKE THEM.

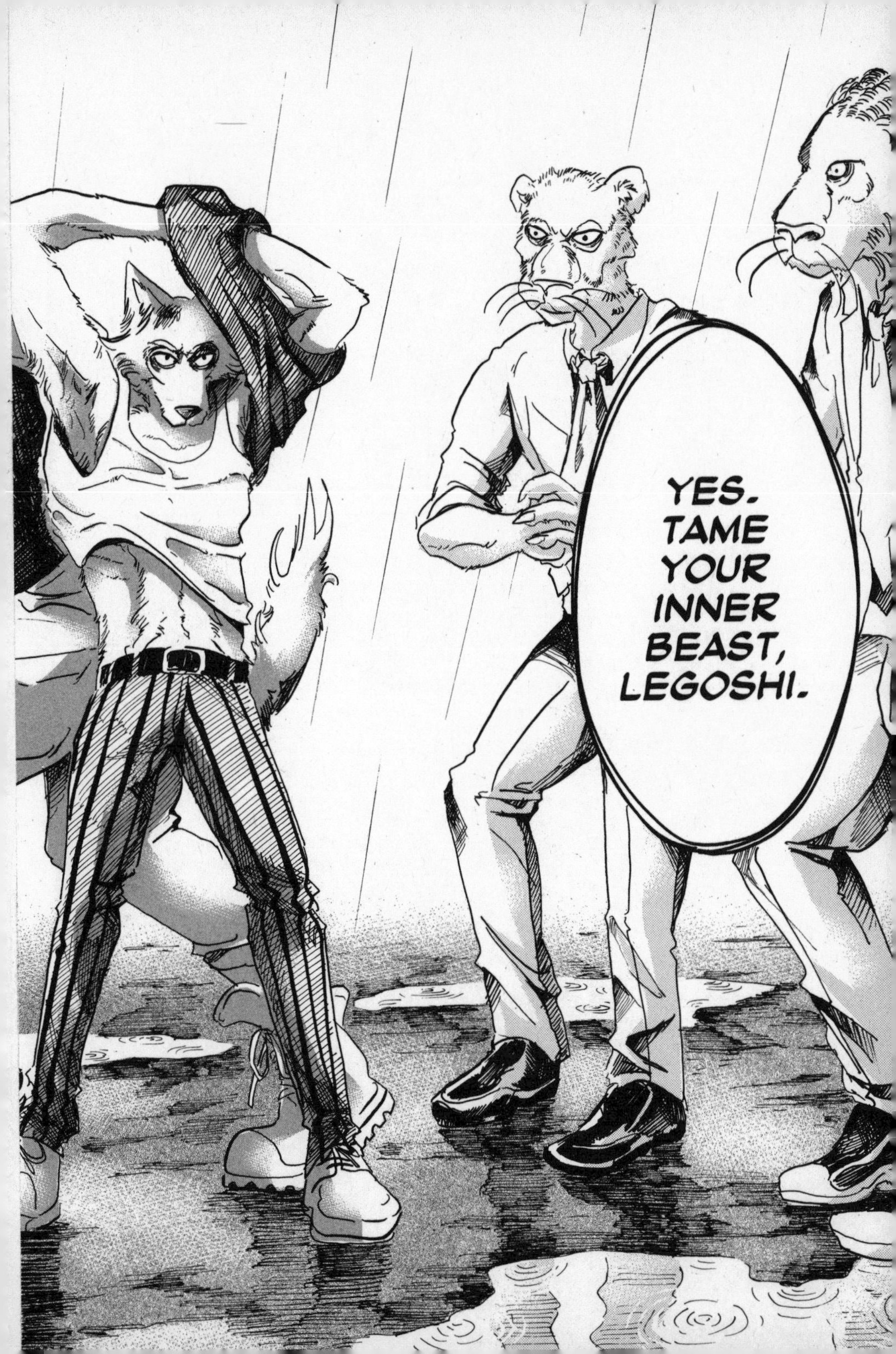
YES. TAME YOUR INNER BEAST, LEGOSHI.

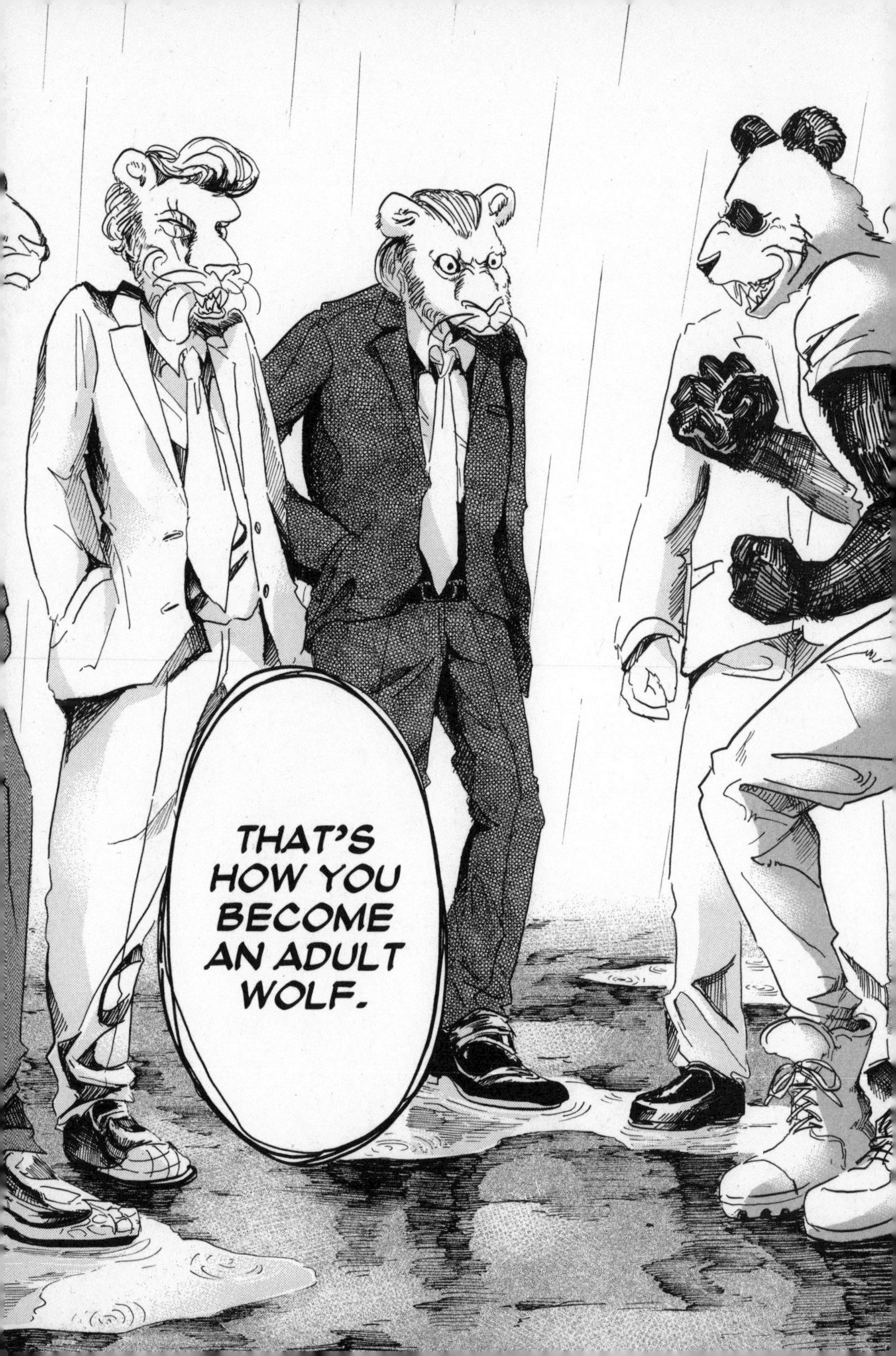
THAT'S HOW YOU BECOME AN ADULT WOLF.

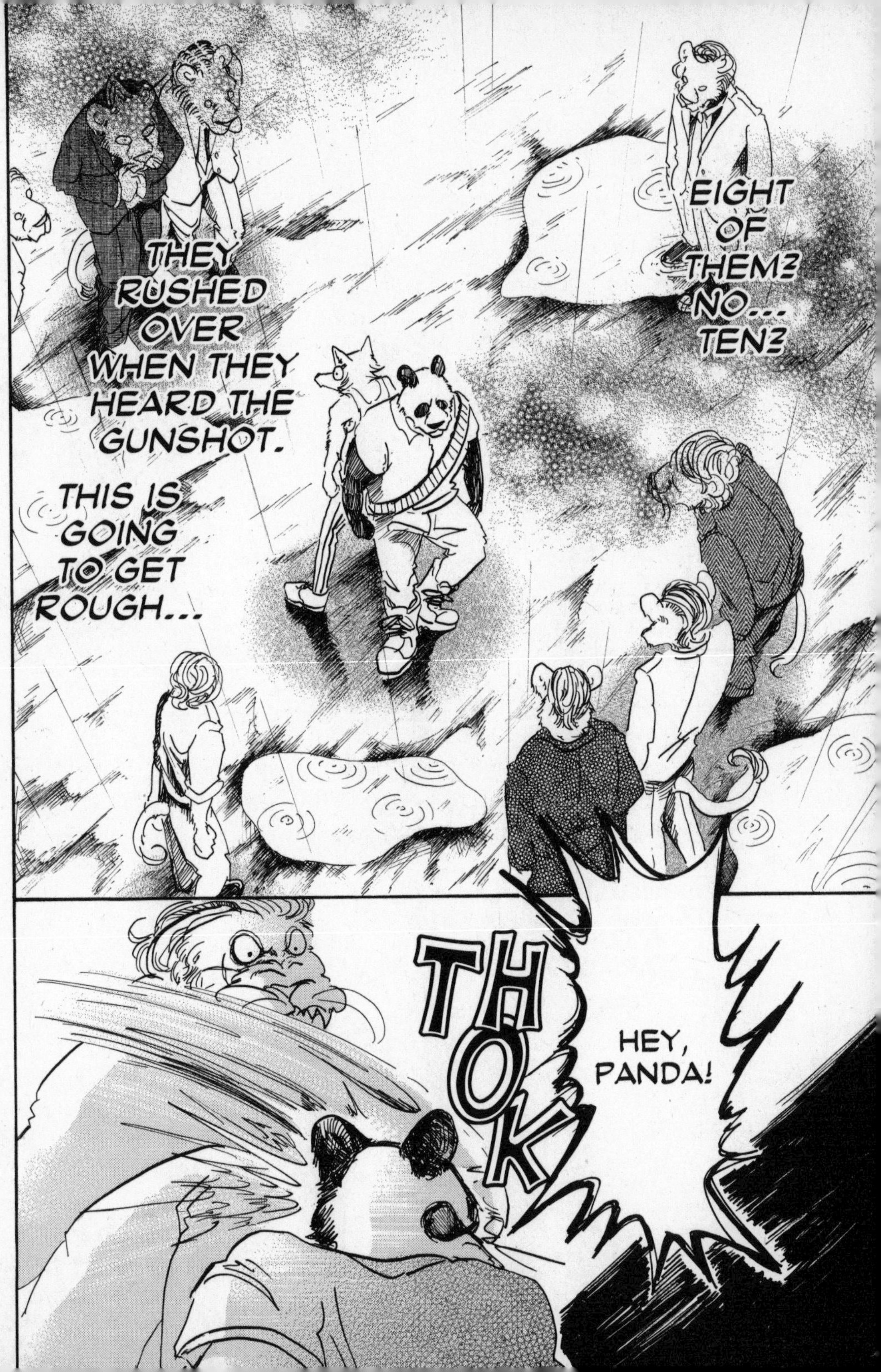
EIGHT OF THEM? NO... TEN?
THEY RUSHED OVER WHEN THEY HEARD THE GUNSHOT.
THIS IS GOING TO GET ROUGH...
THOK
HEY, PANDA!

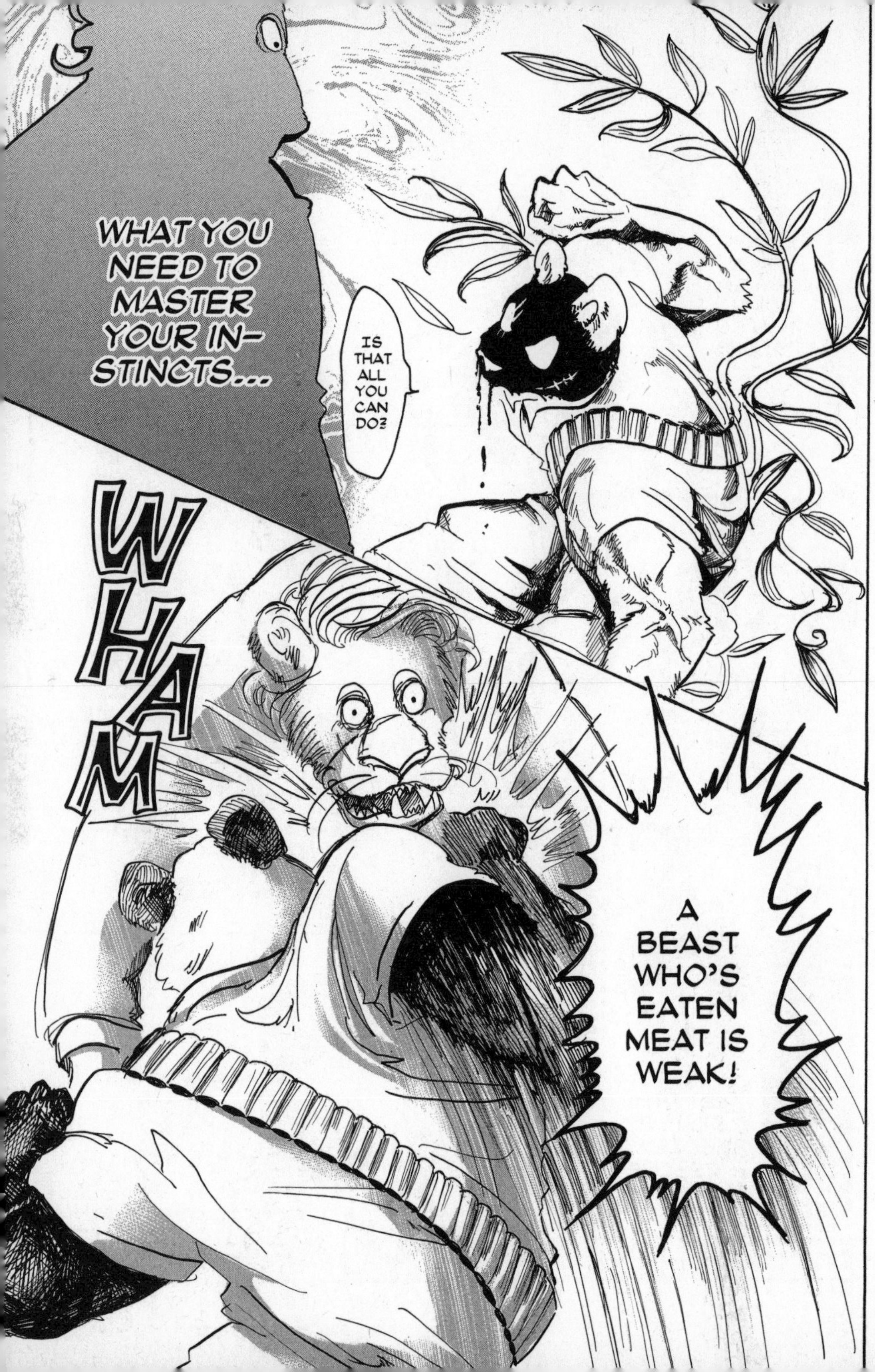

IS THAT ALL YOU CAN DO?
WHAT YOU NEED TO MASTER YOUR INSTINCTS...
WHAM
A BEAST WHO'S EATEN MEAT IS WEAK!

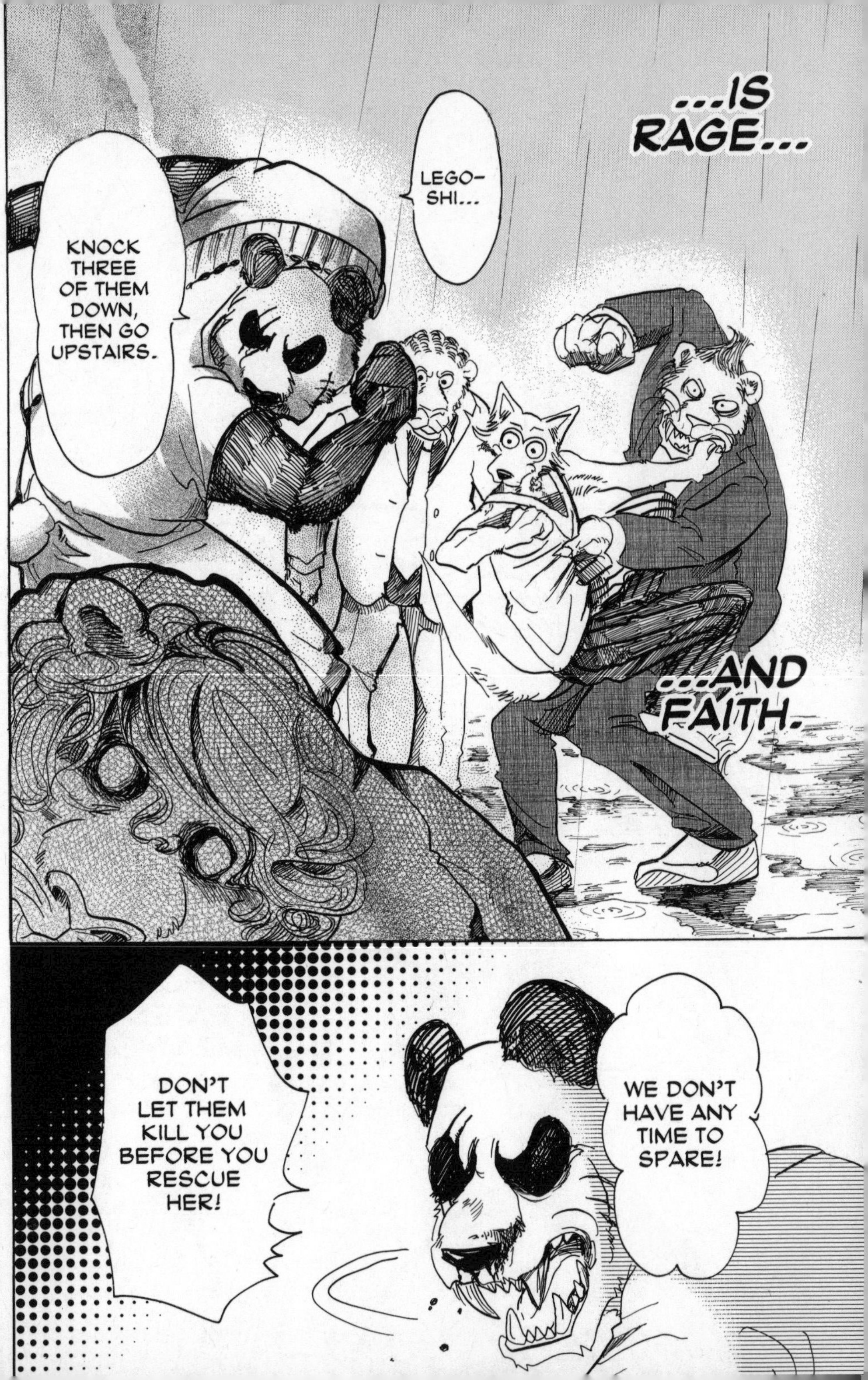
...IS RAGE...
LEGO-SHI...
KNOCK THREE OF THEM DOWN, THEN GO UPSTAIRS.
...AND FAITH.
WE DON'T HAVE ANY TIME TO SPARE!
DON'T LET THEM KILL YOU BEFORE YOU RESCUE HER!

Chapter 40:
My Lungs Are Filled with Your Scent More than My Heart Is Filled with Emotion

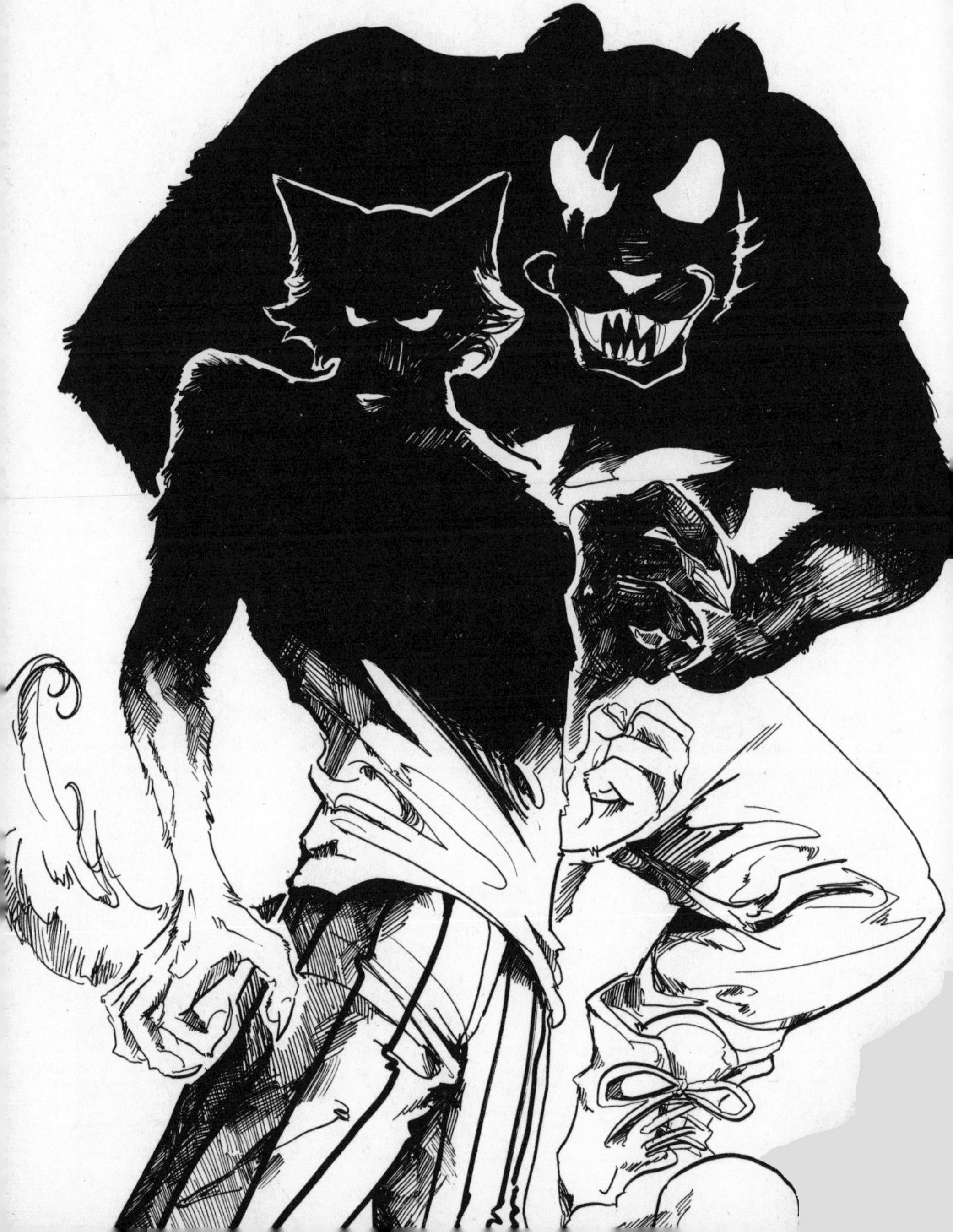

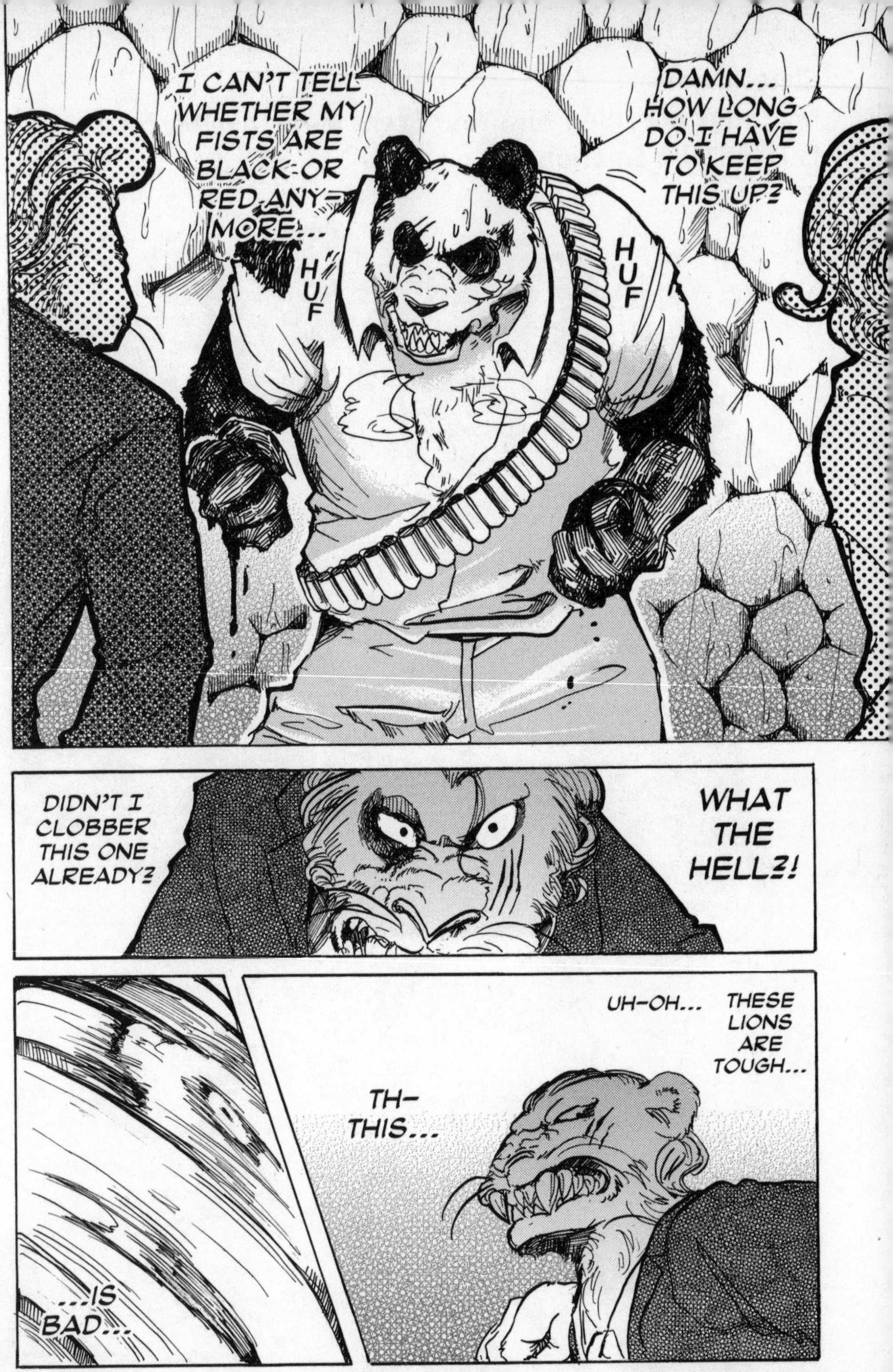
DAMN... HOW LONG DO I HAVE TO KEEP THIS UP?
HUF
I CAN'T TELL WHETHER MY FISTS ARE BLACK OR RED ANYMORE...
HUF
WHAT THE HELL?!
DIDN'T I CLOBBER THIS ONE ALREADY?
THESE LIONS ARE TOUGH...
UH-OH...
TH- THIS...
...IS BAD...

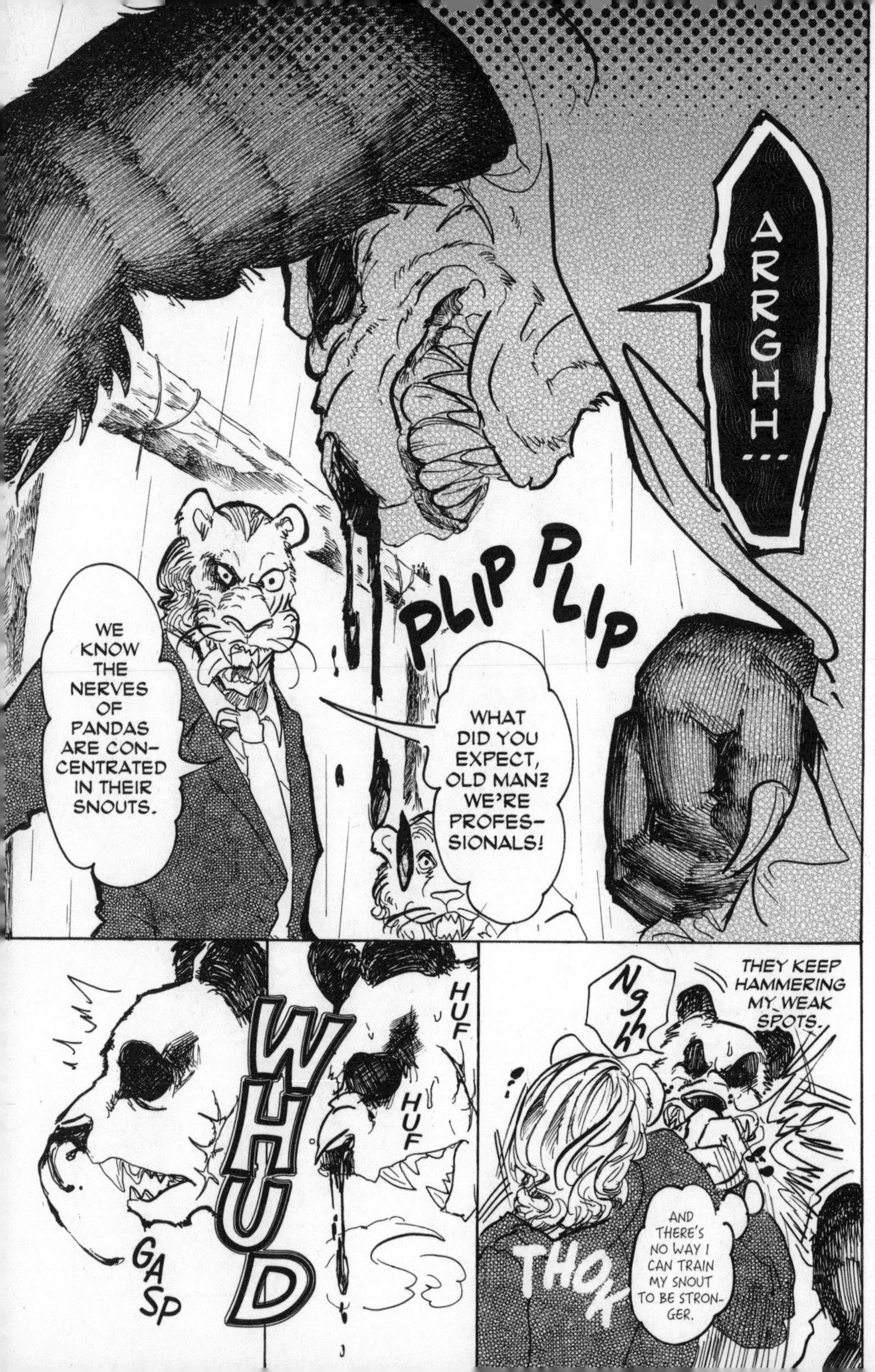
ARRGH...
PLIP PLIP
WHAT DID YOU EXPECT, OLD MAN? WE'RE PROFESSIONALS!
WE KNOW THE NERVES OF PANDAS ARE CONCENTRATED IN THEIR SNOUTS.
THEY KEEP HAMMERING MY WEAK SPOTS.
Ngh
THOK
AND THERE'S NO WAY I CAN TRAIN MY SNOUT TO BE STRONGER.
HUF HUF
WHUD
GASP

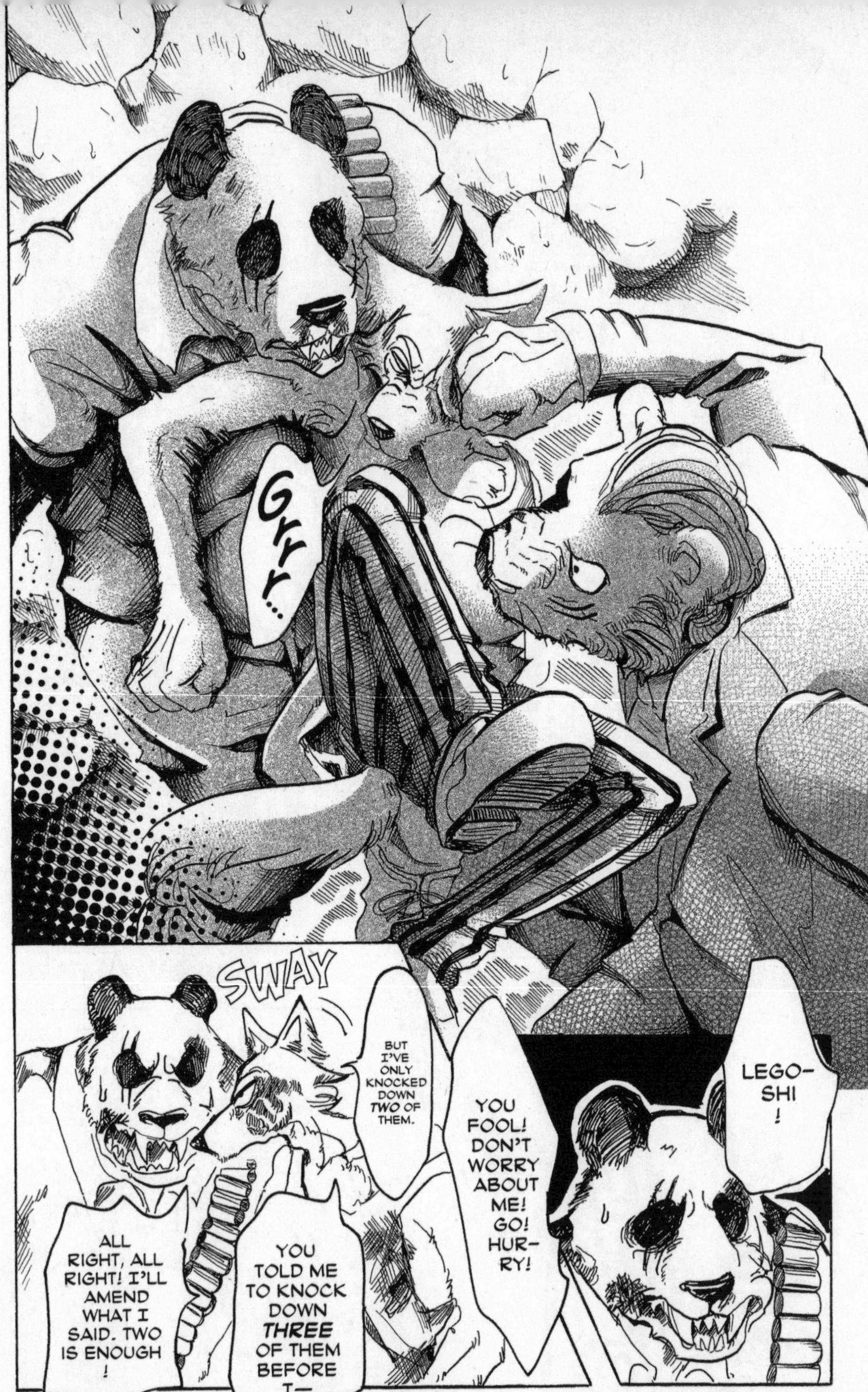
Grrr...
LEGOSHI!
YOU FOOL! DON'T WORRY ABOUT ME! GO! HURRY!
SWAY
BUT I'VE ONLY KNOCKED DOWN *TWO* OF THEM.
YOU TOLD ME TO KNOCK DOWN *THREE* OF THEM BEFORE I—
ALL RIGHT, ALL RIGHT! I'LL AMEND WHAT I SAID. TWO IS ENOUGH!

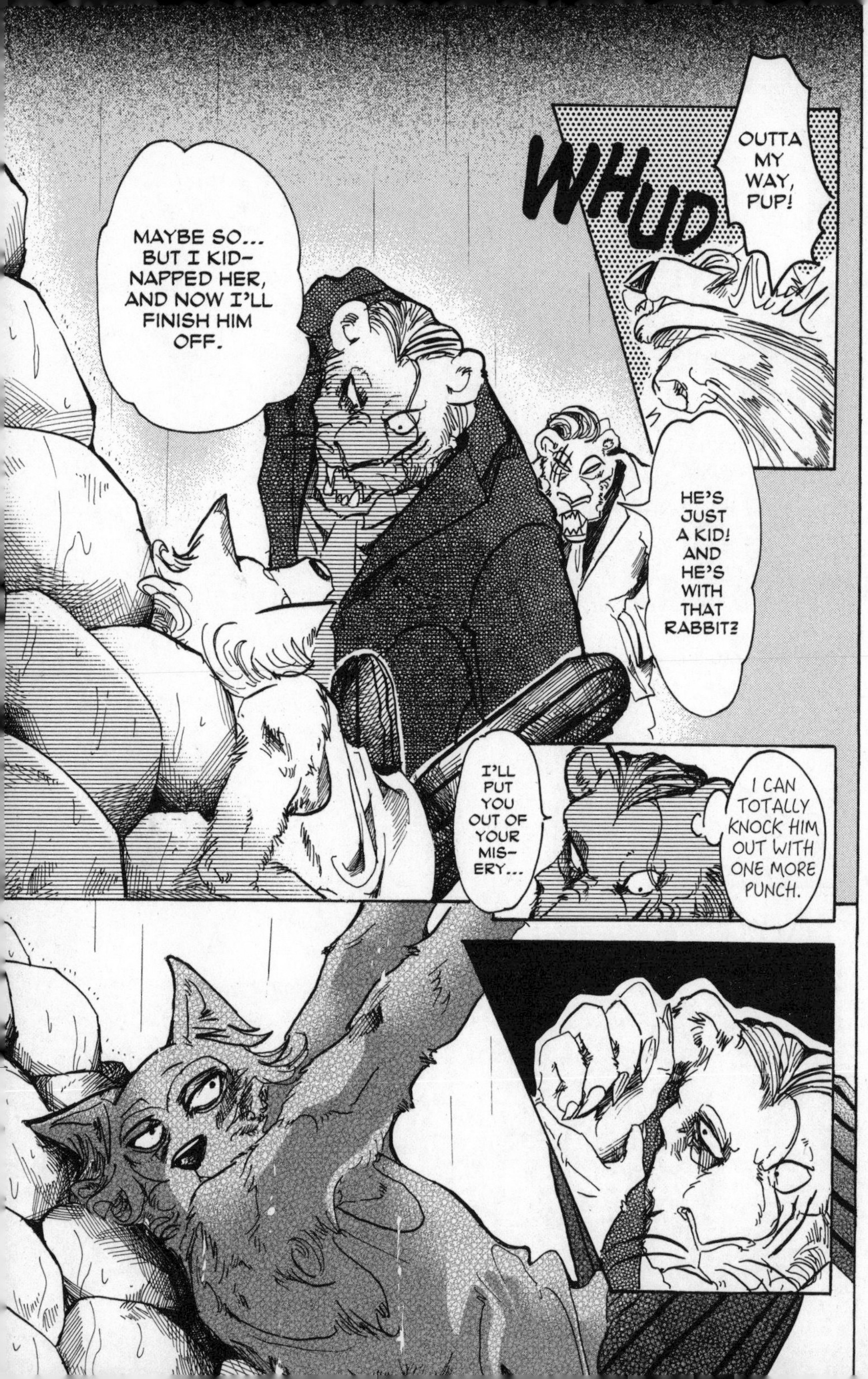
OUTTA MY WAY, PUP!
WHUD
HE'S JUST A KID! AND HE'S WITH THAT RABBIT?
MAYBE SO... BUT I KID-NAPPED HER, AND NOW I'LL FINISH HIM OFF.
I CAN TOTALLY KNOCK HIM OUT WITH ONE MORE PUNCH.
I'LL PUT YOU OUT OF YOUR MIS-ERY...

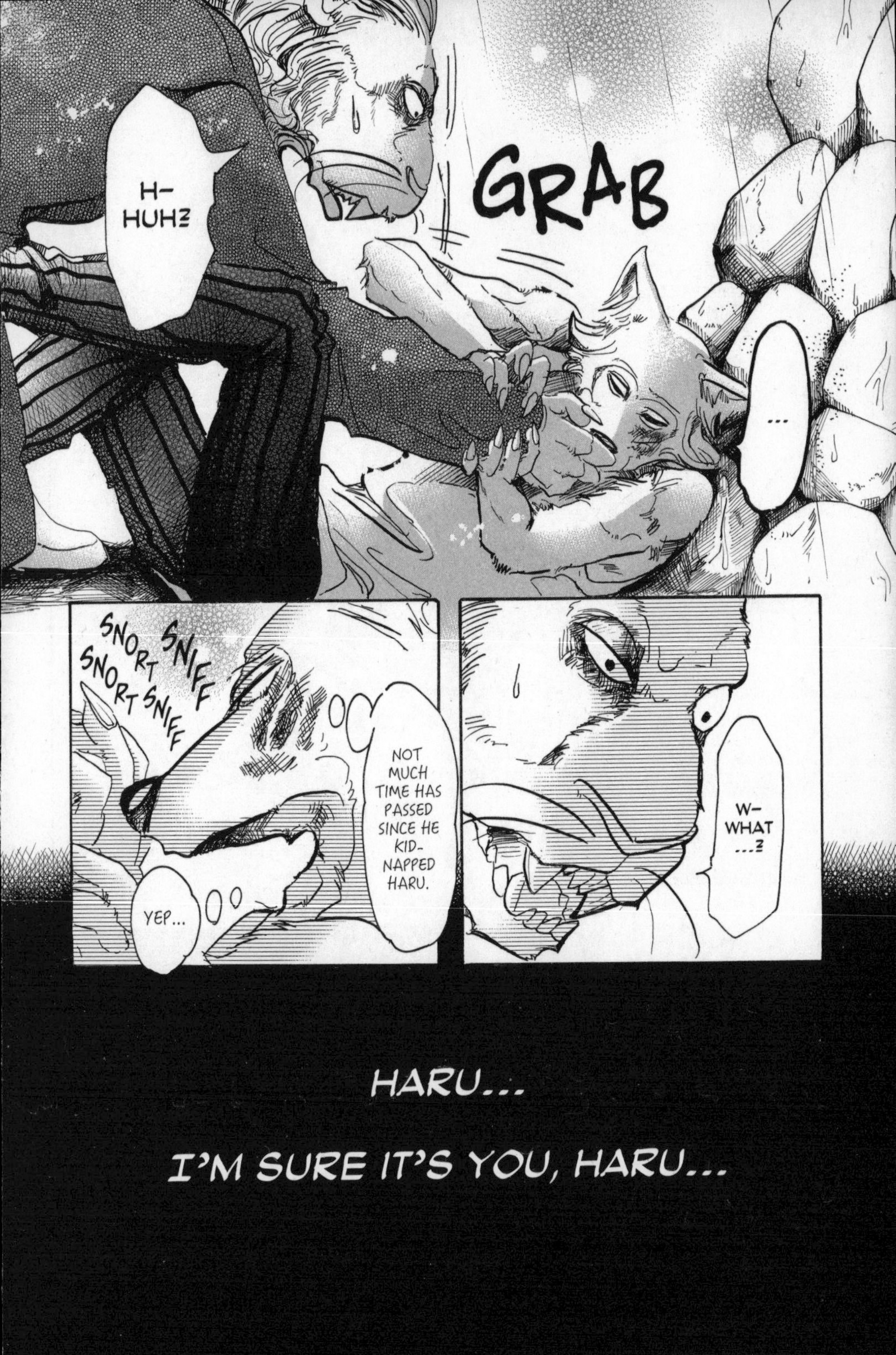
GRAB
...
H-HUH?
W-WHAT...?
NOT MUCH TIME HAS PASSED SINCE HE KID-NAPPED HARU.
SNORT SNIFF
SNORT SNIFF
YEP...
HARU...
I'M SURE IT'S YOU, HARU...

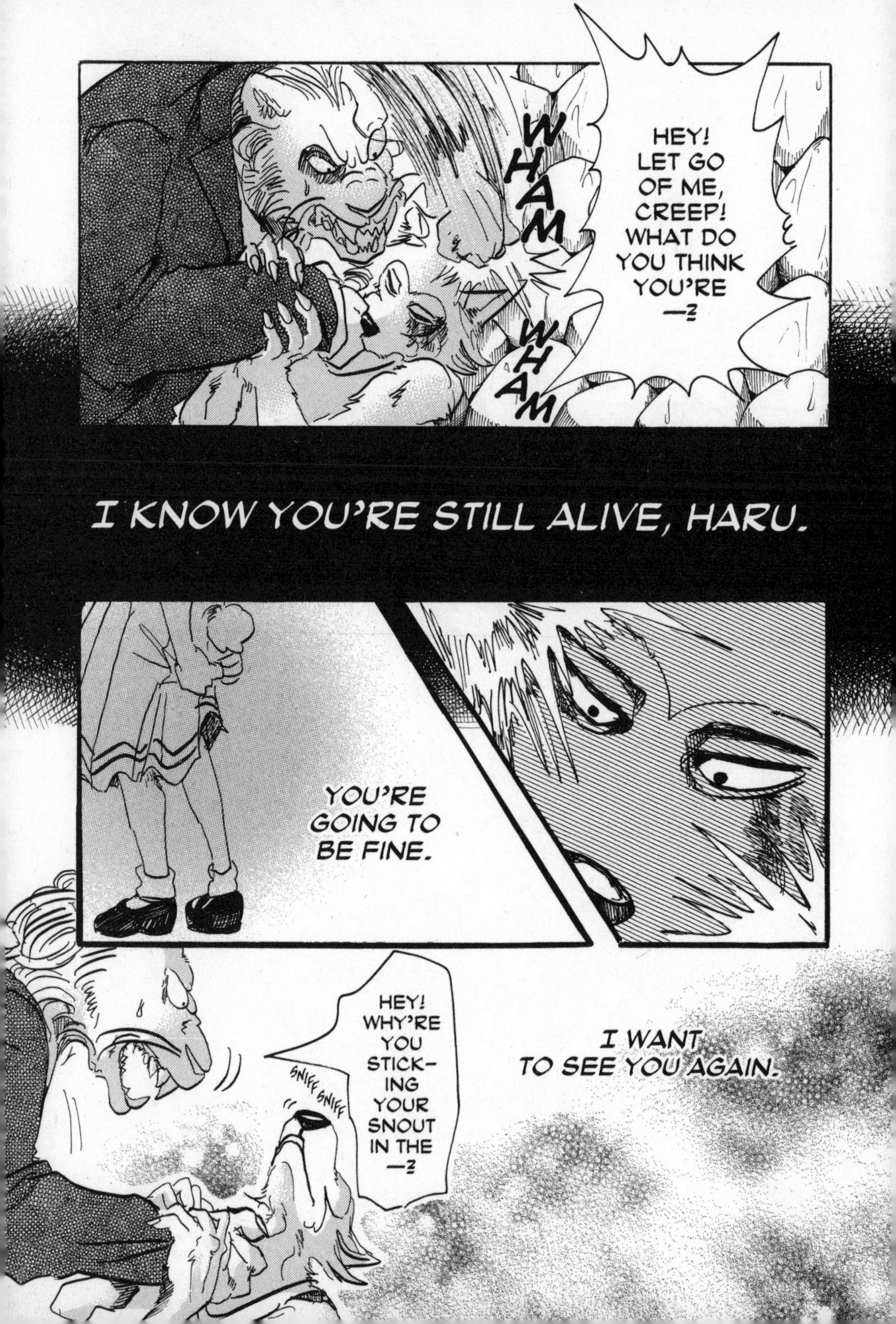
HEY! LET GO OF ME, CREEP! WHAT DO YOU THINK YOU'RE —?
WHAM WHAM
WHAM
I KNOW YOU'RE STILL ALIVE, HARU.
YOU'RE GOING TO BE FINE.
I WANT TO SEE YOU AGAIN.
HEY! WHY'RE YOU STICKING YOUR SNOUT IN THE —?
SNIFF SNIFF

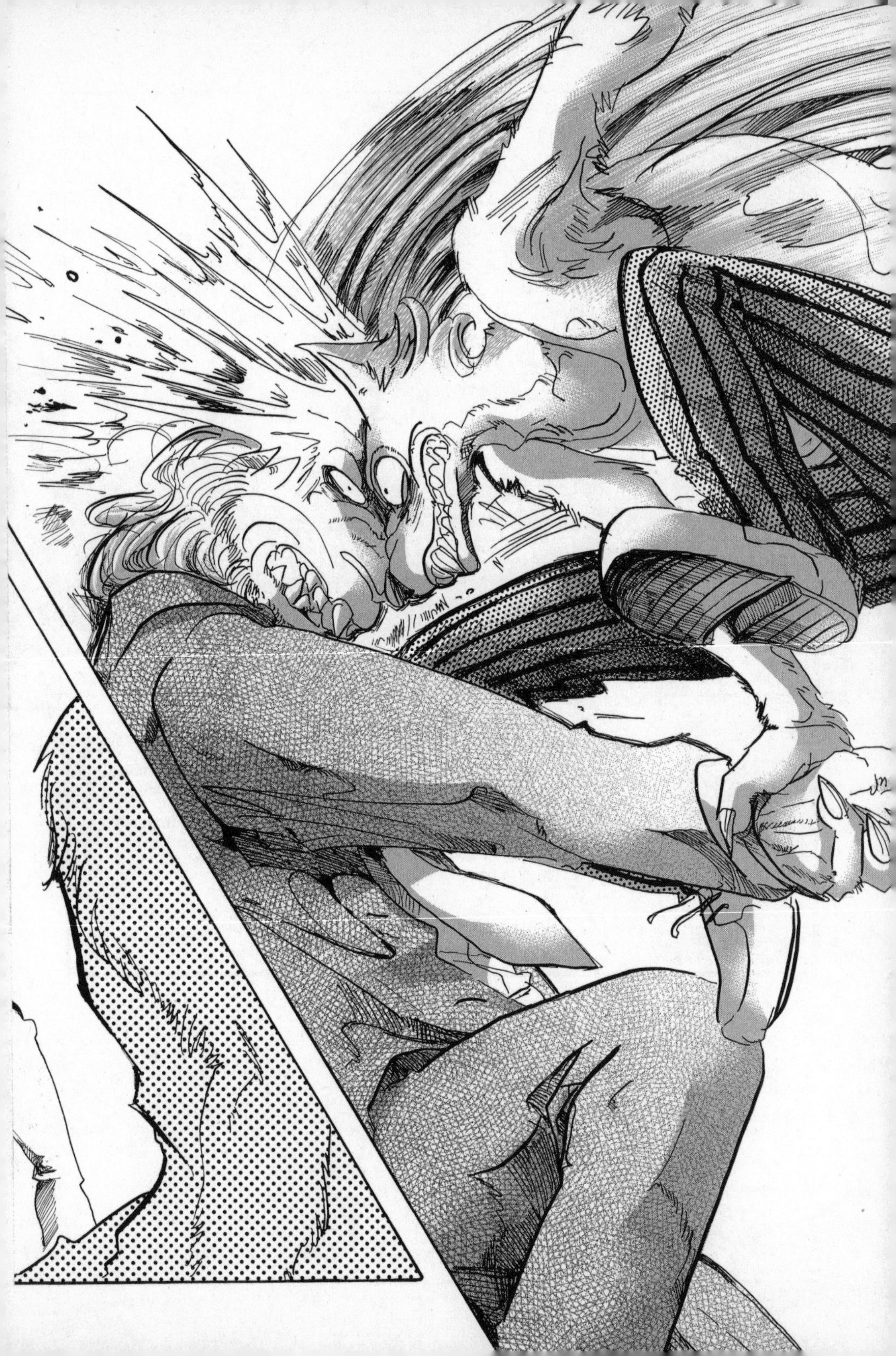

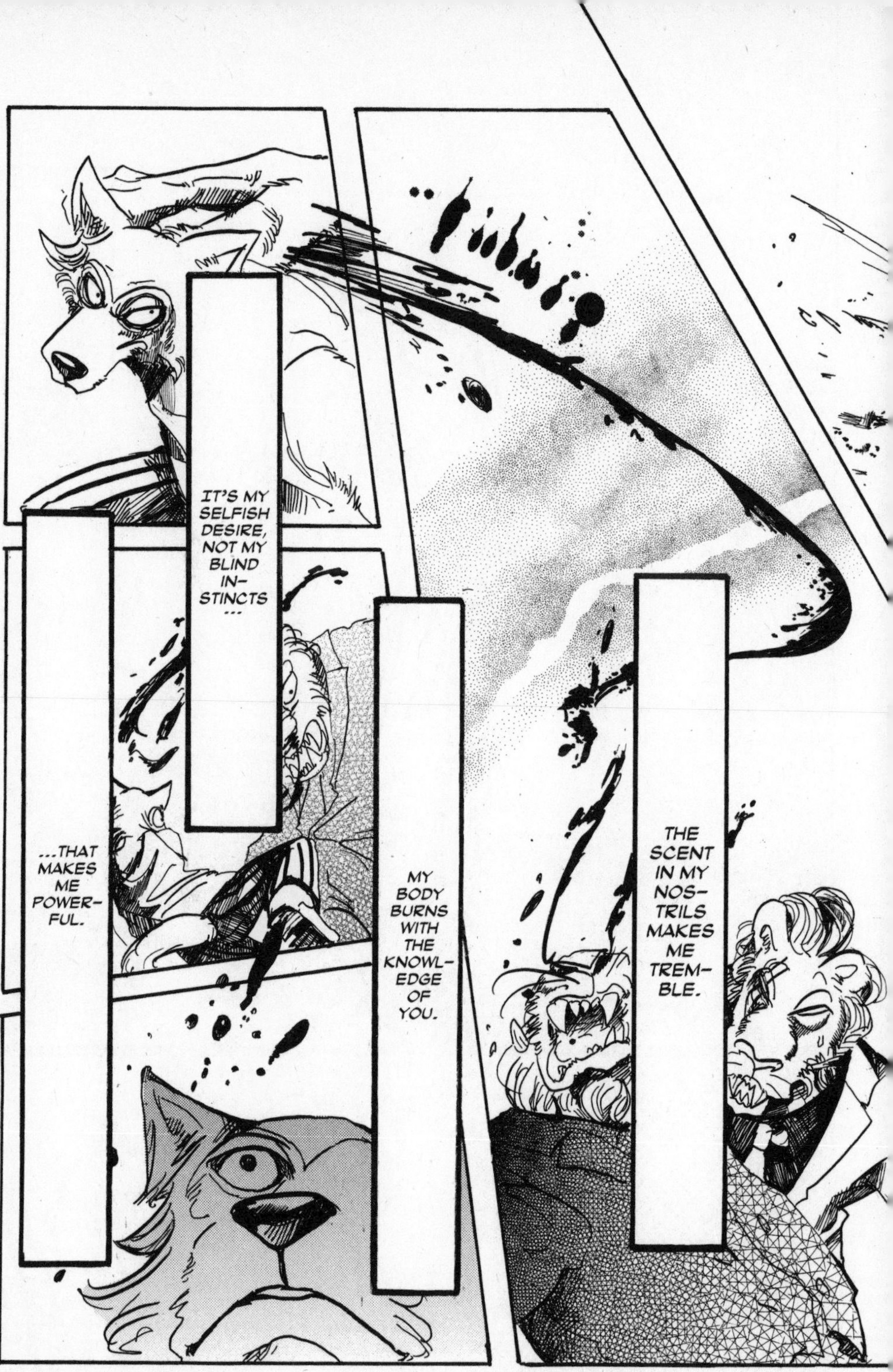
THE SCENT IN MY NOS-TRILS MAKES ME TREM-BLE.
MY BODY BURNS WITH THE KNOWL-EDGE OF YOU.
IT'S MY SELFISH DESIRE, NOT MY BLIND IN-STINCTS...
...THAT MAKES ME POWER-FUL.

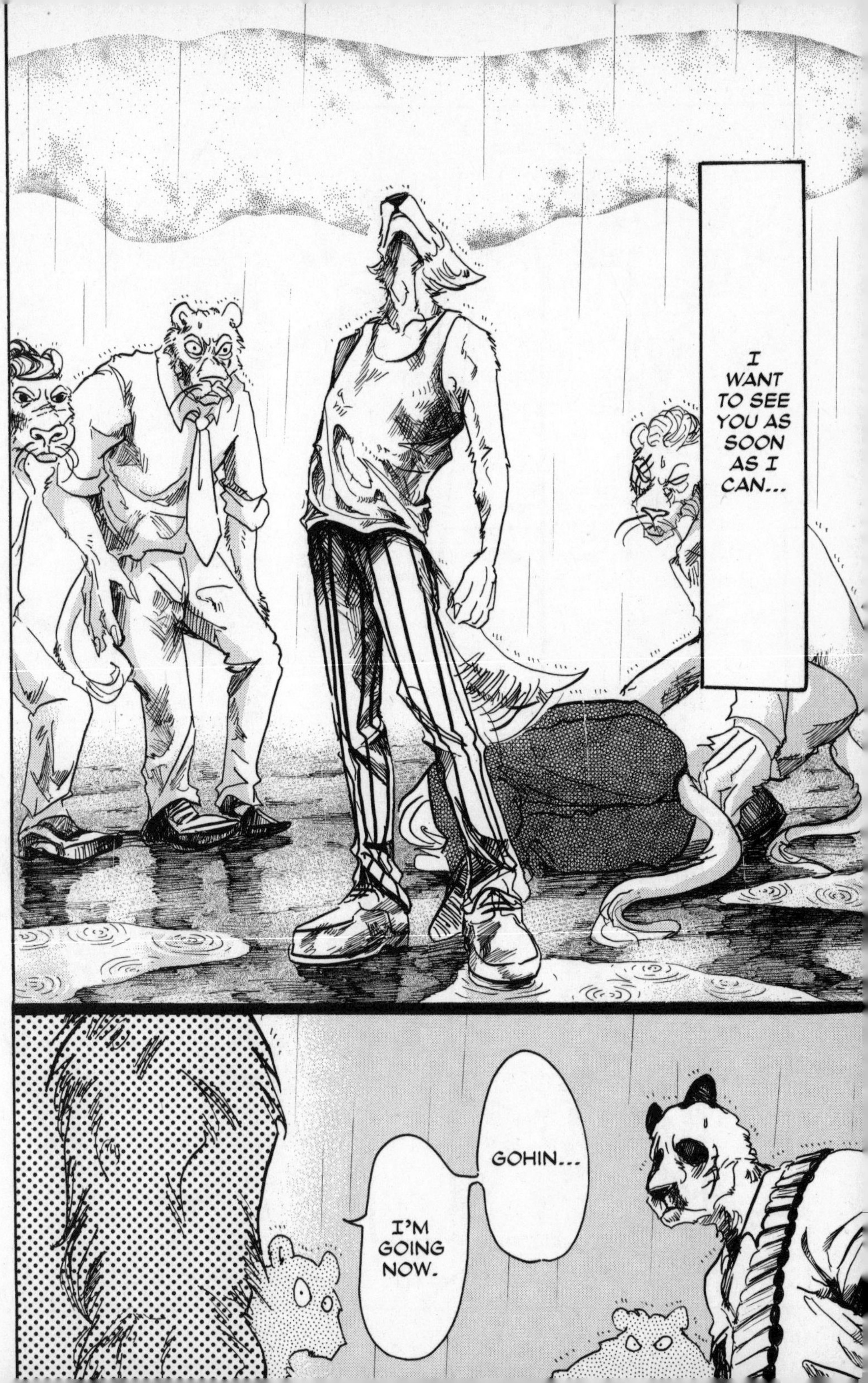
I WANT TO SEE YOU AS SOON AS I CAN...
GOHIN...
I'M GOING NOW.

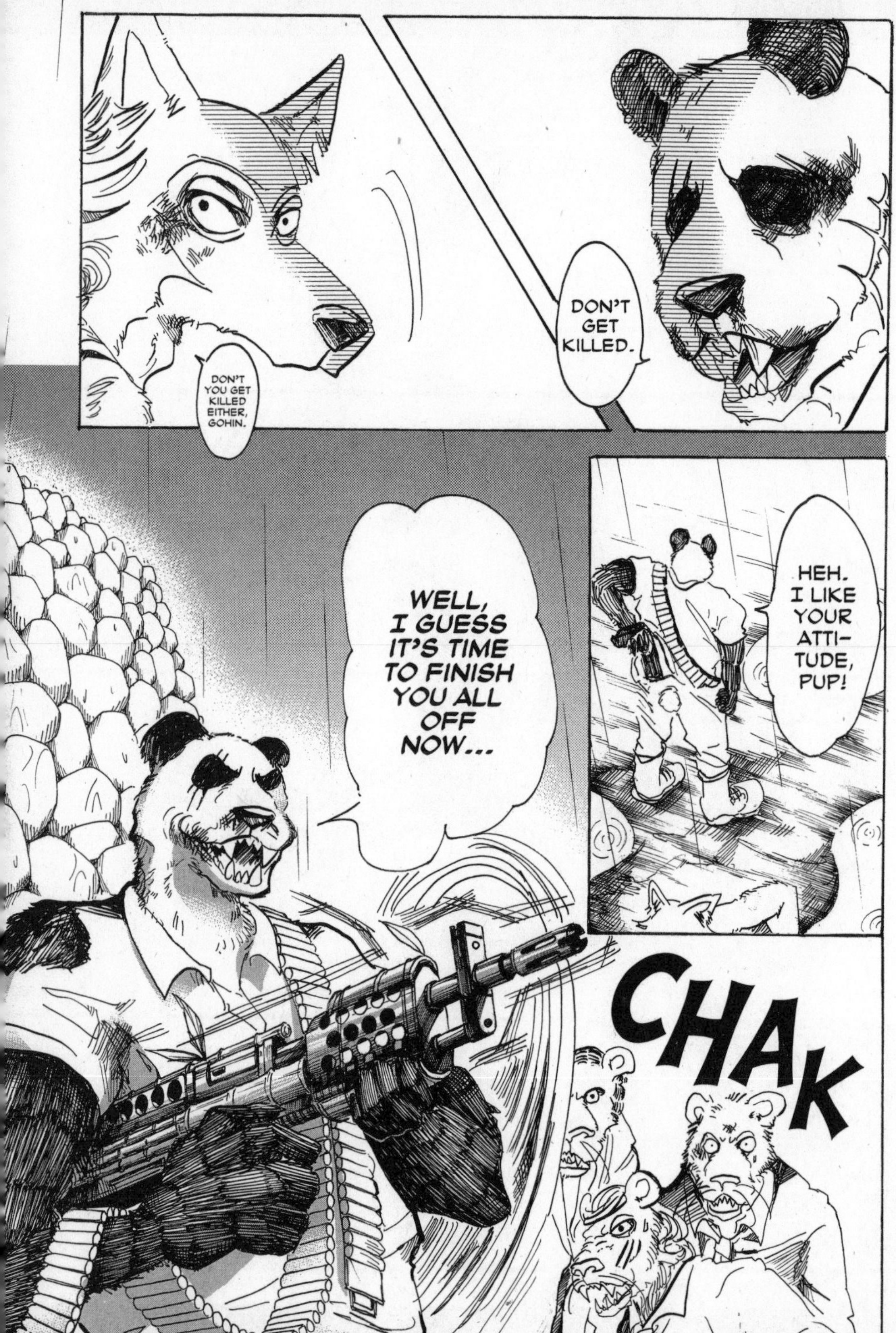
DON'T GET KILLED.
DON'T YOU GET KILLED EITHER, GOHIN.
HEH. I LIKE YOUR ATTI-TUDE, PUP!
WELL, I GUESS IT'S TIME TO FINISH YOU ALL OFF NOW...
CHAK

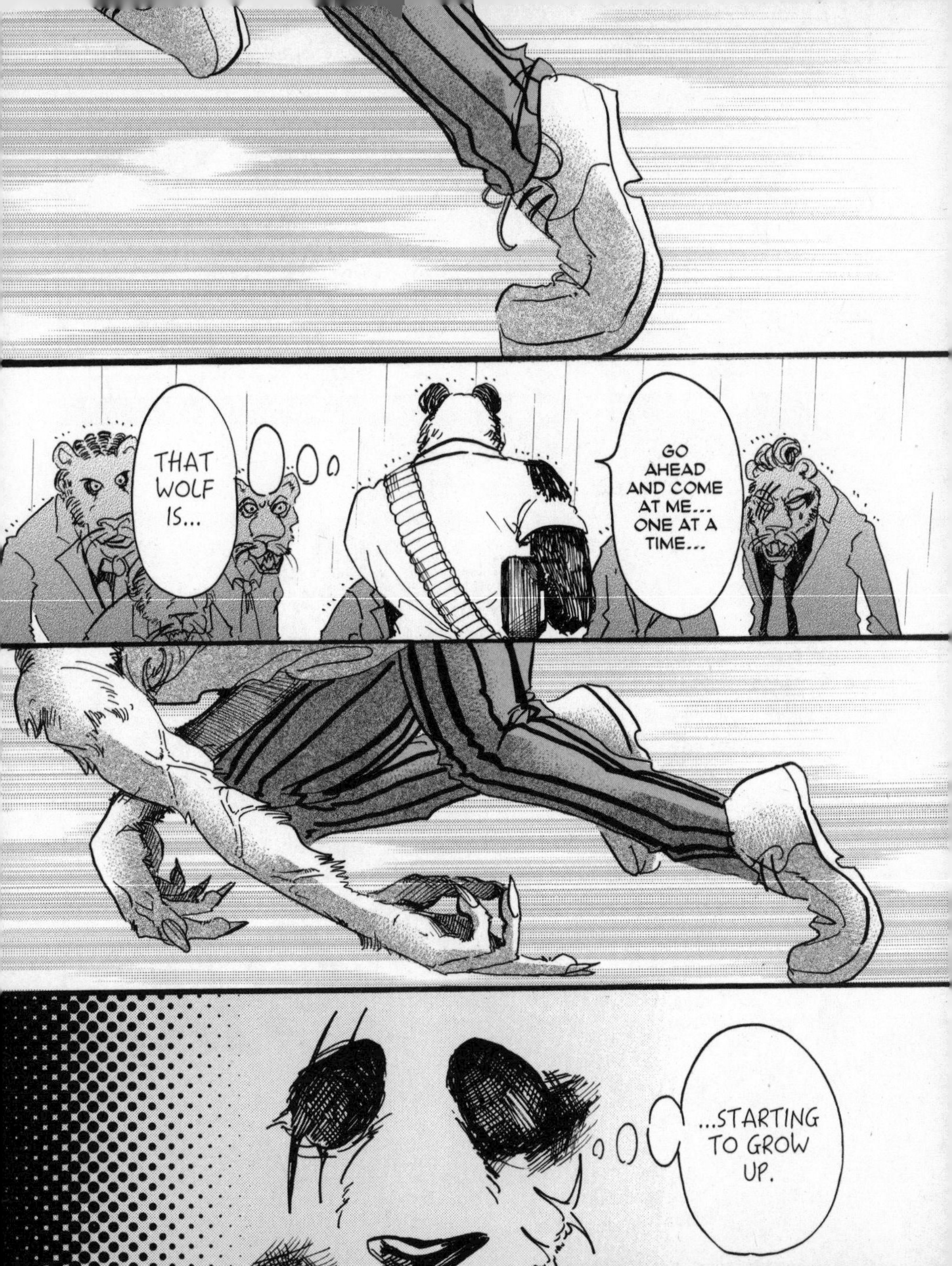
GO AHEAD AND COME AT ME... ONE AT A TIME...
THAT WOLF IS...
...STARTING TO GROW UP.

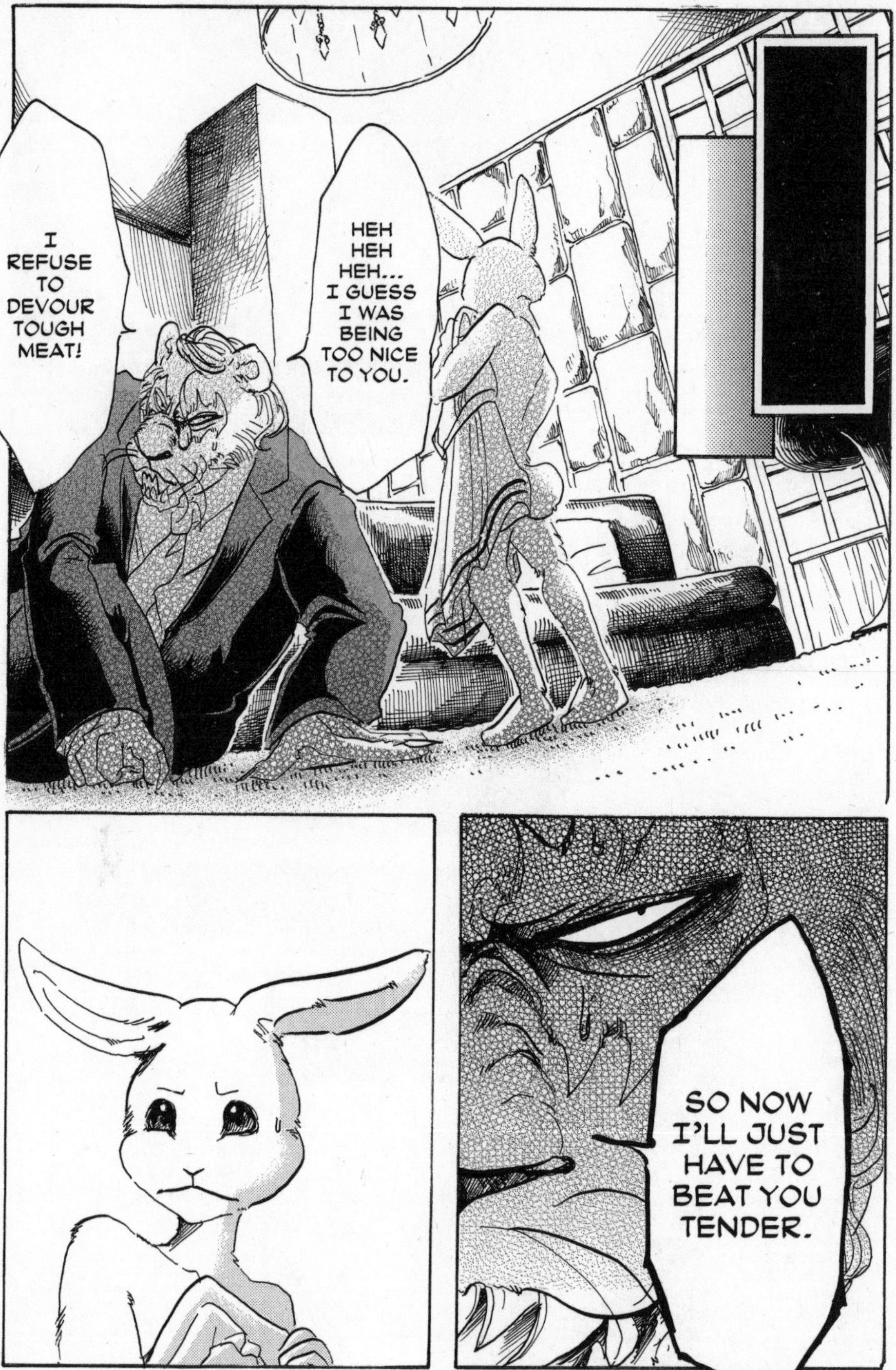
HEH HEH HEH... I GUESS I WAS BEING TOO NICE TO YOU.
I REFUSE TO DEVOUR TOUGH MEAT!
SO NOW I'LL JUST HAVE TO BEAT YOU TENDER.

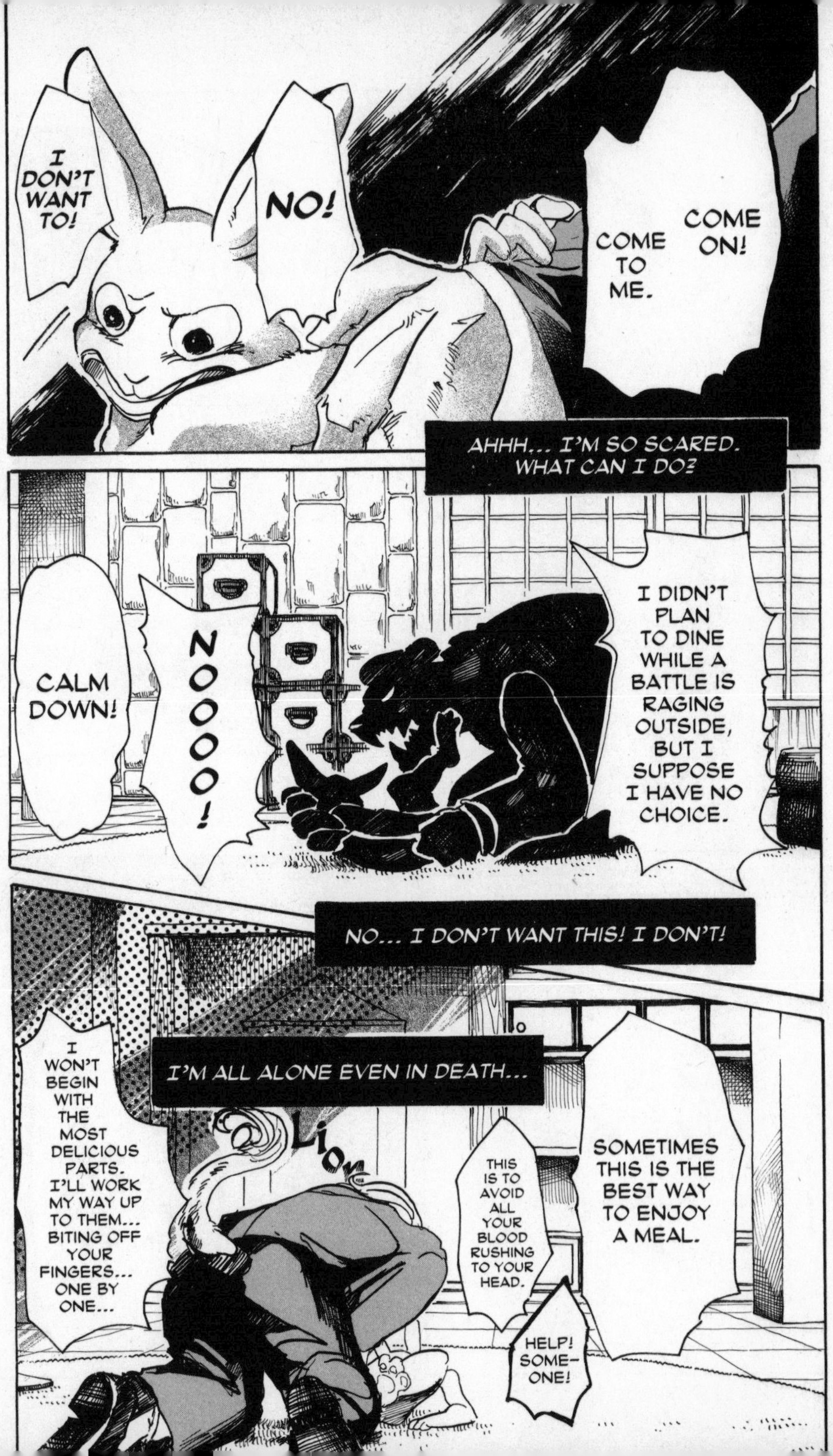
COME ON!
COME TO ME.
NO!
I DON'T WANT TO!
AHHH... I'M SO SCARED. WHAT CAN I DO?
I DIDN'T PLAN TO DINE WHILE A BATTLE IS RAGING OUTSIDE, BUT I SUPPOSE I HAVE NO CHOICE.
NOOOOO!
CALM DOWN!
NO... I DON'T WANT THIS! I DON'T!
I'M ALL ALONE EVEN IN DEATH...
SOMETIMES THIS IS THE BEST WAY TO ENJOY A MEAL.
THIS IS TO AVOID ALL YOUR BLOOD RUSHING TO YOUR HEAD.
HELP! SOME-ONE!
I WON'T BEGIN WITH THE MOST DELICIOUS PARTS. I'LL WORK MY WAY UP TO THEM... BITING OFF YOUR FINGERS... ONE BY ONE...

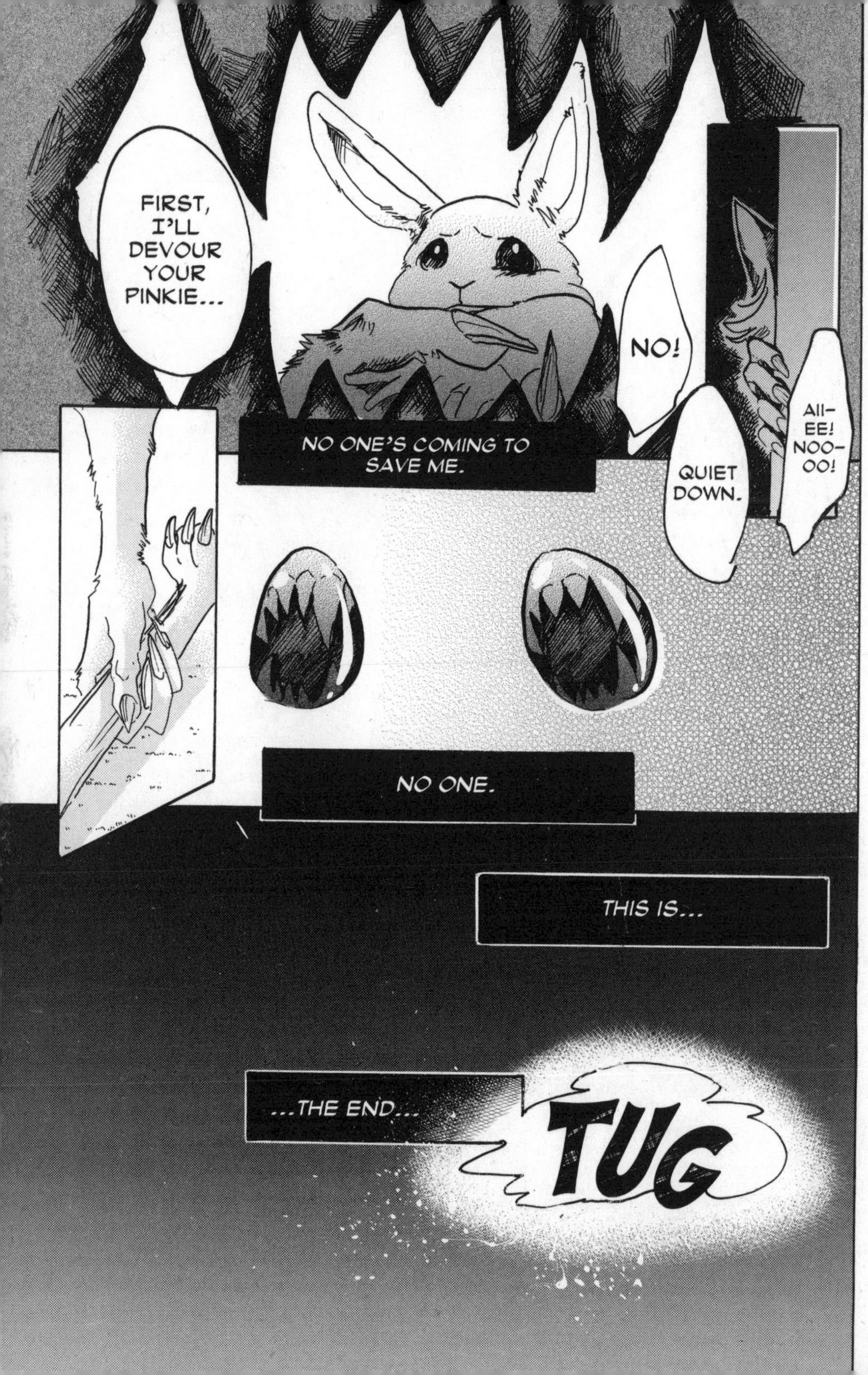
AII—EE! NOO—OO!
NO!
QUIET DOWN.
FIRST, I'LL DEVOUR YOUR PINKIE...
NO ONE'S COMING TO SAVE ME.
NO ONE.
THIS IS...
...THE END...
TUG

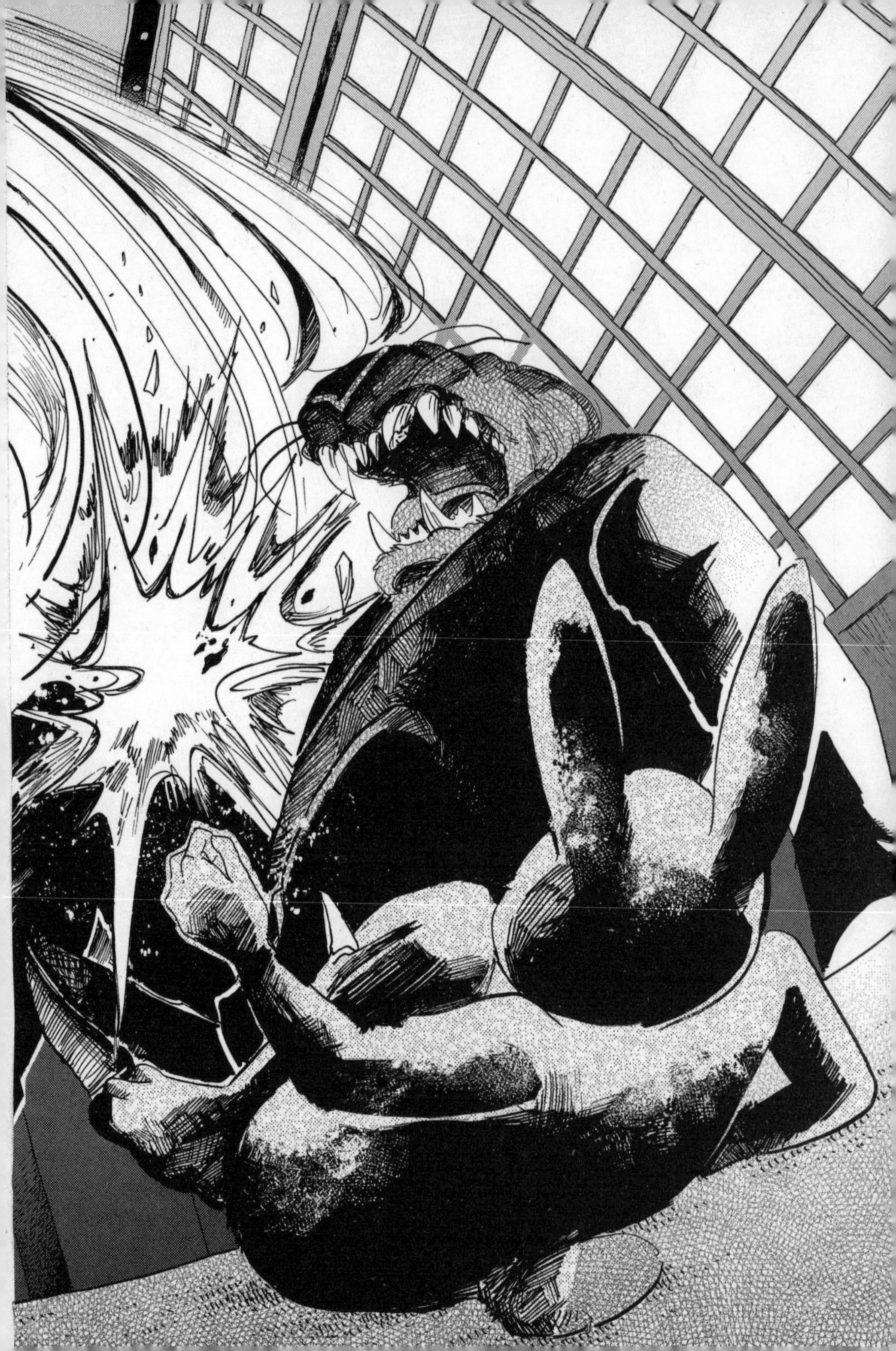

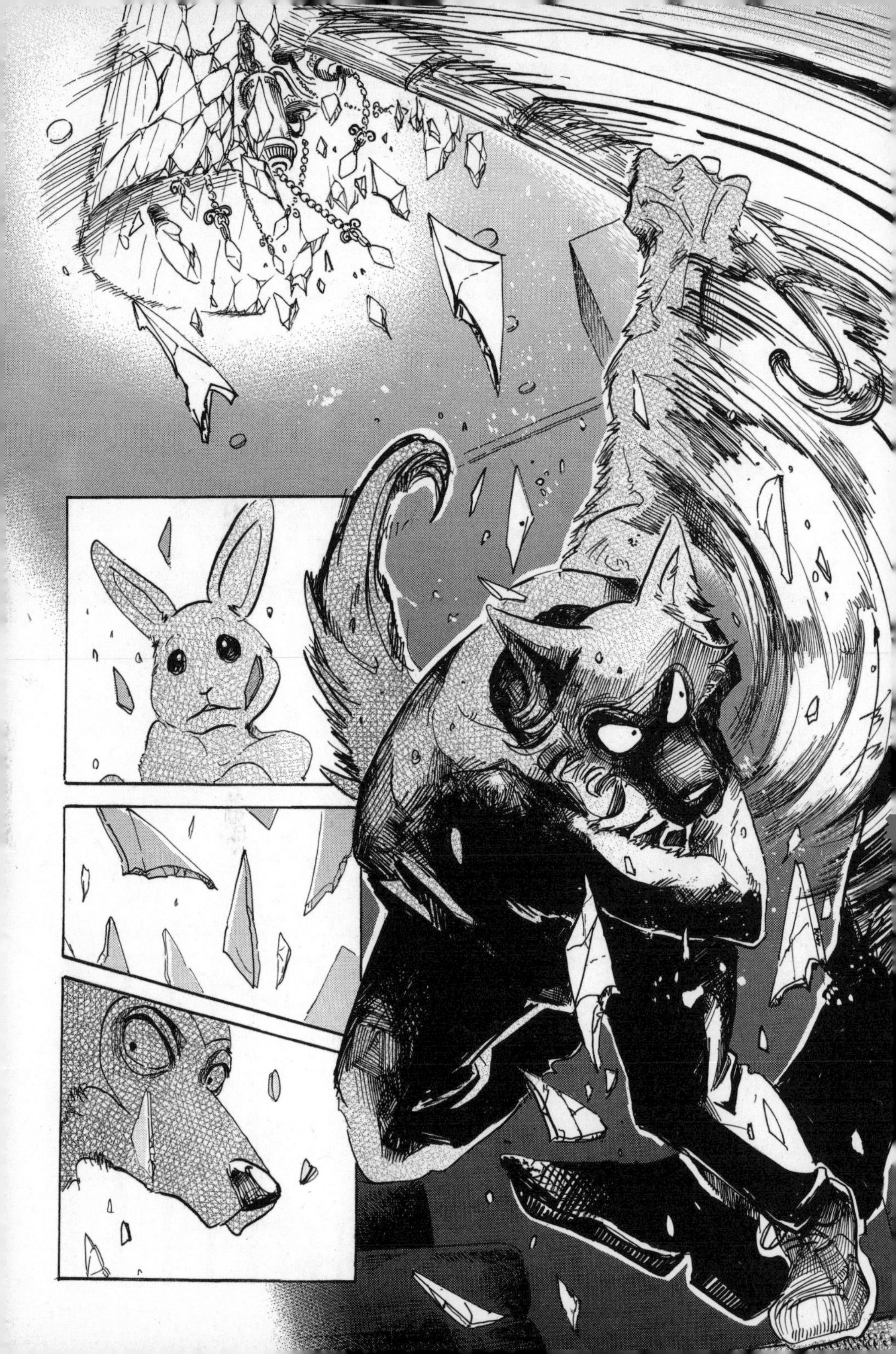

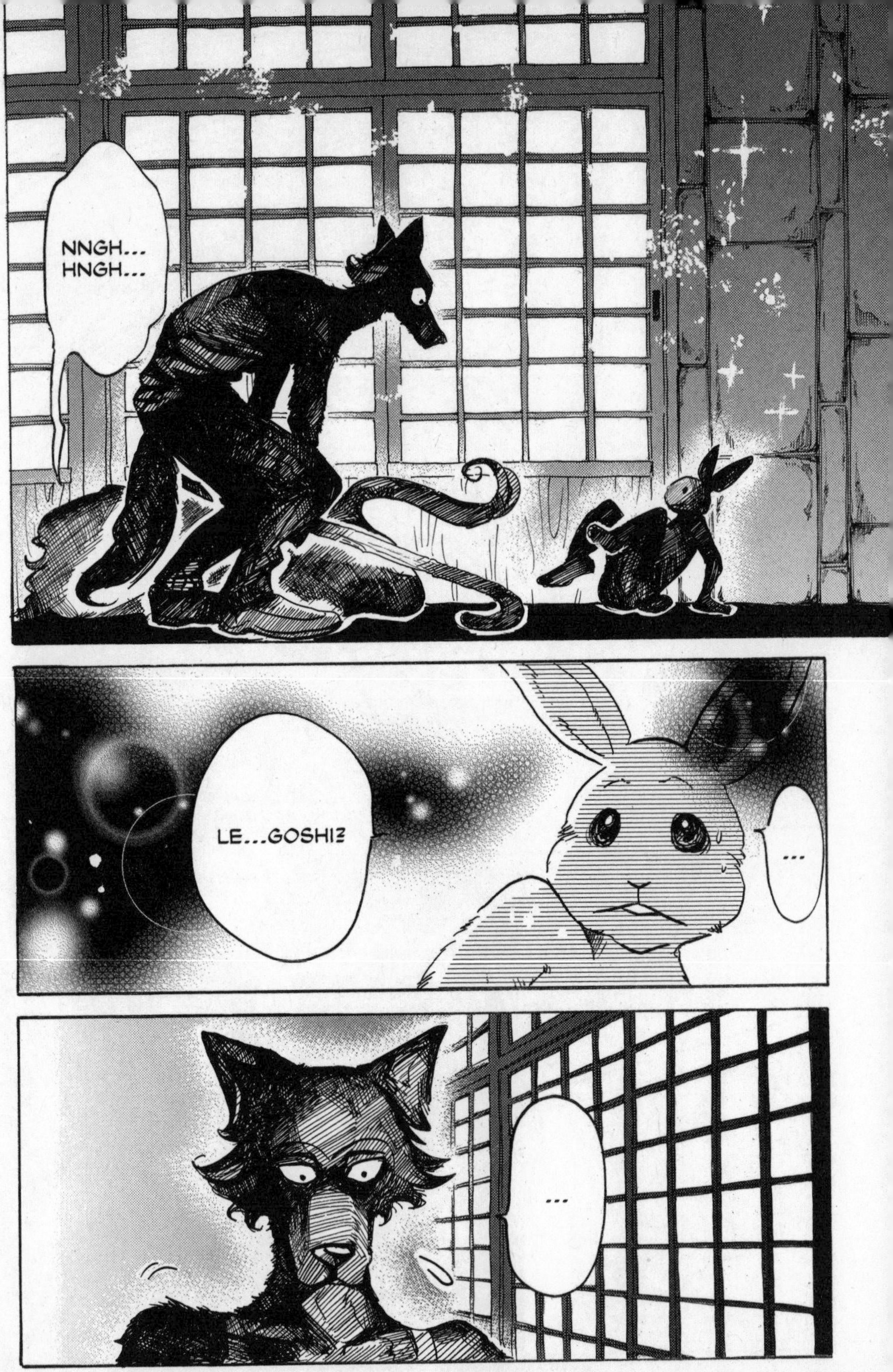
NNGH... HNGH...
...
LE...GOSHI?
...

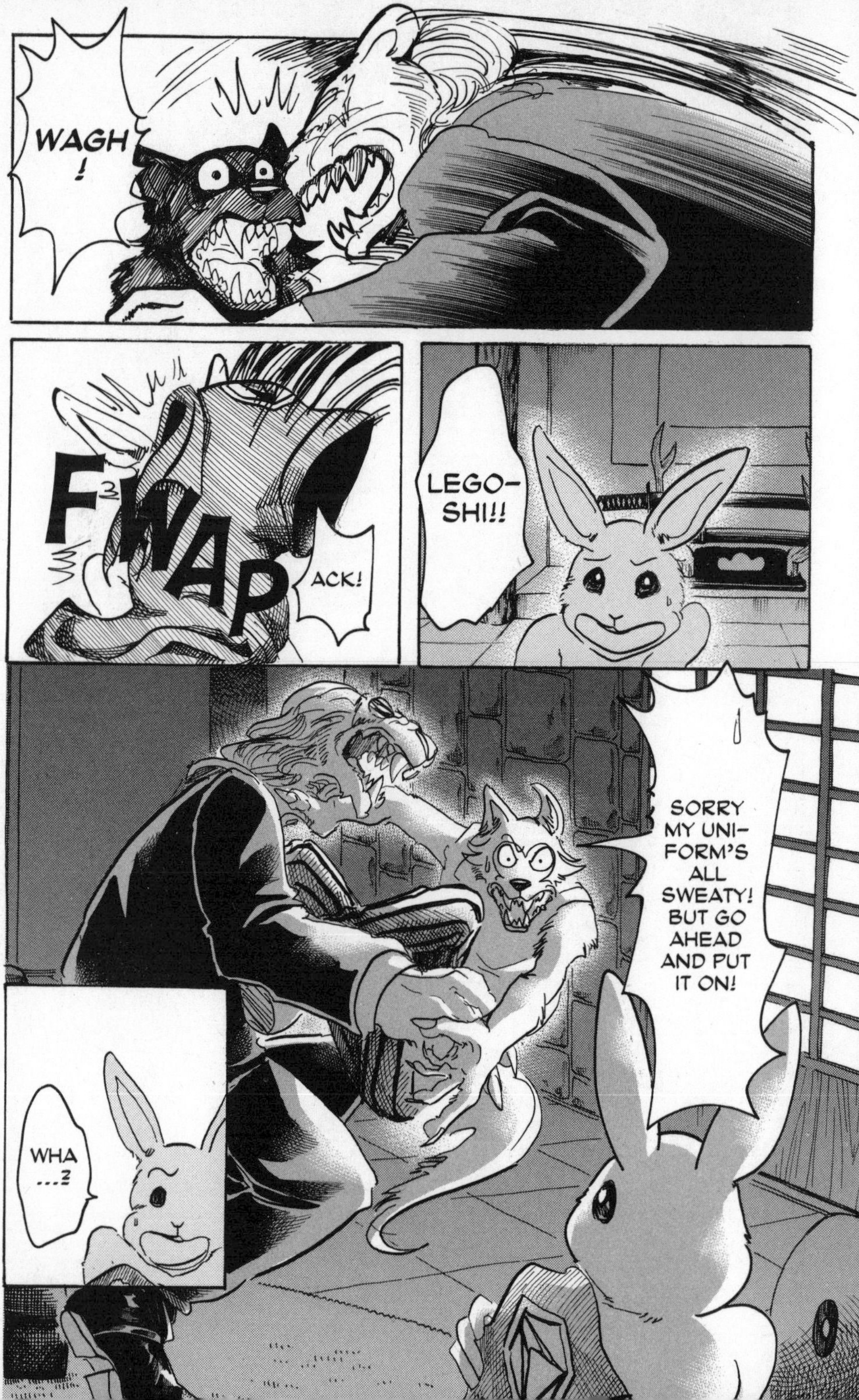
WAGH!
LEGO-SHI!!
FWAP
ACK!
SORRY MY UNI-FORM'S ALL SWEATY! BUT GO AHEAD AND PUT IT ON!
WHA...?

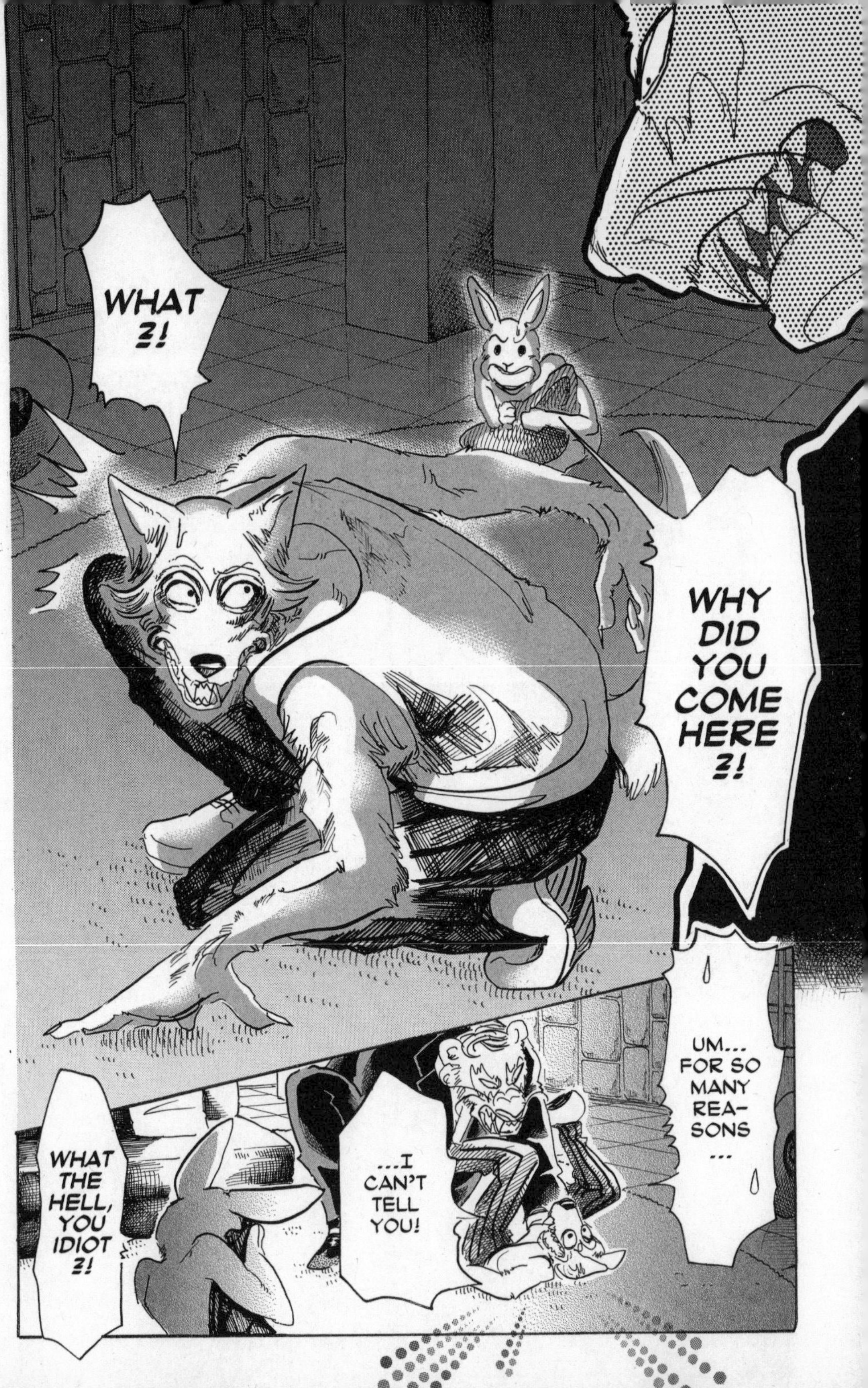
WHAT ?!
WHY DID YOU COME HERE ?!
UM... FOR SO MANY REASONS ...
...I CAN'T TELL YOU!
WHAT THE HELL, YOU IDIOT ?!

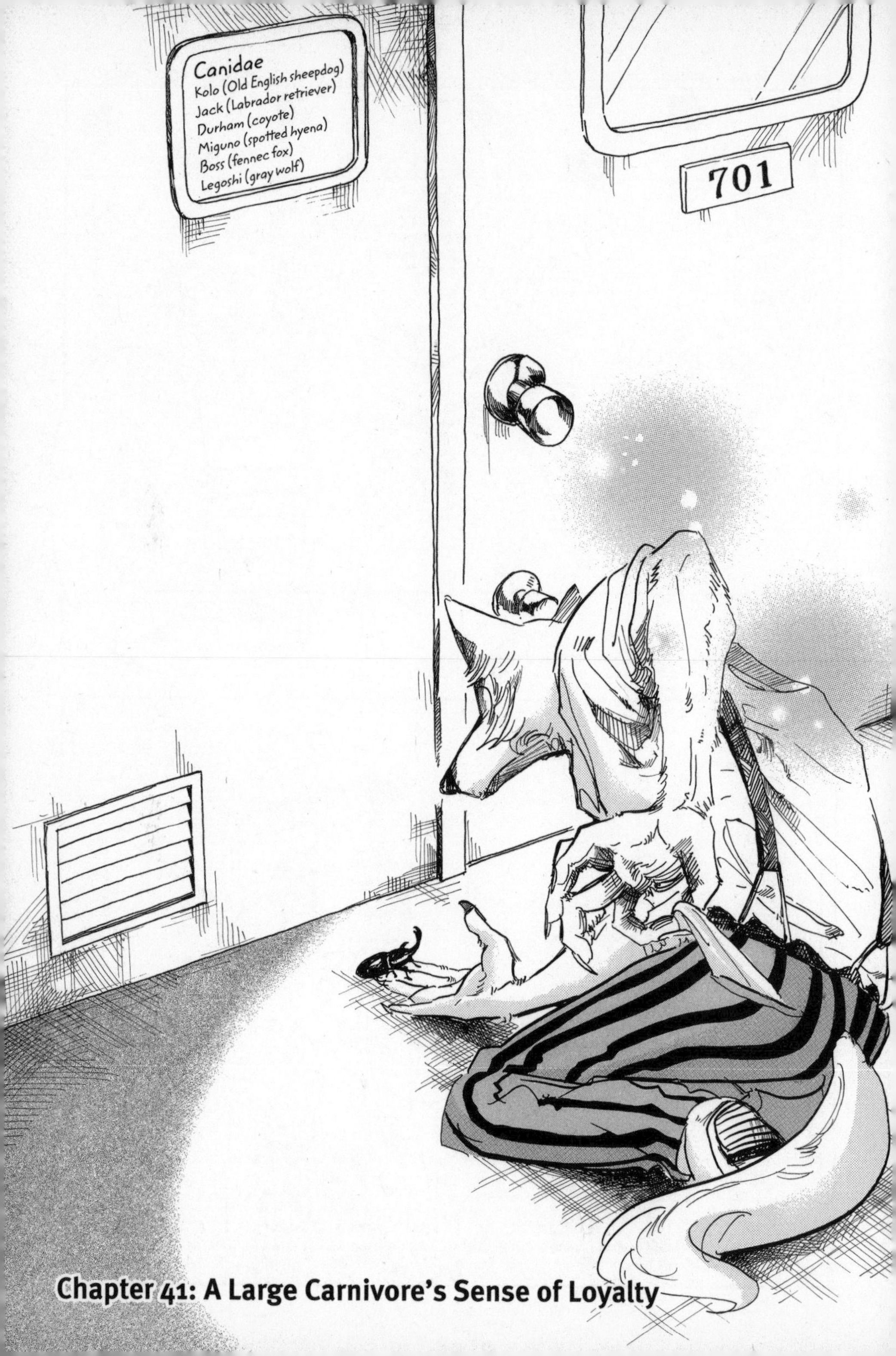
Canidae
Kolo (Old English sheepdog)
Jack (Labrador retriever)
Durham (coyote)
Miguno (spotted hyena)
Boss (fennec fox)
Legoshi (gray wolf)
701

Chapter 41: A Large Carnivore's Sense of Loyalty

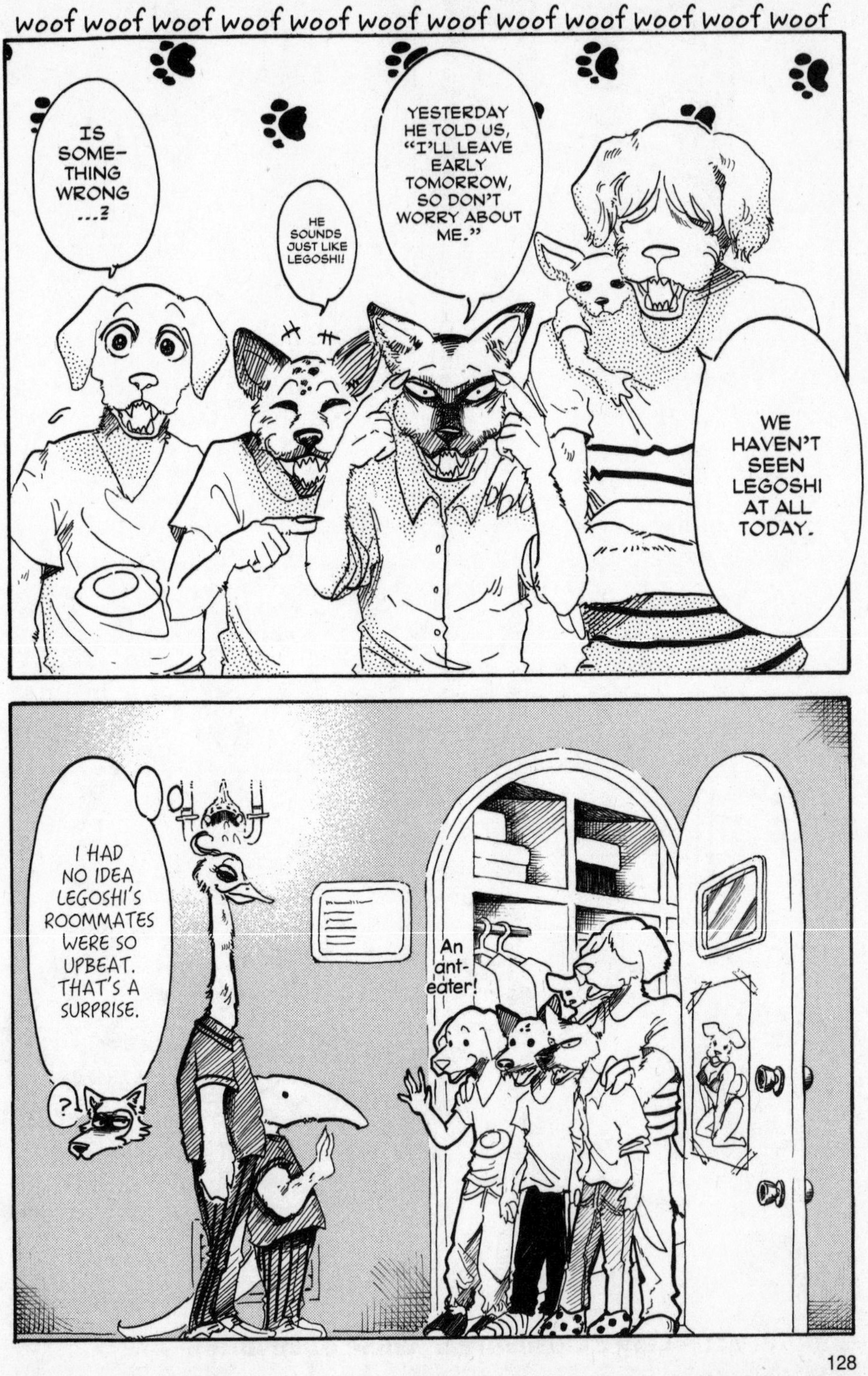
woof woof woof woof woof woof woof woof woof woof woof woof
WE HAVEN'T SEEN LEGOSHI AT ALL TODAY.
YESTERDAY HE TOLD US, "I'LL LEAVE EARLY TOMORROW, SO DON'T WORRY ABOUT ME."
HE SOUNDS JUST LIKE LEGOSHI!
IS SOMETHING WRONG...?
An anteater!
I HAD NO IDEA LEGOSHI'S ROOMMATES WERE SO UPBEAT. THAT'S A SURPRISE.
?

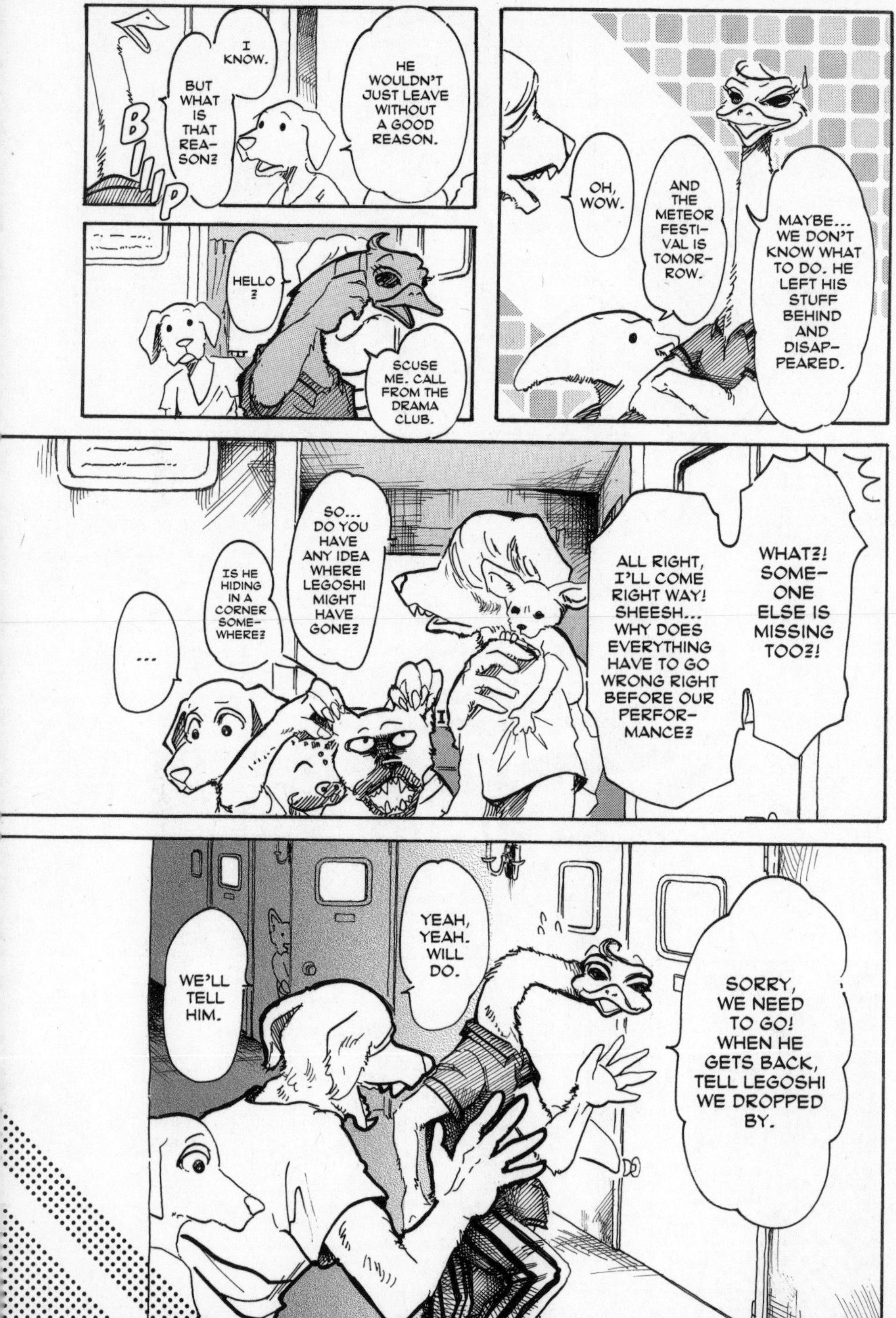
MAYBE... WE DON'T KNOW WHAT TO DO. HE LEFT HIS STUFF BEHIND AND DISAPPEARED.
AND THE METEOR FESTIVAL IS TOMORROW.
OH, WOW.
HE WOULDN'T JUST LEAVE WITHOUT A GOOD REASON.
I KNOW.
BUT WHAT IS THAT REASON?
BIIIP
SCUSE ME. CALL FROM THE DRAMA CLUB.
HELLO?
WHAT?! SOMEONE ELSE IS MISSING TOO?!
ALL RIGHT, I'LL COME RIGHT WAY! SHEESH... WHY DOES EVERYTHING HAVE TO GO WRONG RIGHT BEFORE OUR PERFORMANCE?
SO... DO YOU HAVE ANY IDEA WHERE LEGOSHI MIGHT HAVE GONE?
IS HE HIDING IN A CORNER SOMEWHERE?
...
SORRY, WE NEED TO GO! WHEN HE GETS BACK, TELL LEGOSHI WE DROPPED BY.
YEAH, YEAH. WILL DO.
WE'LL TELL HIM.

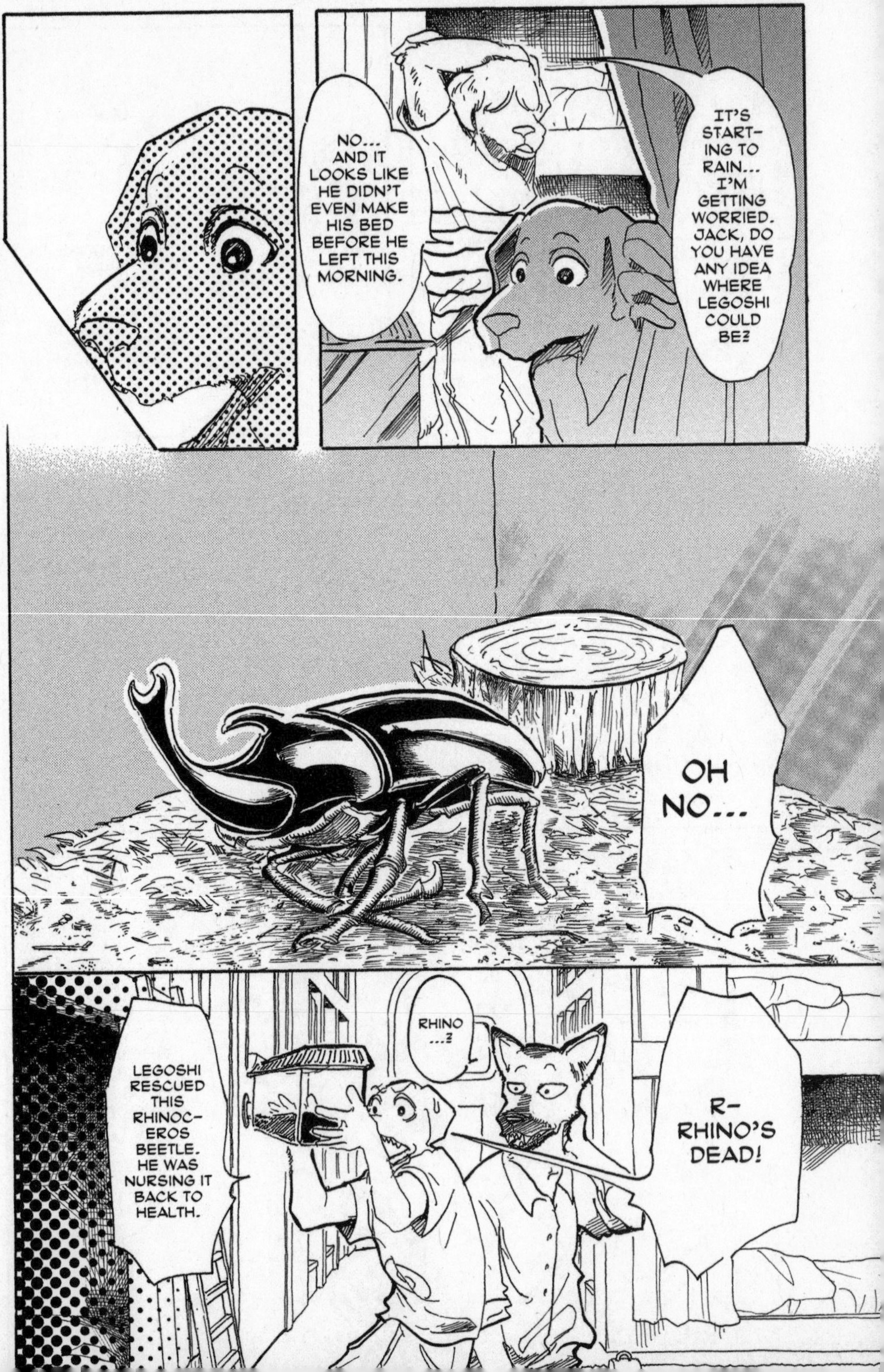
IT'S STARTING TO RAIN... I'M GETTING WORRIED. JACK, DO YOU HAVE ANY IDEA WHERE LEGOSHI COULD BE?
NO... AND IT LOOKS LIKE HE DIDN'T EVEN MAKE HIS BED BEFORE HE LEFT THIS MORNING.
OH NO...
R-RHINO'S DEAD!
RHINO...?
LEGOSHI RESCUED THIS RHINOCEROS BEETLE. HE WAS NURSING IT BACK TO HEALTH.

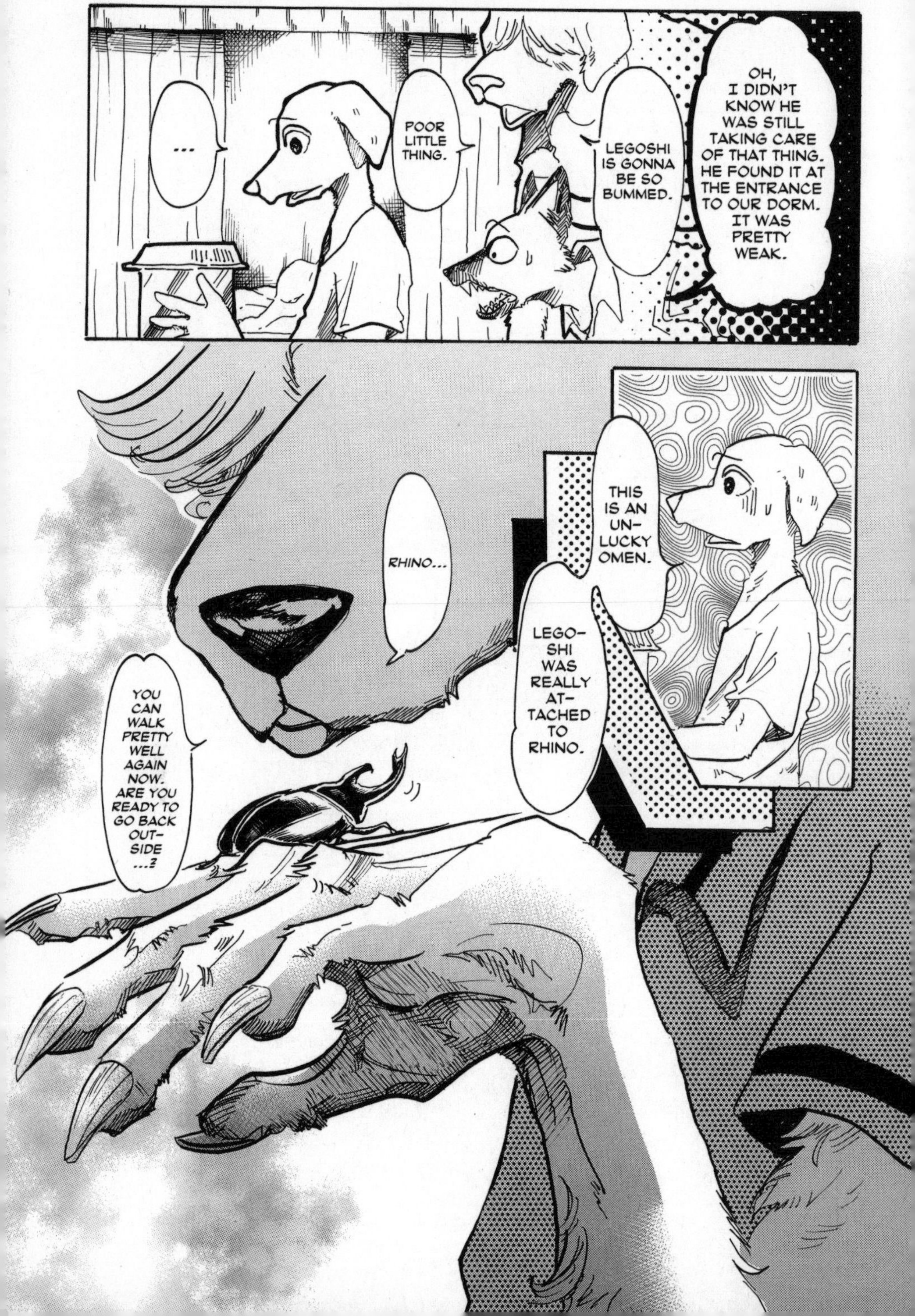
OH, I DIDN'T KNOW HE WAS STILL TAKING CARE OF THAT THING. HE FOUND IT AT THE ENTRANCE TO OUR DORM. IT WAS PRETTY WEAK.
LEGOSHI IS GONNA BE SO BUMMED.
POOR LITTLE THING.
...
THIS IS AN UN-LUCKY OMEN.
LEGO-SHI WAS REALLY AT-TACHED TO RHINO.
RHINO...
YOU CAN WALK PRETTY WELL AGAIN NOW. ARE YOU READY TO GO BACK OUT-SIDE ...?

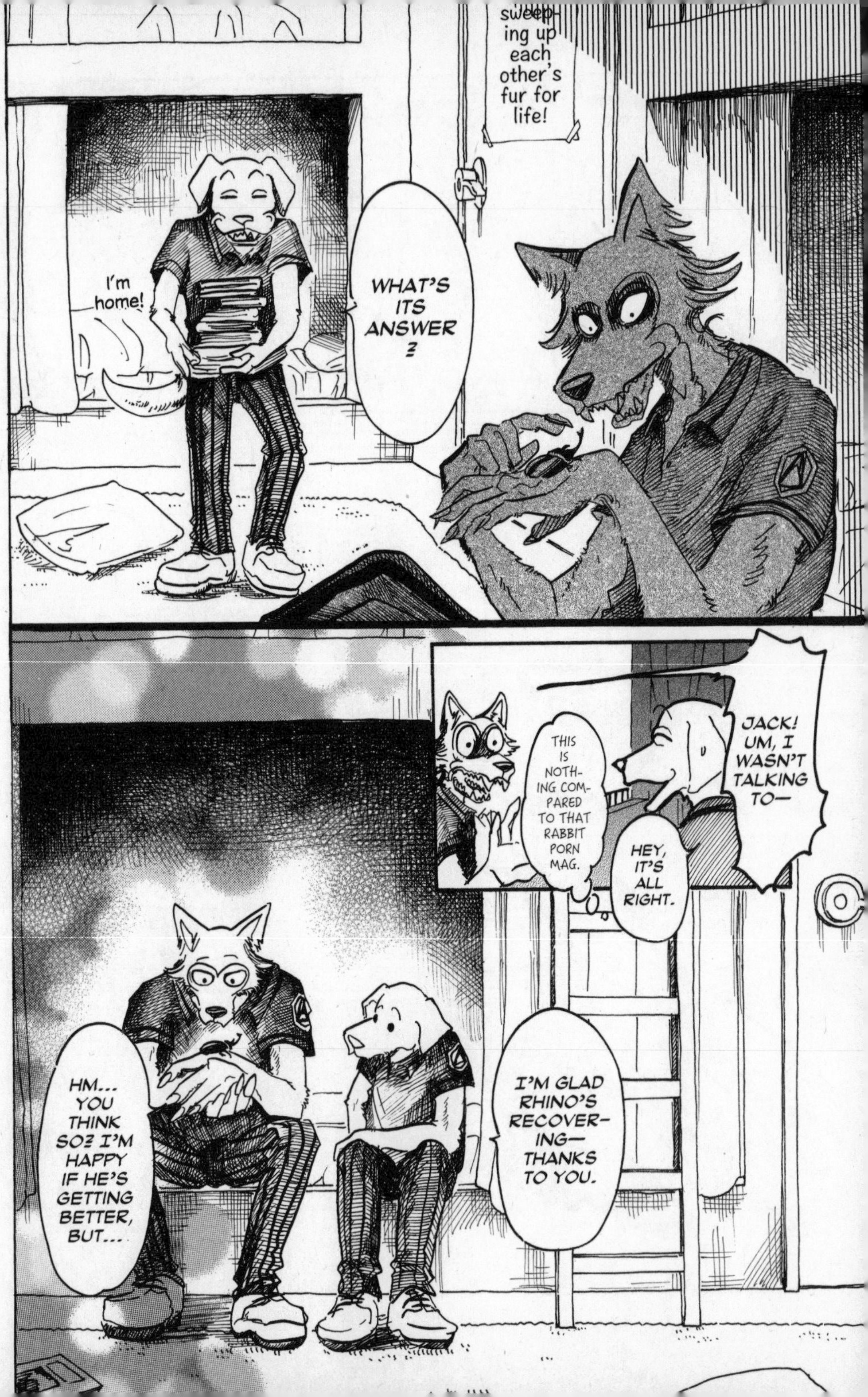
sweeping up each other's fur for life!
WHAT'S ITS ANSWER?
I'm home!
JACK! UM, I WASN'T TALKING TO—
HEY, IT'S ALL RIGHT.
THIS IS NOTHING COMPARED TO THAT RABBIT PORN MAG.
I'M GLAD RHINO'S RECOVERING—THANKS TO YOU.
HM... YOU THINK SO? I'M HAPPY IF HE'S GETTING BETTER, BUT...

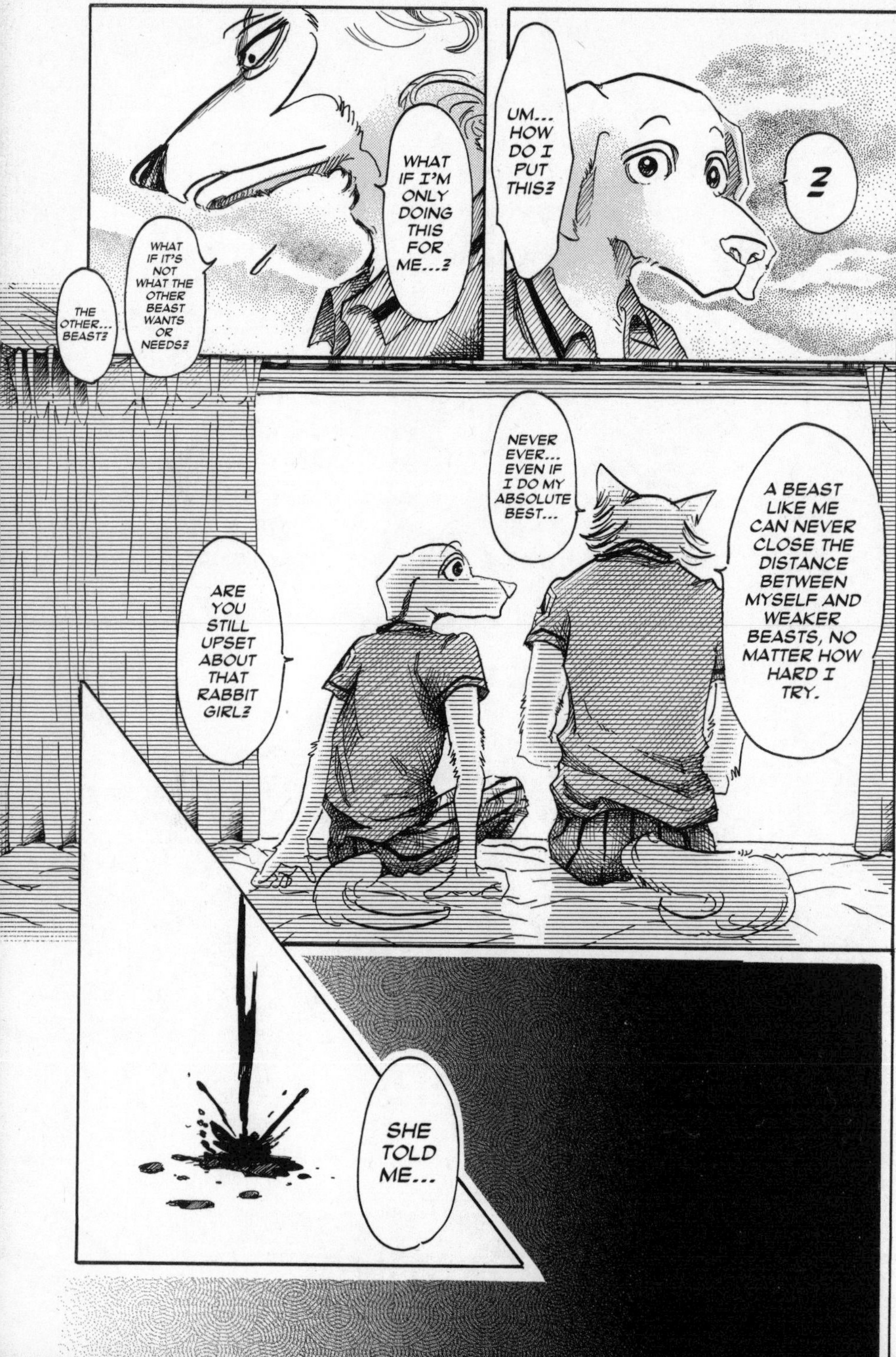
?
UM... HOW DO I PUT THIS?
WHAT IF I'M ONLY DOING THIS FOR ME...?
WHAT IF IT'S NOT WHAT THE OTHER BEAST WANTS OR NEEDS?
THE OTHER... BEAST?
A BEAST LIKE ME CAN NEVER CLOSE THE DISTANCE BETWEEN MYSELF AND WEAKER BEASTS, NO MATTER HOW HARD I TRY.
NEVER EVER... EVEN IF I DO MY ABSOLUTE BEST...
ARE YOU STILL UPSET ABOUT THAT RABBIT GIRL?
SHE TOLD ME...

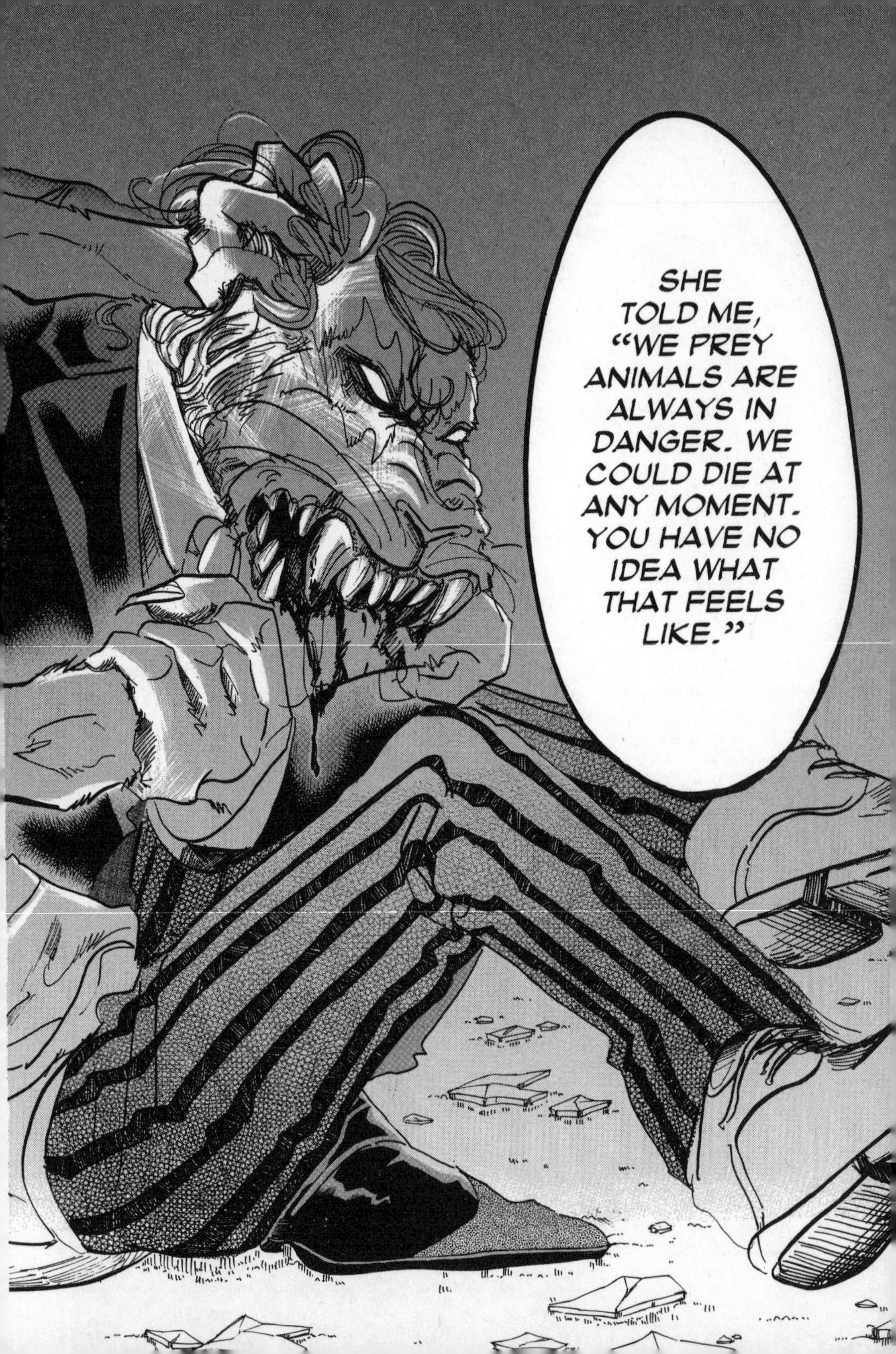
SHE TOLD ME, "WE PREY ANIMALS ARE ALWAYS IN DANGER. WE COULD DIE AT ANY MOMENT. YOU HAVE NO IDEA WHAT THAT FEELS LIKE."

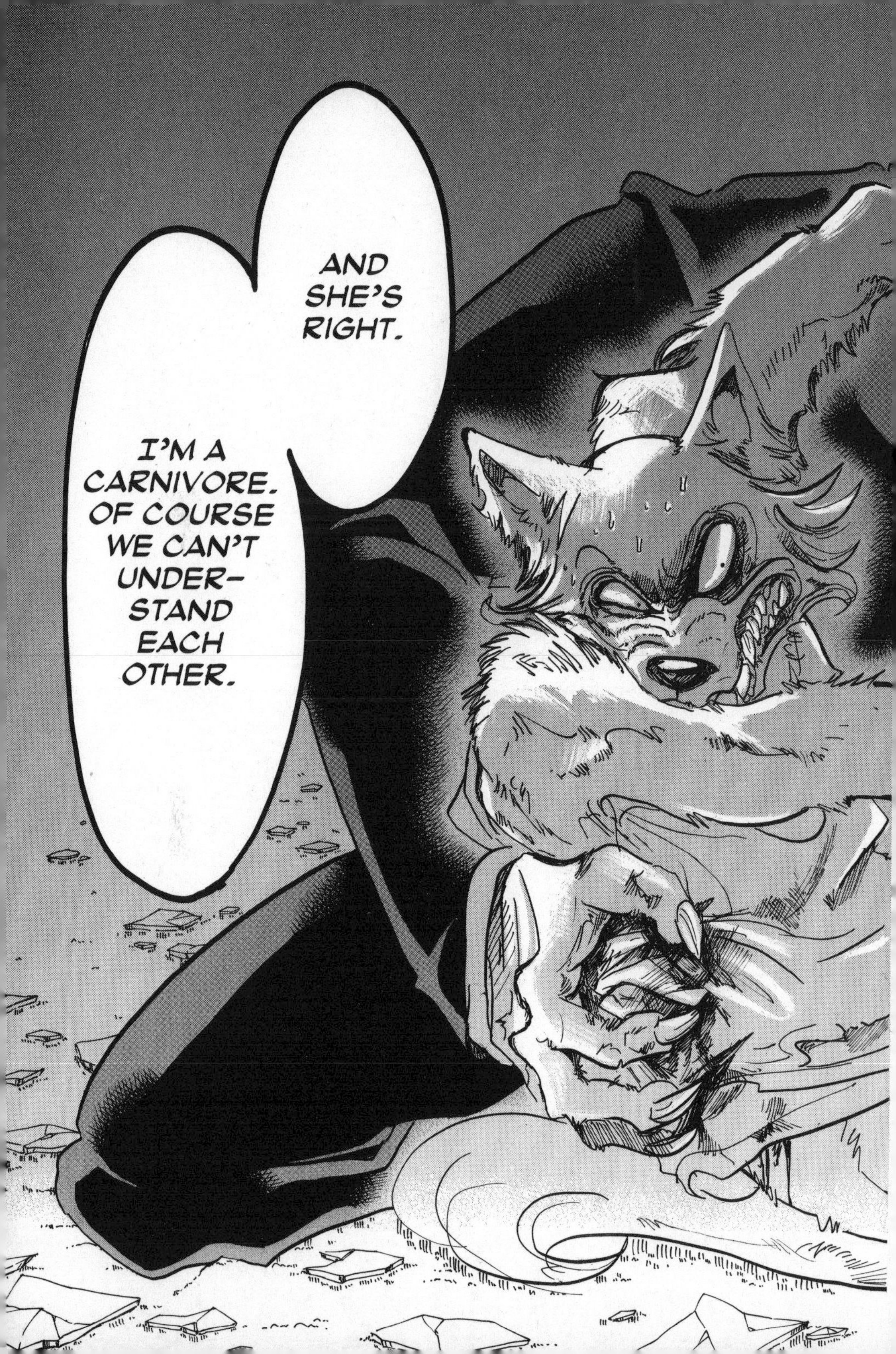
AND SHE'S RIGHT.
I'M A CARNIVORE. OF COURSE WE CAN'T UNDER-STAND EACH OTHER.

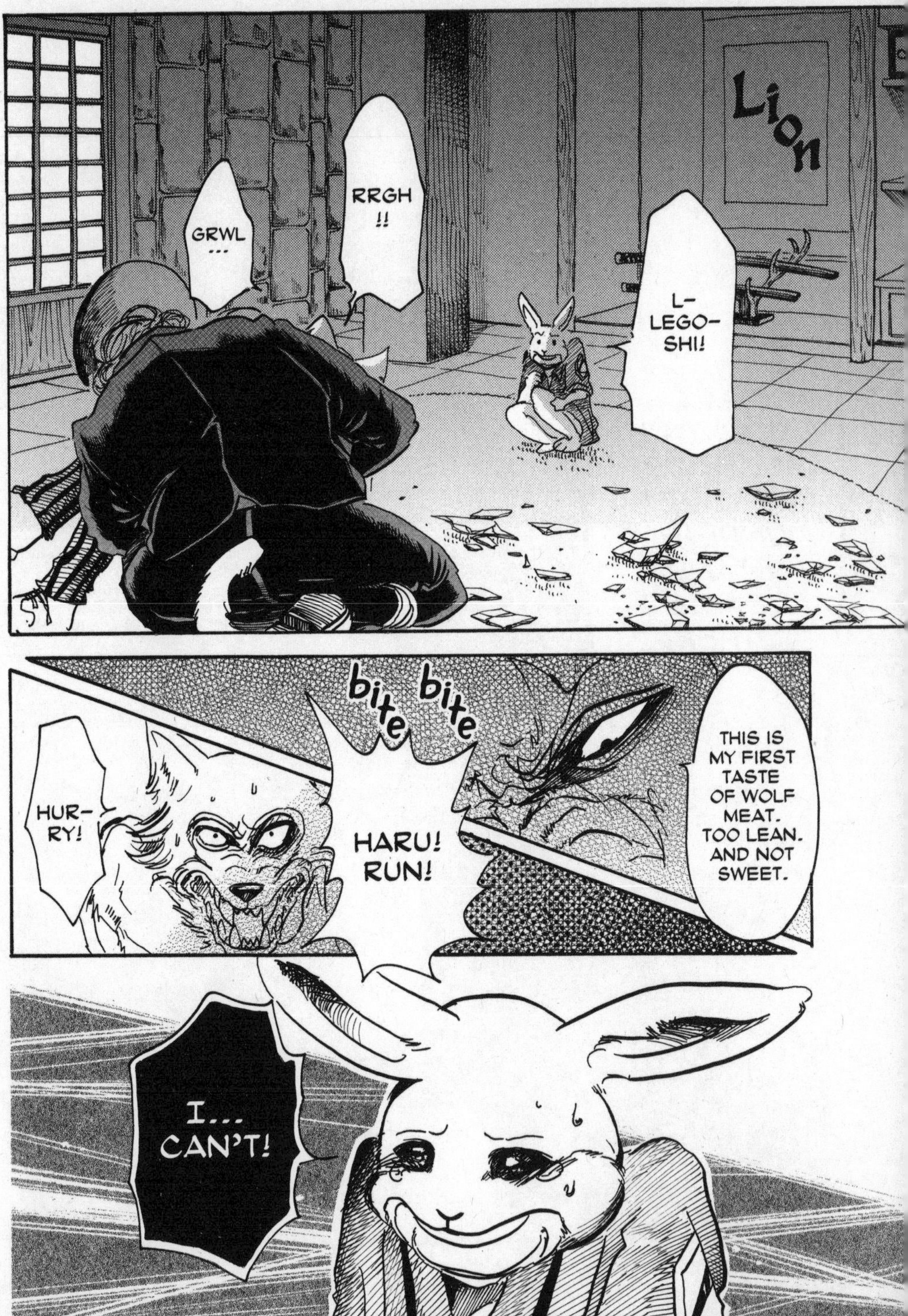
Lion
L-LEGO-SHI!
RRGH!!
GRWL...
THIS IS MY FIRST TASTE OF WOLF MEAT. TOO LEAN. AND NOT SWEET.
bite bite
HARU! RUN!
HUR-RY!
I... CAN'T!

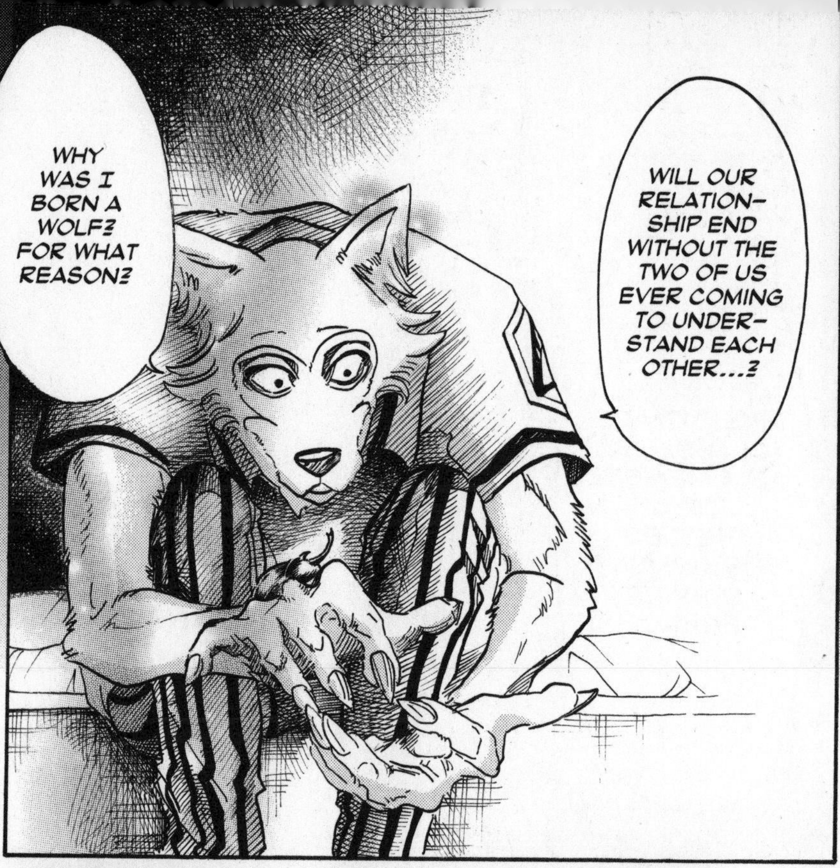
WILL OUR RELATIONSHIP END WITHOUT THE TWO OF US EVER COMING TO UNDERSTAND EACH OTHER...?
WHY WAS I BORN A WOLF? FOR WHAT REASON?

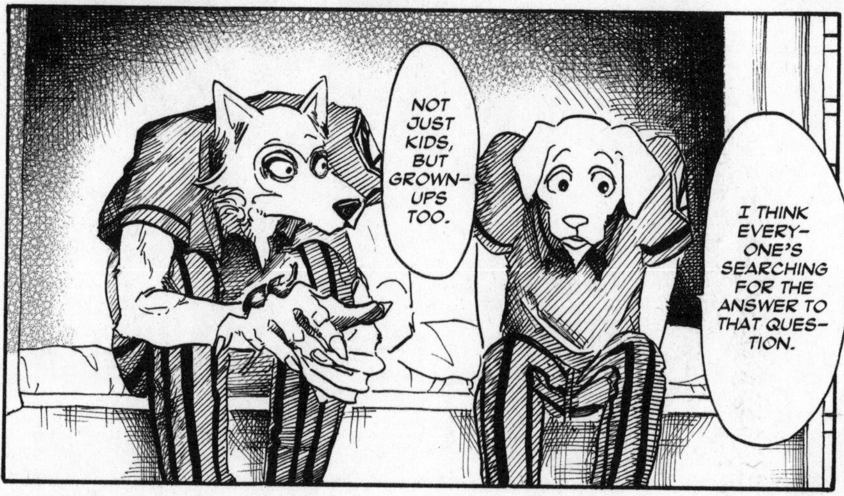
I THINK EVERYONE'S SEARCHING FOR THE ANSWER TO THAT QUESTION.
NOT JUST KIDS, BUT GROWN-UPS TOO.

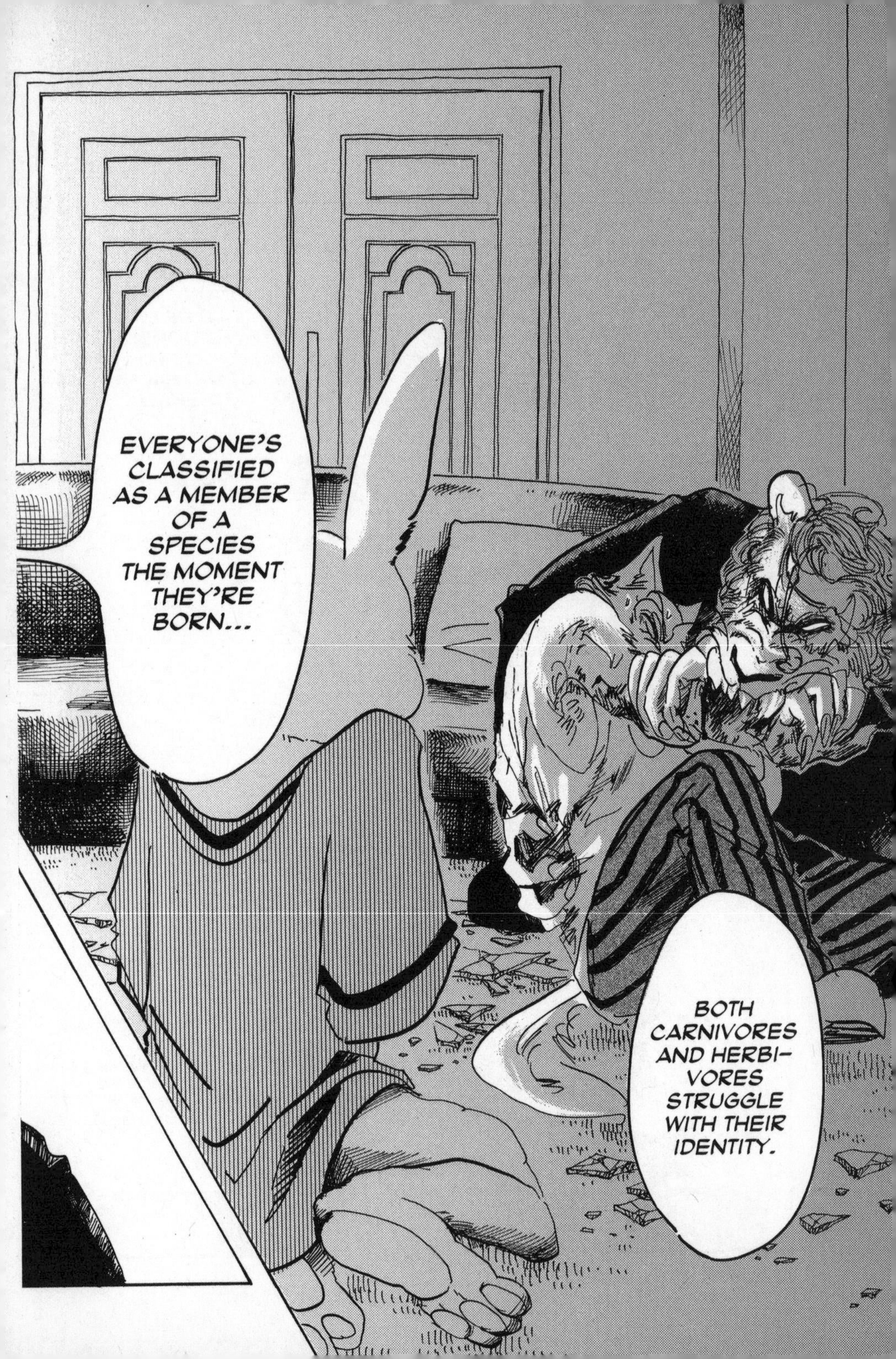
EVERYONE'S CLASSIFIED AS A MEMBER OF A SPECIES THE MOMENT THEY'RE BORN...
BOTH CARNIVORES AND HERBI-VORES STRUGGLE WITH THEIR IDENTITY.

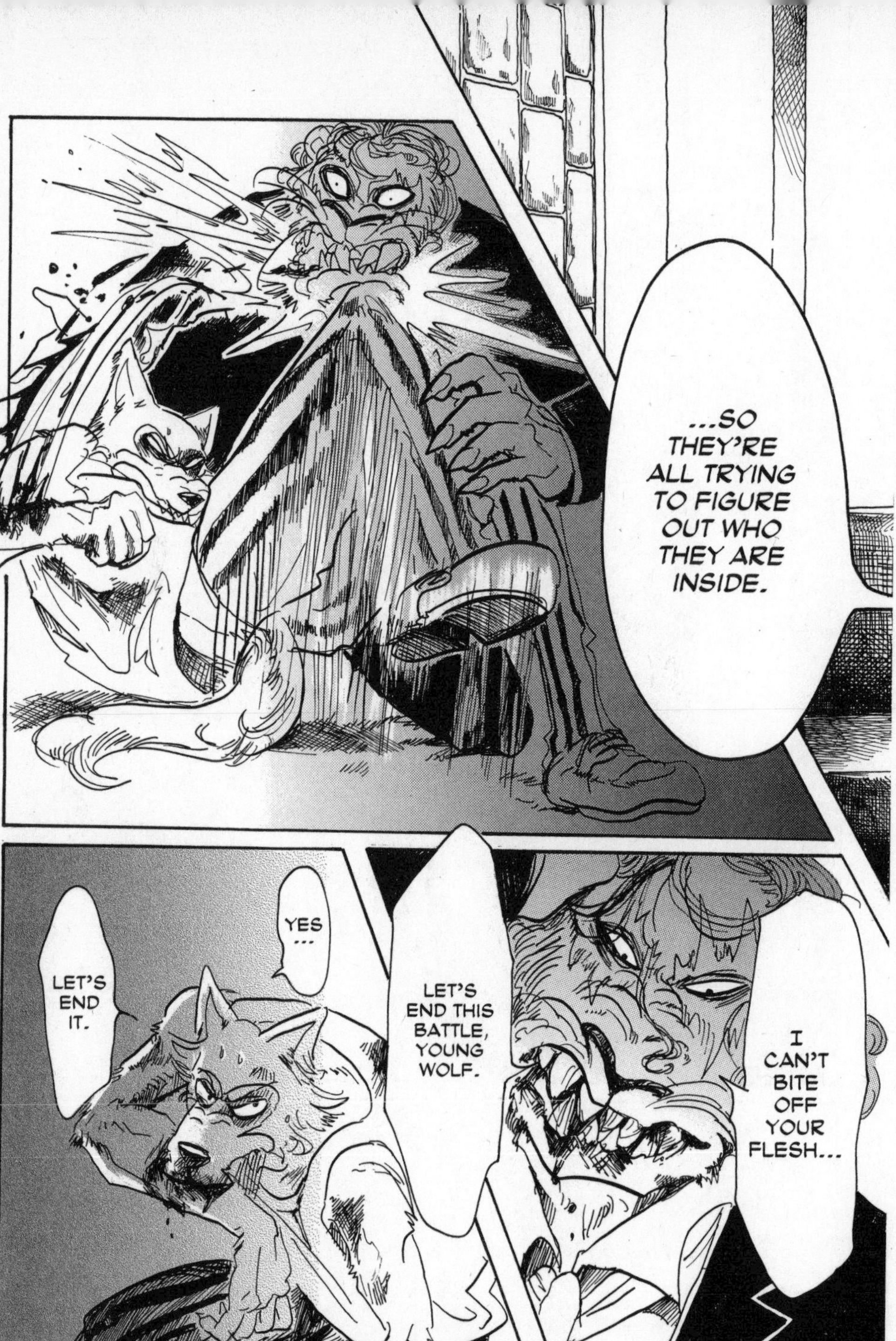
...SO THEY'RE ALL TRYING TO FIGURE OUT WHO THEY ARE INSIDE.
I CAN'T BITE OFF YOUR FLESH...
LET'S END THIS BATTLE, YOUNG WOLF.
YES...
LET'S END IT.

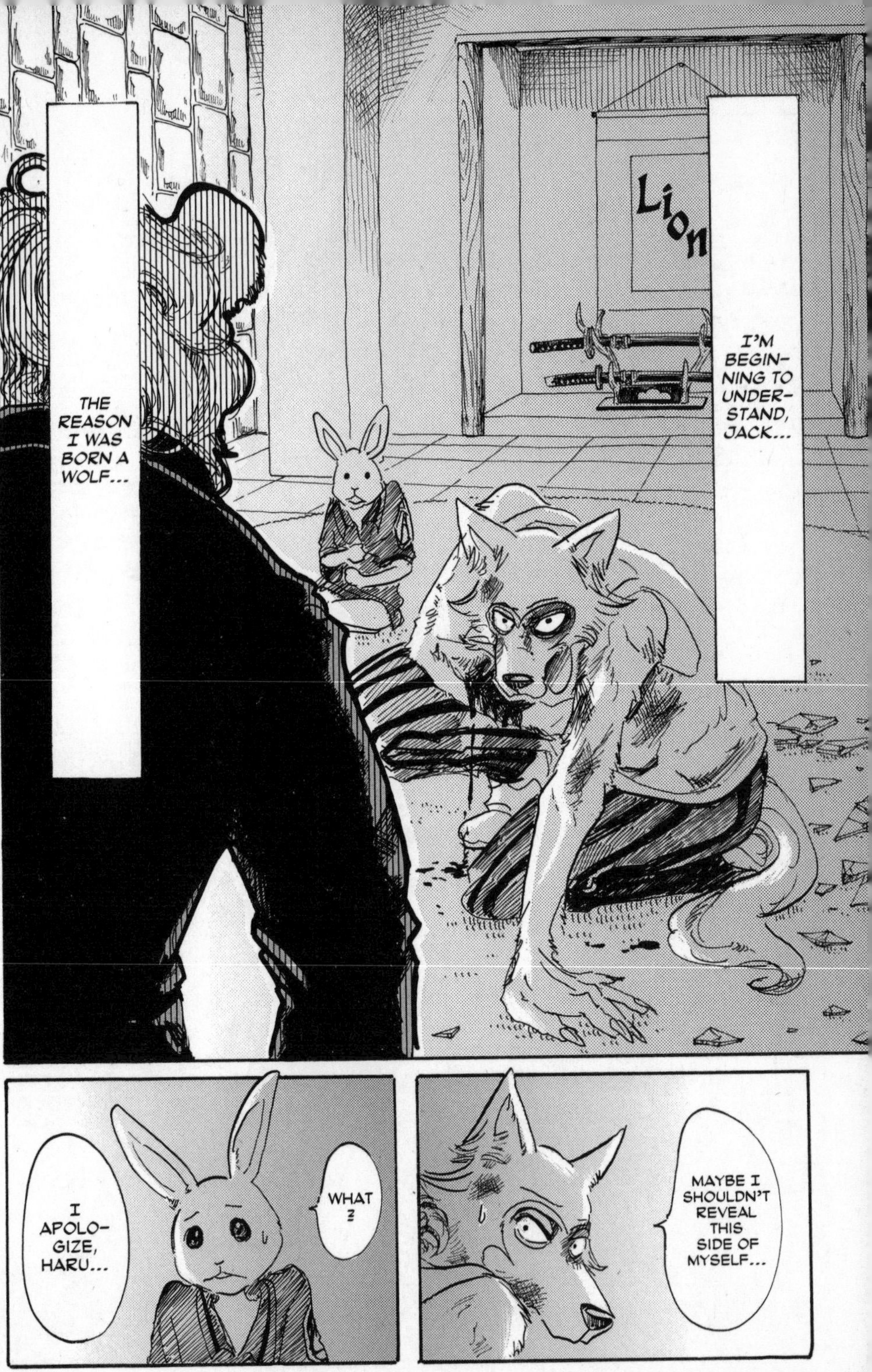

I'M BEGINNING TO UNDERSTAND, JACK...
Lion
THE REASON I WAS BORN A WOLF...
MAYBE I SHOULDN'T REVEAL THIS SIDE OF MYSELF...
WHAT?
I APOLOGIZE, HARU...

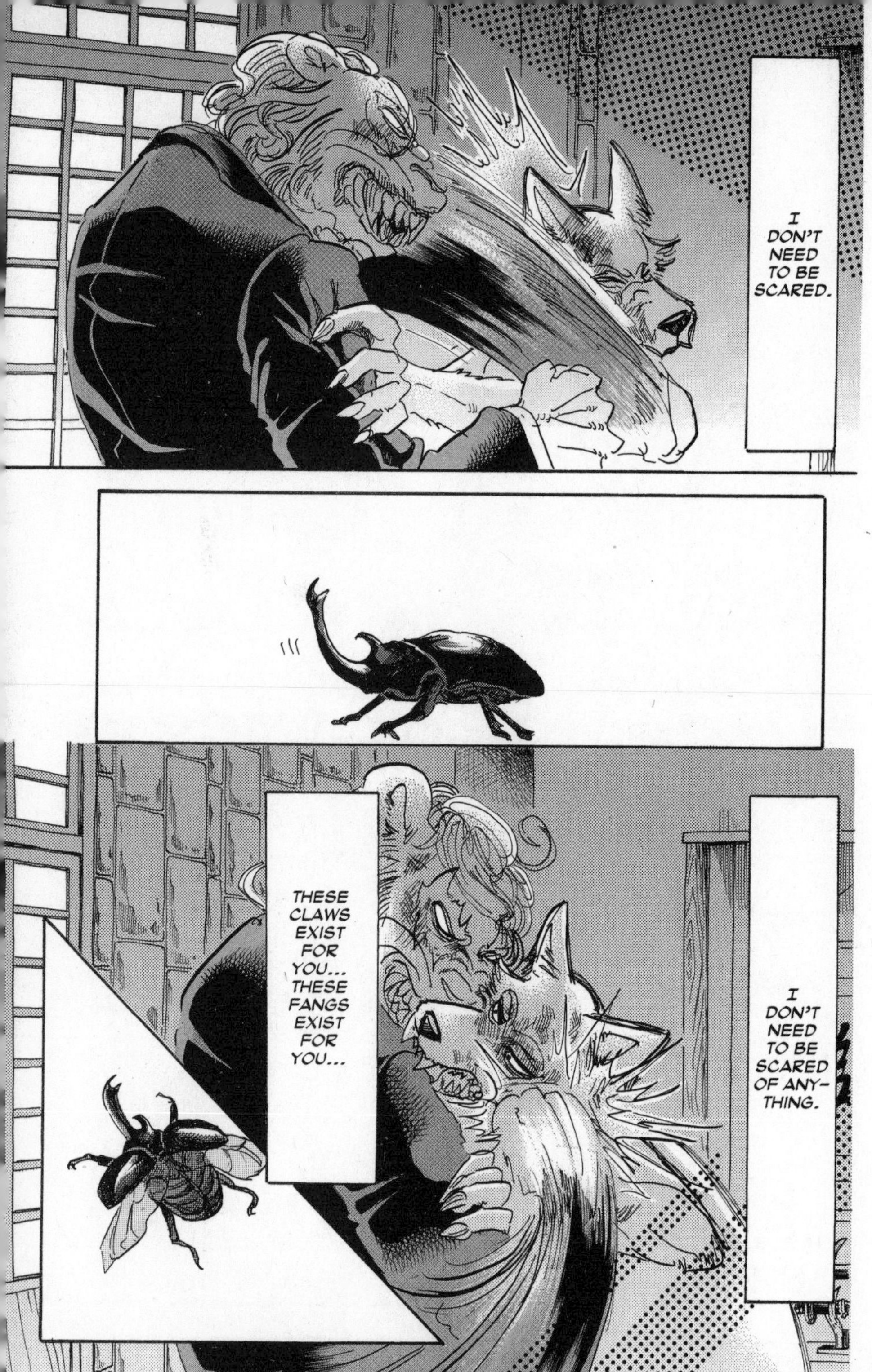
I DON'T NEED TO BE SCARED.
I DON'T NEED TO BE SCARED OF ANYTHING.
THESE CLAWS EXIST FOR YOU... THESE FANGS EXIST FOR YOU...

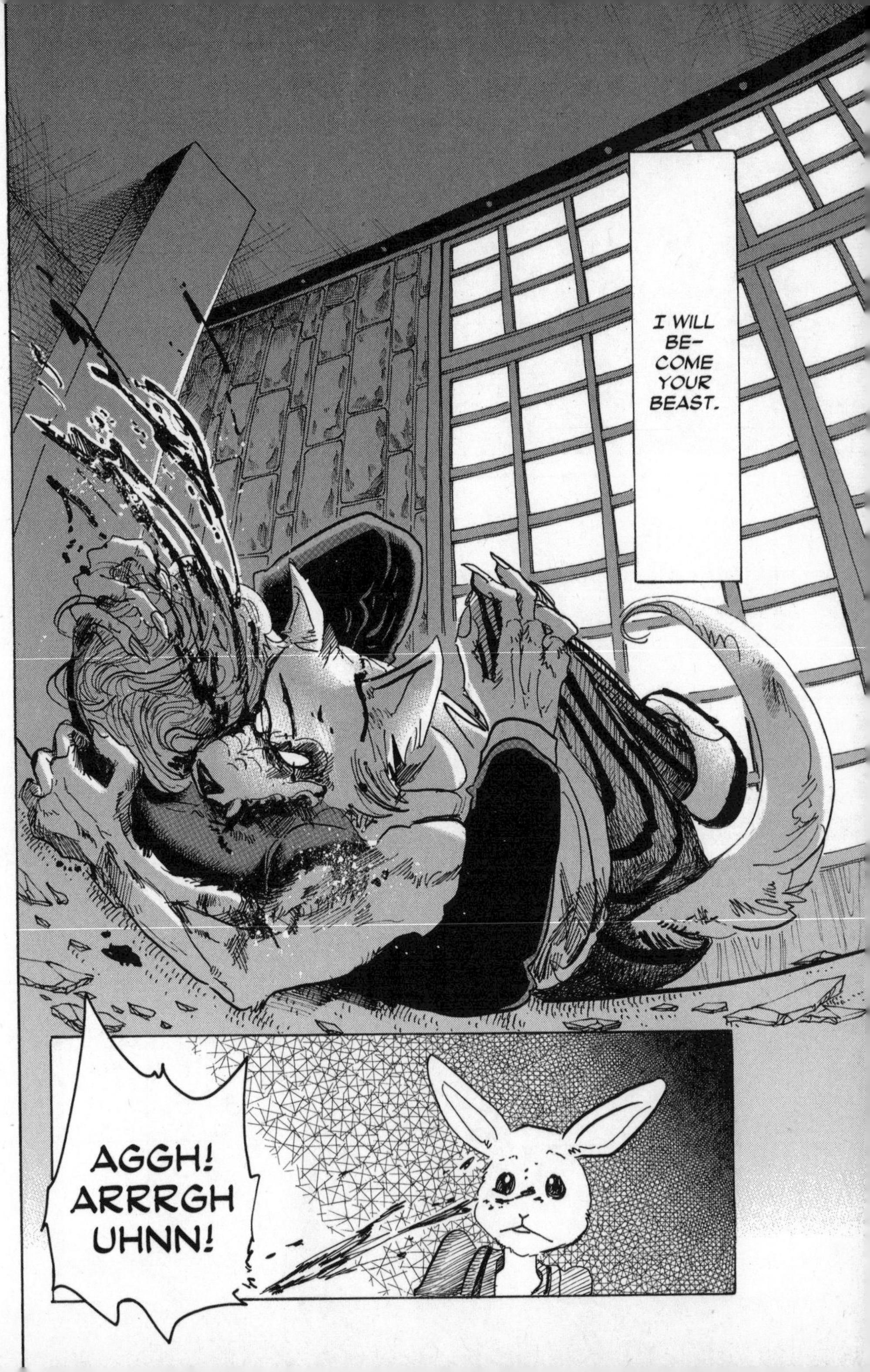
I WILL BE-COME YOUR BEAST.
AGGH! ARRRGH UHNN!

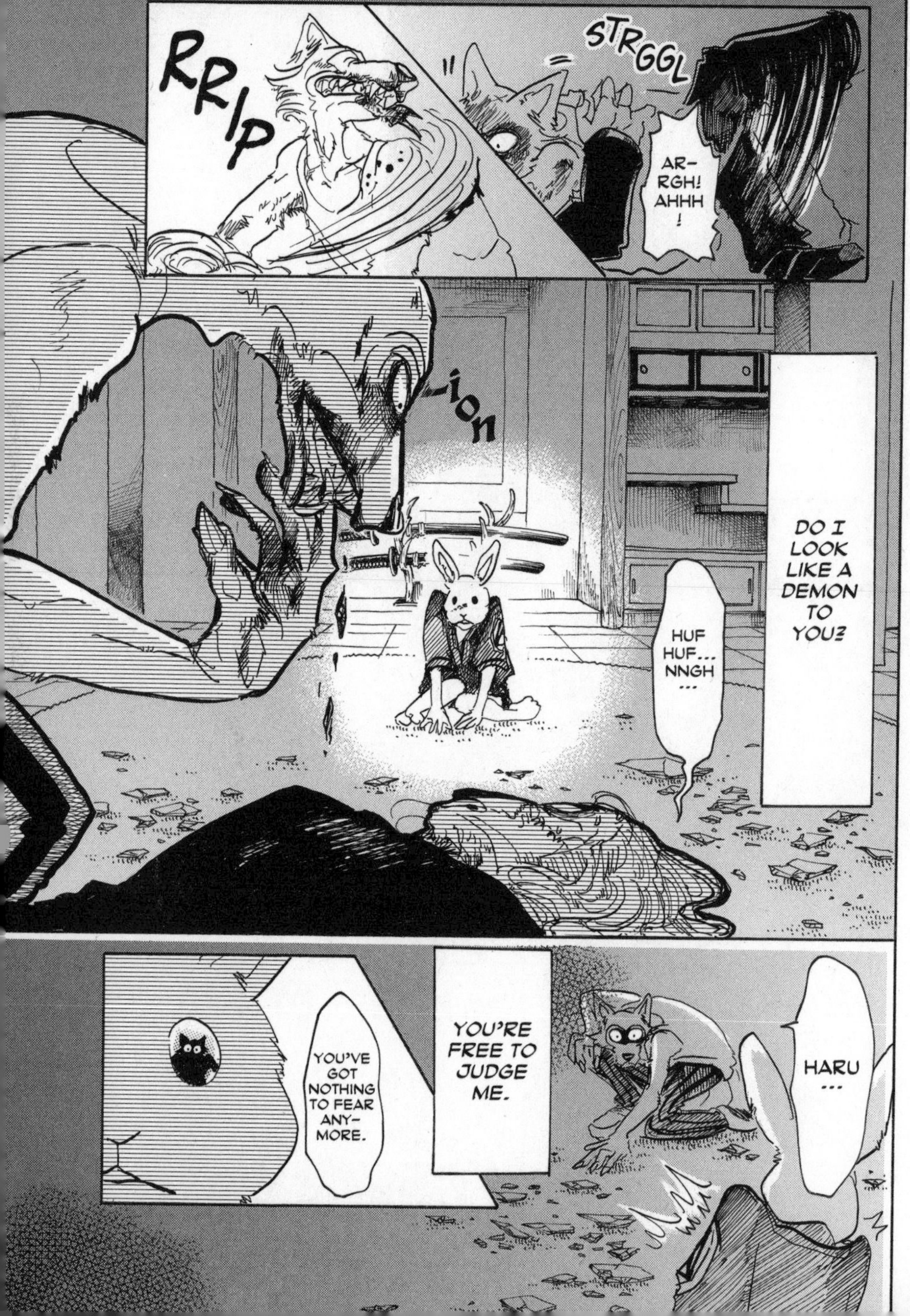
STRGGL
ARRGH! AHHH!
RRIP
DO I LOOK LIKE A DEMON TO YOU?
HUF HUF... NNGH...
-ion
HARU...
YOU'RE FREE TO JUDGE ME.
YOU'VE GOT NOTHING TO FEAR ANYMORE.

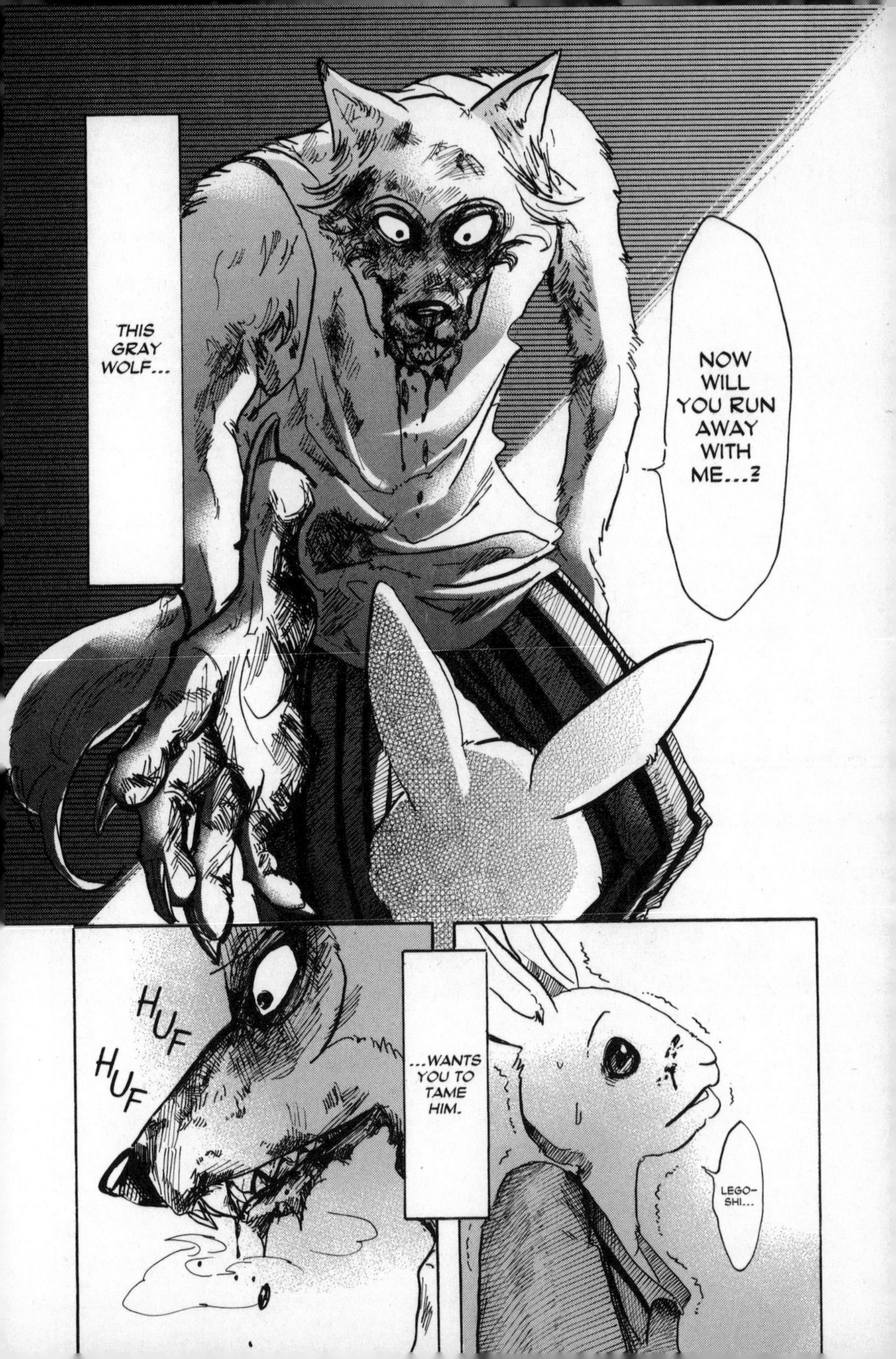
NOW WILL YOU RUN AWAY WITH ME...?
THIS GRAY WOLF...
LEGO-SHI...
...WANTS YOU TO TAME HIM.
HUF HUF

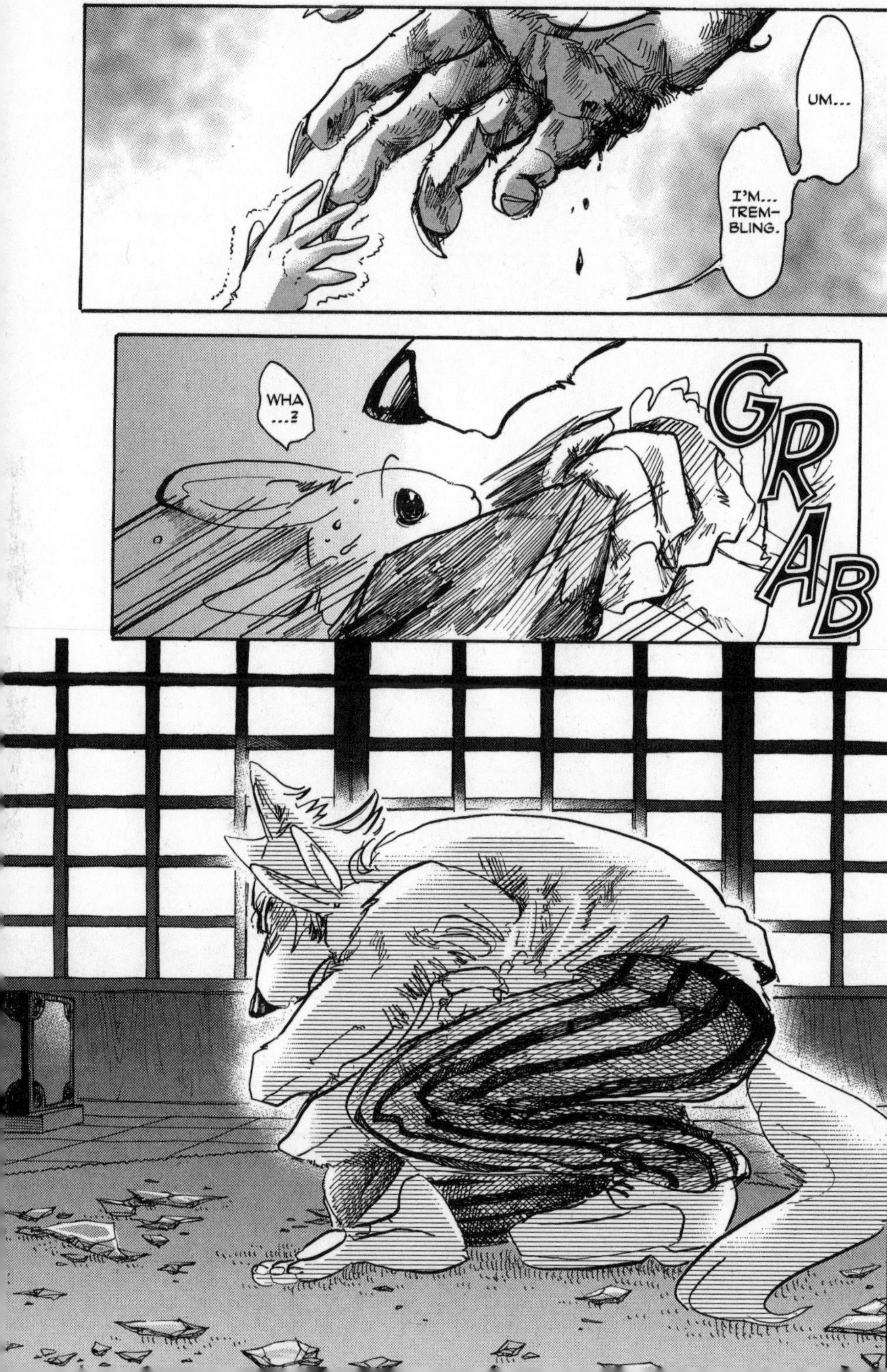
UM...
I'M... TREM-BLING.
GRAB
WHA...?

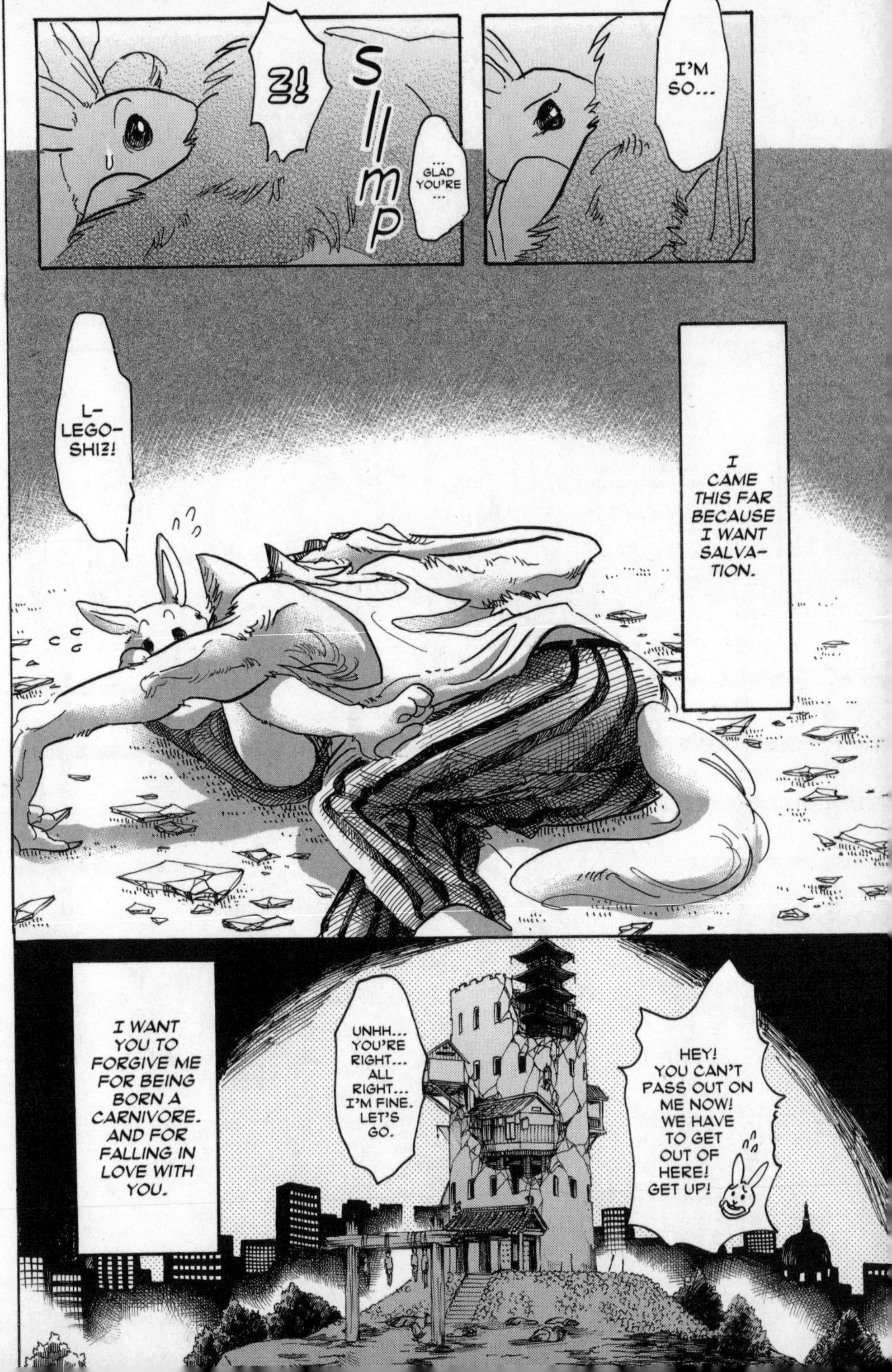
I'M SO...
...GLAD YOU'RE ...
SLIMP
!?
I CAME THIS FAR BECAUSE I WANT SALVATION.
L-LEGOSHI!?
HEY! YOU CAN'T PASS OUT ON ME NOW! WE HAVE TO GET OUT OF HERE! GET UP!
UNHH... YOU'RE RIGHT... ALL RIGHT... I'M FINE. LET'S GO.
I WANT YOU TO FORGIVE ME FOR BEING BORN A CARNIVORE. AND FOR FALLING IN LOVE WITH YOU.

Chapter 42: The Two of Us in This Intense Night

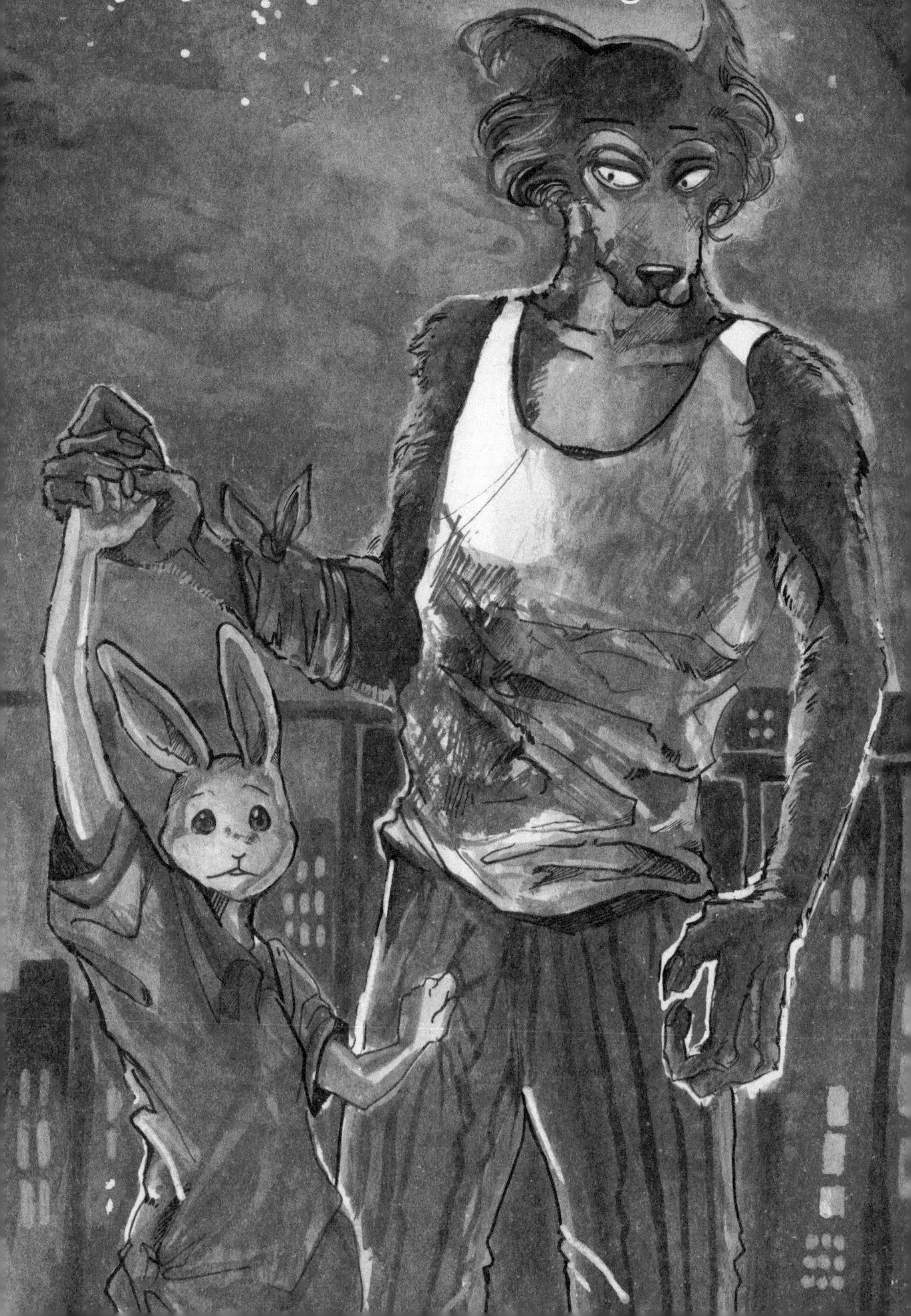

BEASTARS
Vol. 5

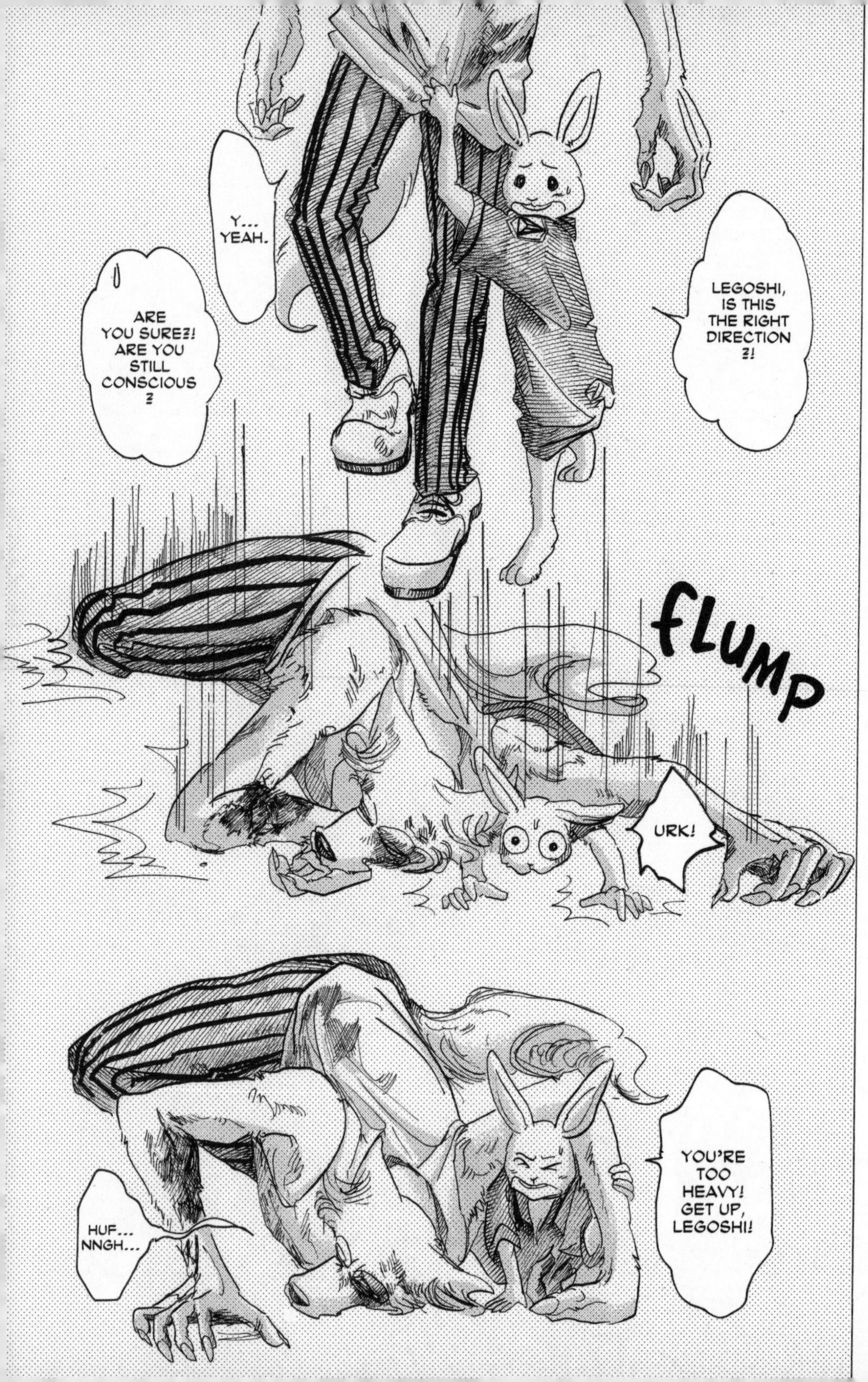
LEGOSHI, IS THIS THE RIGHT DIRECTION ?!
Y... YEAH.
ARE YOU SURE?! ARE YOU STILL CONSCIOUS ?
FLUMP
URK!
YOU'RE TOO HEAVY! GET UP, LEGOSHI!
HUF... NNGH...

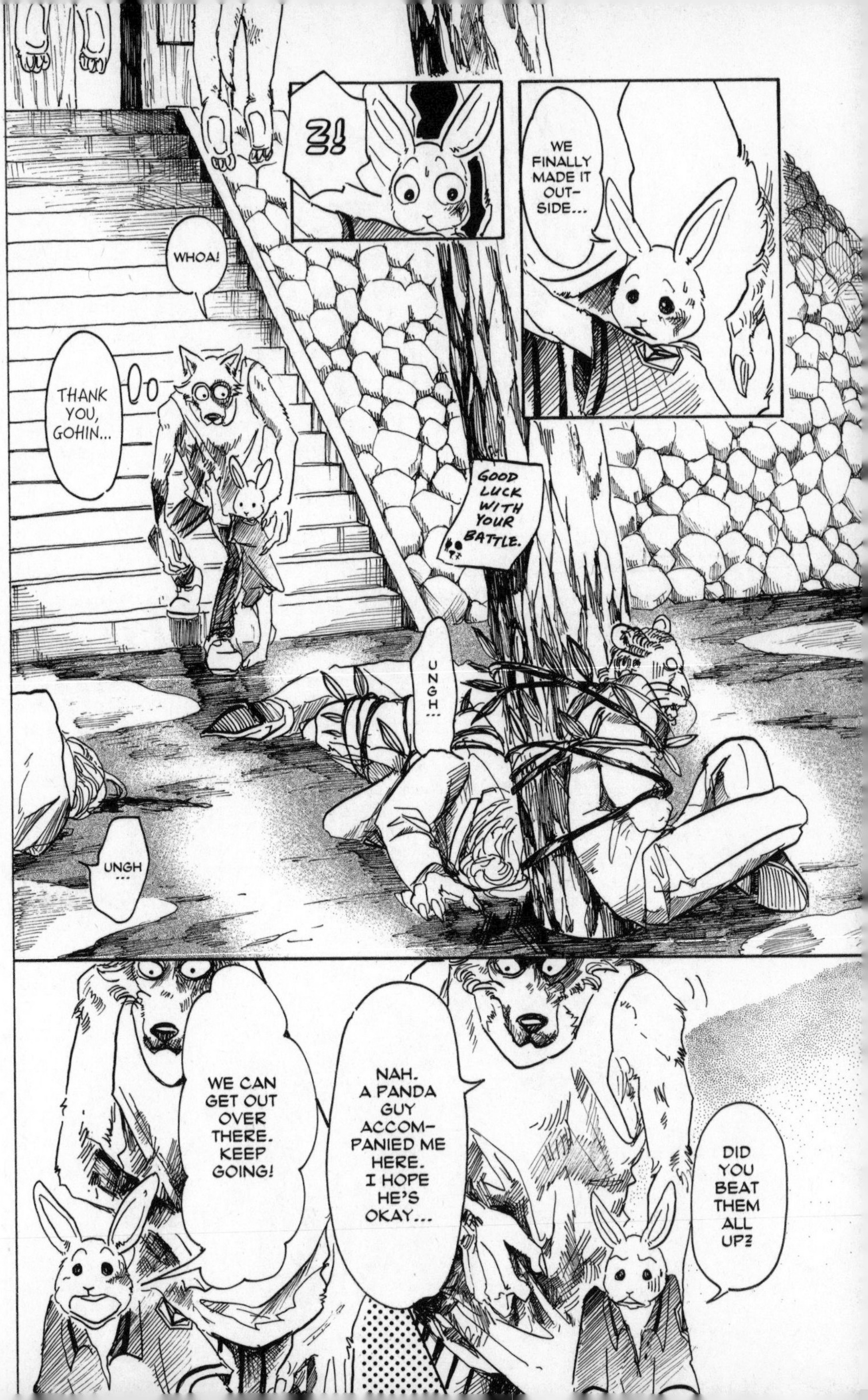
WE FINALLY MADE IT OUT-SIDE...
Z!
WHOA!
THANK YOU, GOHIN...
GOOD LUCK WITH YOUR BATTLE.
UNGH...
UNGH...
DID YOU BEAT THEM ALL UP?
NAH. A PANDA GUY ACCOM-PANIED ME HERE. I HOPE HE'S OKAY...
WE CAN GET OUT OVER THERE. KEEP GOING!

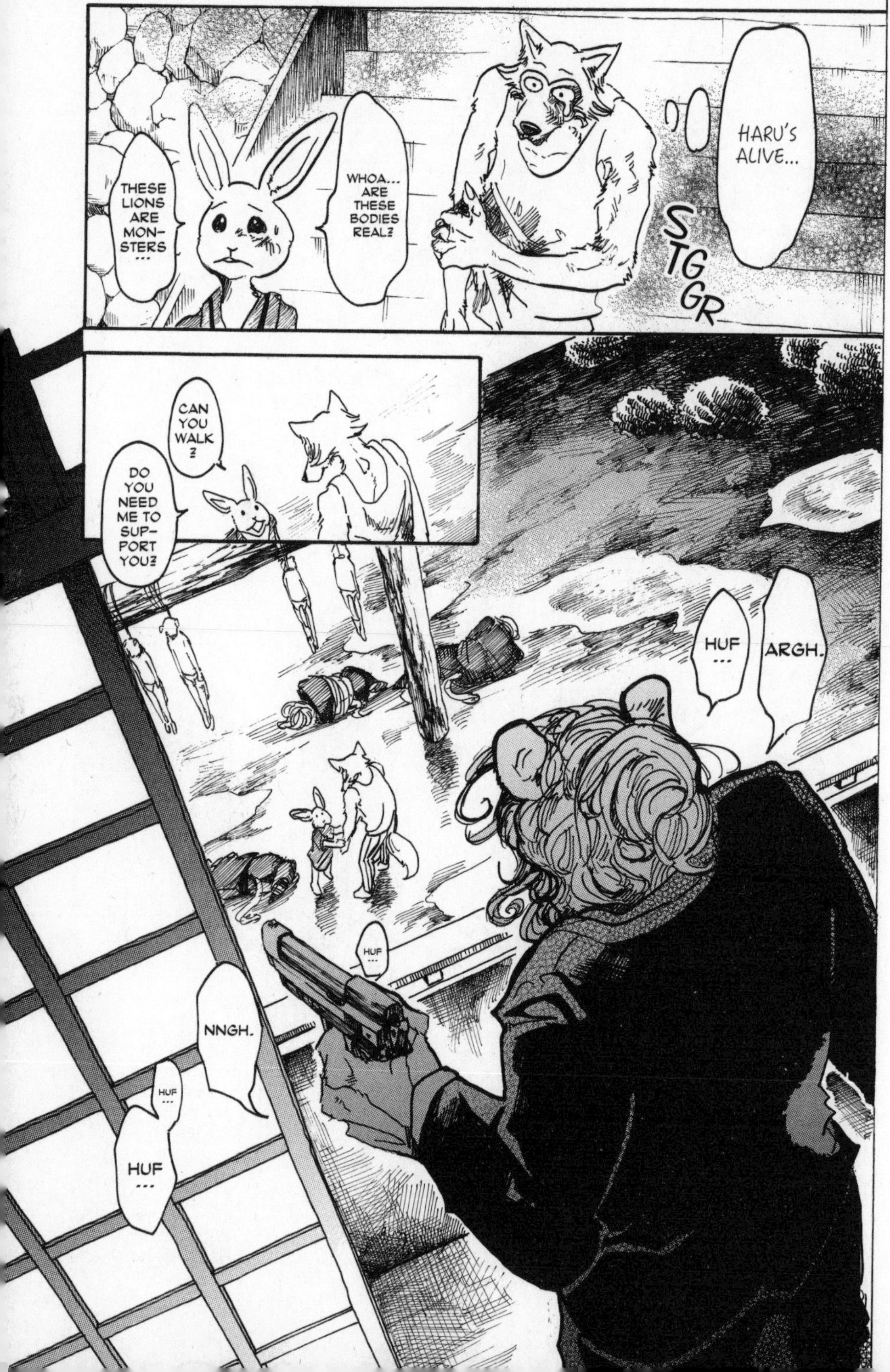
HARU'S ALIVE...
STGGR
WHOA... ARE THESE BODIES REAL?
THESE LIONS ARE MONSTERS...
CAN YOU WALK?
DO YOU NEED ME TO SUPPORT YOU?
ARGH.
HUF...
HUF...
NNGH.
HUF...
HUF...

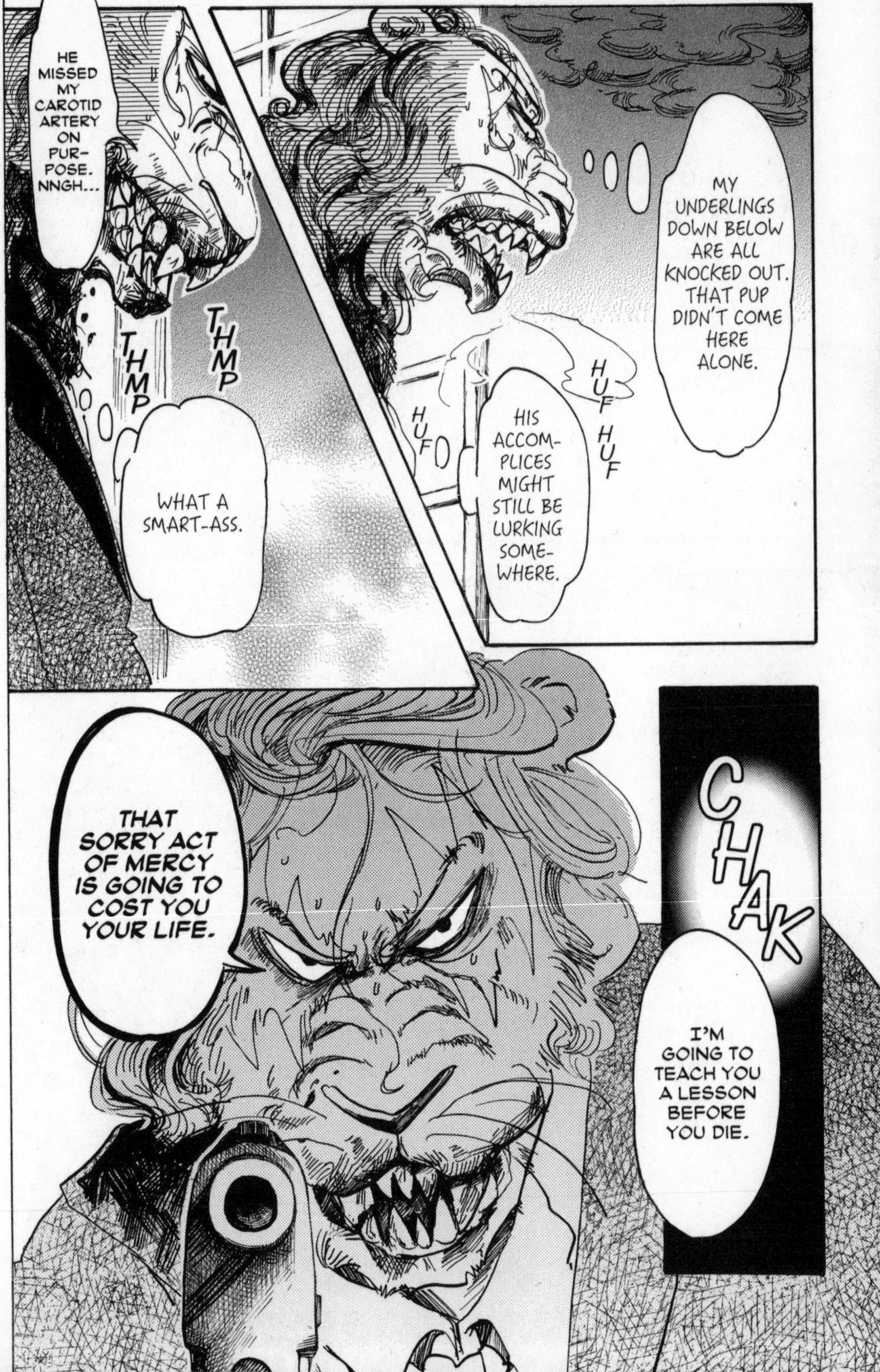
MY UNDERLINGS DOWN BELOW ARE ALL KNOCKED OUT. THAT PUP DIDN'T COME HERE ALONE.
HUF HUF
HUF HUF
HIS ACCOMPLICES MIGHT STILL BE LURKING SOMEWHERE.
HE MISSED MY CAROTID ARTERY ON PURPOSE. NNGH...
THMP THMP
WHAT A SMART-ASS.
CHAK
I'M GOING TO TEACH YOU A LESSON BEFORE YOU DIE.
THAT SORRY ACT OF MERCY IS GOING TO COST YOU YOUR LIFE.

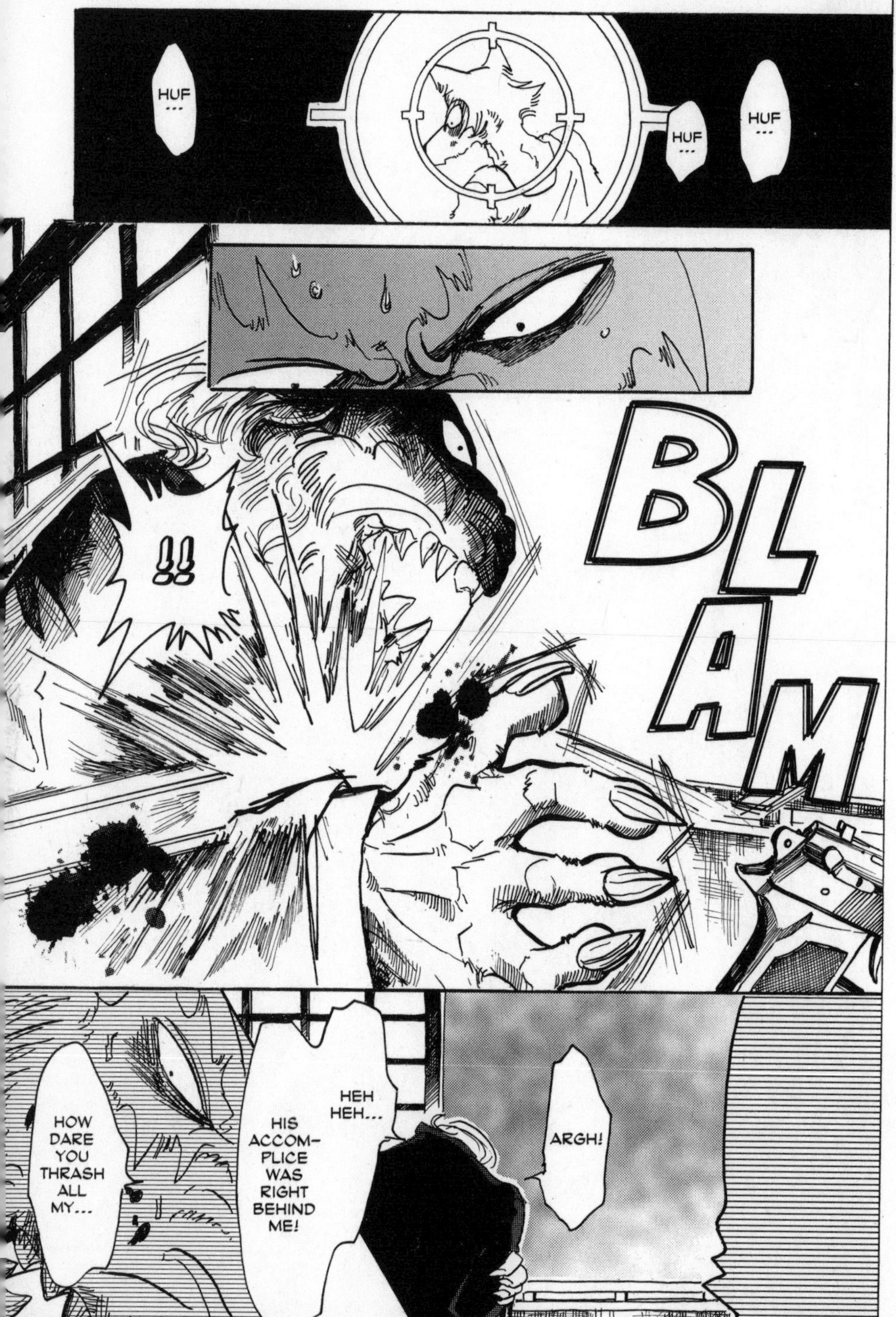
HUF...
HUF...
HUF...
BLAM
!!
ARGH!
HEH HEH...
HIS ACCOMPLICE WAS RIGHT BEHIND ME!
HOW DARE YOU THRASH ALL MY...

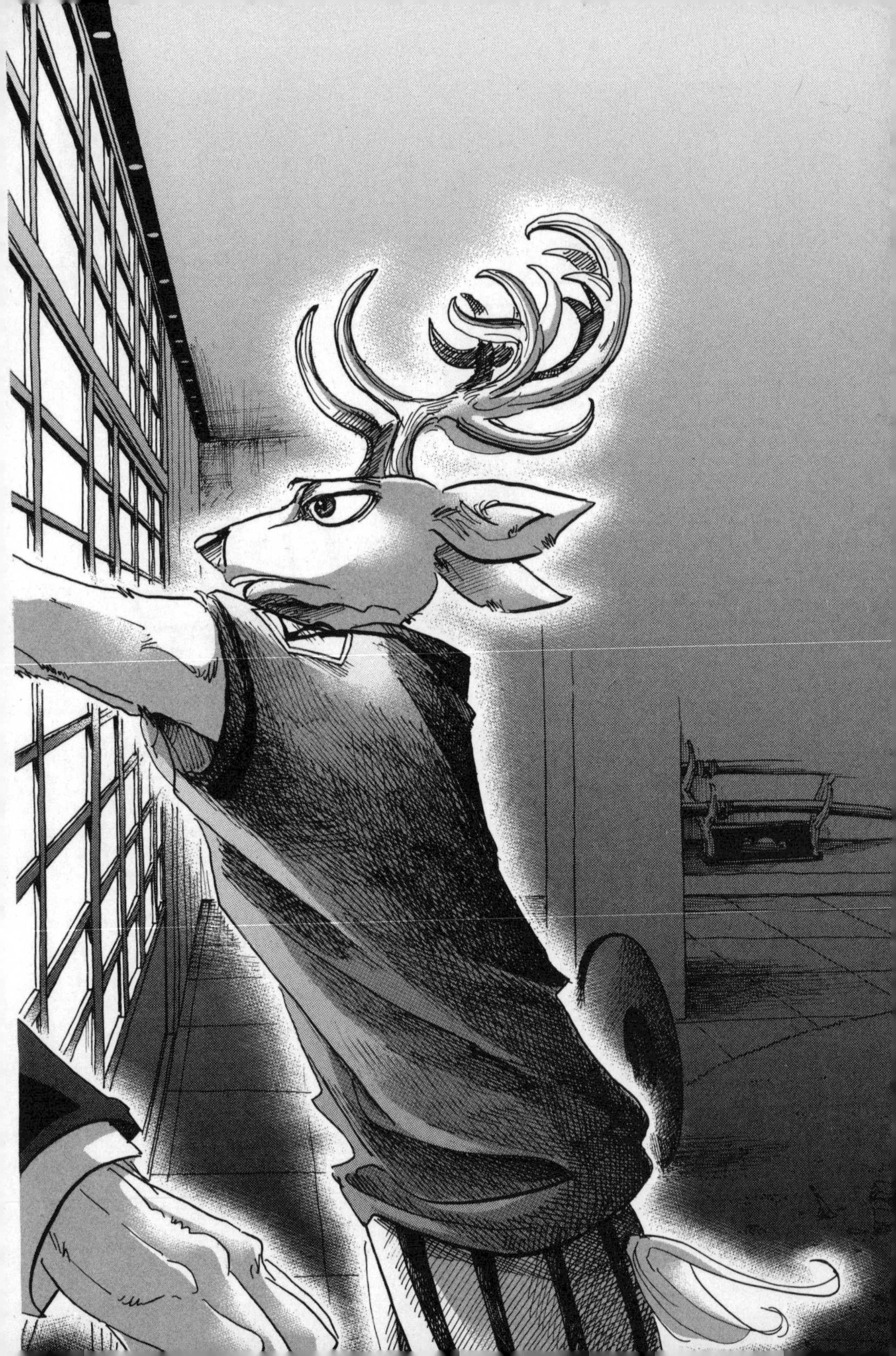

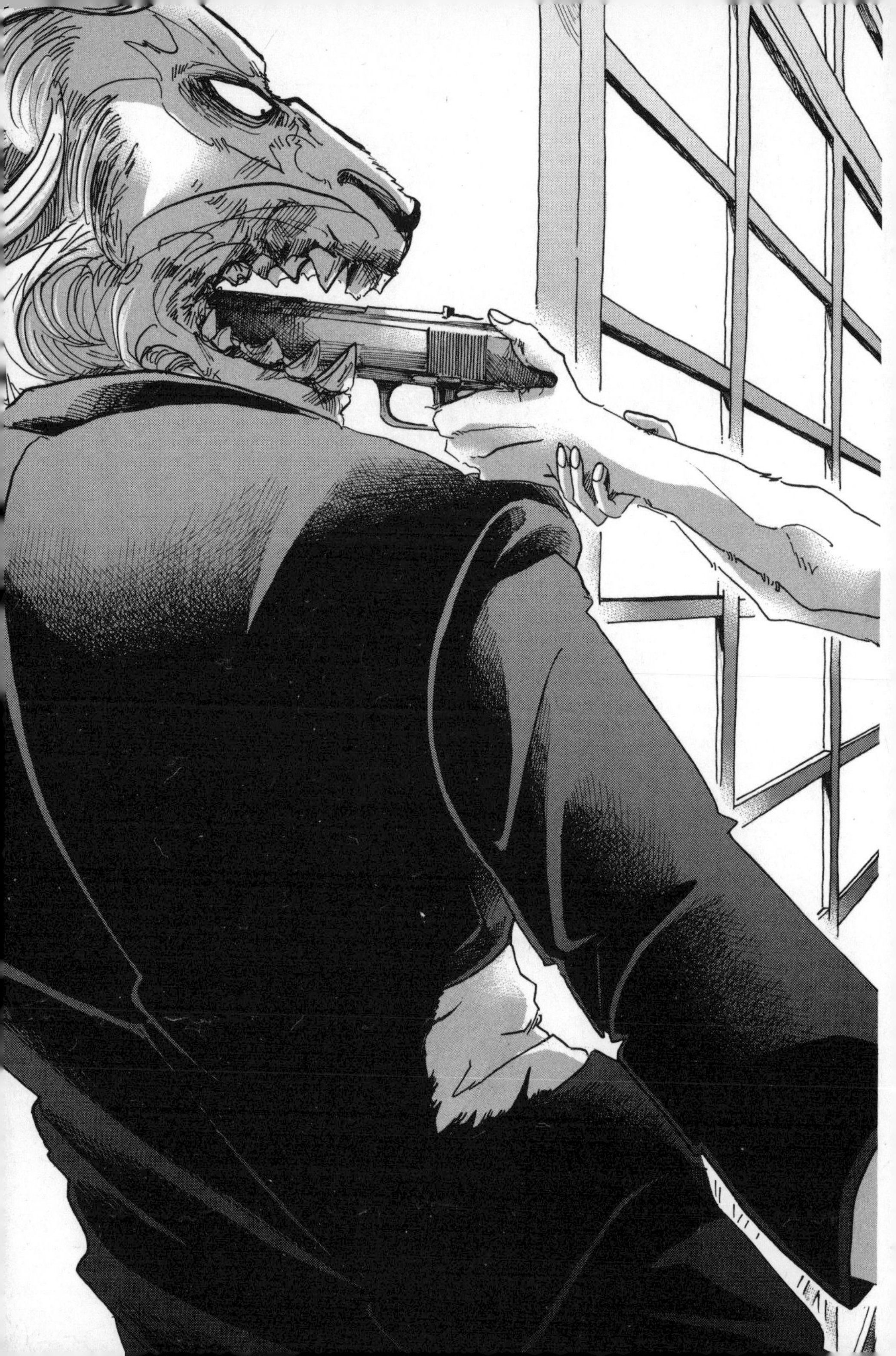

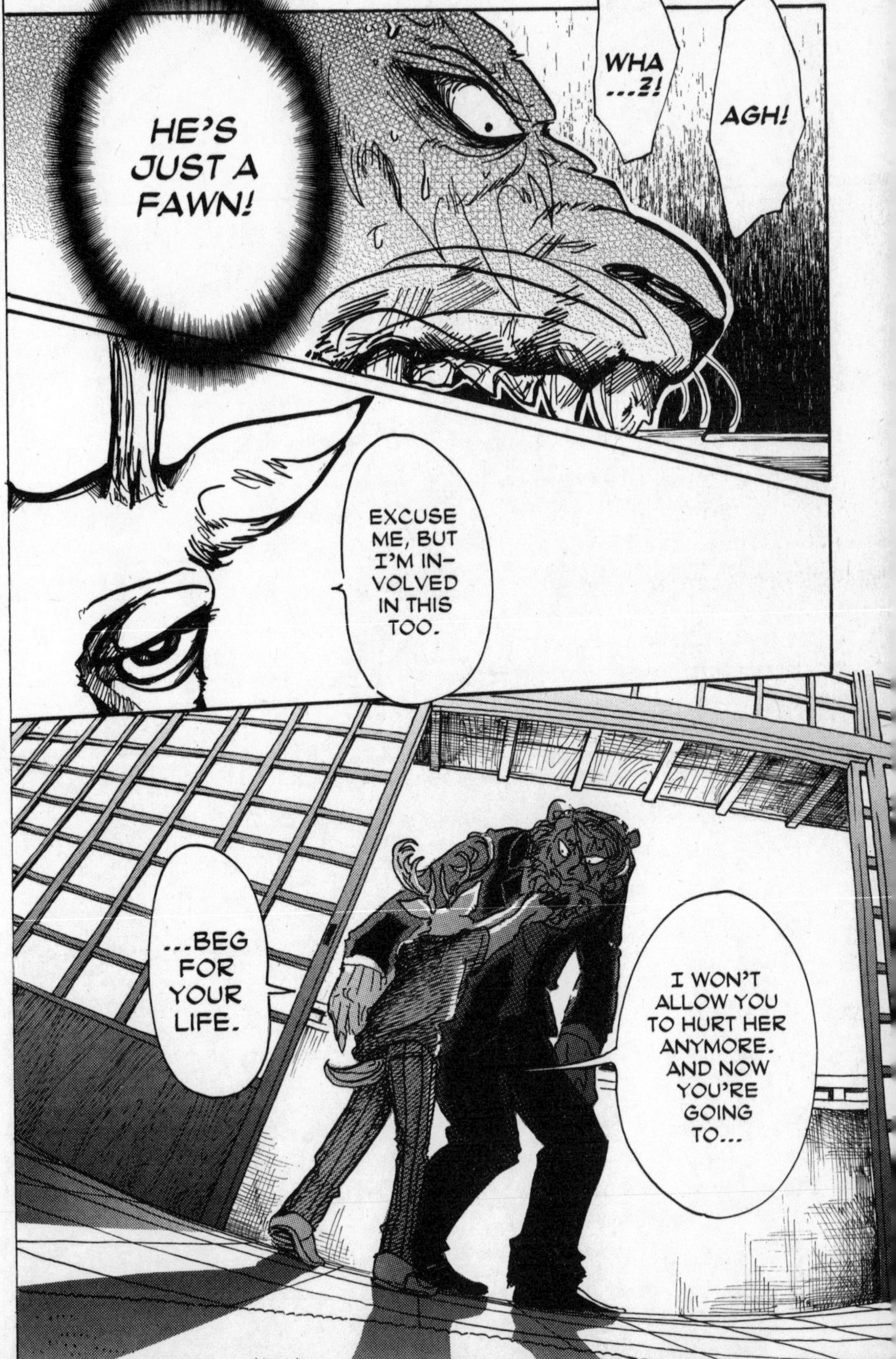
AGH!
WHA ...?!
HE'S JUST A FAWN!
EXCUSE ME, BUT I'M IN-VOLVED IN THIS TOO.
I WON'T ALLOW YOU TO HURT HER ANYMORE. AND NOW YOU'RE GOING TO...
...BEG FOR YOUR LIFE.

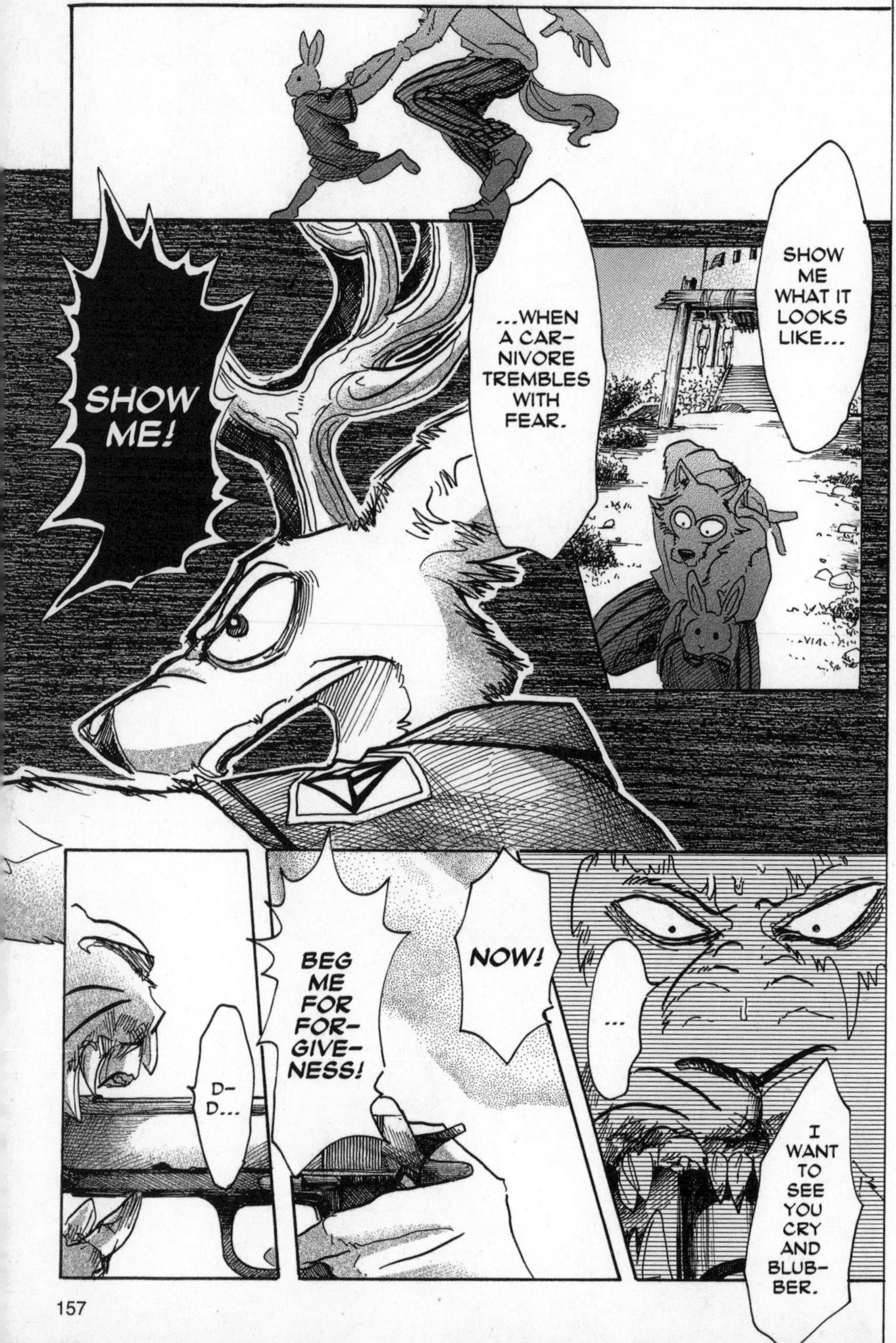
SHOW ME WHAT IT LOOKS LIKE...
...WHEN A CARNIVORE TREMBLES WITH FEAR.
SHOW ME!
...
I WANT TO SEE YOU CRY AND BLUBBER.
NOW!
BEG ME FOR FORGIVENESS!
D- D...

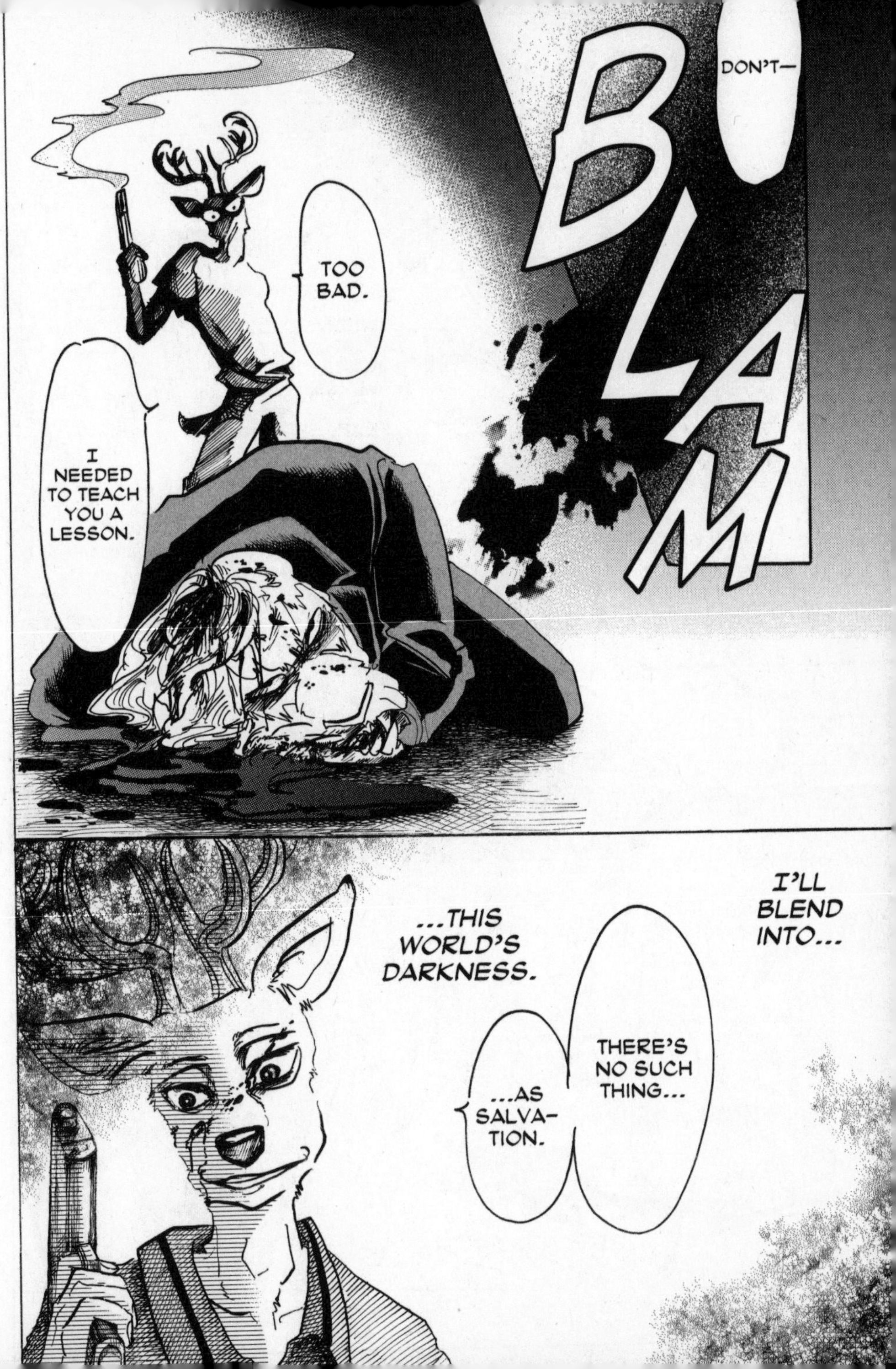
DON'T—
BLAM
TOO BAD.
I NEEDED TO TEACH YOU A LESSON.
I'LL BLEND INTO...
...THIS WORLD'S DARKNESS.
THERE'S NO SUCH THING...
...AS SALVATION.

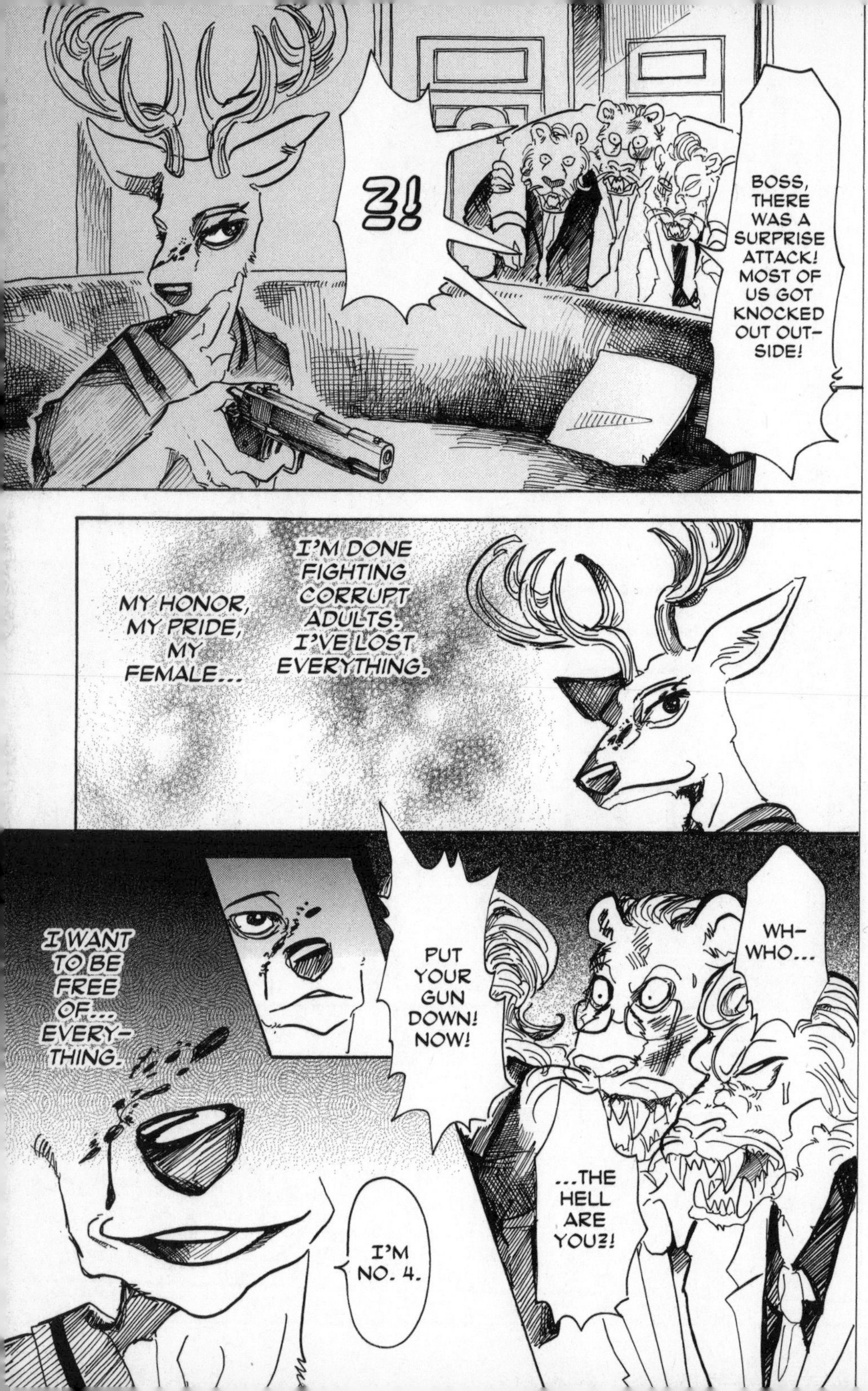
BOSS, THERE WAS A SURPRISE ATTACK! MOST OF US GOT KNOCKED OUT OUT-SIDE!
?!
I'M DONE FIGHTING CORRUPT ADULTS. I'VE LOST EVERYTHING.
MY HONOR, MY PRIDE, MY FEMALE...
WH-WHO...
...THE HELL ARE YOU?!
PUT YOUR GUN DOWN! NOW!
I WANT TO BE FREE OF... EVERY-THING.
I'M NO. 4.

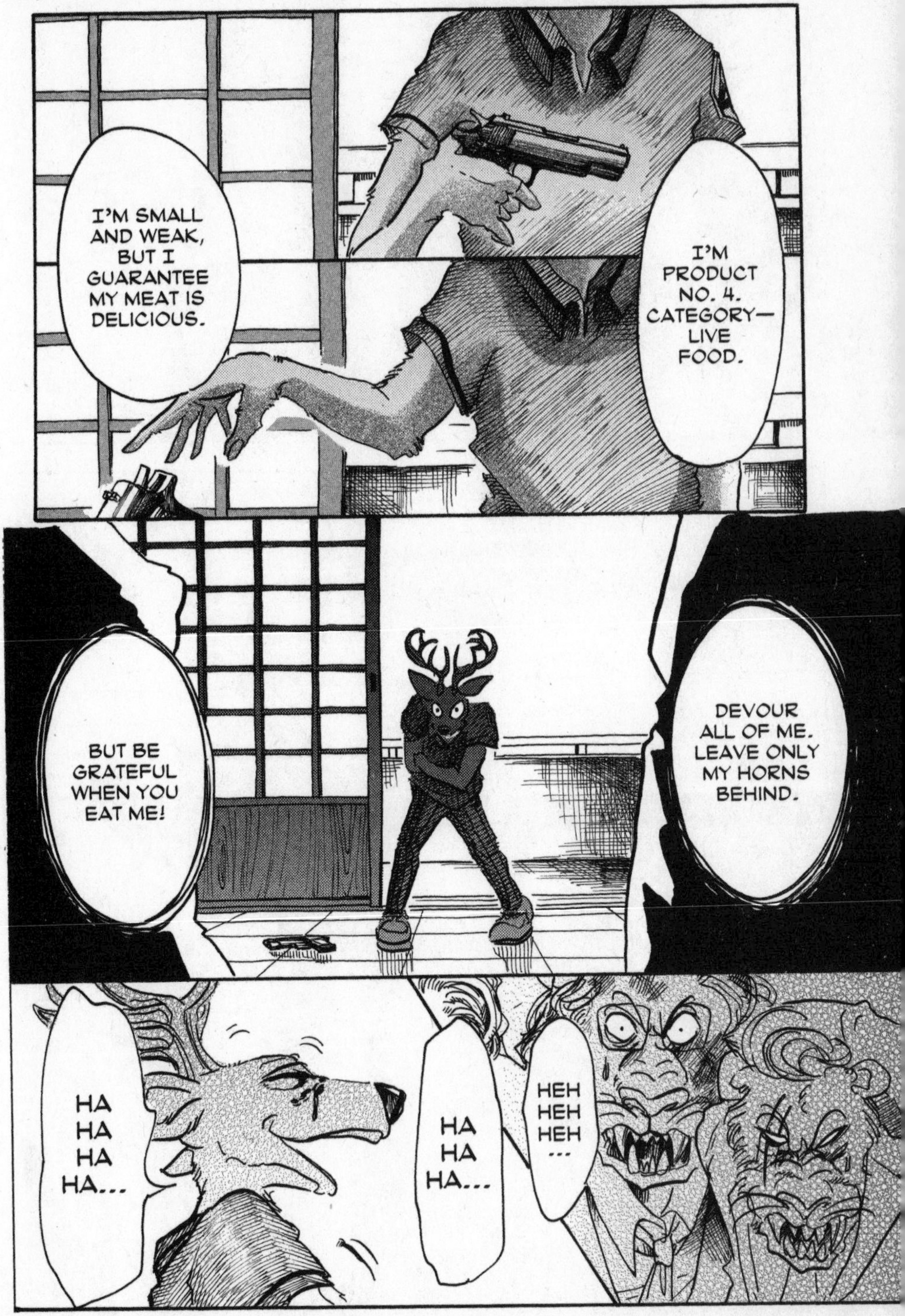
I'M PRODUCT NO. 4. CATEGORY— LIVE FOOD.
I'M SMALL AND WEAK, BUT I GUARANTEE MY MEAT IS DELICIOUS.
DEVOUR ALL OF ME. LEAVE ONLY MY HORNS BEHIND.
BUT BE GRATEFUL WHEN YOU EAT ME!
HEH HEH HEH ...
HA HA HA...
HA HA HA HA...

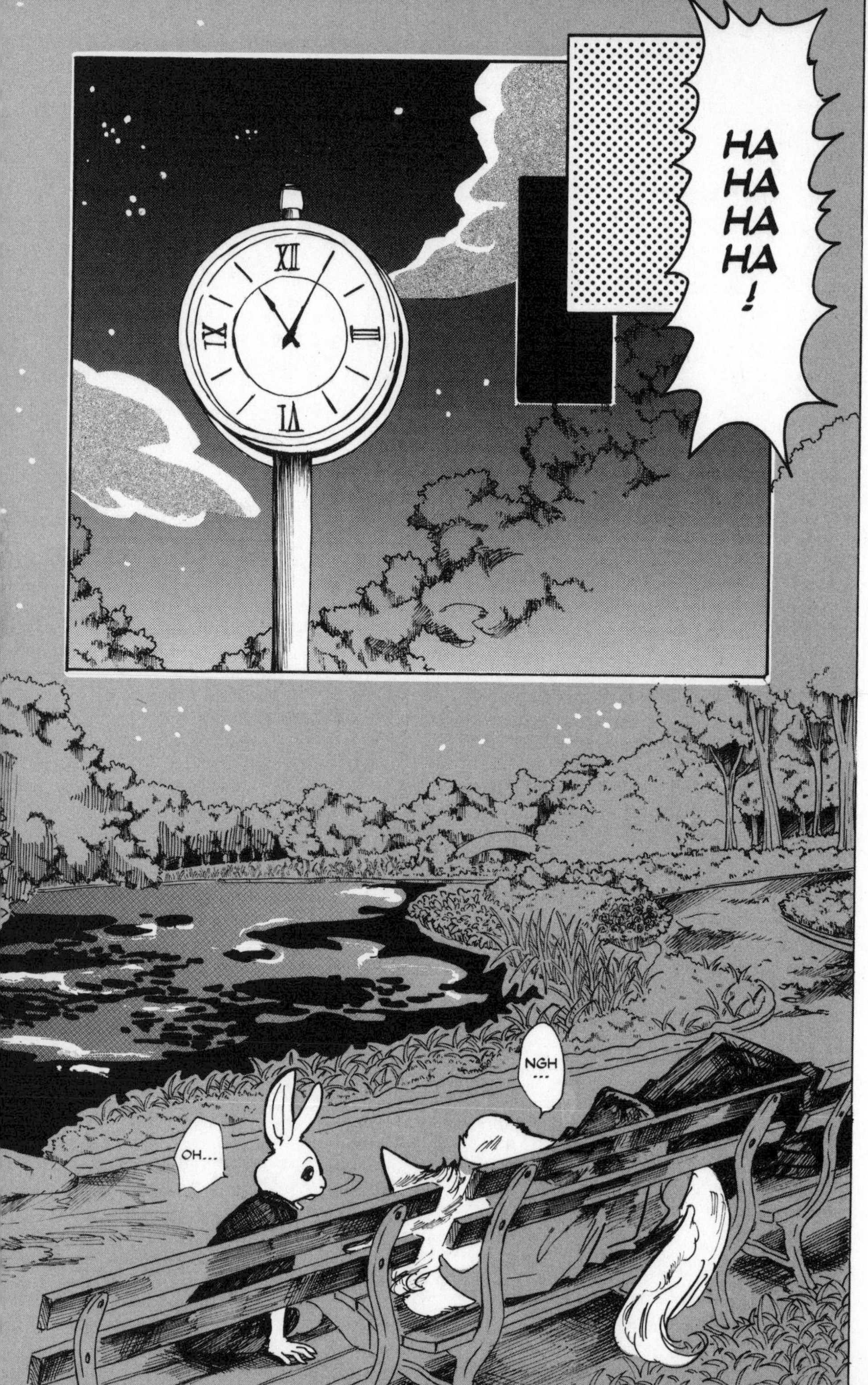
HA HA HA HA!
NGH...
OH...

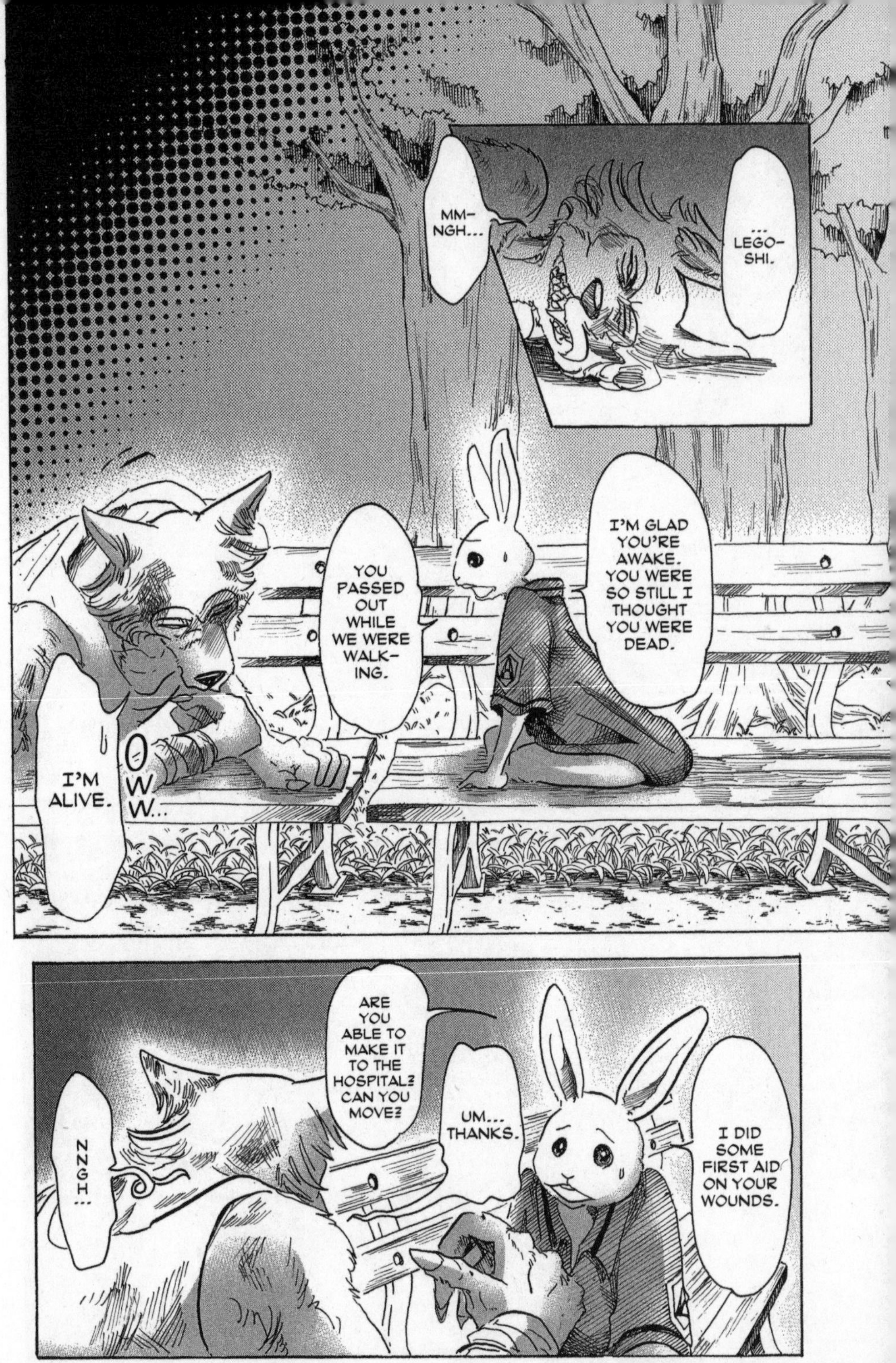
...LEGO-SHI.
MM-NGH...
I'M GLAD YOU'RE AWAKE. YOU WERE SO STILL I THOUGHT YOU WERE DEAD.
YOU PASSED OUT WHILE WE WERE WALK-ING.
OWW...
I'M ALIVE.
I DID SOME FIRST AID ON YOUR WOUNDS.
UM... THANKS.
ARE YOU ABLE TO MAKE IT TO THE HOSPITAL? CAN YOU MOVE?
NNGH...

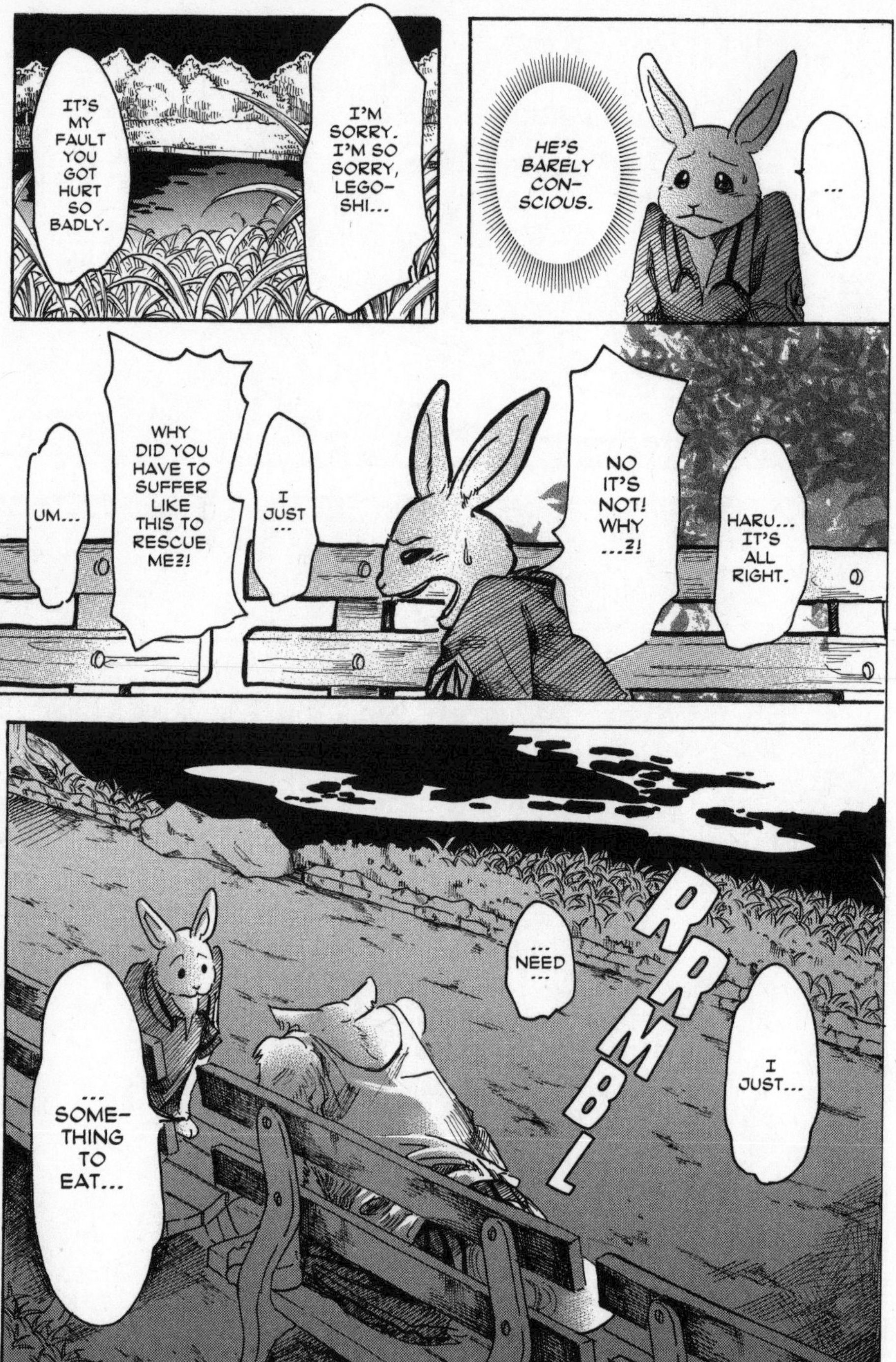
...
HE'S BARELY CONSCIOUS.
I'M SORRY. I'M SO SORRY, LEGOSHI...
IT'S MY FAULT YOU GOT HURT SO BADLY.
HARU... IT'S ALL RIGHT.
NO IT'S NOT! WHY ...?!
I JUST ...
WHY DID YOU HAVE TO SUFFER LIKE THIS TO RESCUE ME?!
UM...
I JUST...
RRRMBL
... NEED ...
... SOMETHING TO EAT...

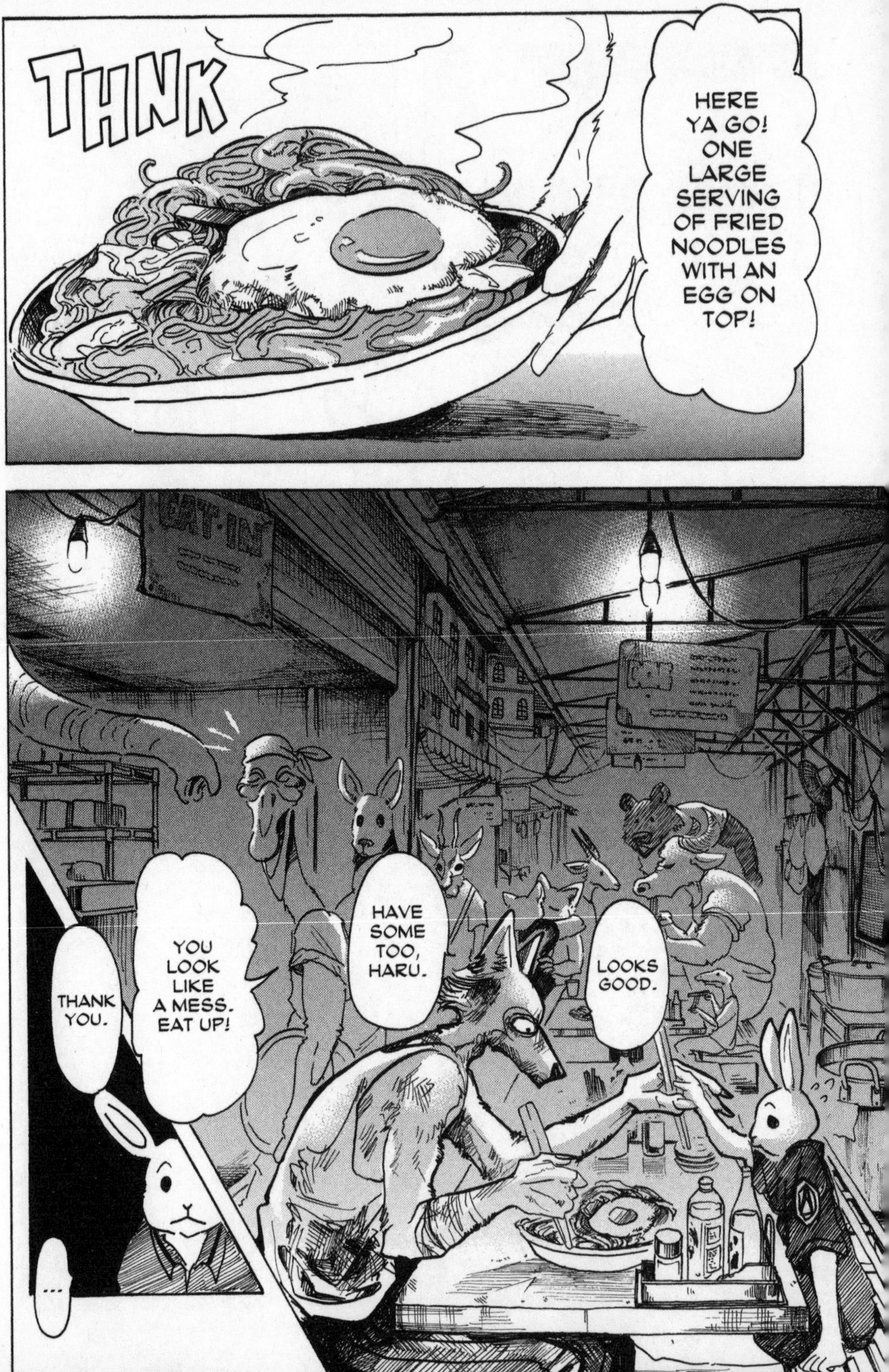
THNK
HERE YA GO! ONE LARGE SERVING OF FRIED NOODLES WITH AN EGG ON TOP!
LOOKS GOOD.
HAVE SOME TOO, HARU.
YOU LOOK LIKE A MESS. EAT UP!
THANK YOU.
...

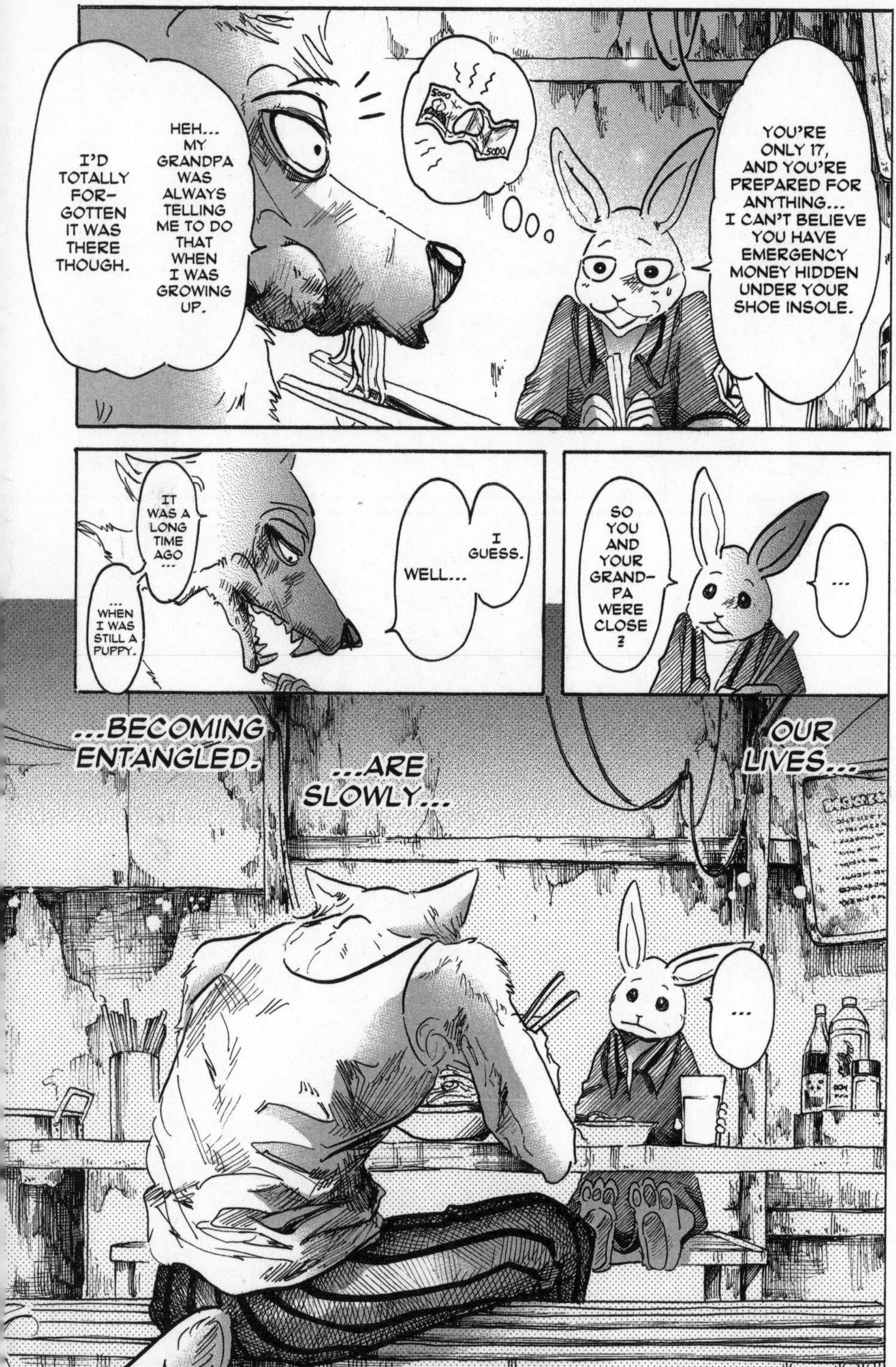
YOU'RE ONLY 17, AND YOU'RE PREPARED FOR ANYTHING... I CAN'T BELIEVE YOU HAVE EMERGENCY MONEY HIDDEN UNDER YOUR SHOE INSOLE.
HEH... MY GRANDPA WAS ALWAYS TELLING ME TO DO THAT WHEN I WAS GROWING UP.
I'D TOTALLY FORGOTTEN IT WAS THERE THOUGH.
SO YOU AND YOUR GRANDPA WERE CLOSE?
...
WELL... I GUESS.
IT WAS A LONG TIME AGO...
...WHEN I WAS STILL A PUPPY.
OUR LIVES...
...ARE SLOWLY...
...BECOMING ENTANGLED.
...

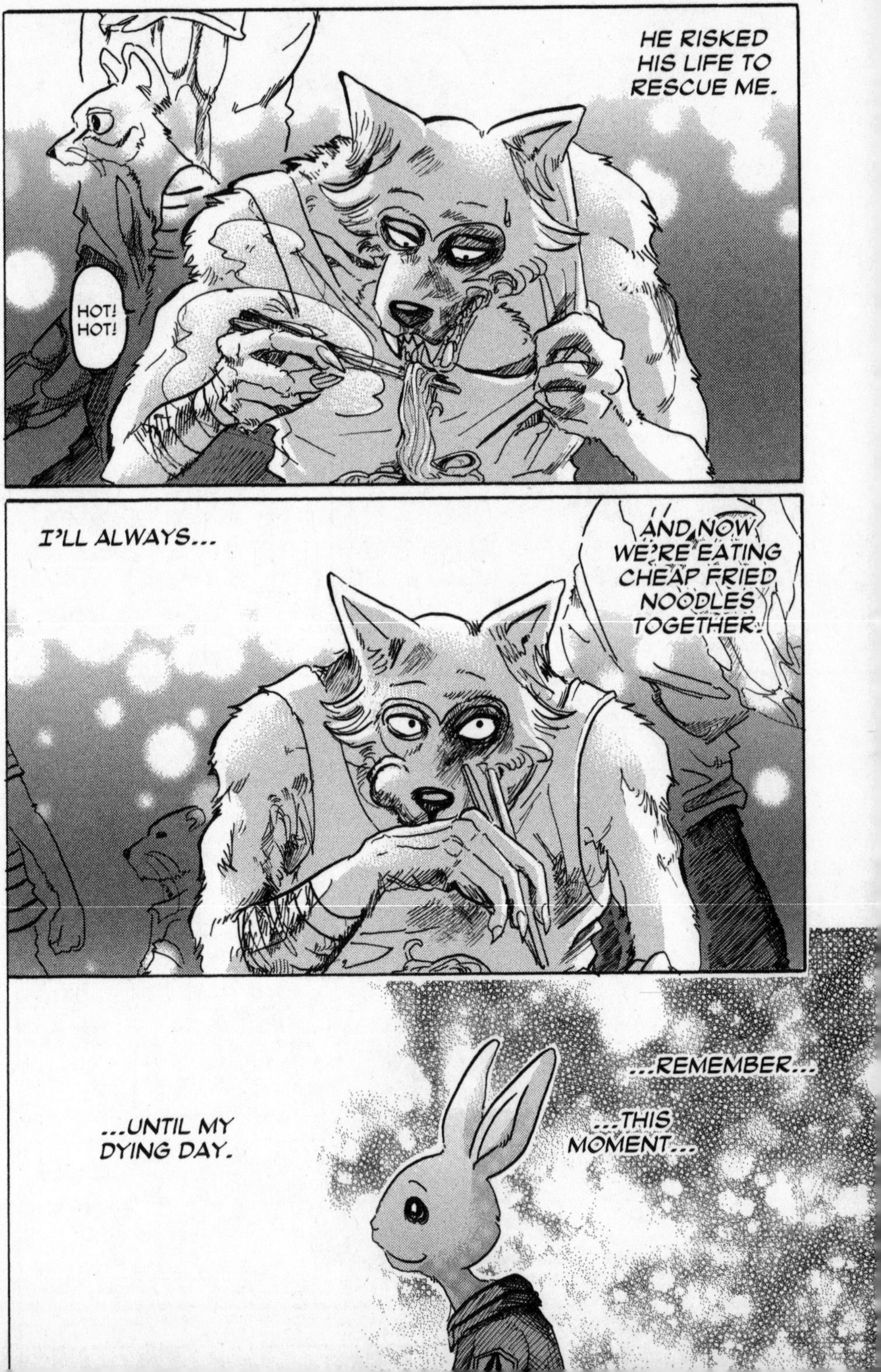
HE RISKED HIS LIFE TO RESCUE ME.
HOT! HOT!
AND NOW WE'RE EATING CHEAP FRIED NOODLES TOGETHER.
I'LL ALWAYS...
...REMEMBER...
...THIS MOMENT...
...UNTIL MY DYING DAY.

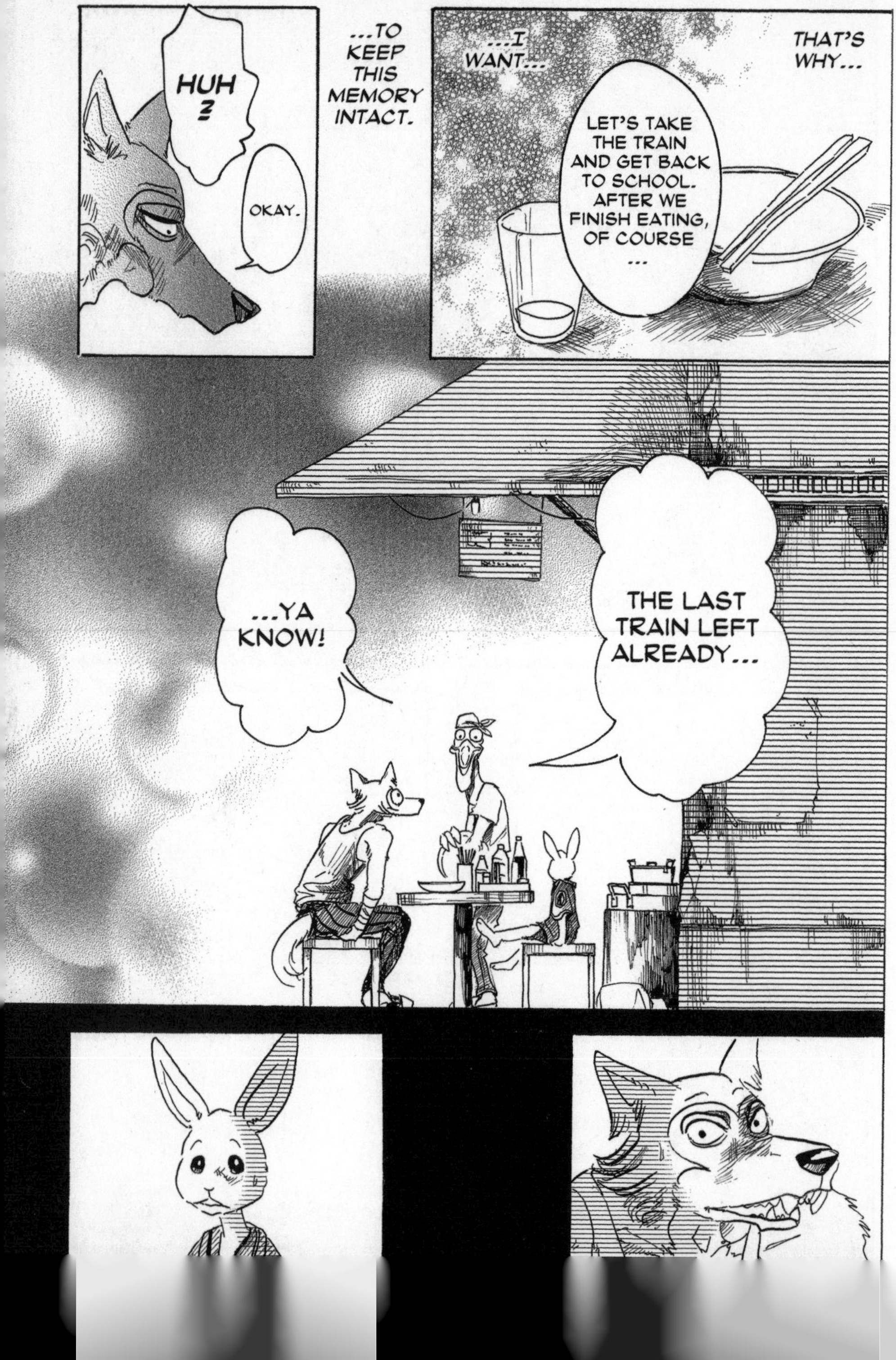
THAT'S WHY...
...I WANT...
...TO KEEP THIS MEMORY INTACT.
LET'S TAKE THE TRAIN AND GET BACK TO SCHOOL. AFTER WE FINISH EATING, OF COURSE...
HUH?
OKAY.
THE LAST TRAIN LEFT ALREADY...
...YA KNOW!

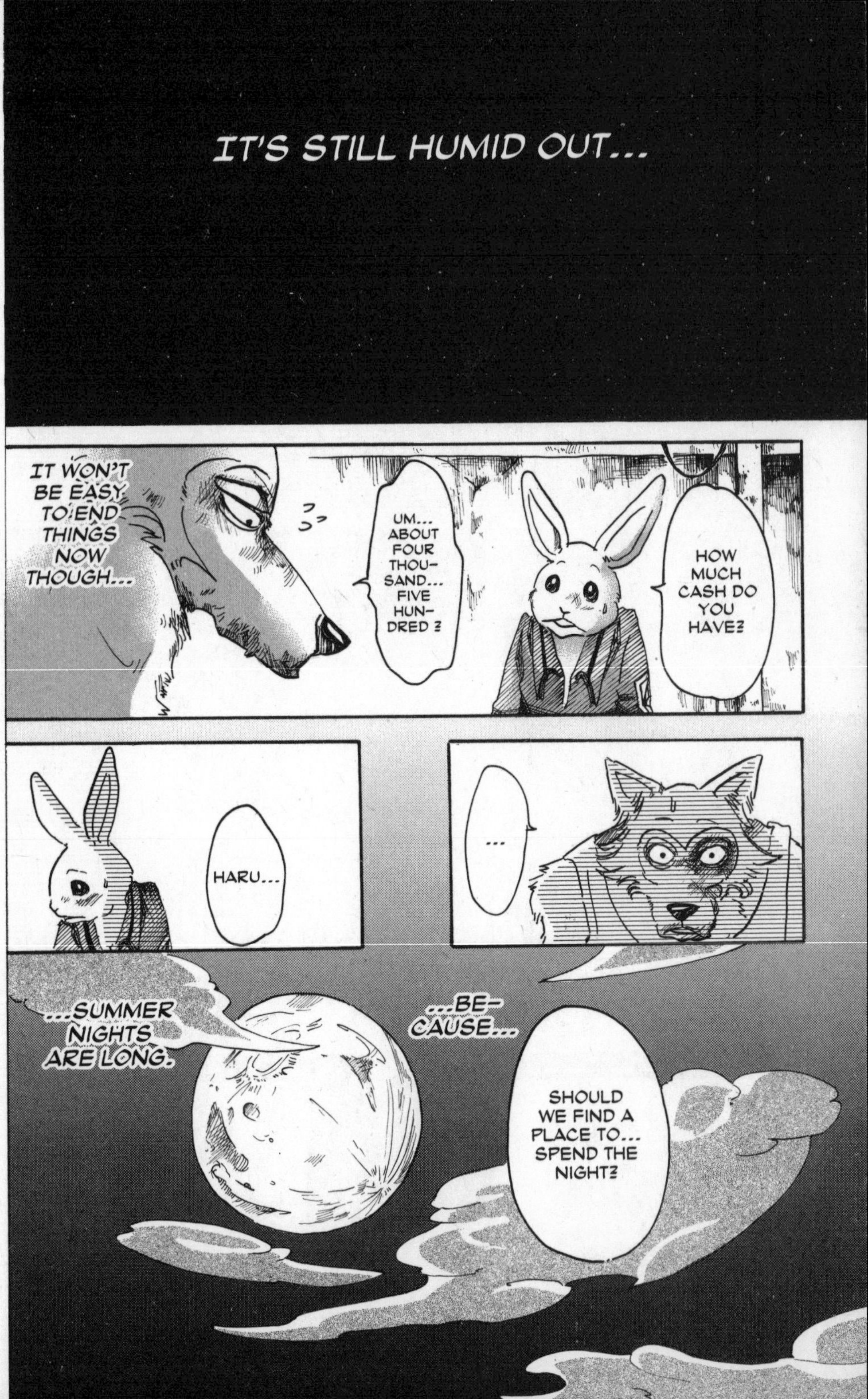
IT'S STILL HUMID OUT...
HOW MUCH CASH DO YOU HAVE?
UM... ABOUT FOUR THOU-SAND... FIVE HUN-DRED?
IT WON'T BE EASY TO END THINGS NOW THOUGH...
...
HARU...
SHOULD WE FIND A PLACE TO... SPEND THE NIGHT?
...BE-CAUSE...
...SUMMER NIGHTS ARE LONG.

Chapter 43: A Young Male's Instincts

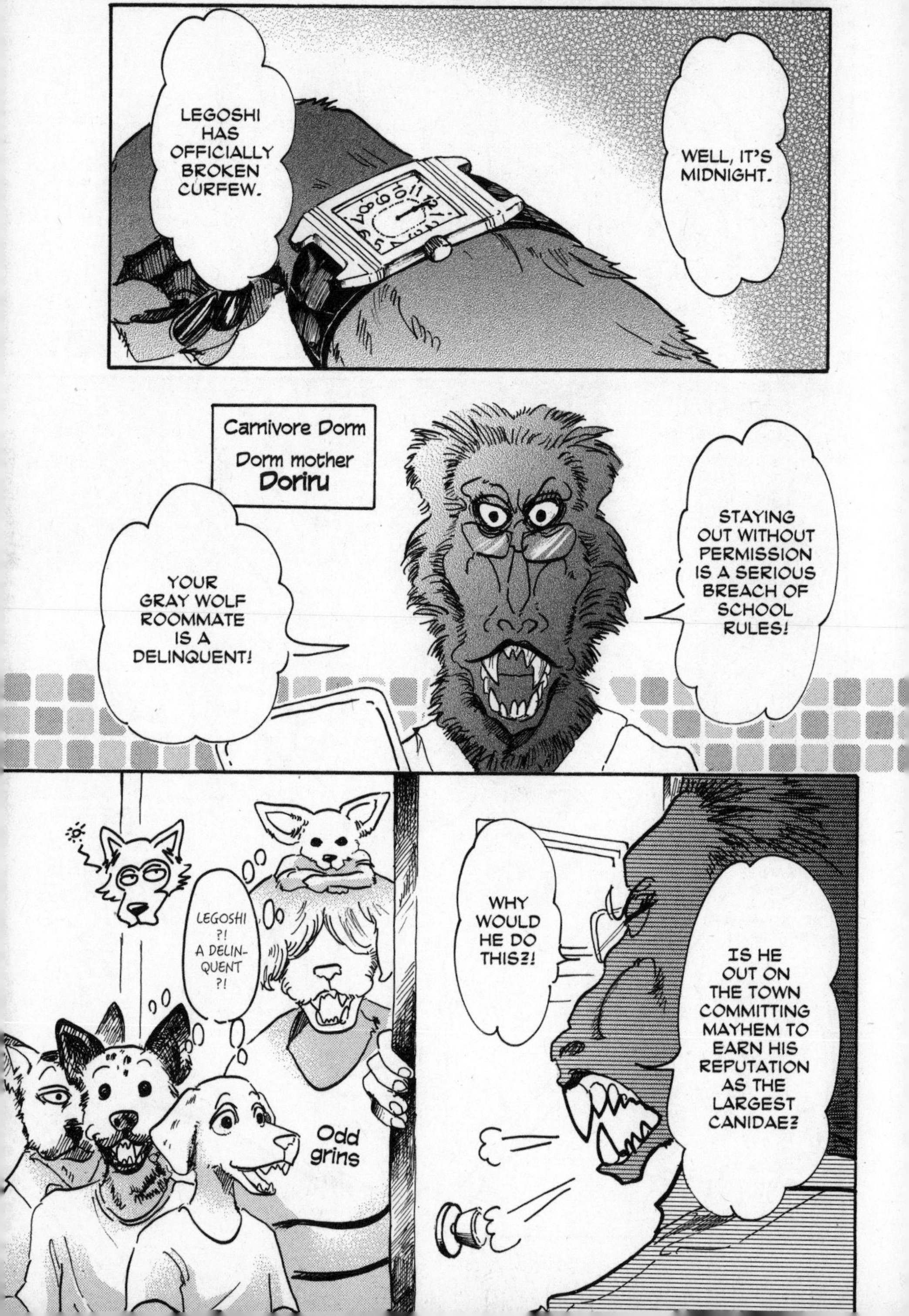
WELL, IT'S MIDNIGHT.
LEGOSHI HAS OFFICIALLY BROKEN CURFEW.
Carnivore Dorm
Dorm mother Doriru
STAYING OUT WITHOUT PERMISSION IS A SERIOUS BREACH OF SCHOOL RULES!
YOUR GRAY WOLF ROOMMATE IS A DELINQUENT!
WHY WOULD HE DO THIS?!
IS HE OUT ON THE TOWN COMMITTING MAYHEM TO EARN HIS REPUTATION AS THE LARGEST CANIDAE?
LEGOSHI?! A DELIN-QUENT?!
Odd grins

Chapter 43: A Young Male's Instincts

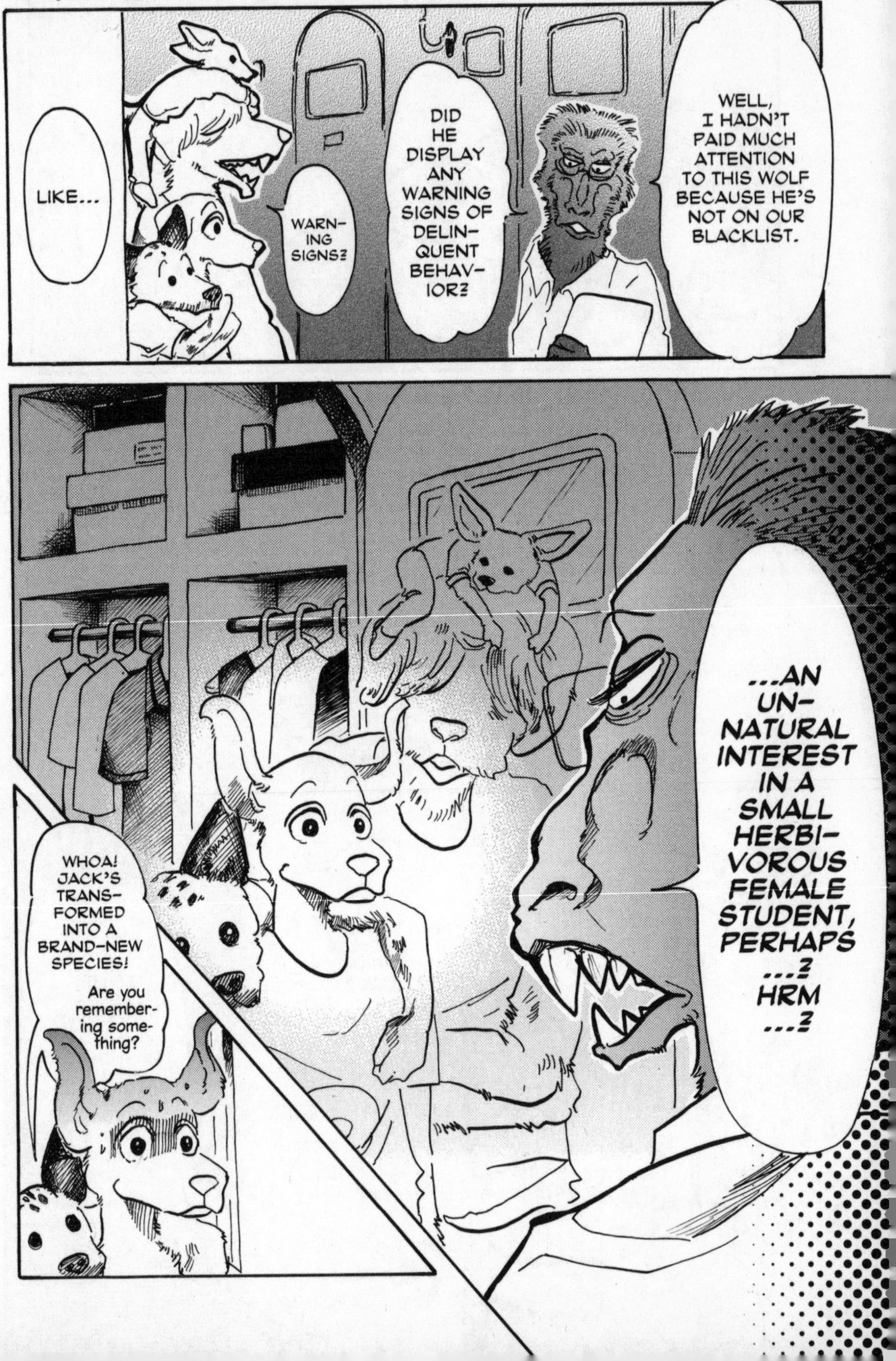
WELL, I HADN'T PAID MUCH ATTENTION TO THIS WOLF BECAUSE HE'S NOT ON OUR BLACKLIST.
DID HE DISPLAY ANY WARNING SIGNS OF DELIN-QUENT BEHAV-IOR?
WARN-ING SIGNS?
LIKE...
...AN UN-NATURAL INTEREST IN A SMALL HERBI-VOROUS FEMALE STUDENT, PERHAPS ...? HRM ...?
WHOA! JACK'S TRANS-FORMED INTO A BRAND-NEW SPECIES!
Are you remember-ing some-thing?

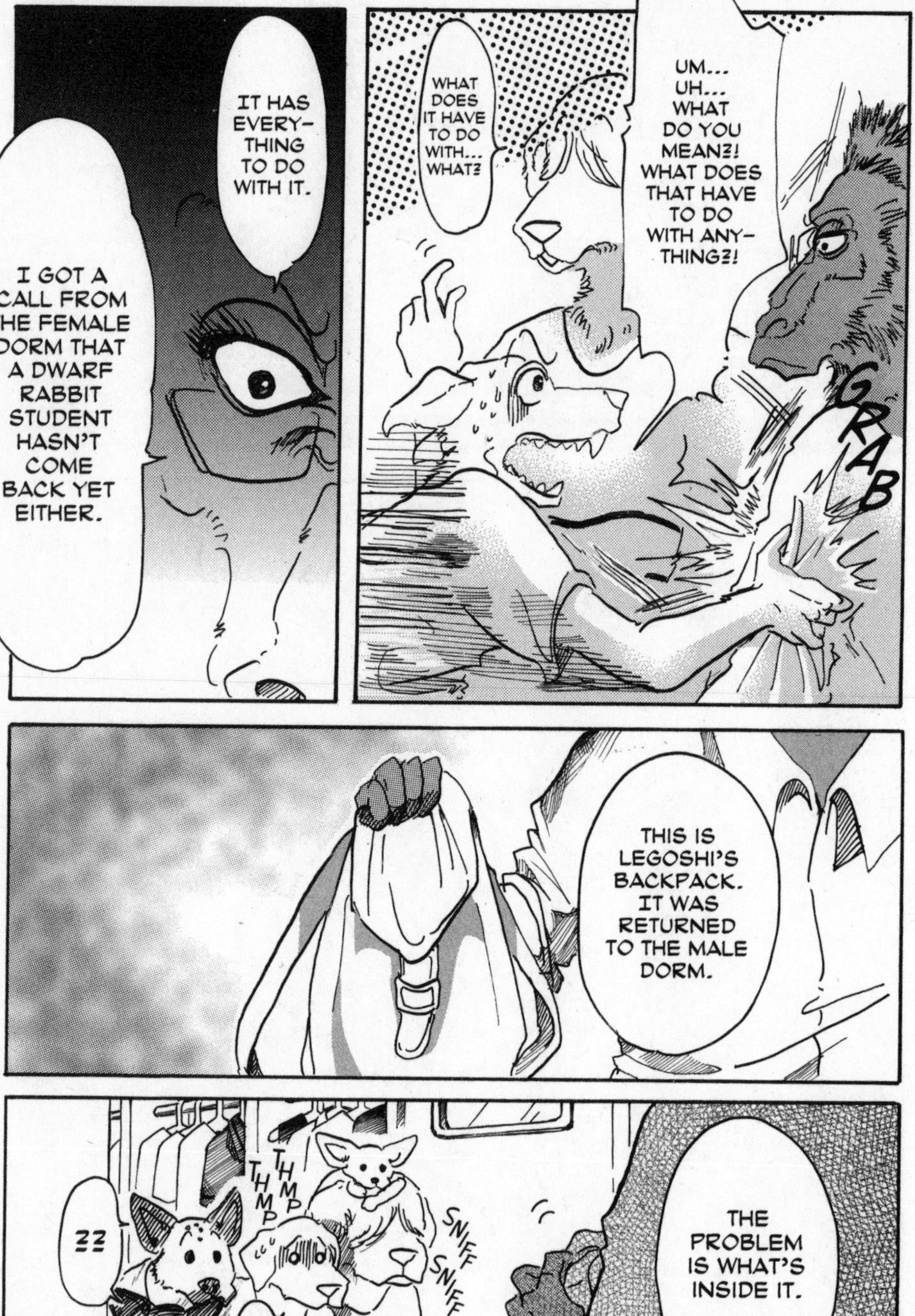
UM... UH... WHAT DO YOU MEAN?! WHAT DOES THAT HAVE TO DO WITH ANY-THING?!
WHAT DOES IT HAVE TO DO WITH... WHAT?
GRAB
IT HAS EVERY-THING TO DO WITH IT.
I GOT A CALL FROM THE FEMALE DORM THAT A DWARF RABBIT STUDENT HASN'T COME BACK YET EITHER.
THIS IS LEGOSHI'S BACKPACK. IT WAS RETURNED TO THE MALE DORM.
THE PROBLEM IS WHAT'S INSIDE IT.
SNIFF SNIFF
THMP THMP
?
...
??

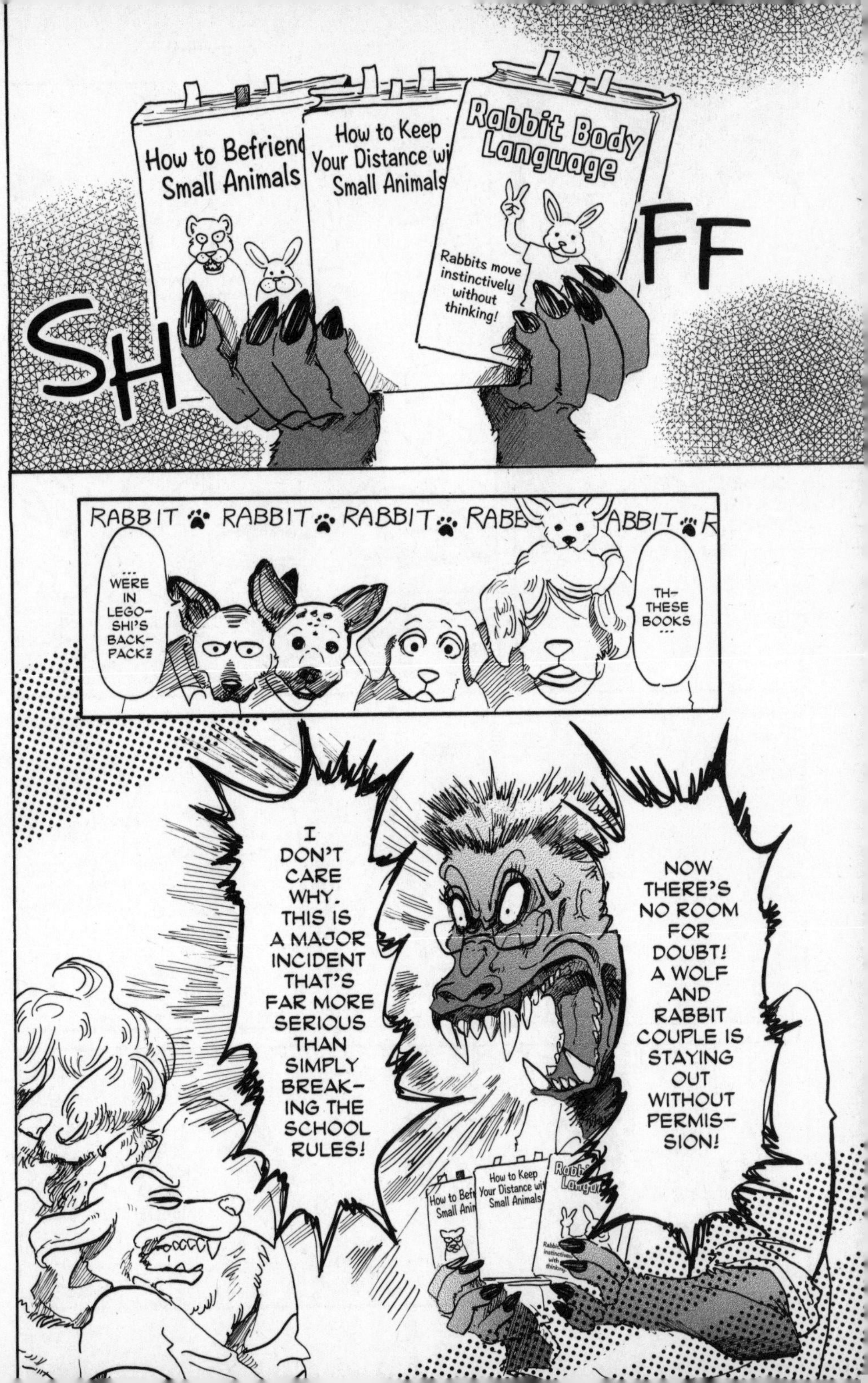
How to Befriend Small Animals
How to Keep Your Distance wi Small Animals
Rabbit Body Language
Rabbits move instinctively without thinking!
SHFF
RABBIT RABBIT RABBIT RABB ABBIT R
TH-THESE BOOKS...
...WERE IN LEGOSHI'S BACKPACK?
NOW THERE'S NO ROOM FOR DOUBT! A WOLF AND RABBIT COUPLE IS STAYING OUT WITHOUT PERMISSION!
I DON'T CARE WHY. THIS IS A MAJOR INCIDENT THAT'S FAR MORE SERIOUS THAN SIMPLY BREAKING THE SCHOOL RULES!
How to Keep Your Distance wi Small Animals

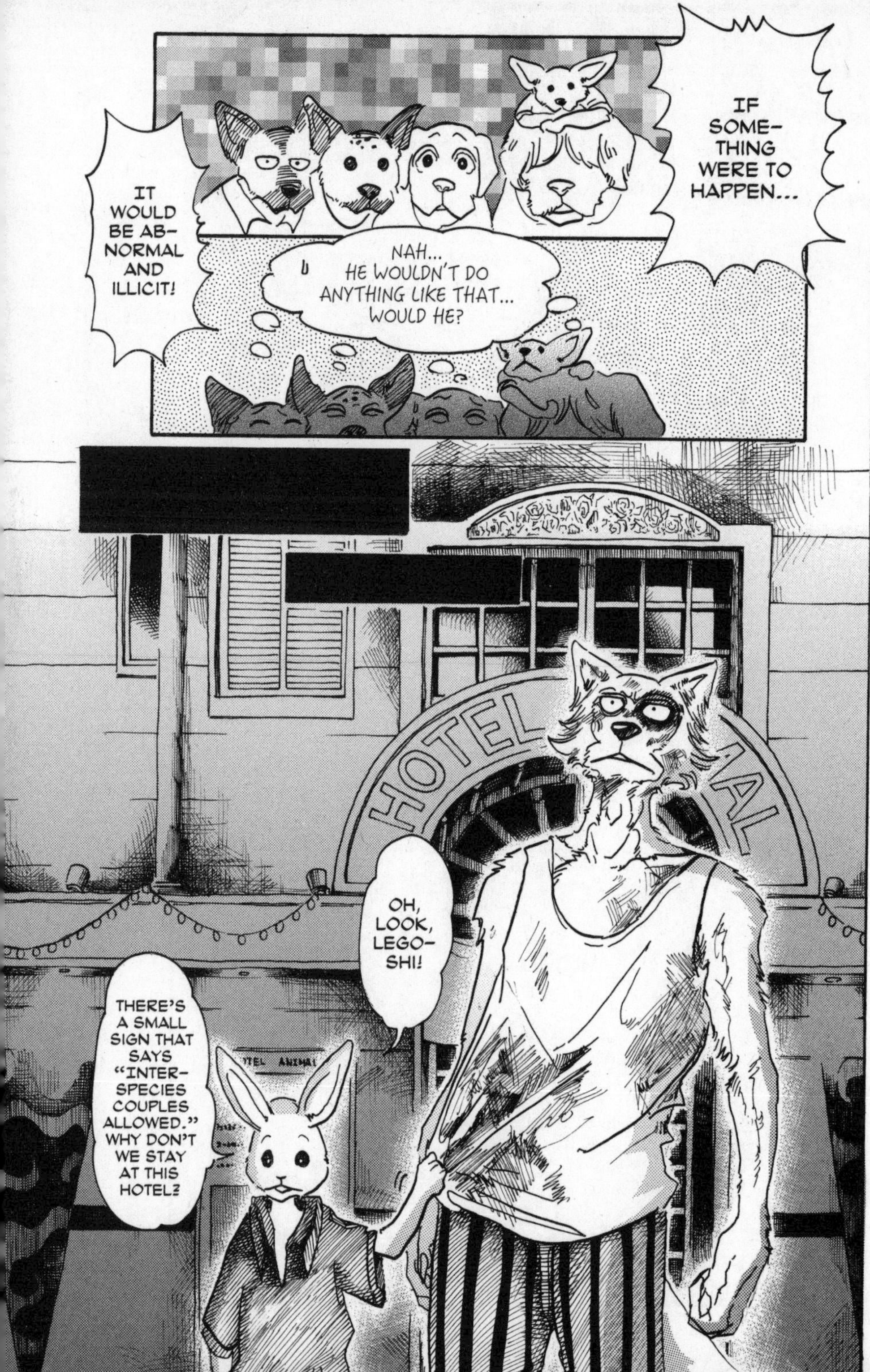
IF SOME-THING WERE TO HAPPEN...
IT WOULD BE AB-NORMAL AND ILLICIT!
NAH... HE WOULDN'T DO ANYTHING LIKE THAT... WOULD HE?
OH, LOOK, LEGO-SHI!
THERE'S A SMALL SIGN THAT SAYS "INTER-SPECIES COUPLES ALLOWED." WHY DON'T WE STAY AT THIS HOTEL?

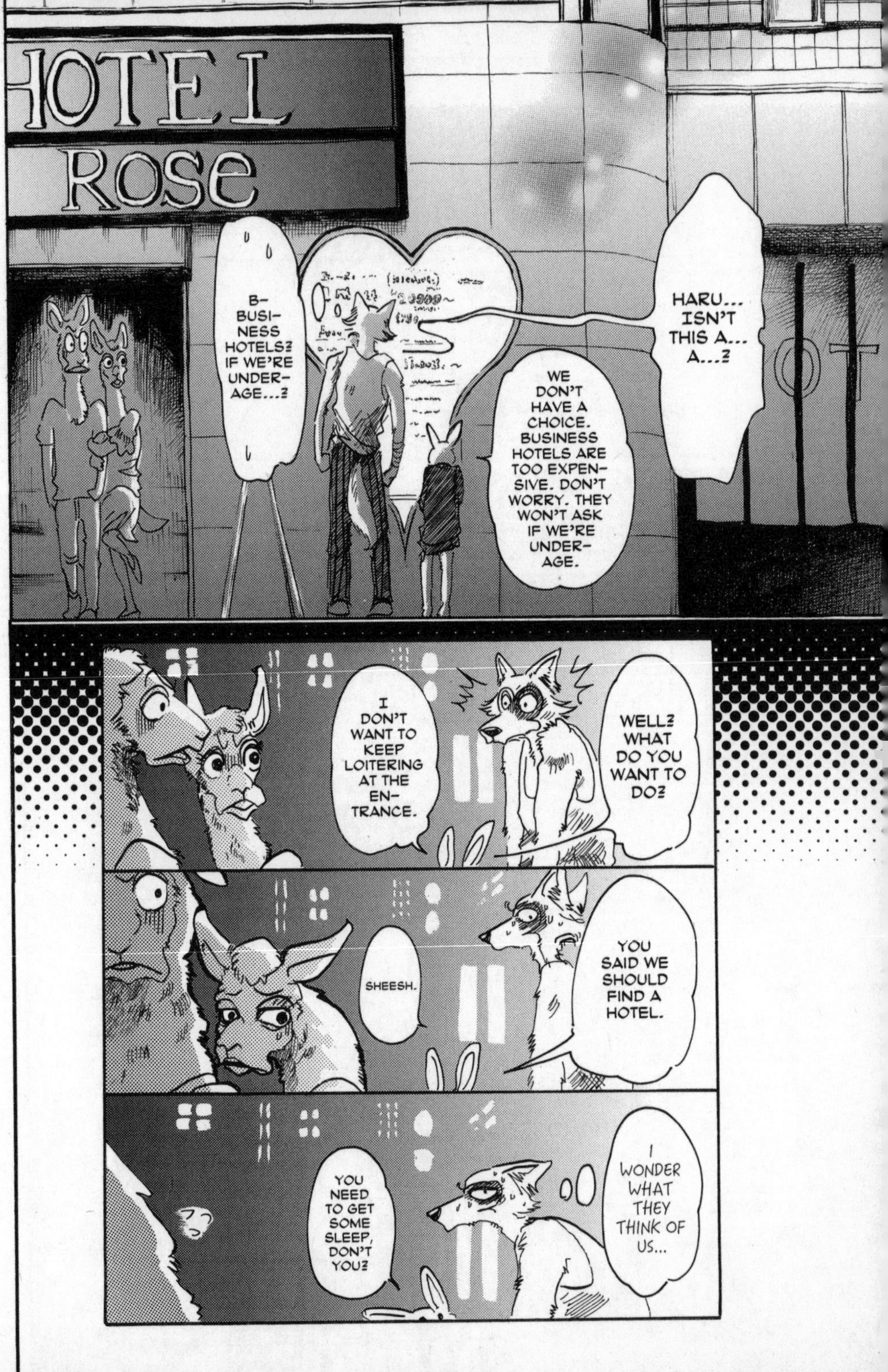
HOTEL
Rose
HARU... ISN'T THIS A... A...?
WE DON'T HAVE A CHOICE. BUSINESS HOTELS ARE TOO EXPENSIVE. DON'T WORRY. THEY WON'T ASK IF WE'RE UNDERAGE.
B-BUSINESS HOTELS? IF WE'RE UNDERAGE...?
WELL? WHAT DO YOU WANT TO DO?
I DON'T WANT TO KEEP LOITERING AT THE ENTRANCE.
YOU SAID WE SHOULD FIND A HOTEL.
SHEESH.
I WONDER WHAT THEY THINK OF US...
YOU NEED TO GET SOME SLEEP, DON'T YOU?

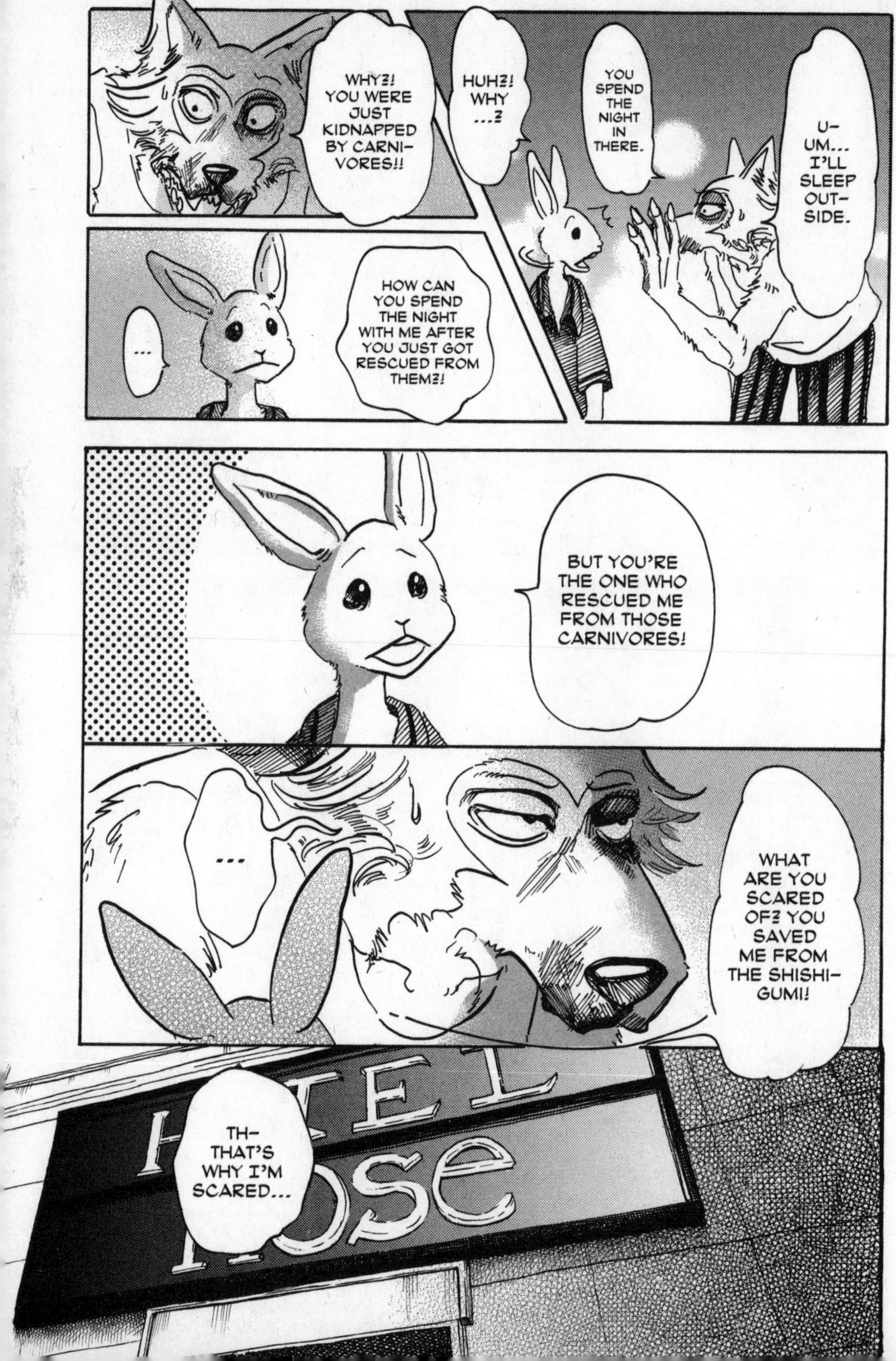
U-UM... I'LL SLEEP OUTSIDE.
YOU SPEND THE NIGHT IN THERE.
HUH?! WHY...?
WHY?! YOU WERE JUST KIDNAPPED BY CARNIVORES!!
HOW CAN YOU SPEND THE NIGHT WITH ME AFTER YOU JUST GOT RESCUED FROM THEM?!
...
BUT YOU'RE THE ONE WHO RESCUED ME FROM THOSE CARNIVORES!
WHAT ARE YOU SCARED OF? YOU SAVED ME FROM THE SHISHI-GUMI!
...
TH-THAT'S WHY I'M SCARED...

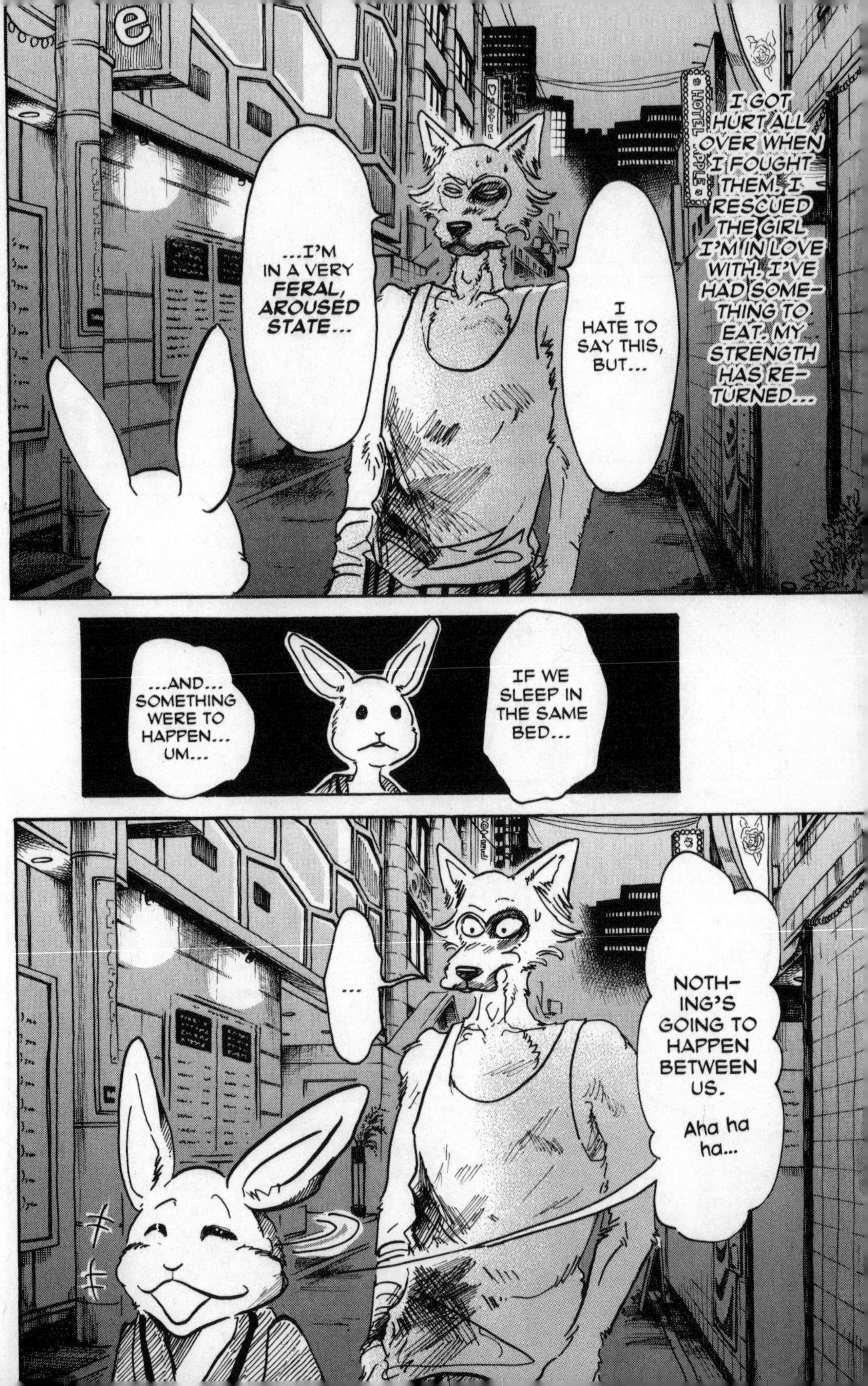
I GOT HURT ALL OVER WHEN I FOUGHT THEM. I RESCUED THE GIRL I'M IN LOVE WITH. I'VE HAD SOME-THING TO EAT. MY STRENGTH HAS RE-TURNED...
I HATE TO SAY THIS, BUT...
...I'M IN A VERY FERAL, AROUSED STATE...
IF WE SLEEP IN THE SAME BED...
...AND... SOMETHING WERE TO HAPPEN... UM...
NOTH-ING'S GOING TO HAPPEN BETWEEN US.
Aha ha ha...
...

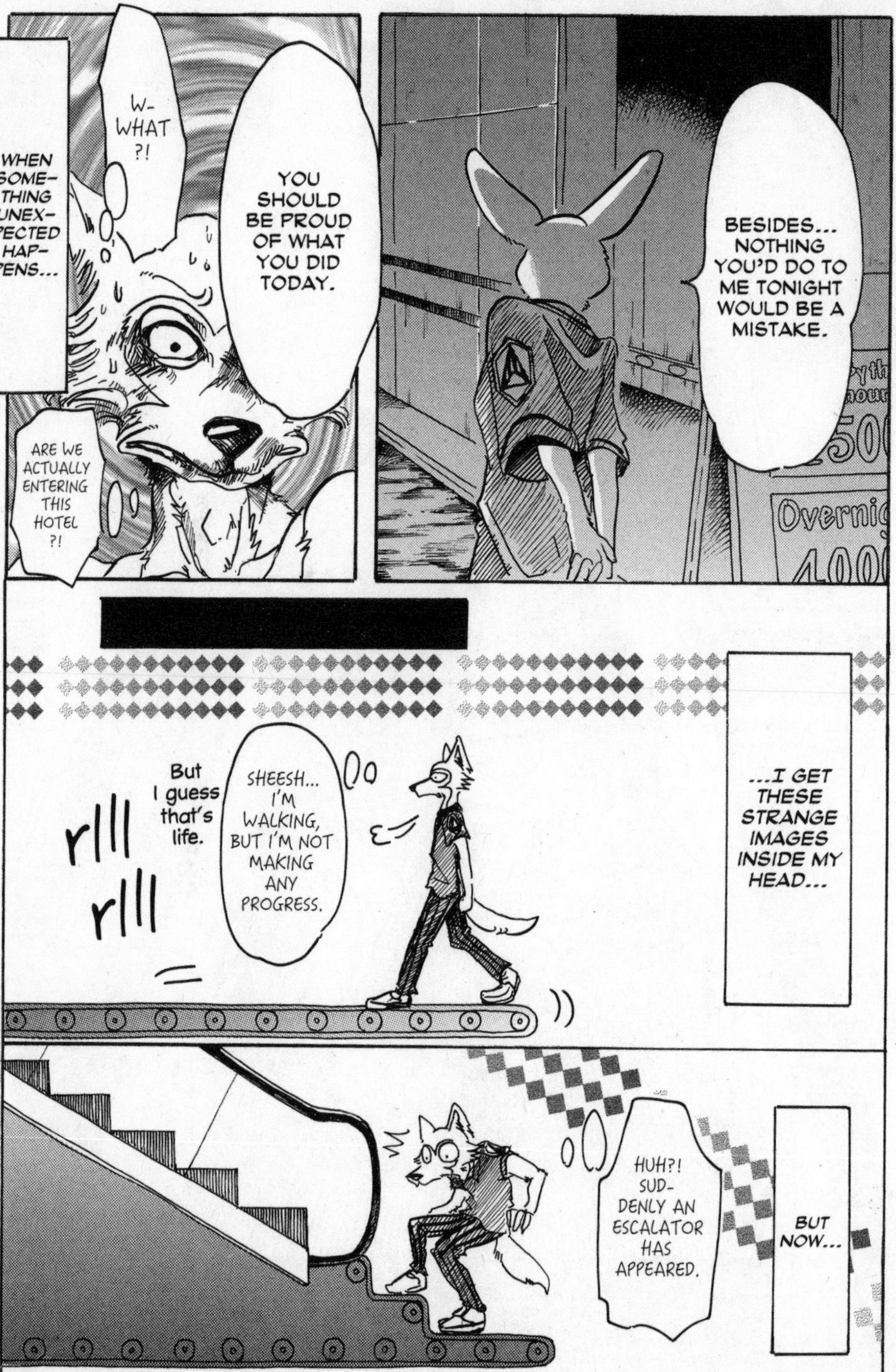

BESIDES... NOTHING YOU'D DO TO ME TONIGHT WOULD BE A MISTAKE.
YOU SHOULD BE PROUD OF WHAT YOU DID TODAY.
W-WHAT?!
WHEN SOME-THING UNEX-PECTED HAP-PENS...
ARE WE ACTUALLY ENTERING THIS HOTEL?!
...I GET THESE STRANGE IMAGES INSIDE MY HEAD...
[redacted]
SHEESH... I'M WALKING, BUT I'M NOT MAKING ANY PROGRESS.
But I guess that's life.
rll
rll
BUT NOW...
HUH?! SUD-DENLY AN ESCALATOR HAS APPEARED.

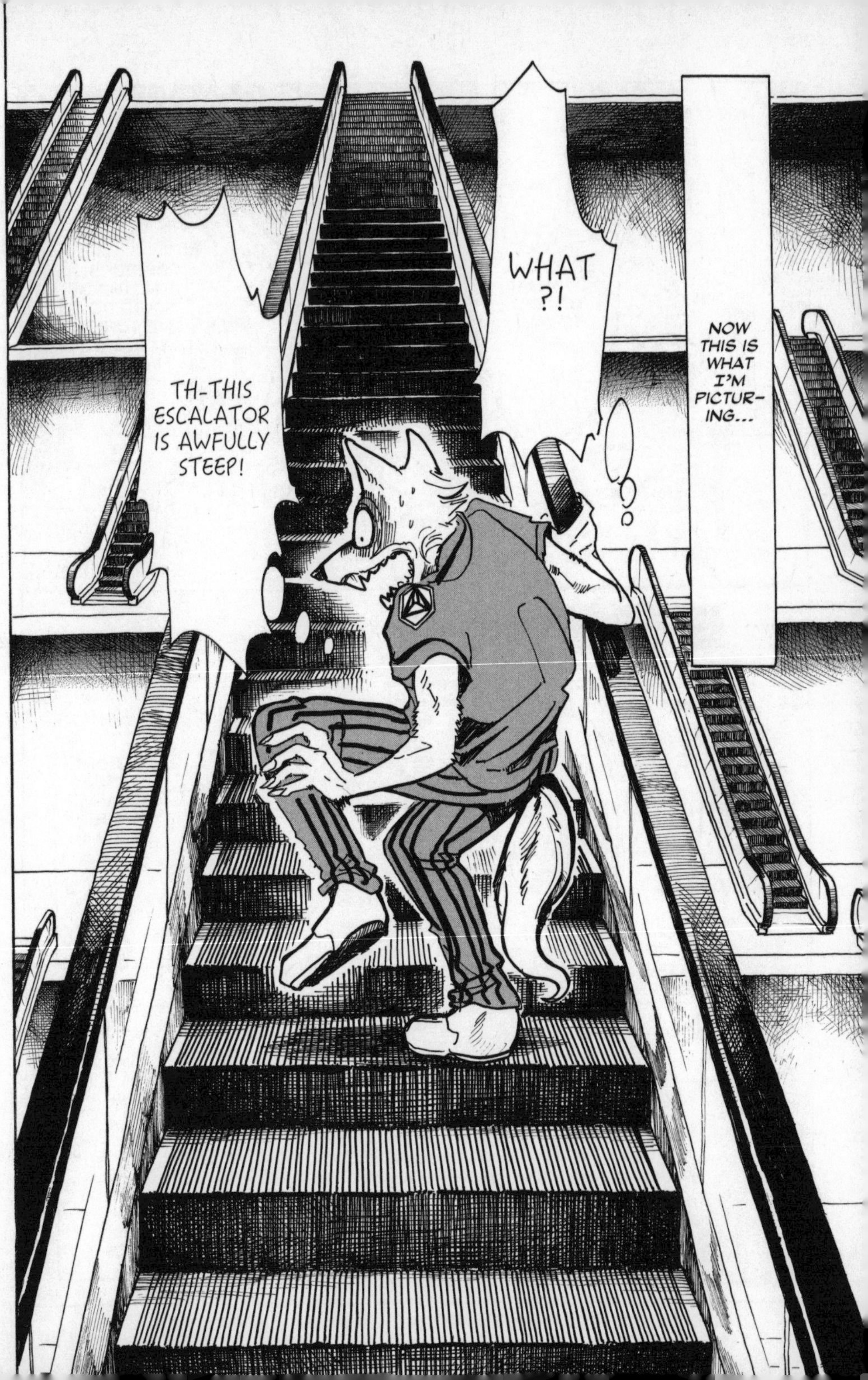
NOW THIS IS WHAT I'M PICTURING...
WHAT?!
TH-THIS ESCALATOR IS AWFULLY STEEP!

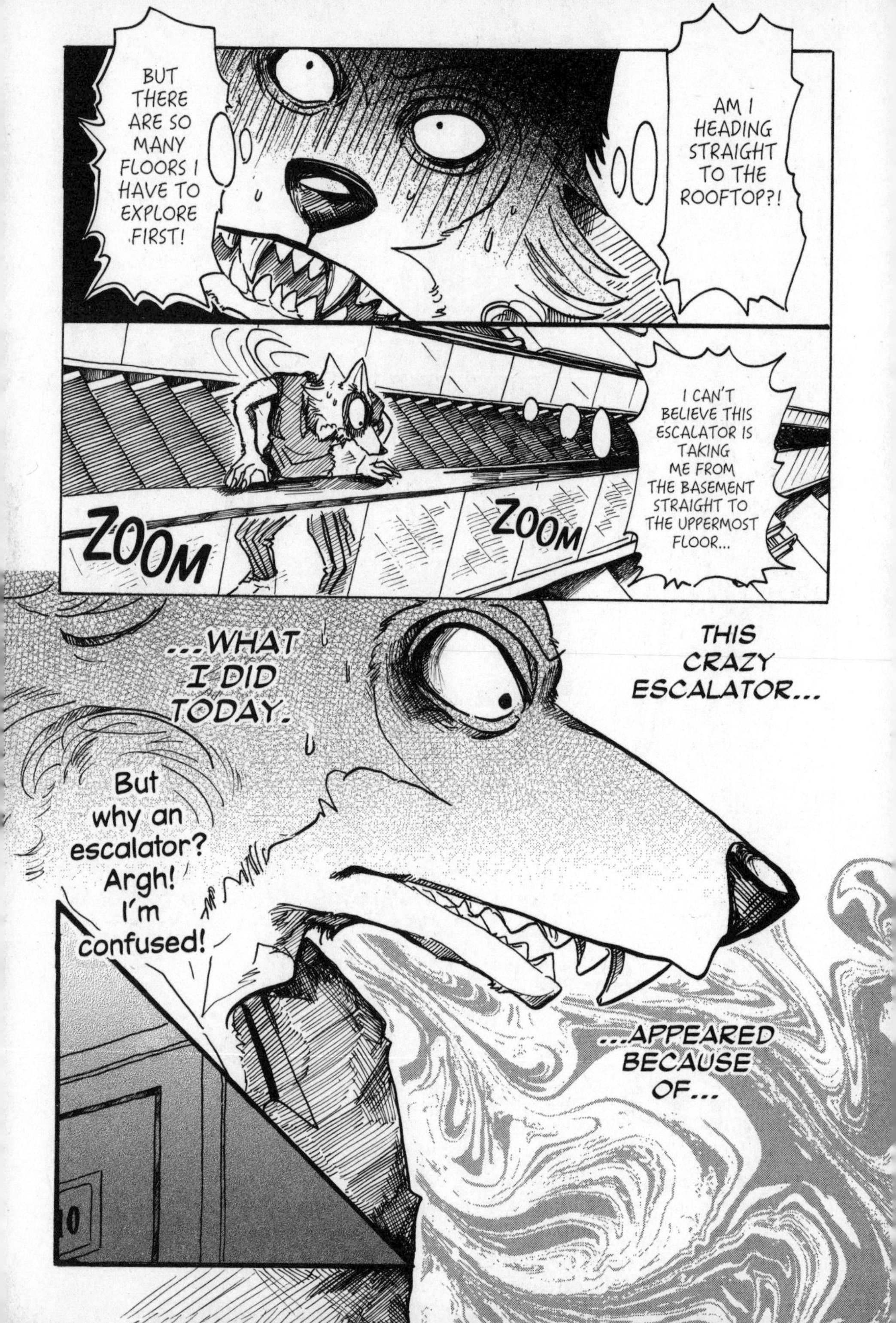
AM I HEADING STRAIGHT TO THE ROOFTOP?!
BUT THERE ARE SO MANY FLOORS I HAVE TO EXPLORE FIRST!
I CAN'T BELIEVE THIS ESCALATOR IS TAKING ME FROM THE BASEMENT STRAIGHT TO THE UPPERMOST FLOOR...
ZOOM
ZOOM
THIS CRAZY ESCALATOR...
...APPEARED BECAUSE OF...
...WHAT I DID TODAY.
But why an escalator? Argh! I'm confused!

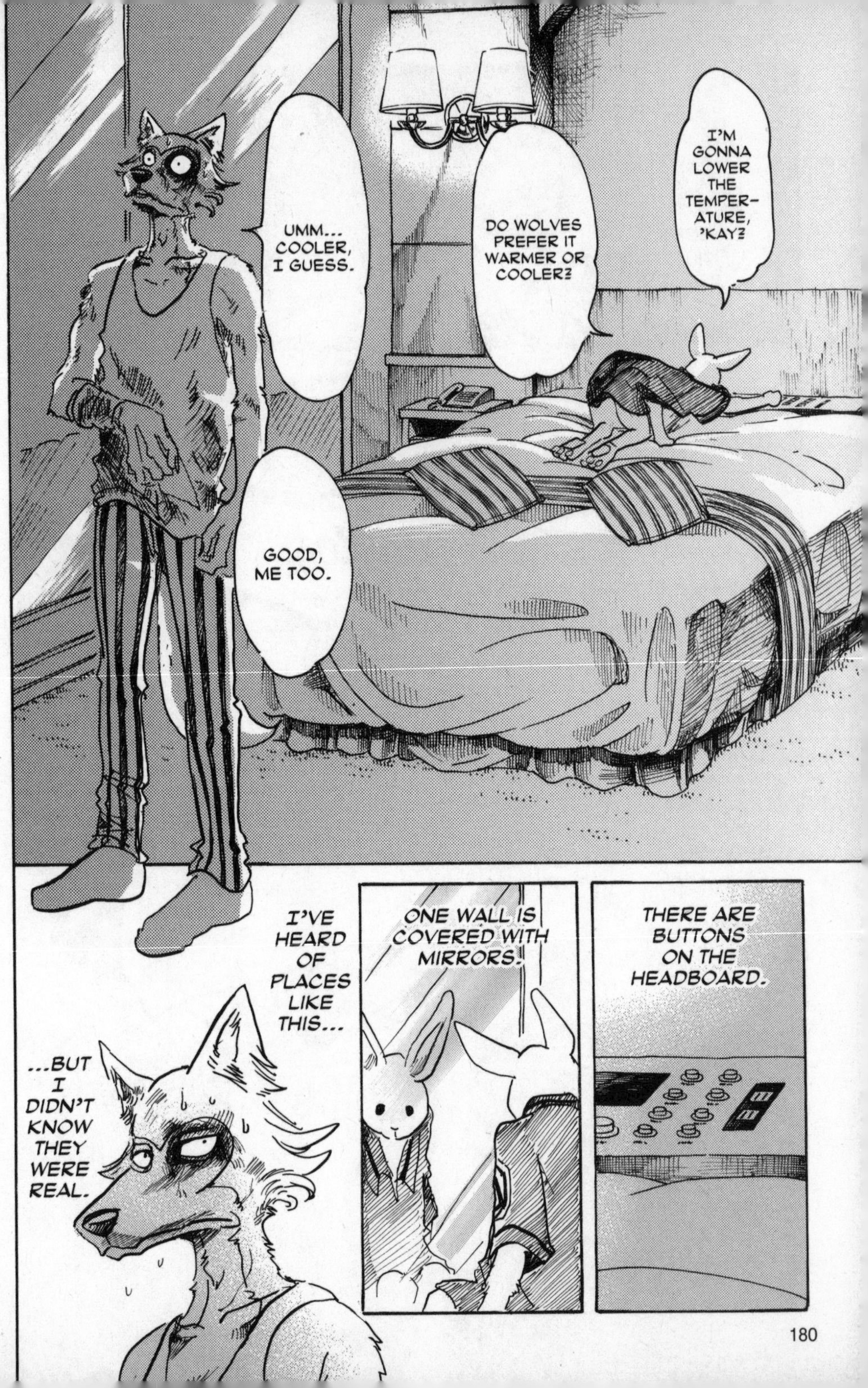
I'M GONNA LOWER THE TEMPER-ATURE, 'KAY?
DO WOLVES PREFER IT WARMER OR COOLER?
UMM... COOLER, I GUESS.
GOOD, ME TOO.
THERE ARE BUTTONS ON THE HEADBOARD.
ONE WALL IS COVERED WITH MIRRORS.
I'VE HEARD OF PLACES LIKE THIS...
...BUT I DIDN'T KNOW THEY WERE REAL.

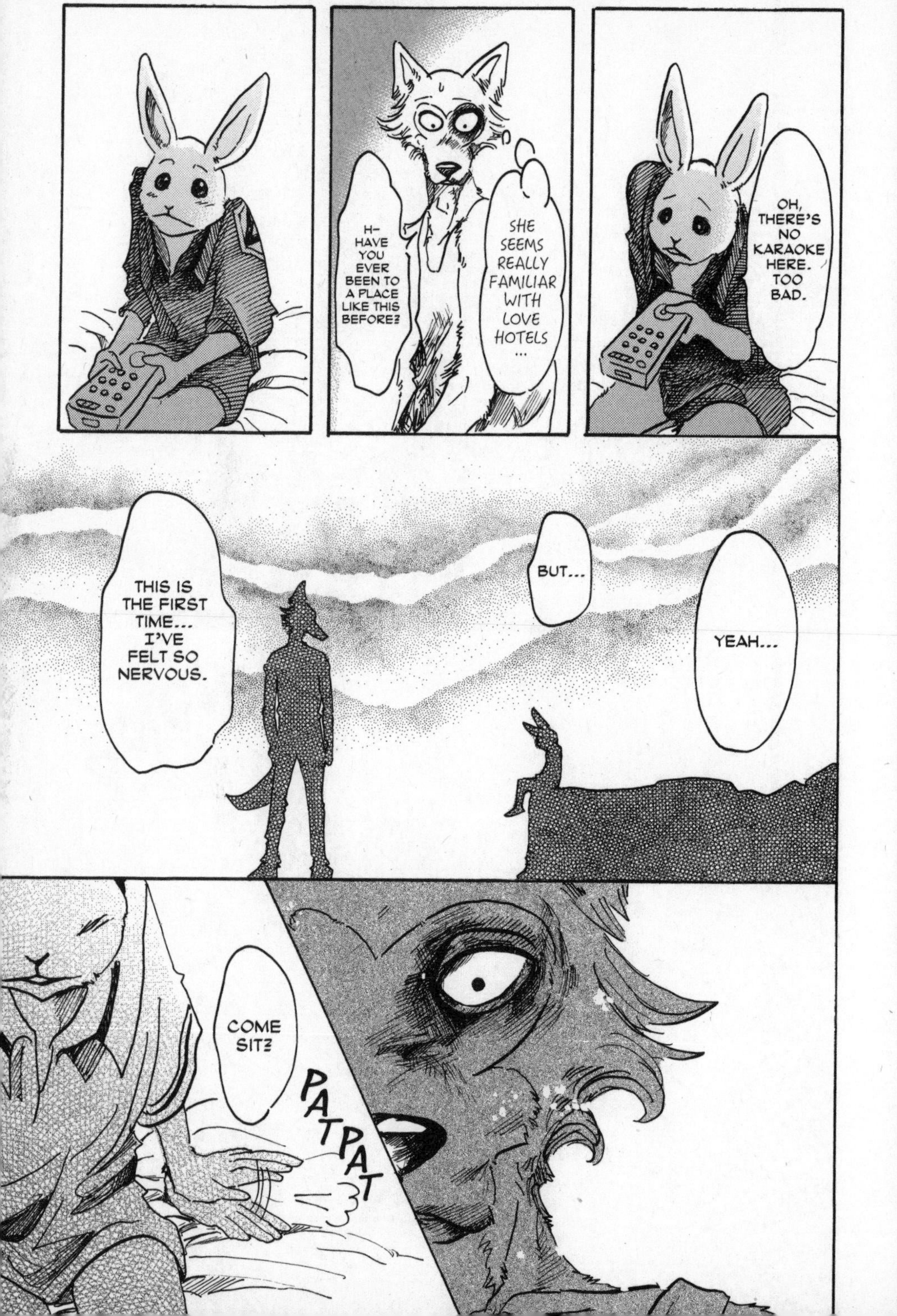
OH, THERE'S NO KARAOKE HERE. TOO BAD.
SHE SEEMS REALLY FAMILIAR WITH LOVE HOTELS...
H-HAVE YOU EVER BEEN TO A PLACE LIKE THIS BEFORE?
YEAH...
BUT...
THIS IS THE FIRST TIME... I'VE FELT SO NERVOUS.
COME SIT?
PATPAT

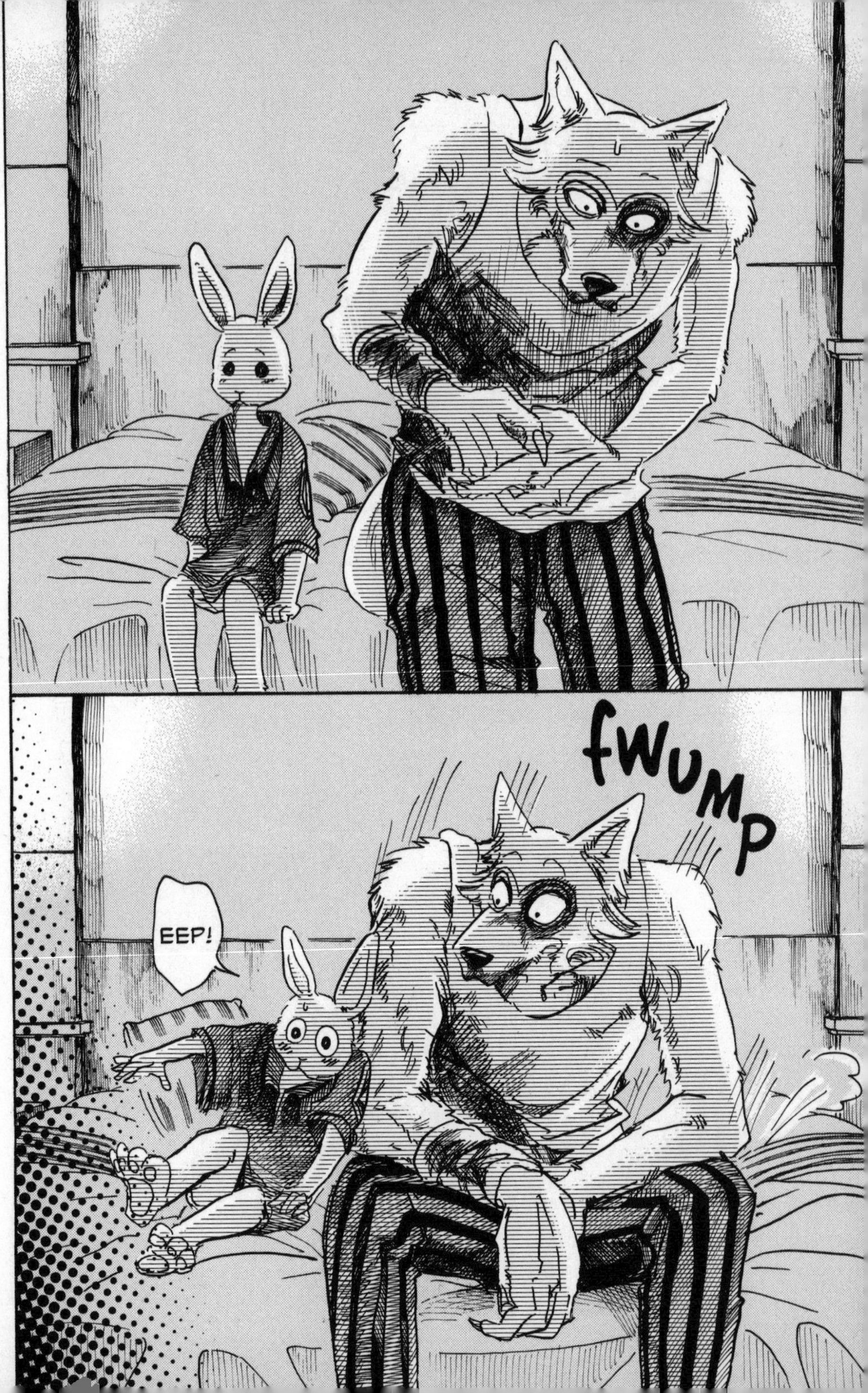
FWUMP
EEP!

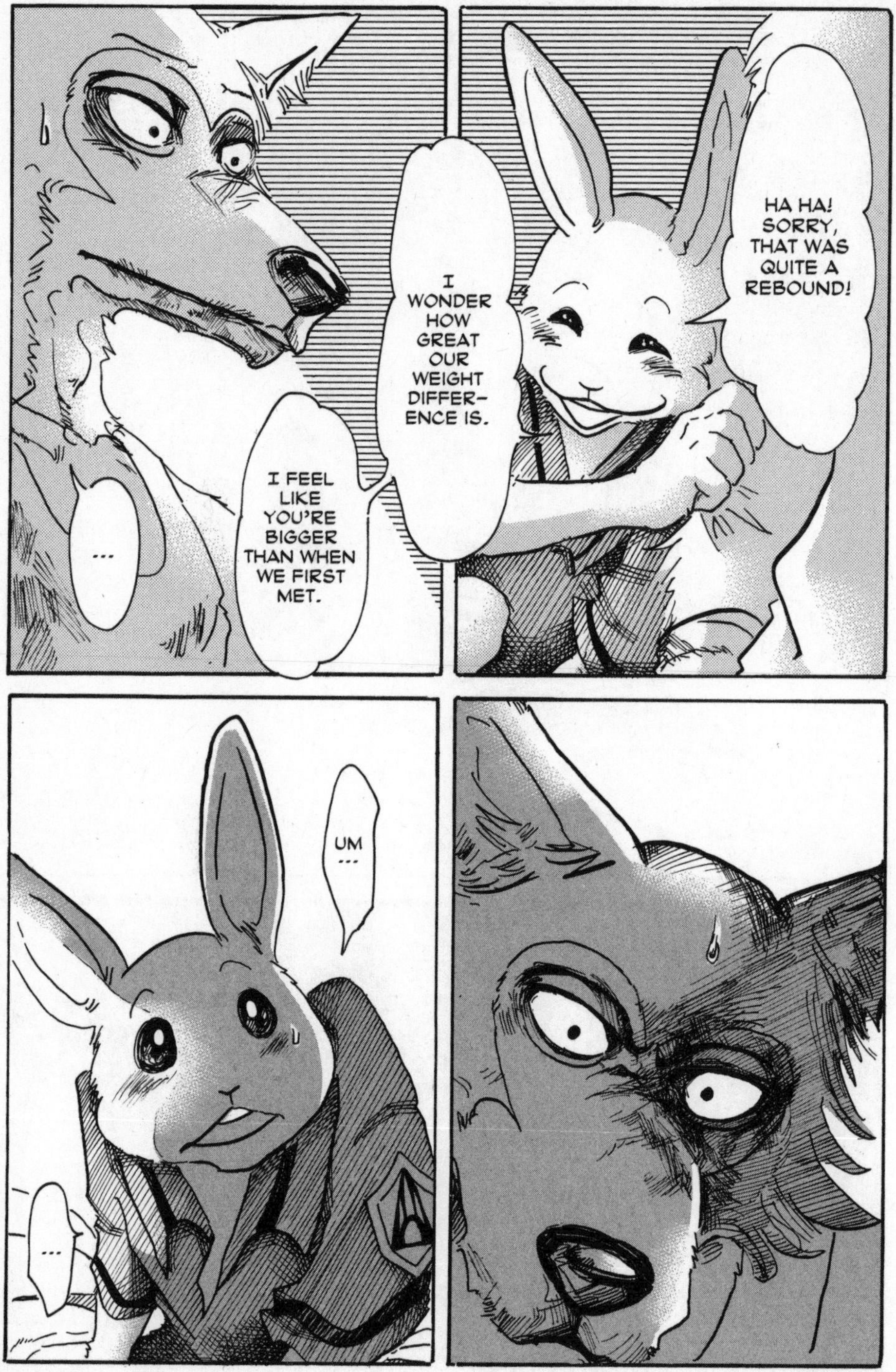
HA HA! SORRY, THAT WAS QUITE A REBOUND!
I WONDER HOW GREAT OUR WEIGHT DIFFERENCE IS.
I FEEL LIKE YOU'RE BIGGER THAN WHEN WE FIRST MET.
...
UM ...
...

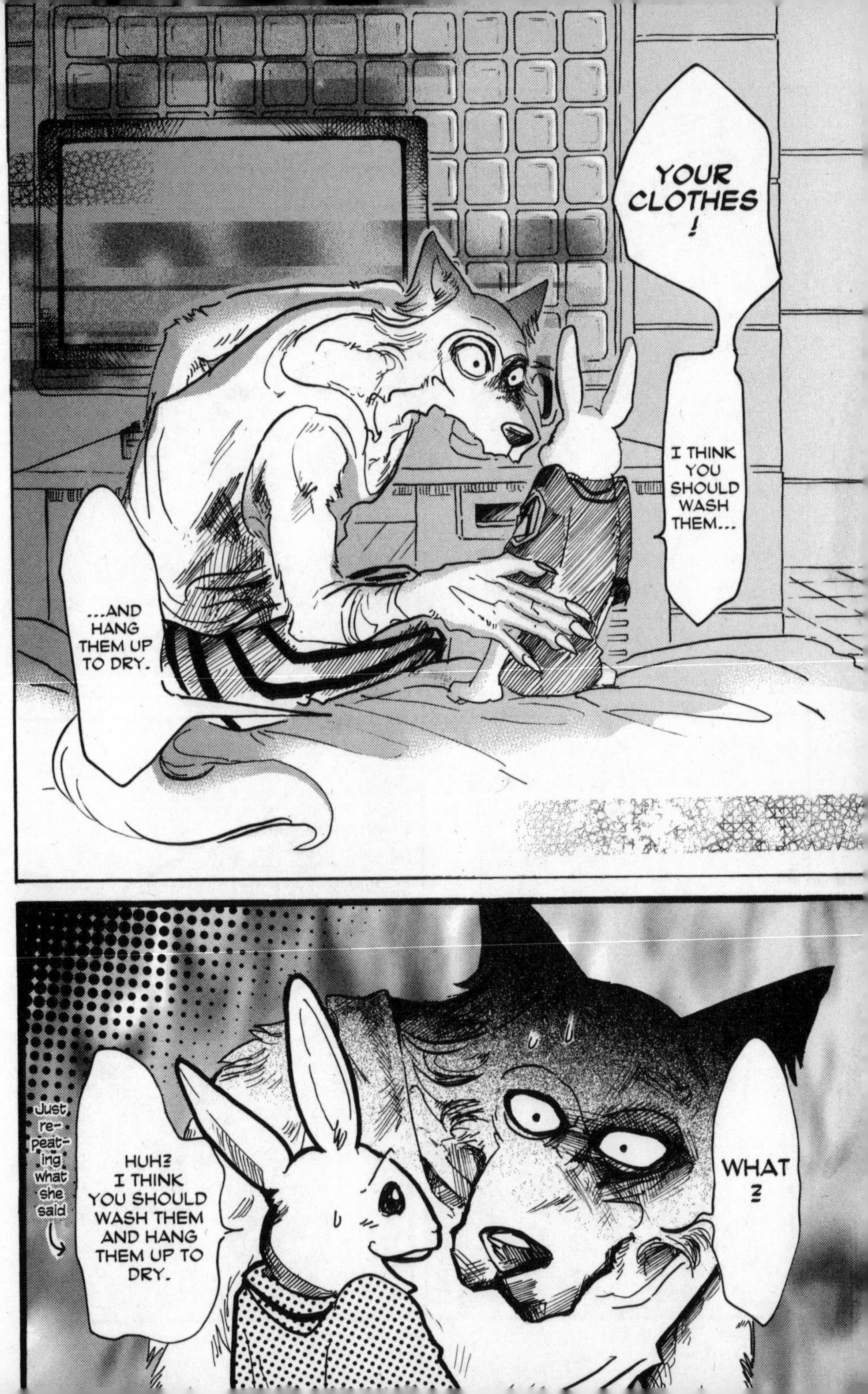
YOUR CLOTHES!
I THINK YOU SHOULD WASH THEM...
...AND HANG THEM UP TO DRY.
WHAT?
HUH? I THINK YOU SHOULD WASH THEM AND HANG THEM UP TO DRY.
Just re-peat-ing what she said

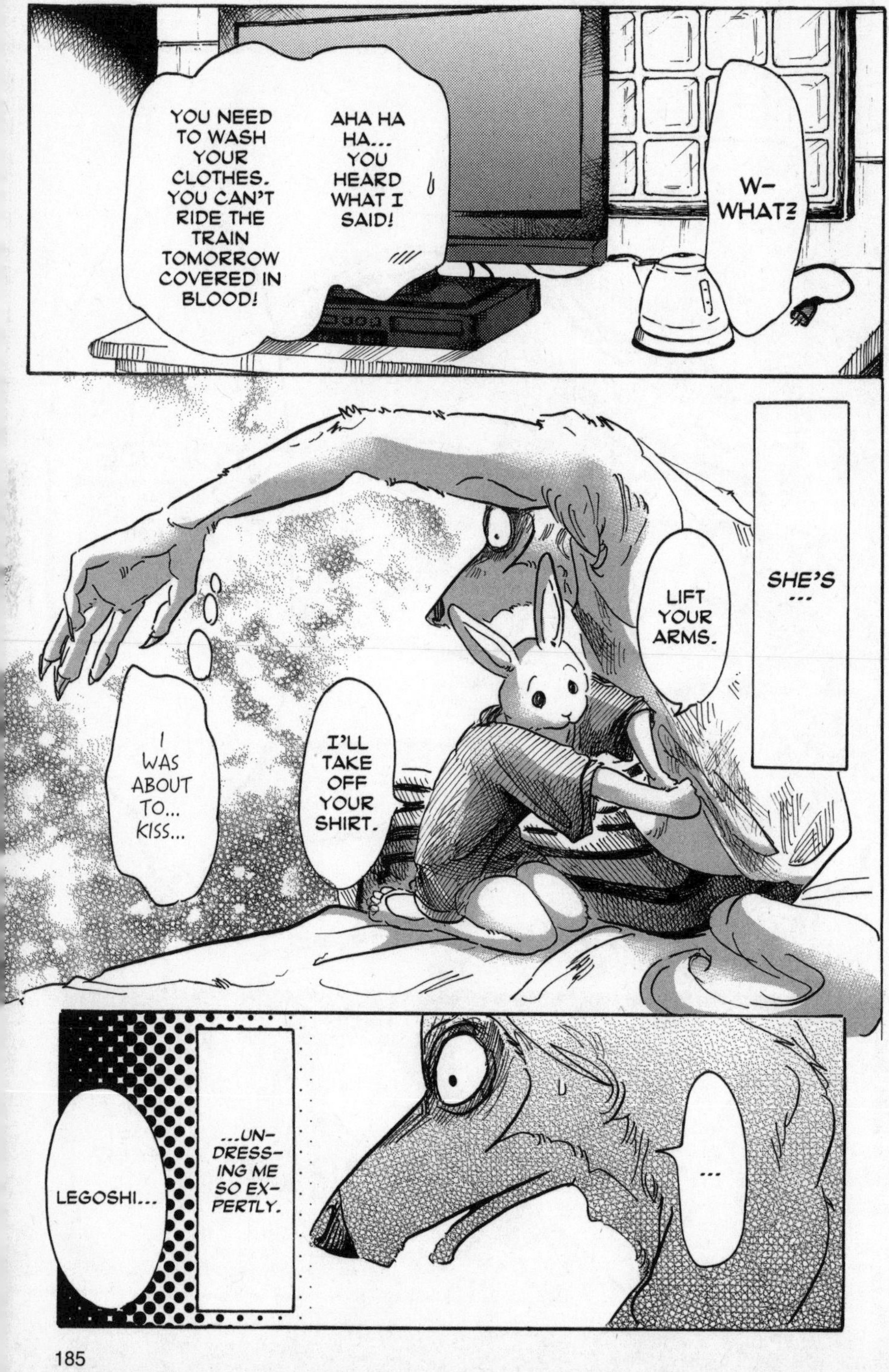
W-WHAT?
AHA HA HA... YOU HEARD WHAT I SAID!
YOU NEED TO WASH YOUR CLOTHES. YOU CAN'T RIDE THE TRAIN TOMORROW COVERED IN BLOOD!
SHE'S ...
LIFT YOUR ARMS.
I'LL TAKE OFF YOUR SHIRT.
I WAS ABOUT TO... KISS...
...
...UNDRESSING ME SO EXPERTLY.
LEGOSHI...

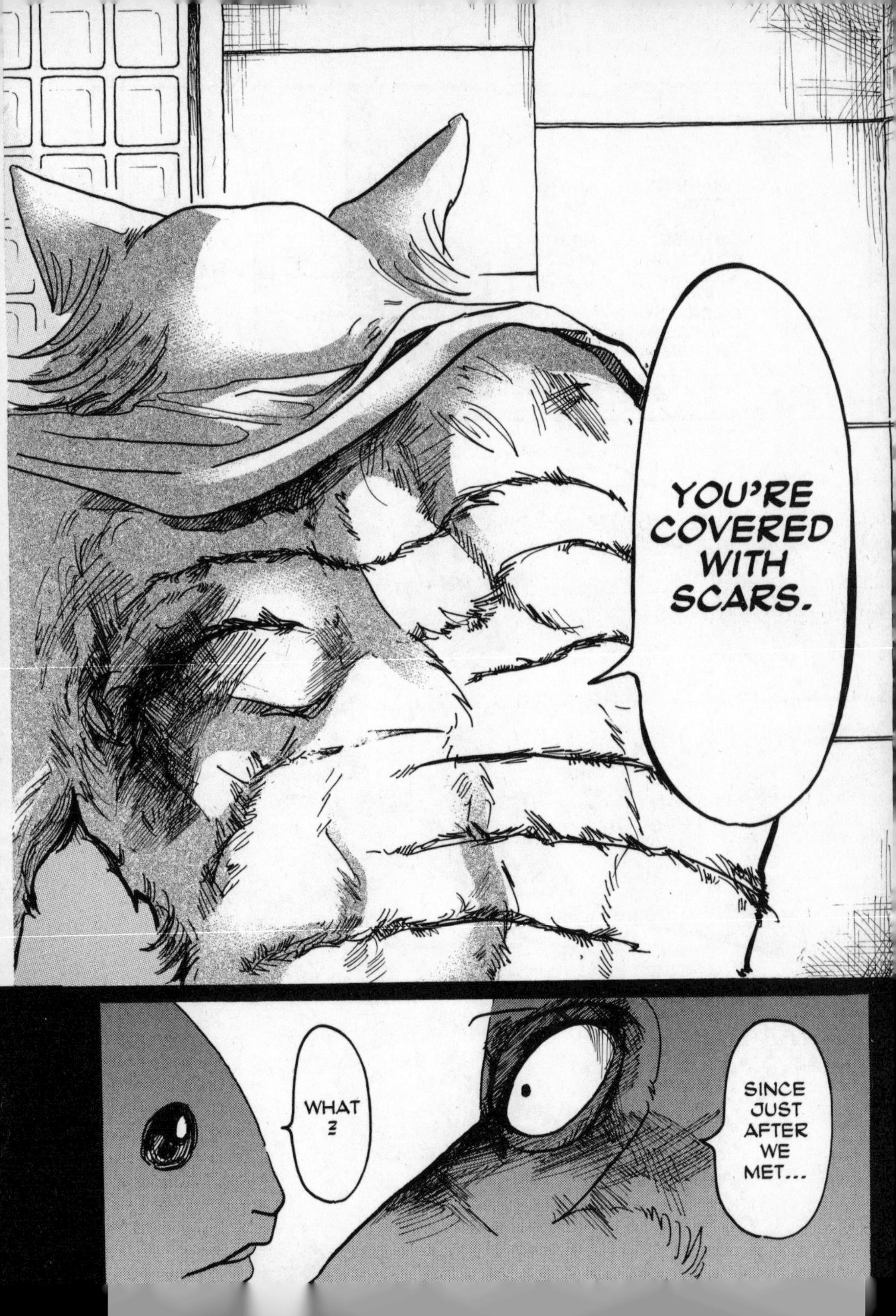
YOU'RE COVERED WITH SCARS.
SINCE JUST AFTER WE MET...
WHAT?

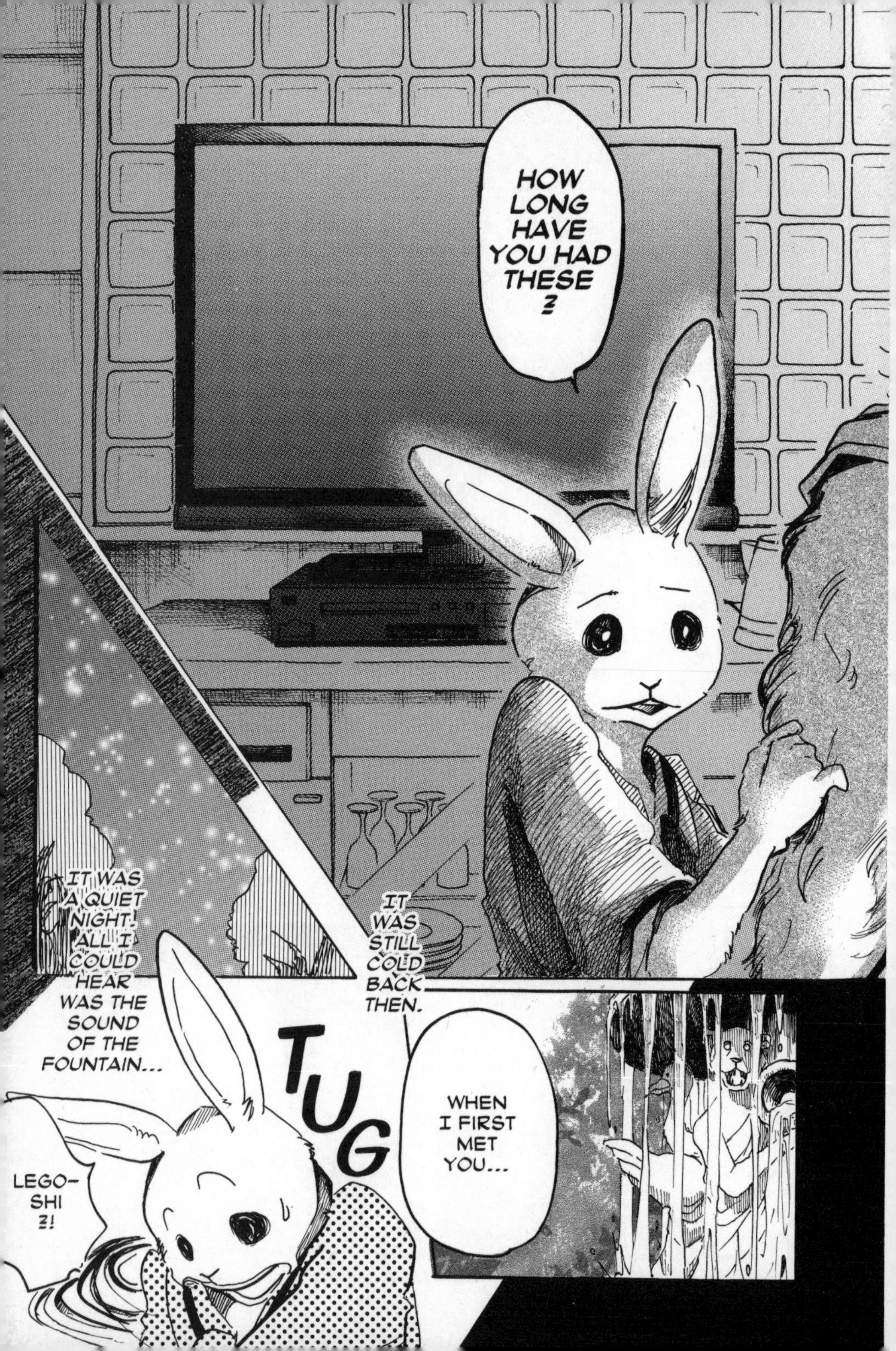
HOW LONG HAVE YOU HAD THESE?
WHEN I FIRST MET YOU...
IT WAS STILL COLD BACK THEN.
IT WAS A QUIET NIGHT. ALL I COULD HEAR WAS THE SOUND OF THE FOUNTAIN...
TUG
LEGOSHI?!

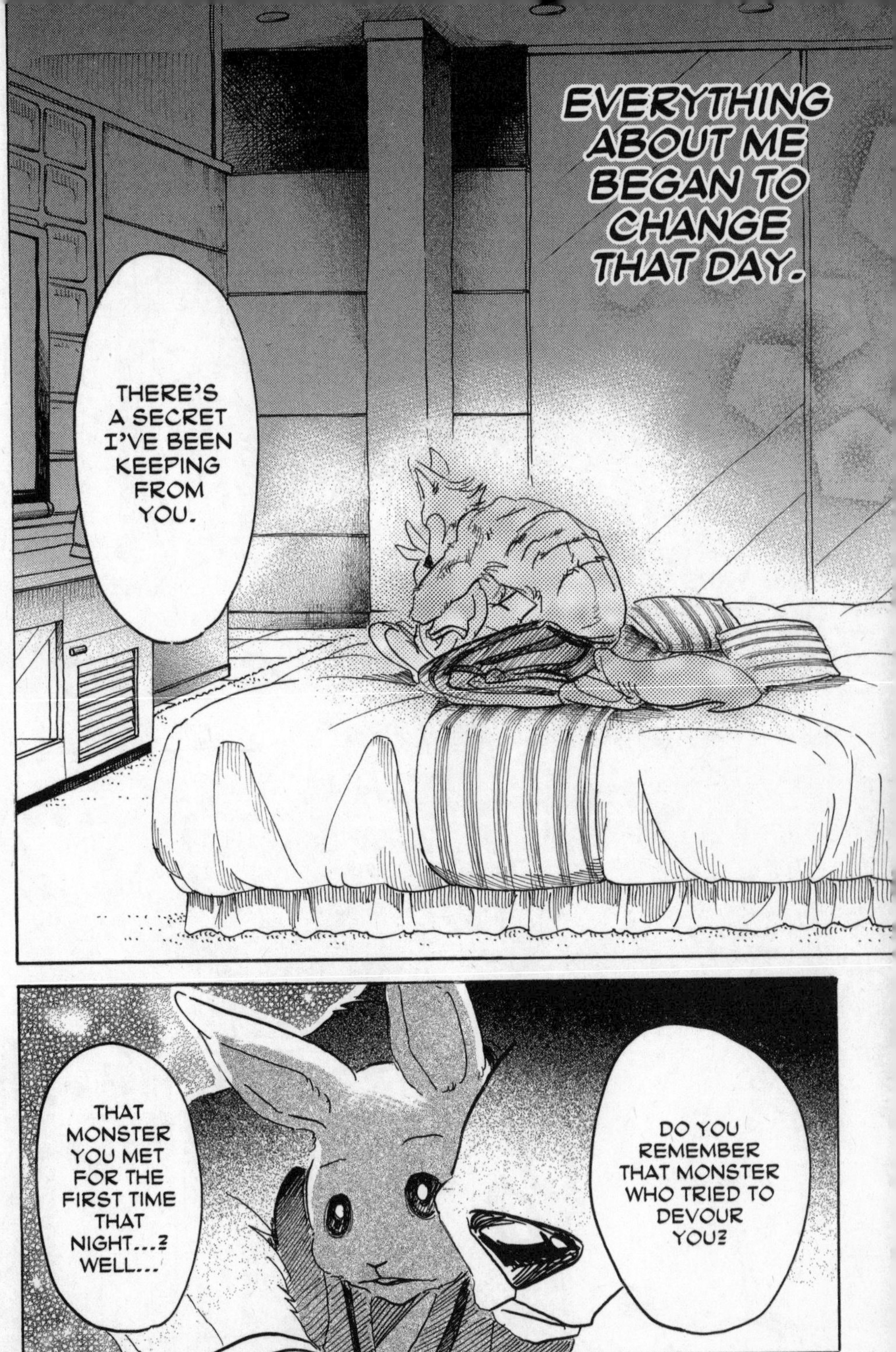
EVERYTHING ABOUT ME BEGAN TO CHANGE THAT DAY.
THERE'S A SECRET I'VE BEEN KEEPING FROM YOU.
DO YOU REMEMBER THAT MONSTER WHO TRIED TO DEVOUR YOU?
THAT MONSTER YOU MET FOR THE FIRST TIME THAT NIGHT...? WELL...

END OF BEASTARS VOL. 5

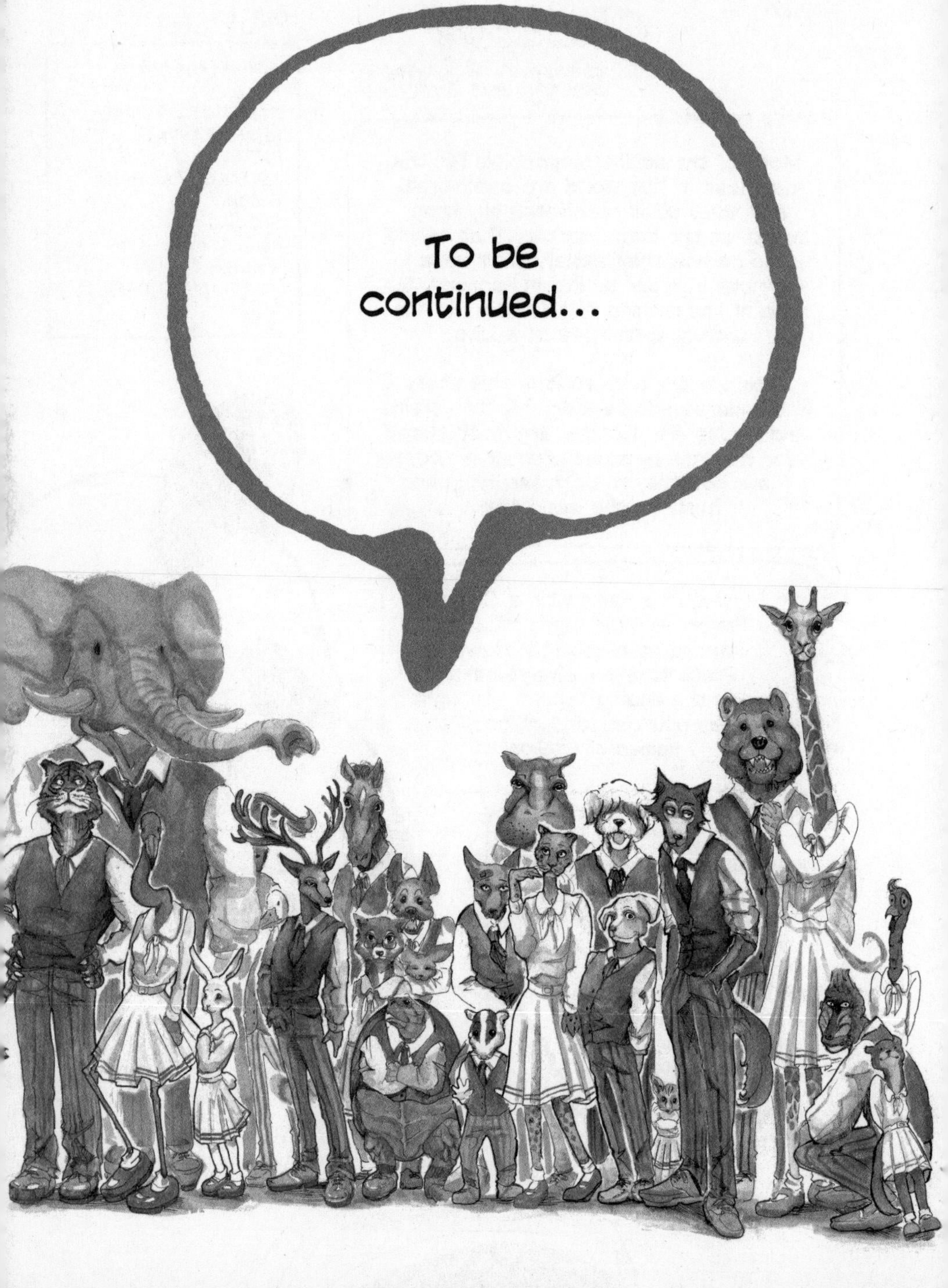
To be continued...

Gohin

Character Design Notes

PROFILE

GOHIN (AGE 39)
MALE
CARNIVORA URSIDAE
(GIANT PANDA)
BIRTHDAY: JUNE 9
ASTROLOGICAL SIGN:
GEMINI
BLOOD TYPE: O
HEIGHT: 6 FT., 7 IN.
WEIGHT: 227 LB.
LOVES BAMBOO AND
ALCOHOL

Gohin's personality

Most of the adults responsible for the darkness in this world are carnivores, and most adult carnivores buy meat to eat at the black market. That seems to be how they satisfy their base instincts in order to live in harmony. So one of the themes of this story is the untrustworthiness of adults.

Gohin is the only adult in this story who understands Legoshi. He also trains and guides him. Pandas are most suited for this role because of their biology. I love how they're both terrifying and funny at the same time.

How did you come up with his name?

I wanted a name with a Chinese flavor, so I did some research. Pandas at a zoo in Wakayama Prefecture are always named with the ending "-hin." I thought that sounded kind of cool, so I named him "Gohin."

Gohin's Appearance

Gohin is like an intelligent, physically powerful middle-aged man. But these characteristics don't go well with pandas because they look like children. However, I stayed faithful to the panda's form, and I think that makes him interesting looking. I'm glad he's on the cover!

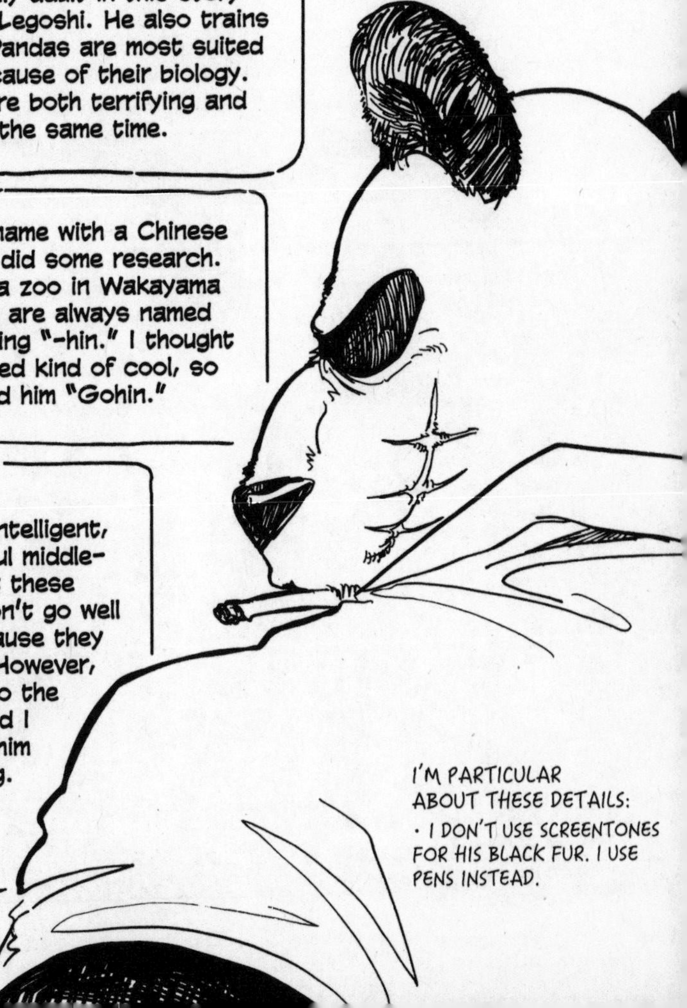

I'M PARTICULAR ABOUT THESE DETAILS:

- I DON'T USE SCREENTONES FOR HIS BLACK FUR. I USE PENS INSTEAD.

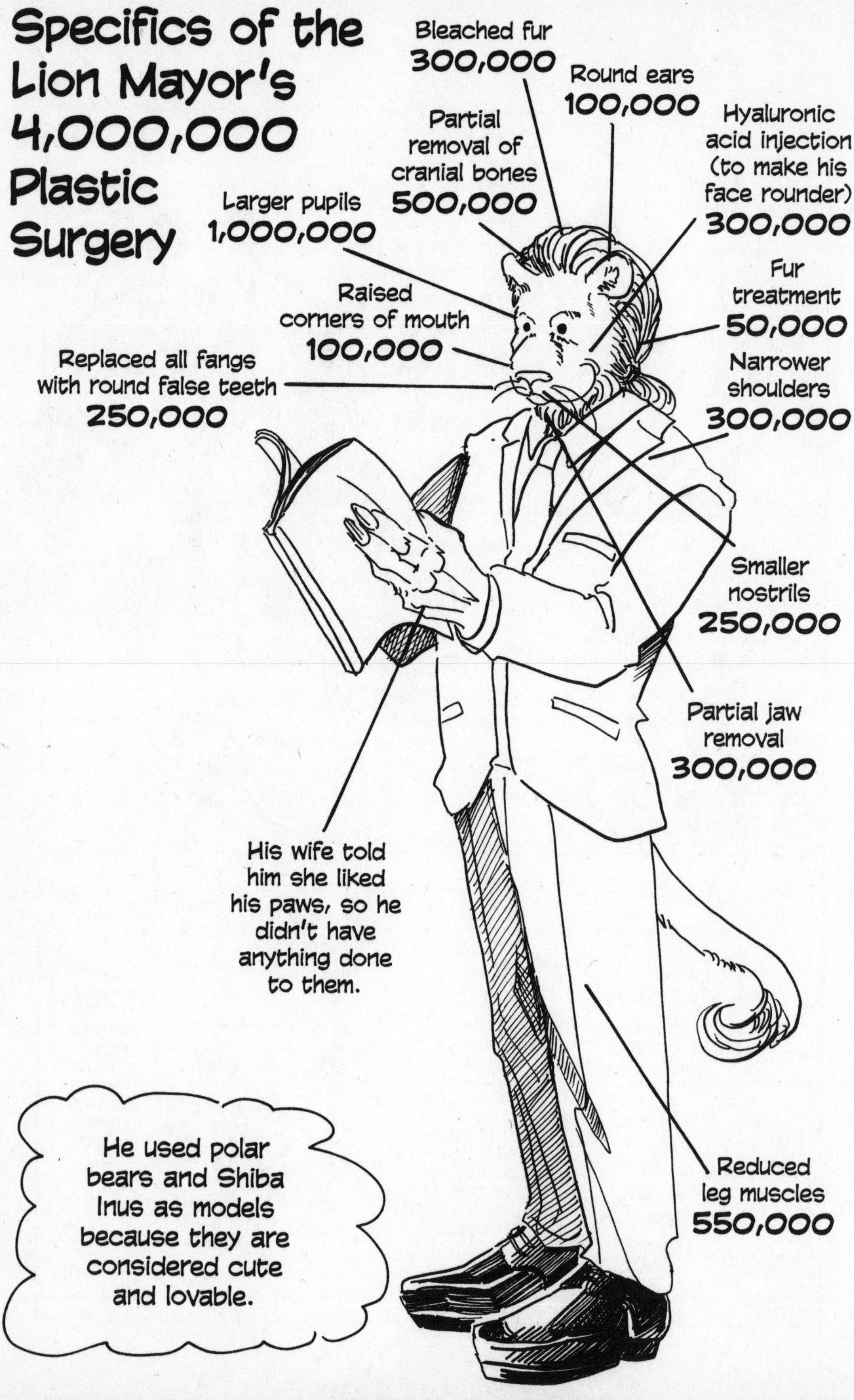
Specifics of the Lion Mayor's 4,000,000 Plastic Surgery
Bleached fur 300,000
Round ears 100,000
Partial removal of cranial bones 500,000
Hyaluronic acid injection (to make his face rounder) 300,000
Larger pupils 1,000,000
Fur treatment 50,000
Raised corners of mouth 100,000
Narrower shoulders 300,000
Replaced all fangs with round false teeth 250,000
Smaller nostrils 250,000
Partial jaw removal 300,000
His wife told him she liked his paws, so he didn't have anything done to them.
Reduced leg muscles 550,000
He used polar bears and Shiba Inus as models because they are considered cute and lovable.

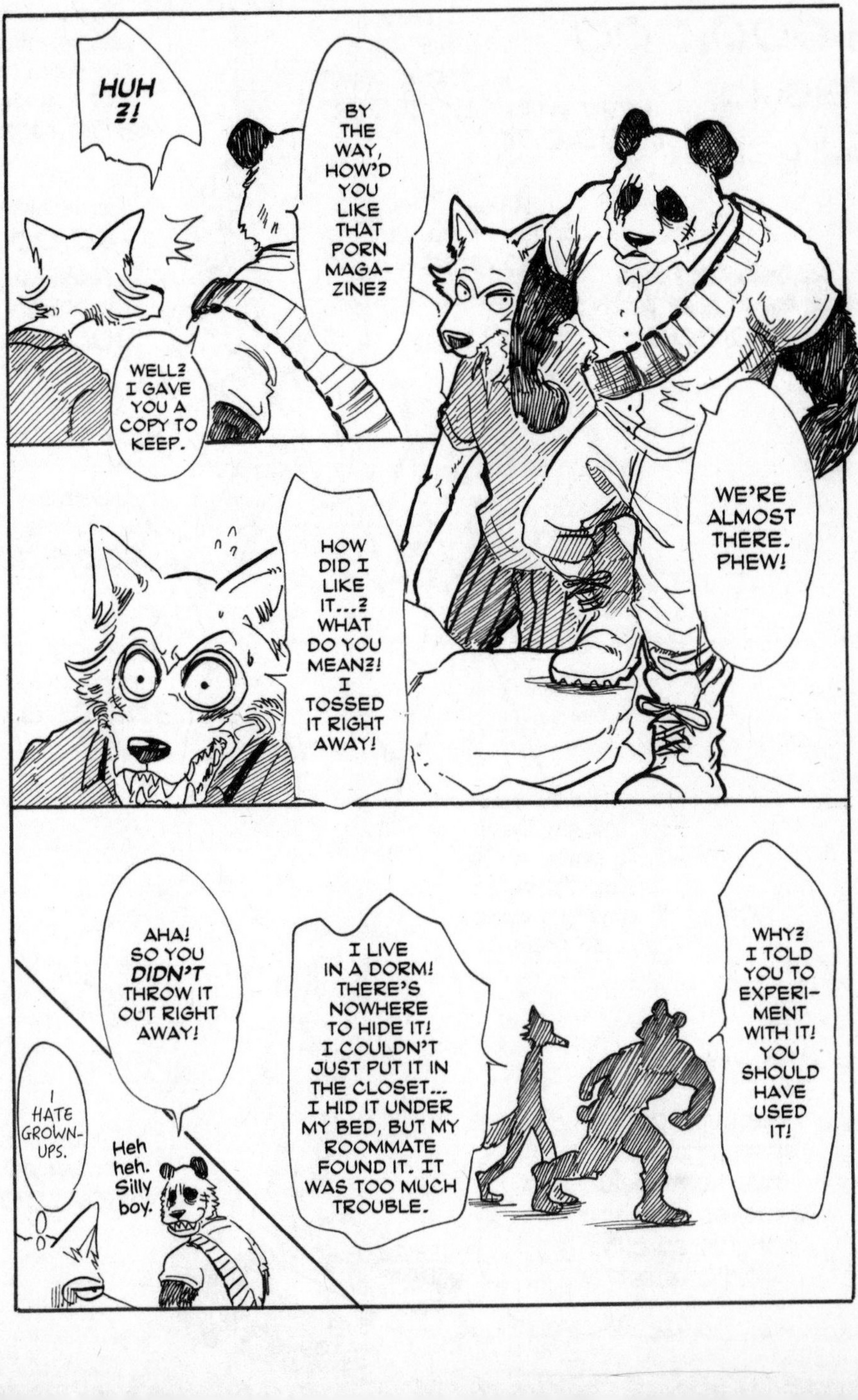

WE'RE ALMOST THERE. PHEW!
BY THE WAY, HOW'D YOU LIKE THAT PORN MAGAZINE?
HUH?!
WELL? I GAVE YOU A COPY TO KEEP.
HOW DID I LIKE IT...? WHAT DO YOU MEAN?! I TOSSED IT RIGHT AWAY!
WHY? I TOLD YOU TO EXPERIMENT WITH IT! YOU SHOULD HAVE USED IT!
I LIVE IN A DORM! THERE'S NOWHERE TO HIDE IT! I COULDN'T JUST PUT IT IN THE CLOSET... I HID IT UNDER MY BED, BUT MY ROOMMATE FOUND IT. IT WAS TOO MUCH TROUBLE.
AHA! SO YOU *DIDN'T* THROW IT OUT RIGHT AWAY!
Heh heh. Silly boy.
I HATE GROWN-UPS.

(Continued from the previous volume...)

Do you prefer dogs? Or cats?

~ Put out your hand ~

~Cats~

They negotiate with you!

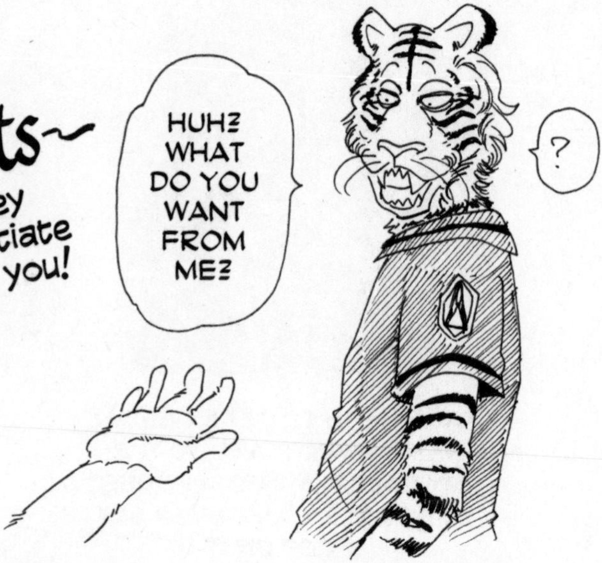
?
HUH? WHAT DO YOU WANT FROM ME?

~Dogs~

They slap your hand!

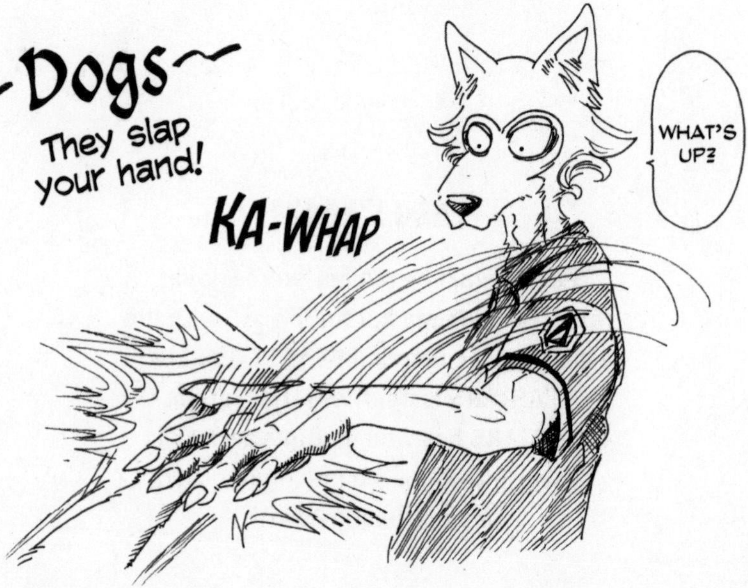
WHAT'S UP?
KA-WHAP

MY GOAL IS TO GET MORE AND
MORE PLANTS AND TO TURN
MY BALCONY INTO A FOREST
SO THAT I CAN'T EVEN SET
FOOT ON IT.

PARU ITAGAKI

Paru Itagaki began her professional
career as a manga author in 2016 with the
short story collection **BEAST COMPLEX**.
BEASTARS is her first serialization.
BEASTARS has won multiple awards in
Japan, including the prestigious 2018
Manga Taisho Award.

BEASTARS

VOL. 5
VIZ Signature Edition

Story & Art by
Paru Itagaki

Translation/Tomoko Kimura
English Adaptation/Annette Roman
Touch-Up Art & Lettering/Susan Daigle-Leach
Cover & Interior Design/Yukiko Whitley
Editor/Annette Roman

First published in 2017 by Akita Publishing Co., Ltd., Tokyo
English translation rights arranged with AKITA PUBLISHING CO., LTD. through Tuttle-Mori Agency, Inc., Tokyo

Printed in the U.S.A.

Published by VIZ Media, LLC
P.O. Box 77010
San Francisco, CA 94107

10 9 8 7 6 5 4 3 2 1
First printing, March 2020

VIZ MEDIA
viz.com

VIZ SIGNATURE
vizsignature.com

RATED T+ OLDER TEEN ratings.viz.com

PARENTAL ADVISORY
BEASTARS is rated T+ and is recommended for ages 16 and up. It contains adult themes, sexual situations and violence.

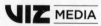

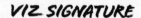

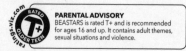

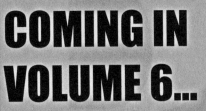

COMING IN VOLUME 6...

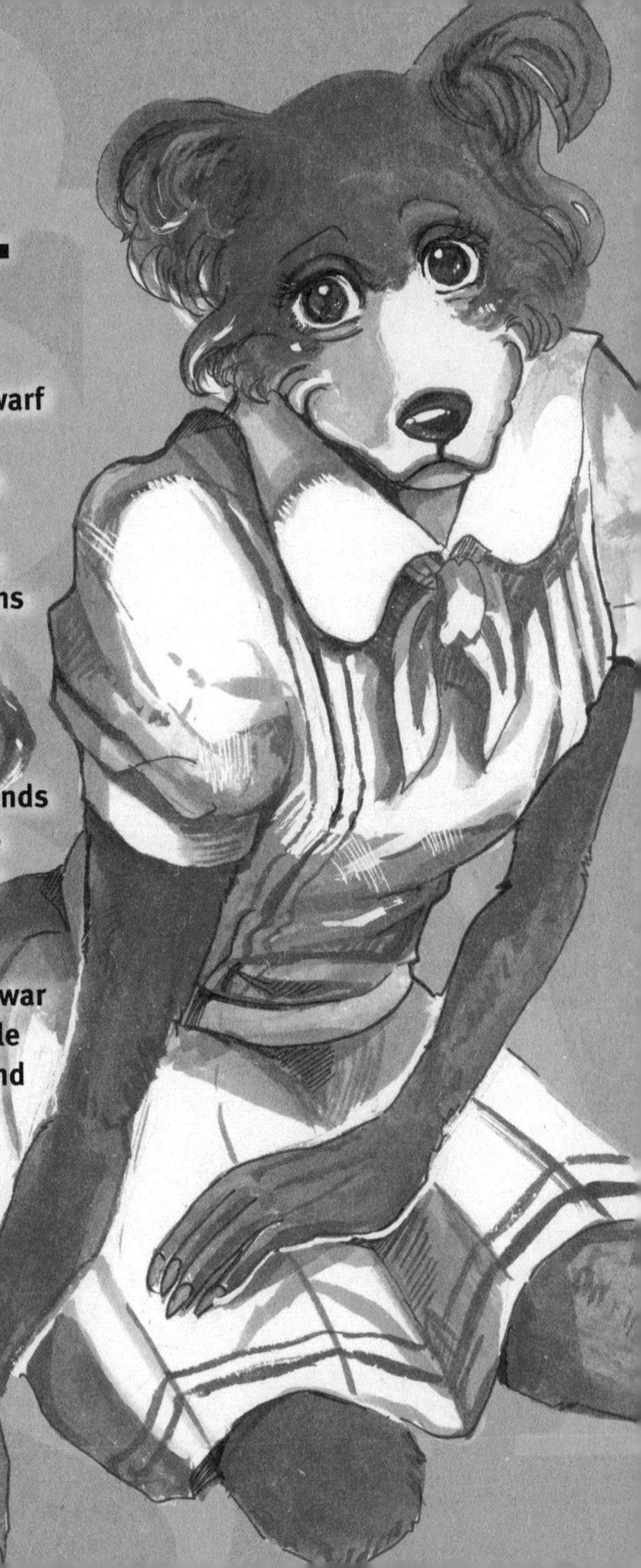

As gray wolf Legoshi and dwarf rabbit Haru's relationship intensifies, gray wolf Juno's jealousy grows. Red deer Louis's mysterious absence from school has ramifications for both his friends and his enemies. And while the lion gang Shishi-gumi chooses a new leader, Cherryton Academy's headmaster attends the Council of Living Beings to choose the school's next Beastar. Plus, a flashback to Legoshi's and Jack's puppyhoods and the world war that led to the current fragile truce between carnivores and herbivores.

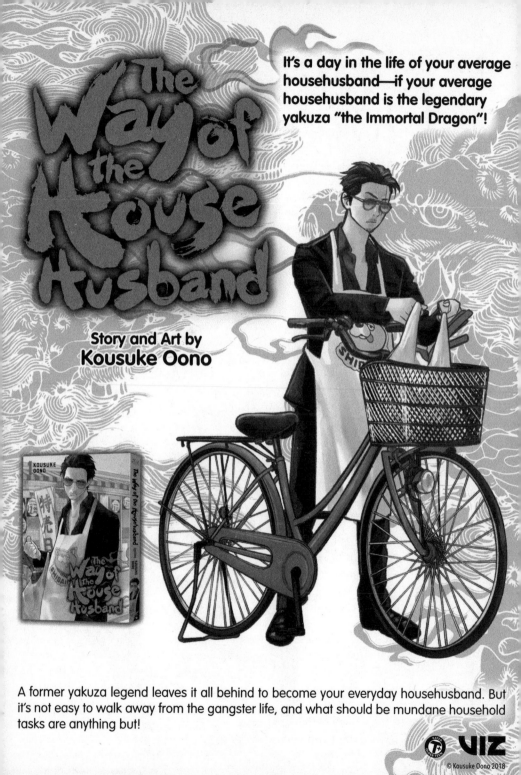

It's a day in the life of your average househusband—if your average househusband is the legendary yakuza "the Immortal Dragon"!

The Way of the House Husband

Story and Art by
Kousuke Oono

A former yakuza legend leaves it all behind to become your everyday househusband. But it's not easy to walk away from the gangster life, and what should be mundane household tasks are anything but!

Sweet Blue Flowers

Story and Art by **Takako Shimura**

Akira Okudaira is starting high school and is ready for exciting new experiences. And on the first day of school, she runs into her best friend from kindergarten at the train station! Now Akira and Fumi have the chance to rekindle their friendship, but life has gotten a lot more complicated since they were kids…

Collect the series!

CHILDREN OF THE WHALES

In this postapocalyptic fantasy, a sea of sand swallows everything but the past.

In an endless sea of sand drifts the Mud Whale, a floating island city of clay and magic. In its chambers a small community clings to survival, cut off from its own history by the shadows of the past.

This is the last page.

BEASTARS reads from right to left to preserve the orientation of the original Japanese artwork.